ALSO BY WALID PHARES

Future Jihad

The War of Ideas

The Confrontation

THE
COMING
REVOLUTION

Struggle for Freedom in the Middle East

WALID PHARES

THRESHOLD EDITIONS
NEW YORK LONDON TORONTO SYDNEY

Threshold Editions
A Division of Simon & Schuster, Inc.
1230 Avenue of the Americas
New York, NY 10020

First Threshold Editions hardcover edition December 2010

THRESHOLD EDITIONS and colophon are trademarks of Simon & Schuster, Inc.

For information about special discounts for bulk purchases, please contact Simon
& Schuster Special Sales at 1-866-506-1949 or business@simonandschuster.com.

The Simon & Schuster Speakers Bureau can bring authors to your live event. For
more information or to book an event contact the Simon & Schuster Speakers
Bureau at 1-866-248-3049 or visit our website at www.simonspeakers.com.

Designed by Renata Di Biase

Manufactured in the United States of America

10 9 8 7 6 5 4 3 2 1

Library of Congress Cataloging-in-Publication Data

Phares, Walid, 1957–
  The coming revolution : struggle for freedom in the Middle East / by Walid
Phares.
    p. cm.
  1. Democracy—Middle East. 2. Jihad. 3. Islam and politics—Middle East.
4. Middle East—Politics and government—1979– 5. Democracy—Africa, North.
6. Islam and politics—Africa, North. 7. Africa, North—Politics and government—
21st century. I. Title.
  JQ1758.A91P43 2010
  956.05—dc22
                                                                    2010024620

ISBN 978-1-4391-7837-9
ISBN 978-1-4391-8049-5 (ebook)

To those whose company I was deprived of because of my choice for freedom . . .

And in memory of my father, Halim, and mother, Hind—my greatest inspirations and heroes, who, before they left us, raised me to appreciate justice and liberty.

As I stay behind, I have dedicated my life to speak on behalf of the weak and oppressed.

ACKNOWLEDGMENTS

My thinking regarding this book's subject has evolved over a span of thirty years as I observed the suffering and struggles of the oppressed in the Middle East. I want to thank each one of those freedom fighters, human rights activists, public figures, and courageous men and women who reached out to me, from Beirut to Washington, to relate their personal tales and the stories of their nations. Born and raised in Beirut, I witnessed the saga of many who wrote about freedom deprivation. Since I relocated to the United States in 1990 and adopted my new homeland, I tirelessly researched and published about the causes of freedom in the Greater Middle East, listening and interacting with dissidents and voices of courage whom I would like to thank for their sacrifices. They are too numerous to be listed.

I would like to thank Fox News's leadership for trusting me to be the channel's expert on Middle East affairs since 2006 and all my colleagues at the network for their support. Between 2004 and 2010, I was a senior fellow at the Foundation for the Defense of Democracies (FDD), whom I thank for hosting me professionally in Washington, D.C.

Over the years, I've interacted with many journalists, show hosts, anchors, and producers in the media—in television, radio, and print—both in the United States and overseas, including MSNBC, CNN, France 24, Russia Today, Canada CTV, and others. I'd like to thank them for giving me the opportunity to share my findings and analysis with the public. From the front lines of the battle of words I wish to cite the very courageous and relentless Lebanese Hamid Ghuriafi of *al Siyassa*, Syrian Nihad Ghadri of *al Murarer*, and Egyptian commentator Magdi Khalil.

Also to be acknowledged are the many lawmakers and their assistants with whom I worked for more than a decade in the U.S. Congress, the European Parliament, and other national assemblies around the world, officials and diplomats in the U.S., overseas, and at the United Nations, for their dedication to the battle of freedom. Although they are too many to list on this page individually, I particularly cite Prime Minister of Spain Jose Maria Aznar, Governor Mitt Romney, U.S. Senators Joe Lieberman and Rick Santorum, MEP Jaime Mayor Oreja, U.S. Congresswoman Sue Myrick, Canadian minister of Justice MP Irwin Cotler, Iraqi MP Mithal Alusi, Lebanese MP Nadim Gemayel, and UN special envoy Teri Rod Larson.

In the world of NGOs and human rights, I salute the efforts of dozens of leaders and activists I worked with who have dedicated themselves to raising the visibility of freedom struggle in the Middle East I must cite a few, such as Portuguese MEP Paul Casaca, as well as Tom Harb, and Rev Keith Roderick.

I'd like to thank my relentless literary agent, Lynne Rabinof, whose encouragement and help made the project happen. I greatly thank my publisher, Simon & Schuster, in the person of Anthony Ziccardi, who valued the proposal and saw merit in it. I thank his entire staff, particularly Katharine Dresser and all those who were part of the technical, administrative, and legal stages of the production.

My deep thanks and appreciation to my editor, Kevin Smith, for his patience and dedication, as well as to other reviewers for shaping and sculpting the manuscript, transforming the first draft into a wonderfully flowing text.

Writing this book needed sacrifices by members of my closest circle in life. I thank the "Commander" and the "Scholar" for being willing to allow me to use "our" time. I owe them every day and hour of writing and editing I spent away from daily life and vacations. My best regards go to my sister, Liliane, my childhood coach, and to my brother, Sami, intellectual mentor during my teenage years.

This book and my writing career are in acknowledgment to my late parents, Halim and Hind, now together on the other side. Their sacrifices and love, basic ingredients for my education and passion for justice, made me understand the sufferings of people in past and current times. At times I regret the years of separation we experienced and I consented to so that I could think and express myself in liberty while they lived behind the wall of oppression. Now we're all free, even though in two worlds, until we meet again.

Virginia, July 30, 2010

CONTENTS

A Revolution against the Caliphate?

In the first decade of the twenty-first century, as terror strikes were widening from Manhattan to Mumbai and battlefields raging from Afghanistan to Iraq, many tough questions had yet to be answered: Where are the "moderates" in the Muslim world? Why do we hear only from the "radicals"? Is the Middle East really rejecting democracy? Do people in the region prefer the Taliban and Hezbollah, Hamas, and the Muslim Brotherhoods over liberals, feminists, and seculars? Or is this perception the work of the stronger, wealthier, dominant forces in the Arab and Muslim world who want us to believe that there is no hope that a war against the terrorists can be won and democracy will never take hold in the region?

In fact it is both, for the reality is that in this dangerous and critically important part of the world, there is a very explosive race going on—a competition to the end between those who want to bring all countries from Morocco to Afghanistan under what they call a "Caliphate" or a totalitarian empire, and those who have been working feverishly to launch a revolution against this empire in construction. This is the untold story of a region that can be described as "Middle Earth," in which the world has invested much hope and which could determine the future of the planet in the decades to come.

After the collapse of the Ottoman Empire in 1919, the Greater Middle East from North Africa to Central Asia witnessed one of the most dramatic struggles in history between the forces pushing backward toward the reestablishment of an Islamic Caliphate or a theocratic regime, and the forces of progress moving in the direction of modernity, democracy, and human rights. The race was deeply affected by Western intervention, World War II, a long Cold War, and the rise of oil power.

Instead of the liberal revolution that many hoped for, coup d'états and ultranationalist ideologies brought the people of the region under authoritarian and oppressive regimes for decades. At the very top of the regimes is the absolute power of rulers; below, the constant challenge by the Islamist movements; and below both layers, the democratic elements at the edges of civil societies. During their half-century confrontation, neither the West nor the communists helped bring democratic change to the region.

With the collapse of the Soviet Union a second historic window opened for democratic revolutions to rise. The liberation of Eastern and Central Europe, the expansion of democracies in Latin America, and the transformations in South Africa were powerful signals indicating the global shift toward freedom, but this was not so in the Middle East. This unlucky region witnessed a further penetration by jihadi forces, a competition between Salafism and Khomeinism, a radicalized political culture, a blocking of the Arab-Israeli Peace Process, and further alienation of minorities, women, and youth. As the world was moving gradually away from totalitarianism, and people were gaining rights and freedoms they never had before, "Middle Earth" was losing liberties.

As a result of 9/11 and the subsequent terror attacks in the West, a third historic window opened abruptly and unexpectedly for the forces of democratic change in the region. Western intervention removed two of the most brutal regimes by military force: the Taliban in Afghanistan and the Baathist dictatorship of Saddam Hussein in Iraq. This post-9/11 earthquake shook the foundations of the regional authoritarian system. The United States and Western powers were battling jihadi forces across the region on two major battlefields and in an intense war of ideas. The fight, with Washington and its allies betting on the success of an electoral democracy and the cohorts of Salafi and Khomeinist regimes betting on an all-out jihad to defeat the Western incursion into "Muslim lands," rages on.

The region's regimes, political parties, intellectuals, and "streets" had to side with one or the other camp. Some, like Saudi Arabia, Turkey, Egypt, and Pakistan, thought they'd profit from the clash of titans by consolidating their existing power. Ruling elites felt they could handle the extremist factions and that the Americans and the West should not get involved.

A two-way struggle spread through the region between the

U.S.-led efforts to provoke a change in the region and the Islamist and jihadists expanding their base. Between 2001 and 2010 billions of dollars were spent on the "war on terror," hundreds of millions on the "war of ideas," tens of thousands were killed in wars and terror attacks, hundreds of leading figures were assassinated, and a whole decade was lost for the peoples of the region, still far from enjoying liberty. But was all hope really lost?

Some among the most oppressed civil societies in the region were granted enough space and freedom to build a democracy. The jury is still out on whether these infant democracies will succeed, and the dangers are significant. Afghan women were liberated from the medieval Taliban, but the country is still assaulted by ferocious fundamentalist militias. Pakistan's seculars are also under attack by the jihadists. Iraqi Shiites were saved from Saddam, but Iranian-backed Islamists are pushing Sharia law across the land. In Lebanon, the Syrian occupation receded, but legislators, journalists, and citizens are still being killed, and Hezbollah is holding power. Last but not least, Darfur's genocide is recognized by the international community, but the massacres continue.

It is true that in the wake of 9/11 and the Western intervention in the region, democratic forces and dissidents felt relief, despite what anti-Western propaganda has been arguing forcefully over the past eight years. From Egypt, Syria, Saudi Arabia, the Emirates, Algeria, and Iran, new faces of dissidence have acquired international visibility. In the region, free bloggers, talk shows, journalists, human rights activists, and even newly elected legislators rise to the surface fighting an uphill battle against the combined forces of the status quo (regimes) and jihadi fascism (Salafists and Khomeinists). A breach in the wall of authoritarianism has opened: Democracy has penetrated the fortress of "Middle Earth." Youths, students, women, minorities, and artists are increasingly expressing their will to see their societies become freer. But will the jihadists and the repressive regimes allow the revolution to happen? Not at all, as events are showing us in this first decade of the twenty-first century. Half a century after the end of the Nazi Reich and twenty years after the fall of one of the most suppressive totalitarian regimes in history, the Soviet Union, their copycats in the Arab and Muslim world aren't letting go of their privileges.

Despite some often irreconcilable ideological differences, a brotherhood against democracy has emerged in the center of the planet.

Absolute monarchies, ultrachauvinist Baathists, antipluralism elites, Islamist movements, and jihadists have formed one of the most formidable walls in history, insulating the region's peoples from the international community. Empowered by their full control of the Arab League, the Organization of the Islamic Conference, OPEC, and most media networks in the region, and influence over the United Nations, the African Union, the European Union, and a large segment of America's elite, the "antidemocracy brotherhood" strikes back against the timid surges of democracy in Lebanon, Iraq, Afghanistan, Sudan, and the rest of the Arab world and beyond. The jihadists lead the assault.

The West backed off and chose another direction as of 2009. A general retreat seems to have begun. In Central Asia and the Indian subcontinent, even as they have waged military operations, the United States and NATO bend over backward by seeking a partnership with the so-called moderates in the Taliban. In Lebanon, Britain is recognizing Hezbollah and U.S. officials have been preparing the public for the same. In Iraq, as the U.S.-led coalition begins its redeployment, the democratic groups have been abandoned in favor of a pragmatic alliance with the Shia and Sunni Islamists. With Assad of Syria, the U.S. administration builds hopes of "engagement" at the expense of reformers. Sudan's regime, accused of genocide against black Africans in the south and in Darfur, is now being sought for "dialogue" by the U.S. administration. Last but not least, Washington has opted to "sit down" with the mullahs in Iran and cut regional deals even after the Tehran uprising in reaction to the latest "election." The jihadists are winning psychologically and the authoritarian regimes are stronger than ever. But are the region's democrats defeated? Are they going back to the catacombs?

The answer is no, they are still in the race. From Beirut to Darfur, from the Berber mountains of North Africa to the marshes of Ahwaz on the Persian Gulf, revolutions are brewing. As of June 2009, demonstrators clashing with the Basiji militia have been changing history in Iran. Young souls have seen freedom and mature adults have had glimpses of fundamental human rights. The violet index fingers of Iraq's voters, women legislators in Afghanistan, and the million-men and -women marches of Lebanon and Iran have sparked in the masses' imagination the wildest dreams of human liberties. From the most fertile soil for jihadism may come the most fiery revolutions of the twenty-first century. The Cedars Revolution in Lebanon, the rise of the marginalized black identity in Sudan, the Amazigh revolt of the Kabyle, the stubborn reformers of Syria, the antifundamentalist Muslim intellectuals, enlightened seculars of Turkey, Iraq's NGOs, Iran's women and students, liberals of the Arabian Peninsula and all their diasporas, are gearing up for a final prolonged showdown in "Middle Earth" with the most extreme forms of jihadi, totalitarian, and racist terror. The retreat of the current Western governments in the face of terror and the power of oil regimes, often sugarcoated as "engagement," is leaving the birthplace of the three monotheistic religions to a looming mother of all confrontations.

Will Middle Eastern democrats succeed in resisting and then reversing the tide against the jihadists? Can they rebel against regimes and fight back against the Islamists while they are unarmed, unrecognized, unfunded, and demonized by militant propaganda as "agents of the West"? The race between the rise of the Caliphate and the democratic revolution in the Greater Middle East is on.

And how should the United States, the West, and the international community deal with this race? Are we to engage the regimes and cut deals with them at the expense of their peoples' freedom? Are we to engage the jihadists and abandon the democrats? Should we support the forthcoming revolutions in these civil societies or allow their theological and authoritarian regimes to dispose of them with ease? This book will help answer these troubling questions and explain to readers the untold story of a struggle that will determine if the Middle East will at last reach freedom and democracy in this century and if the planet will avoid the potential wars set to explode by the followers of Salafism, Khomeinism, and other jihadis in the years to come.

How the West Missed the Story
and May Miss It Again

The 9/11 Commission concluded back in 2004 that the United States was engaged in a war with terrorists and didn't know it, but offered insufficient explanation of why. In a briefing I participated in, one of the commissioners stated that in the end, "It was a failure of imagination on the part of Americans." According to the four-hundred-page study, America as a nation wasn't able to fathom the reality of what was taking place in the days, months, and years preceding the strikes. In other words, Americans weren't able to imagine that people out there could hate their country that much and do such horrible things to it.

I argued that we, as a nation, didn't have a failure of imagination. The United States has distinguished itself throughout modern history with stunning discoveries and achievements primarily because of its fertile imagination. Advancements including nuclear power, landing on the moon, and the internet were possible because of the innovative minds of Americans. These are evidence of an endless capacity to break all walls of intellectual restraint. There was a failure, I countered, but of education. Indeed, Americans and Western democracies in general were deprived of basic information, education, and updates about the real roots of the rising jihadi threat, and thus failed in seeing the terror coming. And they continue to fail in combating this developing worldwide threat.

Chillingly, we were not educated in our classroom by our professors and were misinformed by our own media. Throughout the 1990s I had seen how most of the scholarly establishment blocked the public from seeing the truth and missing the critical connections. Rarely in history have nations been so subverted by their own elite.

While classical Middle East scholars in America and Europe adopted an apologist attitude blaming violence and the rise of jihadism on post-Western colonialism and the so-called foreign policy "blunders" of the United States and its allies, the real antidote to extreme Islamist ideologies was ignored: sound democratic cultures. The mainstream intellectual establishment on both sides of the Atlantic, deeply influenced by postcolonial thinking and manipulated by oil interests, dodged investigation of why Middle Eastern societies weren't moving toward pluralism and democracy and instead promoted the idea that bridges must be built with the "radicals," regimes, and movements. Although strong signs were coming from the region that liberals, counterjihadists, minorities, youth, and women's movements opposed fundamentalism and craved their freedom and secular values, the West stayed on the sidelines.

Western elites didn't understand, or perhaps refrained from accepting, that the multiplication of political parties and elections in Iraq and Afghanistan has unleashed the dreams of the youth and women around the region, especially in Iran, and that the Cedars Revolution in Lebanon has captured the imagination of reformers in Syria. We haven't realized that the genocide of southern Sudan has enflamed Darfur's resistance to the jihadists and that mere debates about a possible democracy in the region have triggered unprecedented liberal narratives in the Gulf, the Maghreb, and beyond.

Today, there is a plethora of analysts, writers, and scholars who are discovering the documents that inspire the jihadists. Over the past few years, a whole school of thought has brought attention to the Salafists and Khomeinists, unveiling them as a foe to be reckoned with that threatens the future of freedom and international law. Yes, the increase in awareness in Washington, New York, London, Paris, Madrid, Berlin, Moscow, and beyond is occurring because the jihadists—their boldest members, at least—have revealed many of their deeper ideas and designs. So much has been disclosed by the ideologues and leaders of the radical Islamists, on al Jazeera, on al Manar, and on YouTube, that ignoring their message completely became impossible. Even as apologists in the West try to avoid the debate on the roots of terror and on the mere existence of a jihadist threat, the latter's noise is too astounding, bloody, and loud not to be noticed and addressed, even though our democracies haven't understood yet the essence of its seriousness.

Most governments and academic elites in the West are attempting to dissipate the concerns of the public by changing the narrative of the confrontation.[1] "There is no war on terror," "These are small factions of extremists," "Real jihad is a spiritual experience," "If we enhance the economic opportunities in the Muslim world things would change," and many other ideas are thrown into the debate to convince the public that in fact there is no such thing as a "global jihadist threat" and that global efforts to change things on the other side are not needed.

Facing off intellectually with the dominant Western powers, small activist groups and writers based in liberal democracies are counterarguing by informing their readers of the theological bases upon which the Islamists have been building their indoctrination and mobilization campaigns. Oddly, the current clash of ideas within the West is between a large "apologist" camp denying that the jihadi threat exists and a small "anti-Islamist" camp scrambling to alert the public of recently made discoveries about "radical Islam."

In short, these are only the first baby steps in a greater clash of arguments that is yet to come. The bigger moment in Western strategic choices will come when the small camp of anti-Islamist commentators can attract greater numbers of citizens and confront the apologist camp with political realities—in the voting booths, demonstrating on the streets, and in mainstream media.

Sadly, nine years after the September 2001 attacks and despite all the signs of potential reform, U.S. and Western policies surrendered to the pre-9/11 dogma that the prospects for change in the Greater Middle East are hopeless, and the only forces with which we can partner are, ironically, the movements that have been blocking the rise of pluralism: the Islamists, Salafists, Wahabis, Muslim Brotherhood, and the Khomeinists as well as the hard-core Baathists and other dictatorships. But those who have undertaken the mission of bringing awareness to the free world for the last half century cannot stop trying. Each one has been doing his or her part: writing, speaking, marching, organizing, lobbying, researching, and disseminating material.

I myself have experienced several stages and tried different paths, on different continents. From the Eastern Mediterranean, I offered twenty years of hard work, from writing graffiti on Beirut's walls at a very young age, to publishing books, broadcasting, and lecturing to thousands. Despite five books, hundreds of articles, and more than a thousand interviews and lectures, the bulk of my work in those lands of violence and repression seemed like one tree falling in the forest, and at the time it had no impact in the West. I had to relocate to America and abandon my native country in order to pass my message on.

I assert that the free world can win the conflict with the jihadists, but certainly not using the tactics and policies it has employed so far. I strongly urge policymakers on both sides of the Atlantic to win the battle of identification. If we can't define the enemy, the threat, its ideology, and its strategies, we surely cannot claim any advance or any so-called victory.

Are Western leaders working to define the enemy? With the exception of some shy discourses made by U.S. leaders and a few European chief executives in the years following 9/11, the answer is no. A huge effort to educate the public must be undertaken, since in democracies one cannot engage in sustained national efforts without sustained popular support. A worldwide coalition to isolate the jihadists must be assembled. However, for the tide to turn, it is necessary to believe in and support a democratic revolution in the Greater Middle East.

In this book, I'll explain how the Middle East failed to evolve toward democracy and how a chance was given to its underdogs to rise again as the clash between the West and the jihadists widened. I'll make the case that this unlucky region has struggled and continues to struggle in a harsh race between the forces, such as the Taliban, aimed at establishing an oppressive fundamentalist Caliphate, and the civil society forces aimed at democracy and social liberation. I have called this race of the two forces a *race in Middle Earth,* where the nature of the twenty-first century will ultimately be decided. Either the jihadists will seize power in twenty-one Arab countries, Iran, Turkey, and large segments of Africa and South Asia, or a younger, determined generation of democrats and humanists will sweep the region from below.

The race is on.

The Missed Century:
How the Democratic Revolution Failed During the Twentieth Century

T he Greater Middle East is the cradle of the oldest civilizations on Earth: Egyptian, Persian, Assyrian, Phoenician, and others. Many of its intellectuals boast about the region's high cultures during ancient times as compared to Europe's state of tribalism in the same period. Historians, poets, and ultranationalist politicians argue that these civilizations practiced sophisticated engineering, advanced sciences, built roads, gardens, and towers, and compiled legal codes while barbarians were roaming in the regions of the Danube and the Rhine. Phoenicians offered the world an alphabet, and their commercial ships established the first multinational corporations some twenty-five centuries ago. Moreover, Eastern Christian, Jewish, and Muslim interfaith assemblies have often asserted that the three Abrahamic religions came from that region.

The wealth of stories about the uniqueness of this old region of the world comes in great contrast with its contemporary hostility to the development of democratic societies. The contradiction between the region's so-called rich history of sophistication and its current poor productivity in human rights advancement and fundamental freedoms is stark. It was the cold continent of the barbarians—Europe—and its emigrants to new worlds that produced charters for democracy and embodied them in modern texts, and not the cities of the Greater Middle East that had produced the letters of the alphabet, the Code of Hammurabi, laws of the seas, and the sciences of humanity.

Furthermore, Latin America's nations, on different scales, have been able to move from Iberian colonialism to acceleration of modernization, to acceptable multiparty systems—with few exceptions—while the Arab world's societies, said to be much older in settlement, failed to do the same. Argentina and Chile, Brazil and Colombia, Mexico and Jamaica were all colonies, and most have experienced military regimes, yet they all gradually accepted the idea of pluralism and the peaceful coexistence of elites, while Saudi Arabia, Syria, Iran, Libya, and Sudan, despite the huge regime differences between them, didn't move beyond the one-party system or the no-party system.

Even more dramatic is the comparison with some African countries, such as Côte d'Ivoire, Senegal, and Ghana, that, despite having fewer resources than the Middle East, in some ways have moved toward plural politics. Even where discrimination is at its worst, in South Africa, the country moved away from apartheid toward the end of the twentieth century, while Sudan dove into practicing slavery and ethnic cleansing.

Last but not least, the treatment of women in their own families and society offers stunning comparative images. While wealth is abundant and construction projects are endless in the Wahabi Kingdom, Saudi women can't drive, or even walk unescorted. Women in Madagascar and Trinidad live poorer, but freer lives. Under the Islamic Republic, Iranian women are severely restricted; they are arrested on the streets by female police to check on their hijab.[1] However, in Sri Lanka, a woman is prime minister. Even within the Muslim world, the oddities of sexual repression are salient. In Pakistan, Benazir Bhutto was elected head of government while her countrywomen in Waziristan are living under laws from the Middle Ages. Not surprisingly, Bhutto was assassinated by the Taliban, the force imposing severe sexual discrimination in Waziristan and other valleys.

The question of why democracy didn't emerge as a winning political culture south and east of the Mediterranean is relevant at a time when many in the West and worldwide are condemning entire societies for their inability to produce a democracy that protects basic freedoms. Some argue that the East by nature cannot bypass authoritarianism. Others assert that the lack of secular democracy is embedded in the canonical texts of the Islamic religion, and many postulate that this part of the world is simply condemned to live unhappily forever, no matter the explanation.

Beyond the debate about the "democratibility" of the Arab world and its neighborhood, scores of hard-core realists in the West claim that it is in the interest of the industrialized world that strongmen continue to rule the region. A surge of unstable democratic culture, they feel, would destabilize the capitalist societies, or, more accurately, would injure those in such societies who live off the oil trade with Arab Muslim petro-regimes. Ironically, as harsh as this equation seems to be, we may see that it really serves the interest of financial elites on both sides of the Mediterranean. Our analysis throughout this book will show the incredibly ferocious interests involved in the obstruction of freedom in the region.

Democracy's Failure to Take Root in Middle Earth

For half a century, scholars and propagandists have charged that colonialism, corruption, and Western foreign policies are the real root causes for the failure of democratic freedoms in "Middle Earth." I disagree.

The classical pressures that have precluded societies in other struggling regions from advancing toward freedom haven't completely blocked the march of human rights toward theoretical and practical victories. Colonialism, postcolonialism, imperialism, Western foreign policies, and multinational corporations have had an impact on Latin America, Eastern Europe, Oceania, parts of Asia, and countries in black Africa, but in all these huge zones of the planet, democracy pierced the layers of obstruction and established home bases. Brazil and Uruguay decolonized from Portugal and Spain, endured their own military regimes, and eventually reached functional multiparty systems with acceptable electoral processes. The Philippines, Japan, and India lived under military occupations but swiftly moved on to sophisticated free governments. Setbacks to democracy have also quickly bred postcolonial experiments, as in Cuba, Venezuela, and Thailand, but sexual equality wasn't reversed dramatically once it had begun to move forward. Women's rights have survived, even when political rights have regressed. Even in communist China and Vietnam, women were still granted equal rights despite general suppression of liberties. In the Greater Middle East, noncommunist regimes have suppressed the very basic rights of women.

One must not overgeneralize, but statistics do show that when communist regimes collapse, liberal democracies are not formed immediately afterward, yet things do move forward eventually. After the Soviet collapse in Central and Eastern Europe, Russia, and many of the Central Asian and Caucasus republics, some form of multiparty system rose. In the Middle East, the crumbling of the Ottoman Empire in 1919, the end of European colonialism in the late 1940s, and the end of the Cold War and of Soviet power in 1991 didn't open the path for democratization, nor did they lead to an expanding space for liberalization and the rise of human rights—quite the opposite.

These events unleashed more lethal oppressive forces to reverse and crush the chances for democracy. The twentieth century offered the region multiple opportunities, but almost all these windows were carefully closed by radical ideologies and oppressive elites. While similar totalitarian regimes rose to block democracy during the same century, almost all their "evil" manifestations vanished or slowly declined. Fascism, Nazism, Soviet communism, military juntas, and populist dictatorships rose and fell from the Atlantic to the Indian Ocean while Wahabism, Salafism, Khomeinism, Baathism, and other totalitarian ideologies persisted and wreaked havoc in civil societies.

The Caliphate's Long History

Before becoming the centerpiece of the twentieth century's conflicts and challenges, the region called the Greater Middle East, stretching from Morocco to Afghanistan, experienced a variety of dynastic rules, wars, breakups, and migrations, with all the human dramas that accompany such events. It isn't that different from any other heavily populated area of the world throughout history. Similar conflicts ravaged Christian Europe, Asia, Africa, and later on, the Americas. Unlike most other regions, Middle Earth has lived under a universal empire for the longest period of time in the history of civilization—a full thirteen centuries.

One of the most fascinating imperial institutions in history, second in lifespan only to the Roman Catholic See (about twenty centuries), is the Islamic Caliphate. Known as *Khilafah* in Arabic, the Caliphate served as an inspiration and theological authority, but also as a center of tremendous power for millions of people from the western tip of Africa's Sahel to the eastern edges of the Himalayas. More important for today's geopolitics, the ideologically revisited concept of

"Caliphate" continues to serve as a long-range goal for hundreds of thousands of militants, determined to reestablish it, and thus block any form of government or identity that contradicts its raison d'être.

It is crucial for readers to understand where the concept came from, how it has affected this gigantic region of the world for centuries, and how it has been used since the early part of the twentieth century as a rallying point for regimes, organizations, and elites determined to delay and obstruct the expansion of democratic institutions and culture. If one doesn't grasp the notion of Caliphate, as advanced by the modern-day jihadists, one cannot understand the nature of the wall obstructing the rise of multiparty societies in the region, or realize how hard and dangerous is the path to fundamental freedoms in dozens of countries in that region. A quick historical review of this institution-empire is necessary for an understanding of the current climate in the region.

After the passing of the Muslim Prophet, Mohammad bin Abdullah, in 632 C.E., his followers had to decide on the future of the religion and the state he founded. Born in 570 C.E. in Mecca, *Rassulal Allah* (Messenger of Allah, per Muslim theology) dedicated his adult life to propagating a new religion he introduced as Islam (*al-Islaam*). Mohammad presented the Arabian society, particularly in Mecca, which was the economic capital of the Peninsula, as a universal system for faith and society (*al Islaam deen was dawla*). The way it was structured, the expansion of the *deen* (religion) had to be managed, organized, and sanctioned by the *dawla* (state). In 622 C.E., Mohammad and his "Muslim" followers left Mecca after being confronted by its pagan elite and took refuge in Medina to the north. In Medina, the Muslims were able to organize themselves as a force headed by a commander in chief and proceeded to engage in battles with the Meccan tribes until the city submitted. It has since been ruled as the original "Islamic state." But after the *Rassul* died, the now-organized force had to move forward without its founder, and the decision of the senior commanders and new elite ruling the "Islamic land" was to create a succession order from their Prophet. They selected a successor to Mohammad to resume the leadership of the *Umma* (understand this term as the universal community of Muslims or "Islamic nation") and set up a council to maintain the succession and the mission moving forward.

In Arabic, the word for successor is *khalifa*, or caliph. The institution of the caliph is *al Khilafah* or the Caliphate. It has two dimensions: The first is the legal and theological structure of the *Umma*'s top spiritual office, which is comparable to the "papacy," "monarchy," or "presidency"; the second is the entire land and resources covered by the authority of the caliph, as in "empire." The geopolitical sense of the Caliphate is "empire."

Immediately after the selection of a successor to the Prophet, Abu Bakr, the father of Mohammad's most beloved wife, Aisha, resumed the geopolitical dimension of the mission. The "armies" of Arab Muslim tribes quickly conquered the other tribes of the Peninsula. Some were conquered militarily while others joined the marching victors without putting up a fight. The easier battles were fought against the pagan tribes, while Jewish and Christian clans offered more resistance.[2]

It is important to note that by 636 C.E. all inhabitants of the Arabian ancestral homeland had converted or been forced to join Islam. Arab historians are unanimous in describing that it was the rise of the Caliphate that united all Arabian tribes—by force or by adhesion—and gave them a historical common identity. Baathist ideologue Michel Aflaq wrote in the twentieth century that "Islam is to Arabism what bone is to flesh."[3]

Thirteen centuries later, the concept of the Caliphate (or the existence of a universal state for the *Umma*) is hard to eradicate. It is the cement that created the Arab, and later the Islamic *Umma*, and was the legitimizing force behind many achievements, including territorial expansion and the rise of dominant political and financial elites who ruled large segments of three continents.

It is crucial to understand that challenging the idea of a Caliphate in modern times is not only a matter of theological reformation but a matter of threatening the legitimacy of a prominent power. It would be the equivalent of challenging ancient Rome, the universal political papacy, or the very essence of traditional empire. It would require a revolution in political thinking. The Caliphate as a political and military institution was the generator of and legitimizing authority for events that shaped the Middle East for centuries.

The Arab caliphs launched several offensive campaigns from the Peninsula after winning the crucial battles of Yarmuk in 636 C.E. in Syria against the Byzantines, and Qadissiya in 637 C.E. in Iraq against the Persians. From that point on, no empire, nation, kingdom, or population was able to stop an invasion undertaken by the Caliphate. In less than a century, a large part of the civilized world fell to the imperial new state: Syria, Palestine (including Jerusalem, which fell to Caliph Umar), Egypt, North Africa, Spain, Persia, Nubia-Sudan, and more. The invasions, called *Fatah*, thrust as far as France, Sicily, and Sardinia to the west, and Armenia, Tashkent, and the Indus River to the east. A formidable empire was established in less than one century, stretching from the Atlantic to the Indian Ocean. It was centered on the Caliphate, even though the institution itself was in decline only a few decades after its inception.[4]

The successions of one caliph to another were often bloody, and many were assassinated. A civil war exploded between the partisans of the fourth successor, Ali, who was a cousin and the son-in-law of Mohammad, and the supporters of a challenger, Damascus governor Moawiya. The "partisans" of Ali became the Shia, and those who opposed them became the Sunnis. This first civil war within the Caliphate generated a deeper division, soon after becoming sectarian between the two factions. The Sunnis held the leadership of the empire. The Arab *Khilafa* was first based in Damascus, then moved to Baghdad in 750 C.E. as a result of the first coup d'état in the empire. A new Arab dynasty, the Abbasids, butchered the Umayyad dynasty, expanded the Caliphate even farther inland into Asia and Africa, and ruled almost until the destruction of their capital by the Mongols in 1250 C.E.

This Arab-dominated Caliphate produced political, economic, and social elites comparable to those of the feudal system of Europe, which was attached to the papacy for ultimate legitimacy. The ruling establishment settled in Damascus, Cairo, Baghdad, and Tripoli. The rest of the conquered territories owed their new status to the higher authority of the Caliphate. They became the national elites of these governorates, which became countries later, thanks to appointments made by the Prince of the Believers (a title of the Caliph). Sultans, walis, emirs, and subdynasties were an extension—or sort of viceroys—of the supreme leader of the empire.

Even though many powerful princes and military commanders rose against individual caliphs, and killed them, the umbilical connection to the concept of the Caliphate was indestructible. From it came the legitimacy of jihad and the ability to call on "brothers" to come to the rescue when infidels threatened one or another Muslim principality (called *Jihad al Fard* and *Jihad al Ayn*). The authorization for *Fatah*, to resume conquests into the *kuffar* (infidel) lands, also emanated from the Caliphate. In short, the *Khilafa* did far more than provide the theologically necessary successor to the Prophet; it was a moral and political authority that allowed the expansion of the empire and its provinces (soon to become countries), and most important, it provided an authority to the elites installed by its power in cities and *wilayat* (governorates). And since the nature of the Caliphate was based on a command by Allah, or so believed its founders after the passing of the Messenger, reforming it, dismantling it, or going against its initial mission was impossible. The concept was made of iron, and politically it was the foundation upon which the ruling elites of the empire established themselves. Take away its fundamental legitimacy, and the entire system would collapse.

In fact, the Caliphate resembled the European Christian, the Asian, and to some extent the Mesoamerican empires. The "divine" was the center of power, making any challenge to authorities almost impossible, short of a radical revolution. Just as no Christian was able to challenge the authority of the pope on strategic affairs, no Muslim was able to challenge the caliph on war and peace, or on conquest and expansion. In risings against the caliphs throughout the years, the aim was to replace the individual ruler, not the Caliphate as an institution working in the name of Allah. For thirteen centuries, the region controlled by that Caliphate was molded intellectually and ideologically by clerics and rulers to be faithful to the successor of the Prophet as a guardian of the Islamic lands and rulers, the *Hukkam* of the *Umma*.

In other regions of the world ruled by theological empires, absolute monarchies, and colonial enterprises, challengers rose from among their own people. From revolution to revolution, the religious geopolitical spaces crumbled and were replaced with nation-states. Deteriorating religious empires didn't bring about democracy and human rights immediately, but created an opportunity for constant challenge. Until the early twentieth century the global Islamic Caliphate wasn't yet opposed by a revolutionary movement, even though its authority and direct power was in decay.

One must distinguish between the history of the institutions of the Caliphate and the political culture it firmly established in the region. The main tenets of that political culture were as follows:

1. The lands seized during the march of the caliphs must remain "Islamic" and cannot revert to any other identity. Whatever the Caliphate-empire covered geographically is the core of the "Islamic world." Hence these spaces cannot change civilizational or, some would argue, religious identity.

2. The Caliphate-empire created an irreversible "political and legal space" that can only grow or stay constant, it cannot shrink or regress. It has become a slice of the planet and its fate is to cover the globe. Even if it is invaded, occupied, or some parts of it revert to other civilizational identities, it must be restored.

3. The Caliphate was supposed to survive all human conflicts and eventually expand. Even when it collapsed in the early twentieth century, the basis upon which it was created, such as Sharia law[5] and the concept of jihad, remained. No social or ideological construct would undo Sharia and jihad, even as the physical empire collapsed. These two ingredients, Sharia and jihad, can and would restore the empire.

4. Last but not least, religious minorities living within the universal boundaries of the Caliphate may survive under legal and political proscriptions but cannot reestablish sovereign entities in the empire's territory, even if the countries these minorities seek to rebuild are located on their own ancestral lands.[6]

The Collapse of the Ottoman Empire and the Historic Opportunity

The Arab dynasties that ruled the Caliphate enjoyed a multicentennial era of power from the seventh century C.E. to the early sixteenth century. In 1517, the unexpected occurred: a non-Arab ethnic group, the Turks, emerged in Arab-speaking lands, defeated the regional dynasty of the Mameluk, and claimed the leadership of the Islamic world.

The Ottoman sultan seized the title of caliph from the Arabs and moved the capital of the Islamic empire to Istanbul (formerly Constantinople). To assert its leadership of the *Umma,* the sultans-caliphs resumed jihad in all directions. They thrust farther into *kuffar* lands, conquering the remnants of the Byzantine Empire (in addition to Constantinople), Greece, the Slavic Balkans, Romania, parts of Hungary, Moldavia, all the way to Crimea and most of the Caucasus. They were stopped at the gates of Vienna. As a reward for their success in their mega-jihad in Christian Europe, the Ottomans swept over Syria, Mesopotamia, and all of North Africa. In addition, they seized the biggest prize: Mecca and Medina.

The Ottoman Caliphate-Sultanate survived another four centuries before it was defeated at the end of World War I. During the hundreds of years of Turkish rule on three continents (Asia, Africa, and Europe), the base of a pyramid of conquered, occupied, and oppressed peoples widened. Below the ruling Ottoman establishment at the top of the pyramid came the other Muslim elites from Arab, Balkan, Kurdish, Berber, and Caucasus ethnicities. Below them came the non-Muslims—Christians, Jews, Baha'is, and others. African Muslims were theoretically above the non-Muslims but were treated in the same discriminatory manner. Until the nineteenth century, black *Abeed* (Arabic for slaves) were captured in the Sudan, East Africa, and Mauritania and, despite the fact that they shared a religion, were sent to serve masters in the palaces and homes of Ottoman and Arab elites.[7]

The rulers on top of this pyramid and throughout its layers established their privileges on the moral and theological legitimacy of the Caliphate, and were solidified by the Ottoman Sultanate. Emancipation of slaves, religious freedom, ethnic and national liberation, as well as female equality and fundamental political rights, were all trapped within the confines of an unchallengeable order, which, according to the ruling elite, was set by Allah and carried out by a caliph, whose *Walis,* along with the urban upper classes, managed and maintained the social order. Even outside the physical frontiers of the Ottoman Caliphate, the suppression of peoples' liberties, internal and external, was carried out by dynasties, monarchs, emirs, and khans in reverence to the highest divine will embodied by the remote Sultanate.

Surprisingly, the concept of the Caliphate served as a counterinsurgency tool, even if the actual Islamic Ottoman Empire was weak and in decline. The ideology of Caliphate, which was grounded in the doctrines of Sharia and jihad, was the real cement binding the interests of powerful social, economic, and political interests of the ruling establishments in a vast region. Regardless of the original intention of its founders, historical evolution transformed the Caliphate into a megapower, central for those forces that dominated the vast lands conquered under jihad. In comparative perspective, it certainly resembled the mutation of Christendom from a community of believers into a powerful empire ruled from Rome or Constantinople, and later from European palaces. Certainly there are theological differences. The right to struggle geopolitically was granted to the Islamic *Umma* under the exceptionally powerful concept of jihad, yet "crusading" was performed against the essential teaching of the early Church.

These differences aside, the historical practices were similar, not only between Abrahamic religious power centers, but also between all other religious empires and dynasties. The question in modern times is whether reforms and revolutions transformed all "religious empires," real or virtual, into secular and pluralistic societies.

Aside from the rise of smaller modernist renaissance movements in the Greater Middle East, many of which borrowed European democratic and liberal ideas, the critical mass revolution or reform against the essence of the Caliphate has yet to happen. In Europe and the Americas religious monarchies were abolished and separation between state and theological ideologies was achieved through a series of reformations, reforms, revolutions, and secularization. In the Muslim world, however, there was no parallel track. Despite many reform attempts and the rise of nationalist and secular movements in the nineteenth century, the Ottoman Sultanate continued to retain the power of the Islamic Caliphate until the defeat of the Ottoman Empire in 1919 and the abolishing of the Sultanate in 1924. So, the Caliphate survived until the launching of the League of Nations, the parent of the current United Nations.

European Mandates and Modernization

As of 1920, the British and the French were mandated by the League of Nations to manage the affairs of the former Ottoman provinces of the Levant until they were ready for independence. Britain was to oversee Jordan, Palestine, Iraq, and Kuwait. It already administered (or had colonized) Egypt, Sudan, Eastern Africa, and the Indian sub-continent. France was granted responsibility for Lebanon and Syria, and was already the colonial ruler in North and West Africa. The mandate powers combined covered large parts of what was the Caliphate. With the exception of Kemalist Turkey, central Arabia, and Persia, the rest of the *Umma* had come under Western rule, including Italian control in Libya and Eritrea and Dutch control in Indonesia.[8]

During the period of modern-day European colonization, three main trends characterized the political development of most of these countries with large Muslim populations. First, as the Western colonial powers controlled and enjoyed the resources of these countries, their civil societies were just being introduced to modern institutions, including secular constitutions and various forms of electoral democracies. Second, in most of these countries, local nationalist elites rose to power domestically and eventually snatched authority from the Europeans. Egypt, Syria, Iraq, Jordan, and Algeria mutated from provinces inside the Caliphate to colonies, and finally to independent nation-states. The collapse of the Ottoman Sultanate and, ironically, the structural modernization brought about by Westerners created these new modern republics and constitutional monarchies. The third trend, however, was a significant political current that can be considered "reactionary" in the sense that it wanted to return the Caliphate, the previous regime. Followers of this political movement are known as Islamists.

What the European mandates actually did was to push back against the Ottoman Sultanate, defeat the Islamic powers one after another, from North Africa under the French to Egypt, Sudan, and India under the British, and gradually reduce the geographical Caliphate into its last stronghold, Istanbul. But even as the "empire" borders shrank to Ottoman Anatolia and the Levantine provinces by the early twentieth century, the political establishment in the entire *Umma* (with the exception of Shiite Persia) remained nominally attached to the legitimacy of the Caliphate held by the Turks. Even though the Wahabis in Arabia and many khans, sultans, and royalties in the Muslim world were dissatisfied with the Ottoman rule politically, they never doubted the idea of a world Caliphate. During World War I, the Central Powers convinced their ally the Turkish sultan to declare jihad against the "infidel" Allies. Berlin hoped orders of jihad by the supreme caliph of Istanbul would enflame the vast Muslim populations under Franco-British rule. This brilliant theologically grounded strategy was confronted with a similar British strategy. Through the good offices of agent T. E. Lawrence, who promised British recognition of Sherif Hussein as the king of the Arabs, the Hashemite ruler of Mecca declared his own jihad against the Turks. In fact, the latter wasn't a revolution against the Caliphate, but rather a move to bring back the Caliphate from Turkish to Arab hands. The result was that the Turkish jihad and the Arab jihad negated each other's impact, and soon enough the Ottomans lost the war.

From the ashes of the Ottoman Sultanate, for the first time a fully secular revolution was led by a Turkish general, Mustafa Kemal, known as Ataturk. He actually crossed the forbidden line and abolished the Caliphate-Sultanate in 1924. For the first time since the seventh century, a Muslim leader eliminated the institution of the *Khilafa*. Kemal Ataturk acted quickly, in an authoritarian manner, with no significant opposition from Arab and Muslim powers. His very secular, almost anticlerical, new republic emerged as a result of wars with the Greeks who were removed from Smyrna on the Aegean coast, and with the Armenians who were removed from Van, their capital, and most of their ancestral land in Asia Minor, as well as with campaigns to bump the British and the French out of the country. His "nationalist" achievements and land acquisition for the Turks earned him forgiveness for his sacrilege of disbanding the Caliphate. The majority of Turks were too busy carving out a spot for their nation on the Mediterranean among the other modern nation-states to worry about the fate of the "global empire."

The ruling classes among Arabs in Syria, Lebanon, Iraq, the Gulf states, Egypt, Sudan, and the rest of the region were also not focused on the big picture. Other issues, including decolonization and the shaping of borders, were the top priorities of Muslim ruling classes in the Indian subcontinent, South Asia, and Africa.

The only forces frustrated with the collapse of the "empire" arrived at the scene too late: Wahabis of Arabia and the Muslim Brotherhood of Egypt emerged as influential factors only as of the mid-1920s. Under colonial and mandate power, the upper classes, the financial and intellectual elite of the once-universal Islamic *Khilafa*, were in some way inheriting the Caliphate, by building their own little "caliphates" within the boundaries of their new nation-states.

Even after the crumbling of the Caliphate as a regional entity, the national and regional heirs didn't openly state that they were emerging from the ashes of a thirteen-centuries-old empire and that the *Khilafa* had been abolished, and that its return would be against international law, just as a return of the Holy Roman Empire would be forbidden.

The new elites, absolute and constitutional monarchs, dictators, and authoritarian rulers, turned silent on the path that was before them. They moved forward in creating modern institutions (in most cases) adaptable to the modern era in international society, though these were not democratic. They did not go so far as to declare the Caliphate an "old regime." To do so, they needed to perform an intellectual and ideological revolution against the rule of the *khalifa*, which necessitated a fundamental reform and a rereading of history. Such reformation would require a recognition that most of their countries were established at some point in history by conquest and thus rights to ethnic minorities had to be granted. Should ethnic minorities be granted equal rights, it would amount to another admission that the law prevailing under the Caliphate was not compatible with modern-day secular democracy, which meant that Sharia law had to be reformed as well.

The two conditions that would result from rejecting the old order meant adapting the political culture of democracy, which obviously meant that an alternation in power had to be the rule. Most of the post-Caliphate elites of the region weren't ready to accept liberal democracy yet. Since they didn't seek a democratic state after the Caliphate, the twentieth century basically missed the opportunity for political revolution.

The European mandates ended the Caliphate geopolitically and introduced modern state institutions, but failed to develop full democratic cultures. The historical debate about this failure continues, but the real obstruction to modern democracy appeared within the new countries that emerged. In fact, a triangular relationship was established involving three forces: the new dominant elites—heirs of the past regime but not willing to go forward—the forces that wanted to go back to the past, and the forces that wanted to move forward to the future. Eventually the ruling elite and the fundamentalists would defeat the reformers.

Rise of All Ideologies: Preparing for D-Day

The first decades of the twentieth century produced all the ideologies that would affect the Middle East in the latter part of the century and beyond. The root cause of what was to happen decades later was the rise of several ideologies after the collapse of the Turkish Sultanate. Each of these ideologies was produced by specific elites and claimed authority in the post-Ottoman region. Here is an overview of the main ideologies, which rose almost simultaneously:

1. Arab Nationalism or al Qawmiya al Arabiya

Known also as "Pan Arabism," this movement was launched by secular and liberal intellectuals at the end of the nineteenth century in response to the ailing Turkish Caliphate and to the Wahabi Islamist challenge. The promoters of this ideology claimed that all Arab-speaking peoples of the region belonged to one nation, *al Umma al Arabiya* (the Arab Nation).

Historically the ideologues who called for "Arab" nationalism were from a Christian or Muslim progressive background. They were influenced by the new European nationalism, including the French, German, and Italian unification movements. They wished to do away with the notion of an Islamic religious authority and replace it with a secular notion of a Pan Arab republic or constitutional monarchy. In essence the "Arab nationalists" were proposing a trade: The Islamic dimension of the Caliphate would be confined to religious clerics while the political dimension of that Caliphate would become secular. They wanted to change the substance of the ruling institutions, but not the shell of the empire.

Pan Arab ideologues still wanted to reestablish an "Arab" *Umma* from the Atlantic Ocean to the Arab Gulf, rejecting the rise of other, smaller nationalist ideals within that *Umma*, such as Egyptian, Lebanese, or ethnic movements such as the Kurdish or Berber. Arab nationalism maintained that Persian and Turkish, let alone Indian (especially Pakistani) and Indonesian nationalisms were not Arab, but were cousins in history and religion. Arab nationalists valued the contribution of Islam to the formation and expansion of Arabism. The caliphs were Muslim, but were essentially Arab dynasties until the Abbasids. The idea was to create a secular Arab "Caliphate."

Although non-Islamist in its inception, Pan Arabism kept a number of totalitarian features from the preceding Caliphate rule, among them suppression of ethnic minorities and intolerance toward pluralist ideas that can challenge Arab identity. Later on, after decolonization, Arab nationalists would mutate into chauvinistic elites, ultimately resulting in xenophobia. Movements such as the Baath of Syria and Iraq, the followers of Nasser of Egypt, the doctrine of Muammar Qaddafi, and to some extent those who would form the Palestine Liberation Organization abandoned the original liberalism of the intellectuals and replaced it with extreme forms of supremacist nationalism.

Arab nationalism as of the mid–twentieth century had mutated into the force behind massacres of minorities, suppression of liberties, and military juntas' crushing democracies across the region. Pan Arabism splintered into conservative, progressive, and even Marxist groups, but all were authoritarian. They awaited the crumbling of Turkish authority to reestablish Arab power.[9]

2. Islamic Fundamentalism

Under the Caliphate, including the Ottomans, Islamism as an ideology was the state doctrine. Hence, movements calling for the "establishment" of a Caliphate didn't make sense as long as the Caliphate existed. However, many ultrajihadist ideologues such as Mohammad Abdel Wahab of Arabia, in the eighteenth century, and Hassan al Banna of Egypt in the early twentieth century, criticized Istanbul for being too liberal. They assailed the Turkish sultans for departing from the ways of the founders of the Caliphate, known as *al salaf al salih* (from which the term "Salafist" came).

Under the Islamic empire the Salafists were the extreme right wing of the Caliphate, those who rejected reform, opposed interpretation of the Koran and Hadith, fought modernization, and criticized adopting constitutional texts. They advocated a strict application of the Sharia, and strongly opposed codes produced by Western revolutions or constitutional reforms. Ironically, the Islamists of today, who carry the ideology of the ancient Salafists, would have been the most extreme within a Caliphate. They were influenced by Ibn Taymiyya, a scholar in the Middle Ages who warned that straying from the strict vision of the Salaf (founders of the Caliphates of the seventh century) would bring about the collapse of the Caliphate and the Islamic *Umma*.[10]

The premodern Islamists built a fortress of resistance against the natural evolution of the Muslim world toward sciences, human knowledge, women's liberation, tolerance, and opening up to the outside world. This was known as the *Man' al Ijtihaad* (the blocking of jurisprudence.) They constituted, even under an Islamic Caliphate, the opposition to progress and liberty. A deeper historical analysis would place them as defenders of the old regime within the empire, protective of the privileges of the ruling elites, both clerical and political, opponents of any change that would challenge those elites. They waited for the collapse of the weak and ailing Ottoman Sultanate to reestablish a strong world Islamic Caliphate, and were ready to resume jihad and *Fatah*.[11]

3. Nationalist and Ethnic Movements

The crumbling of the "empire" opened the doors to myriad nationalities, ethnicities, religious groups, and other communities to seek freedom, self-determination, or amelioration of their status in their native lands. From the largest to the smallest, peoples who had been subjected to conquest (*Fatah*) since the seventh century C.E. by Arab dynasties, and since the fifteenth century by the Ottomans, rose to acquire a new status. Some were successful; most weren't. Some ended up with fairly democratic institutions, but a large majority of these nationalities and ethnicities were not so lucky. Let's start with the three big ethnonational groups.

Throughout the twentieth century, the Arabs ended up achieving statehood in twenty-one separate states—the present members of the Arab League. Few Arab populations were left behind as borders shifted. The inhabitants of an enclave in northern Syria, Antioch, were annexed by modern Turkey; the Arab population of the Ahwaz on the eastern coast of the Persian Gulf was annexed to modern-day Iran; and the Arabs of the former British mandate of Palestine, who lost the opportunity to join Transjordan and, despite the fact that the UN has recognized their right for statehood, couldn't form their own state because of the Arab-Israeli conflict. But 96 percent of all Arabs were part of independent countries formed from Morocco to Oman.

The Turks, as we noted earlier, developed a nation-state in Asia

Minor and a piece of the Balkans surrounding Istanbul. That modern
Turkish republic, freed from the Sultanate, was built on two ethnic
conflicts: the evacuation of the Greeks from Smyrna on the Aegean
coast and of the Armenians from their ancestral lands in Asia Minor.
Another Turkic-speaking population formed the state of Azerbaijan,
but a large Azeri population was annexed by Iran to the south. A
small Turkic community was left in Kirkuk in Arab-dominated Iraq.

The third nationality that regrouped after the end of the Caliphate
was the Persians, who after centuries of Arab colonialism were able
to reform ancient Persia under the name of Iran in the sixteenth century. Shiite in religion, the Persians became a majority in their modern country, with a number of other ethnic minorities.

Hence the three largest national and ethnic groups were able to
surge toward independence and reclaim all or most of their ancestral
lands. The Arabs, the Turks, and the Persians had all regrouped, but
what about the other ethnicities?

The Jews, absent from activism in the region for centuries since
being confined to the status of *Dhimmis* (second-class citizens, according to Sharia law), and victims of rising anti-Semitism in Europe,
leaped into a nationalist revival known as Zionism in the nineteenth
century. Rejecting victimhood, they developed an ethnonationalist movement claiming their goal was the return to Palestine, their
"ancestral land." From that perspective, political Zionism was a nationalist revolt of the Jews against the Caliphate, which forbade the
emergence of non-Islamic entities within its own perimeter.

There were also Muslim ethnonationalities that were dominated
by other, larger Muslim groups. The Berbers in Algeria, Morocco,
and the rest of North Africa; the Kurds in Arab Iraq and Syria, Turkey, and Persian Iran; African blacks in Sudan under Arab rule; and
African blacks in Mauritania and the Sahel confronted by Arabo-
Berbers in the north of the region. Last but not least, there were
those Christian ethnonationalities that preceded the Arab Islamic
conquest—Copts of Egypt, Assyro-Chaldeans in Iraq, Aramaeans
in Syria and Lebanon, and others dispersed in the rest of the region.
Smaller religious groups such as Baha'is, Zaidis, and Zoroastrians
lived in Iran and Iraq.

All these minorities sought separation, independence, or some
form of autonomy and formed their own "claims movements."
Minorities often competed among themselves when commingled

territorially, in the case of the Assyro-Chaldeans and Kurds in Iraq or that of the Maronites and Druses in Lebanon, but the main race toward statehood was between these small groups and the larger nationalities. Some call the ethnic race to freedom a mosaic, while others are resigned to seeing it as chaotic. Under both the Arab and Ottoman Caliphates, the peoples seeking liberation from the "empire" had ups and downs in their endeavor.[12]

The Europeans in the Balkans were first to extract themselves from the Caliphate; Serbs, Croats, Romanians, Bulgarians, and Greeks achieved statehood by the end of the nineteenth century. North African Arabs and Berbers moved out of the Turkish zone only to fall under European powers; Copts, Berbers, and Africans fell under Arabs. It became a virtual layer cake. Similar scenarios occurred after 1919 in the Levant: In Iraq and Syria, Kurds, Aramaeans, and other Christians were at the bottom, Arab Muslims above them, and the Franco-British on top. In British-mandated Palestine, the Jewish population rushed to form ethnic enclaves while the Arabs of Palestine rejected the newcomers as an ethnic community seeking statehood. As they were awaiting decolonization, both groups engaged in confrontation. Lebanon, where the Maronites and other Lebanese Christians were lifted up to become first-level citizens along with their Arab Muslim co-citizens, was an exception.

In short, all the inhabitants of the former Ottoman Empire, clustered in nationalities, ethnicities, and religious groups, spent the years of Western colonialism and mandates preparing for their respective "D-Days." Arab nationalists planned on Pan Arabism; the Turks on consolidating their "Turkish-only" republic; the Persians on strengthening Iran and maintaining its borders; Jews and Arabs in Palestine on carving up states for their own future; Berbers and Copts on obtaining autonomy; Africans on obtaining their own entities. In Lebanon, the Christian intelligentsia promoted a "Pluralist Mediterranean Lebanon" while the Islamic establishment was set to "re-Arabize" Lebanon.

4. Democracy and Human Rights Groups

Oddly, democracy movements didn't always correspond to liberation movements or nationalist claims in the post-Ottoman Middle East. Liberal and democracy forces were scattered across the region, adapting to the various ethnonationalist claims, but not always satisfied in their quest for human rights. The region was too crowded with visions, ideologies, identity struggles, and inherited conflicts for reformers and humanists to take the lead in each movement. The Islamists, Pan Arabists, ethnonationalists, separatists, and the like were too chauvinistic and nervous about their agendas to allow too much space for liberalism and humanitarianism. Leaders in majority nationalities, as in the Arab, Turkish, and Persian movements, feared "democratization" would weaken the nationalist gains and allow separatism to shrink the national territory.

Ironically, often politicians within minorities acted in authoritarian fashion, alleging that the time was not yet ripe for the "democratic debate," but for a focused struggle for "group rights." Democracy and human rights movements were dispersed and fragmented across the region, unable to mount a transnational effort. Among all forces seeking surges on postcolonial D-Day, the democracy forces including women, students, artists, labor, and writers were the weakest and least-prepared segments of society to take part in the race to build the new states.

In the first rows of the vast arena of competition were the already established elites, heirs of the past Caliphate provinces and regional and local dynasties, and other upper classes co-opted by the colonial powers. In most cases, they were the same rich and powerful groups that had ruled cities under the Sultanate and Caliphate and were often the first partners of the incoming European administrations. Ironically, these urban or tribal forces were sometimes also first to lead anti-Western revolts. Second in that arena were the newly emerging ideological factions, Islamists, Pan Arabists or military juntas. Third were the leaders of separatist communities, solidly entrenched within their groups and not always democratic. Last were democracy and individual rights elements.

In some cases, politicians within minorities were educated as liberals and remained so, as in the case of Lebanon, until future crises marginalized them. In other cases the ruling classes accepted ingredients of multiparty systems, as in Turkey and Jordan. In Israel, the mostly Westernized society of the Jewish Yishuv was unique in establishing a pluralist liberal democracy at the departure of the British, but in a country encompassing two parallel societies: Jews and Arabs.

The advocates of liberal democracy and secular revolution were in the minority, at the bottom of the scale, and about to be further suppressed at the end of the region's European era. Ironically, as indicated earlier, the British and French were the ones to introduce basic representative institutions such as parliaments, constitutional courts, tribunals, bureaucratic methods, and public secular teaching. Even more ironic, the "colonial powers" were mostly acclaimed by the weakest elements of society, ethnic minorities and liberals, because of the protections and rule of law they introduced, while the highest levels of society, the nationalists, Islamists, and upper classes, saw in the Europeans not only a foreign force to be expelled, but promoters of dangerous ideas. The colonial rulers, particularly the local governors and military commanders, were oppressive, and their rule, no matter how profitable to the indigenous populations, had no future but withdrawal.

One hidden truth during colonial times was that often the local elites posing as the alternative ruling choice were much worse oppressors, harsh opponents of democracy, and enemies of democratic institutions. In the decades that followed decolonization, the new masters of the land made sure to perpetuate the blaming of miseries on "imperialism" and the former colonial powers, disguising their own destruction of human liberties within their own societies.

Decolonization and the Defeat of Democracy

In most regions around the world, the departure of a colonial power signals an immediate advancement toward democracy, or at least a step in that direction. This wasn't always the case in the Greater Middle East. It is almost impossible to make global statements about an entire region stretching from Morocco to Afghanistan in terms of democratic advancement, for some countries leaped toward multiparty systems and pluralism while others regressed to absolutism.

The differences between Turkey and Saudi Arabia, Lebanon and Iran, Jordan and Syria, for example, are vast. Some, such as Lebanon and Turkey, grant many rights to more citizens, including women and the political opposition, than the others. But in the wake of decolonization throughout the region, the dominant political culture retained common characteristics that resisted the advance of civil societies toward the norms achieved by the international community, at least in the free world.

The first of these characteristics was the common view that a "regional cause" superseded all other causes for internal freedoms. In the Arab world it was "Arabism" or *al Uruba*, synonymous with a transnational ethnic identity that must be defended and imposed at the same time. The promoters of *al Uruba* claimed no higher cause could overshadow this virtual hypertribe, and anyone who would challenge it from the inside would be considered a traitor. Thus, gradually, a regional political culture was firmly grounded across borders and defended by the Arab League and Arab leaders, regardless of their political systems. This explains how the Kurds, Berbers, southern Sudanese, Darfur Africans, Lebanese Aramaic Christians, Copts, and all other non-Arab ethnicities were crushed for many decades with almost unanimous approval by all Arab states and Pan Arab elites.

The second common characteristic was the view that the region, and a much larger slice of Asia, Africa, and a chunk of Europe, formed a "Muslim world" *Aalam Islamee*, which had to be defended and strengthened as a political, cultural, religious, and economic bloc, almost in the same manner as the Soviet Bloc. A modern mutation of the older concept of *Umma*, the Muslim world was presented as a geographical space with marked territories.

Another more troubling notion was advanced in the more ideological theorizing—that these were therefore "Islamic lands" or *Aradee Islamiya*. This implied that these "lands" could not revert to any other identity. So, in a postcolonial Greater Middle East there was no room anymore for "non-Islamic" lands, states, countries, and homelands. The Copts of Egypt, the Assyro-Chaldeans of Iraq, the Christians of Lebanon, the Animists and Christian Africans in southern Sudan, and the Biafrans were denied any hope of self-determination. Astonishingly and ironically, all "Islamic lands" found under the sovereignty of non-Muslim nation-states had to be reclaimed and granted independence or separation. These included Eritrea, Kashmir, northern Cyprus, Ceuta and Melila, the southern Philippines, and the Palestinian territories under Israeli occupation.

A third common characteristic was a general attitude against the so-called Western democracy. Apart from Lebanon, Turkey, Israel, and to some extent Jordan, elites in other countries expressed criticism of what they called "Western-style democracy." The idea was that constitutions that mirror those of European liberal democracies are not indigenous and thus cannot represent the region's "identity." The real meaning of this notion is that since these Western pluralist systems recognize the rise and fall of new elites and the emergence of new identities, they are in fact a threat to the well-established regional elite of the Middle East. Across the board in the Arab world, and to a lesser degree in Muslim South Asia, both conservative and progressive elites—each from a different perspective—lashed out against "importing" the institutions of the former colonial powers. They resented the adoption of the principles of laws and constitutional stipulations that would permit their political demise through universal elections and a challenge to the so-called regional identity.

However, one cannot make sweeping generalizations about how different countries in the Middle East adopted different aspects of democratic institutions. The advances made in one sector were counterbalanced by failures in other areas. On the top of the list, Israel's advanced democratic system was limited in that fewer rights were granted to ethnic Arabs, as a result of national security considerations. In Turkey, all citizens enjoyed voting rights and the right to assemble, with the exception of rights of autonomy for Kurds and the right to recognize the Armenian genocide. In Lebanon, all nationals may vote for the parties of their choice, but posts in government are cast in stone as the property of particular religious communities. These are the states with the most advanced democratic systems in the region, and yet they still suffered from inconsistencies.

Once the colonial powers left the region, gradually, and in different ways, the peoples of the Middle East were transferred from living under European colonialism to living under either Arab or Islamic imperialism and, in most cases, Arab-on-Arab authoritarianism. Let's review the main failures in the movement toward freedom, democracy, and recognition of ethnic and religious minorities in the region throughout the twentieth century:

1. As early as the 1920s, the Wahabis seized power in Arabia and formed an absolute monarchy based on Salafism: Non-Muslim religions were banned, Shia Muslims were suppressed, women's basic rights restrained, and fundamental political freedoms annulled. By law, no political parties were allowed.

2. In Egypt, as the British departed, the constitutional monarchy was removed by the military coup d'état that installed a quasidictatorship under Pan Arabist leader Gamal Abdel Nasser in 1954: Political freedoms were curtailed for all citizens and the ethnic rights of the Coptic minority suppressed.

3. In Libya, following the withdrawal of the Italians and British, the constitutional monarchy collapsed in a coup d'état in 1970: Muammar Qaddafi declared himself the leader of the "revolution" and has since aspired to become the "Islamic Arab" leader of the whole region. Naturally, all freedoms perished.

4. In Syria, a limping multiparty democracy following the departure of the French in 1945 was removed through a series of military coups bringing the Baath Arab Socialist Nationalist Party to power in the 1960s. After internal palace coups within the party, a hard-line faction took over in 1970 under Hafez Assad.

5. In Iraq, following the withdrawal of the British, the same Pan Arabist officers bloodily removed the king in 1958. The Baath established a one-party dictatorship in the 1960s, seized ultimately, in 1979, by Saddam Hussein, one of the most lethal dictators in the region. Since then, Kurds, Shia, and liberal Sunnis have been oppressed.

6. In Iran, after the pullback of British and Russian influence in the 1950s, a monarchic authoritarian regime survived the Mossadegh revolution in 1953 but didn't survive the revolution led by Ayatollah Ruhollah Khomeini, which removed Shah Reza Pahlevi in 1979 and replaced him with a highly oppressive Islamist "republic."

7. In Algeria, after years of violent struggle against French colonialism, the National Liberation Front (FLN) finally obtained independence in 1962, but only to create a one-party regime that banned political freedoms and suppressed the cultural rights of the Berber Kabyle minority.

8. Lebanon became the most successful multireligious democracy of the Arab world when it gained its independence from the French in 1943, until domestic and foreign forces shattered its precarious political system. Pan Arabists in the region, as well as their supporters in the former "Switzerland of the Middle East," feared the exportation of that little country's "model" to the region and coalesced to cripple Lebanon's institutions, provoking a ravaging ethnic war in which most rights of all sects and individuals were pulverized.

9. As soon as the British left Sudan in 1954, the northern Arab elite rejected calls by the southern African population for federation and self-determination. A hellish civil war ensued for decades, leaving more than a million killed, mostly in the south, with massive ethnic cleansing and blacks taken into slavery.

The rest of the Greater Middle East didn't fare much better, from Morocco and Mauritania to the Gulf and Afghanistan. Unlike the situation in Latin America, where democracy had its ups and downs, swinging between military regimes and multiparty elections, Middle Earth knew only oppression as a common characteristic for its peoples: at different times, in different circumstances, and at the hands of different oppressors, but the twentieth century did not bring peace, freedom, and democracy to the region.

2.

The 1990s: A Dark Tunnel
for Dissidents

By the end of the twentieth century, nine months before Bin Laden's strikes at the heart of the West, the Greater Middle East was still riddled with the worst forms of oppressions, and with genocide, massacres, ethnic cleansing, slavery, executions, torture, and political jailing. From Morocco to Afghanistan, more than one million individuals had been detained for political reasons, as many as the entire population of Gaza. About 750,000 black Africans had been forced into modern-day slavery in Sudan and Mauritania. Armed occupations were still a reality in Lebanon, the Palestinian territories, and Cyprus, and a state military presence was rejected by ethnic minorities in the Algerian Kabyle, southern Sudan, the Kurdish territories in Iraq, Turkey, and Iran, and the Arab province of Iran.

Eleven years after the end of the Cold War, oppression in the region hadn't unclenched its fist a bit. Regimes had solidified their political machines, radical ideologies had expanded wider and deeper, and the West seemingly had abandoned hope for democratic solidarity among these nations. By the last decade of the twentieth century, the American and European departure from freedom policy in the Middle East was astonishing, when contrasted with Western interest in dissidence, pluralism, and human rights during the Cold War.

The 1990s offered evidence of the realities that preceded the international conflict against terror forces with jihadi roots that the United States and other democracies, along with Russia, India, and the moderate Arab and Muslim governments, found themselves involved in as of 2001. In the immediate aftermath of the 9/11 attacks, and again after strikes in Madrid, London, Beslan, Mumbai, and other cities outside the Middle East, many observers and scholars saw a link between the state of civil societies in the region and the surge of jihadist forces.

Contrary to what some experts alleged, there wasn't a direct cause-and-effect relationship between socioeconomic conditions and terrorism, but rather a link between the lack of democratic culture and the rise of radical ideologies, particularly militant Islamist doctrines. One unavoidable conclusion was that all jihadi terrorist actions stem from ideologies that reject pluralist societies and democracy. There is no exception to this rule: The stated motive of violence is ideological. Al Qaeda, the Taliban, Jemaa Islamiya, Hezbollah, the Pasdaran, Hamas, and the Abu Sayyaf faction all stated different geographical goals, but unequivocally called for the establishment of regimes based ultimately on one totalitarian force.

The growth and success of early-twenty-first-century terror was proportional and directly related to the expansion of radical ideologies. And the rise of these ideologies is inversely proportional to the failure of democratic culture in the civil societies from which these radical factions arose.

Four Fundamental Questions

The answers to four crucial, fundamental questions must be determined in order to understand how the Middle East was left behind while the international community moved beyond the Cold War, and how a new window of opportunity subsequently opened, but may be closed again.

1. How did the antidemocracy forces win the battle in the Greater Middle East despite the end of the Cold War, and how were they able to maintain control of the peoples of that vast region under authoritarian rule for a decade and beyond as other nations freed themselves?

2. Why did the West abandon its commitment to freedom and democracy for the region's people while assisting other nations around the world?

3. Why are these values perceived as being different in the Arab and Muslim world than in all other regions of the world?

4. How did the West fail to hear the dissident voices from the Middle East, and why?

Last Years of the Cold War in the Middle East

The Soviet Union's crushing of the Budapest democratic revolution of 1956 signaled an important reality: People oppressed by totalitarian ideologies and military regimes will surge when the opportunity is available, or when their tolerance of suppression is breached. The Hungarians suggested that civil societies under Pan Arabism or other Islamist regimes in the Middle East would eventually explode. Even though in the end the Czechs were put down, the Prague revolt in spring 1968 showed that people on the streets could defy the most powerful oppressive machine of the twentieth century. The Polish workers' strikes of 1980 opened another hole in Soviet domination. The Gdansk workers, by organizing and moving en masse, were able to influence the future of their own nation, opening the door for another generalized uprising in the late 1990s. *Solidarność* was possible on the Baltic shores, so why not on the Mediterranean coasts as well?

Aleksandr Solzhenitsyn, Andrei Amalrik, Vaclav Havel, and others have shown that totalitarianism can be challenged by individuals and that ideas are stronger than secret police. This brewing democratic revolution, coupled with the murmur within the Russian population against all deprivation of freedom, led to the surge of reform forces within the ruling Communist Party, brought Mikhail Gorbachev to the Kremlin, and before our eyes, led to the collapse of European communist regimes one after another, leading to the dismantling of the Soviet Union. What was happening in the Soviet Bloc during the 1980s brought hope into the minds and hearts of Middle Eastern dissidents and reformers.

Ironically, though, while the Soviet Union was much more powerful than all the dictatorships of the Arab and Muslim world combined, the ability of the oppressive regimes in the Greater Middle East to deflect the democratic waves coming from Europe was very strong. The forces of oppression in the Muslim world are rooted in the Caliphate doctrine and are much more pervasive within the political culture than anything the communists were able to achieve under the Soviets. Additionally, the legacy of the Caliphate used by the dominant elites in the region is about thirteen centuries old, compared to the short sixty years or so of communist domination experienced by the peoples of the Soviet Bloc.

Despite robust strikes in the Gdansk factories, the demonstrations in the rest of Europe, the singing revolution in Estonia, the Velvet Revolution in Prague, and finally the fall of the Berlin Wall, it was hard to imagine a similar movement breaking out in the Levant. The regimes, as they'd done in the past, would send tanks to roll over the bodies of the demonstrators. In Syria, the Assad regime leveled the city of Hama when Sunni protesters rose up against the regime in February 1982. In Iraq, Saddam gassed the Kurds in Halabja. In Sudan, the regime's militias captured slaves among the black community in the south. In Iran, thousands of opponents were exterminated. In Algeria, the Berbers were surrounded by tanks. Most of the region's regimes had no intention of reforming, opening, or engaging as they saw the events unfolding in Eastern Europe. Rather it was very much the opposite in the Middle East—as the USSR was going down, the heirs of the Caliphate moved upward.

Regimes' Rush to Crush Democracy

As long as the Cold war was on, Wahabis, Khomeinists, Baathists, Pan Arabists, and other authoritarians perceived themselves as a sort of third bloc between NATO and the Warsaw Pact, their fingers holding the global oil pump and keeping a lid on the democratic aspirations of their own peoples. The West was too consumed by its confrontation with the East to risk prodemocracy policies in the region, and the Soviets had no freedom agenda for the Middle East.

The communist regimes and radical ultranationalist regimes had something in common: Both were undemocratic. So, as long as Washington and Moscow were in conflict, the "sultans" of the region and the would-be leaders among Islamists could secure their reigns, using a platform of Pan Arabism, Pan Islamism, and the eternal conflict against "Zionism." As long as the two superpowers were locked in a world struggle, the dictatorships in Baghdad, Damascus, Tripoli, and Tehran, as well as the authoritarian regimes across the region, had a free hand in suppressing any shred of political liberation in their own societies.

Similarly, the so-called Islamist alternative to the secular Pan

Arabism of the time was also taking advantage of the Cold War to further penetrate Muslim societies. Since the regimes were suppressing all liberal and human rights activities, the Islamists—with support from oil-producing powers within Saudi Arabia, other Gulf principalities, and later on Sudan and Iran—were filling the void.

However, with the spread of dissidence and unrest in the Eastern Bloc as of the mid-1980s, ruling elites in the Middle East got nervous. Supportive or not of Moscow's communist leaders, the dictatorships of the region were extremely sensitive to the rise of popular movements against authoritarianism next door in Eastern Europe. "Socialist" regimes such as those in Syria, Iraq, and Libya were mostly concerned with the weakening of their Soviet allies, while the Islamist regimes in Iran, Sudan, and the Wahabi and Muslim Brotherhood quarters were wary about the rise of democracy that could follow the downfall of their communist foes. Gorbachev's reforms and his slow demobilization of Soviet military aggressiveness between 1985 and 1989 pushed the authoritarians in the Middle East to speed up their preventive measures. After seven years of bloody battles, the Iranian and Iraqi regimes agreed to stop their war in 1987 and since then have dedicated their energy to crushing domestic challengers. The Khomeinists went after the internal ethnic minorities and ended secular and progressive dissidence inside the country. Saddam Hussein completed his oppression of his own minorities, culminating with the gassing of the Kurds in the north in 1988 and further persecution of the Shia in the south. Hafez Assad escalated his campaign in Lebanon against his Muslim opponents in the zones he already occupied and began a new campaign to destroy the last free enclaves of the Christians in East Beirut. There were similar campaigns in Algeria against the Berbers and in Sudan against the southern blacks. Simultaneously, the jihadi Islamists hurried their penetration of Arab societies and hastened their preparations to inherit Afghanistan and other Soviet Muslim republics, including inside Russia in Chechnya.

The year 1989 was of grave symbolic importance to Middle Eastern authoritarians, both secular and Islamist. Across Eastern Europe, one after another, one-party systems were collapsing like dominos. The masses, erupting after decades of complete suppression, were crushing the communist parties, militias, propaganda, and leadership. As Syrian shells exploded during a ravaging war against the "free areas" of Lebanon, in the former Eastern Europe, East Germans,

Poles, Czechs, Hungarians, Romanians, Bulgarians, and others took to the streets of their cities.

In fall 1989, two centuries after the French Revolution, another gigantic revolution against absolutism and totalitarian power was taking place. The Berlin Wall was falling, brick by brick, signaling to the world and particularly to the post-Caliphate Middle East that people can eventually get it right and make it happen. Decades of forced state indoctrination shattered as youths broke the Berlin Wall into pieces. Baghdad and Khartoum's regimes watched live as the Baltic republics quit the Soviet Union, while trembling at the idea that the Kurds and the Africans of southern Sudan could do the same. Soviet forces were asked to leave Eastern Europe, and Hafez Assad feared a similar demand for his troops to eventually withdraw from Lebanon.

But perhaps the dramatic development that created the greatest shock and awe in the hearts of all the dictators of the eastern and southern Mediterranean was the arrest and execution of Romanian dictator Nicolae Ceausescu and his wife, Elena, on December 25, after the bloody repression of demonstrators in Timisoara. In this last tragic episode of the decade, the rulers of the Middle East who had ordered many "Timisoaras" in Syria, Iraq, Iran, Sudan, and other places saw visions of a future they didn't want to happen. Middle Eastern rulers knew the risks of their business: coup d'états, assassinations, and regime change have occurred in their region, but not because of democratic revolutions, or at least not yet.

Abrupt changes of power have been common in the region, but they have always ended in the rise of other authoritarian elites, never in the ascendancy of the rule of the people or the liberation of minorities. Eastern Europe's revolution was sending a dangerous message to the regional elite of the Arab world and its wider neighborhood. Totalitarian regimes were crumbling and the people were establishing democracies. The bottom line was obvious: If it could happen to the Soviets, it could also happen to the Baathists, the Wahabis, the Khomeinists, and all authoritarian rulers in the Greater Middle East.

Even the failed student uprising in Tiananmen Square that same year perturbed the absolutist commanders of "revolutions" and seekers of Caliphates and Imamates in the region. Here was the other communist superpower putting down unarmed youths facing a column of tanks. At that point, the events of 1989 seemed a bad example for civil societies, thought the regimes of the Middle East.

The following two years offered a benchmark. In those years the forces of totalitarianism in the Arab world unleashed hell on earth to maintain power for one more decade before lethally dangerous democracy had another chance to loom on the horizon.

The Region's Response to the Soviet Collapse

The year 1990 witnessed two important indicators of how the radicals, particularly the Baathists, would behave after the collapse of the USSR. On August 2, 1990, Saddam's armored divisions invaded Kuwait to claim it as Iraq's seventeenth province. In fact it was a move, among other things, to allow the Baghdad elite to preemptively strike at any possibility of an uprising inside Iraq by Kurds, Shia, and anti-Saddam Sunnis who could be aided by outside forces. With Soviet support gone, Iraqi Baathists felt the West might be tempted to assist the internal opposition.

As seemingly unreal as it was, Saddam's invasion was a coup aimed at the future. The objective was to consolidate Iraq's power while acquiring additional oil reserves so that the outside powers would be unable to touch the "republic of fear."[1] Saddam's miscalculation was inspired by events in Eastern Europe. Seeing Soviet tanks withdrawing in retreat from Estonia sent chills into Saddam's elite, who feared the rise of an independent Kurdistan. So he sent his own armor against his neighbor.

Hafez Assad sent his tanks rolling into East Beirut, the last free enclave of Lebanon, on October 13 of that same year. Shrewd like no other Arab leader, the dictator of Damascus calculated almost perfectly. As he saw his Soviet ally in decline, he knew that once the collapse commenced, those whom he had oppressed for decades within Syria and his neighbor Lebanon might rise against him.

Without the Cold War, Assad and scores of other rulers feared that the West might turn against the Middle Eastern dictatorships. Exploiting the Saddam threat fully, the Syrian president promised U.S. secretary of state James Baker in September that his regime would join the coalition against Saddam if, among other things, the United States would give Assad carte blanche in Lebanon, which would allow him to invade the last resisting pocket. Under pressure by oil lobbies to restore Kuwait fast, Washington agreed to sacrifice the little country of the Cedars on the altar of overarching interests. Syria's Baathists rejoiced that they were able to score two victories: They weakened Saddam's regime on the one hand, while they finished off the potential free resistance of Lebanon on the other. On October 13, 1990, Syrian divisions overran the smaller Lebanese army and seized the presidential palace, the Ministry of Defense, and other government institutions. The Lebanese were then put under the diktat of their neighbor for the next fifteen years. Freedom was lost for those who believed in democracy and pluralism.[2]

In August 1991, pro-Soviet regimes in the region experienced their last glimpse of hope that all was not yet lost. For a few days, a coup organized by the KGB and other hard-core communists in Moscow was about to turn back the clock. Gorbachev was under house arrest and a military state of emergency was declared. If the USSR came back, Eastern Europe would inevitably suffer, as would the captive nations of the Middle East.

Saddam rushed to congratulate the red Kremlin for the reversal of perestroika. Muammar Qaddafi expressed the same satisfaction. In Damascus, the more cautious Assad preferred to wait for a few more days. Across the region, the authoritarians who counted on the Soviets to supply them with weapons and spare parts were celebrating. In Khartoum, the Bashir elite breathed at last.

The joy was short-lived. The coup failed, Gorbachev temporarily came back to power, and the hard-core generals were jailed. The most troubling moment for Middle Eastern dictators after the defeat of the Moscow coup came when Boris Yeltsin stood up on a tank and called on the Russian military and people to follow him and bring down the communist dictatorship. This was the pivotal moment that brought the Soviet Union down and dismantled the totalitarian power of the Communist Party.

In Tehran, Baghdad, Damascus, and Khartoum this scene had a more ominous meaning. Yeltsin was a member of the Communist Party but had revolted against it. What if members of the ruling parties in the Middle East followed suit? That question was, to some extent, answered years later when high-ranking officials from the Syrian Baath broke away in 2005 and when former leaders of the Iranian regime rose against Ahmadinejad during the Tehran uprising of June 2009.

In August 1990, the region's regimes finally understood that the Cold War was really over and the Soviet big brother was no more. The "powers that be" in the region had to move fast to head off any future attempt within their own civil societies to push for change, reform, and liberation.

The Scramble to Crush Freedom

Incredible as it may seem, the decade that followed the collapse of the Iron Curtain in Europe and large parts of Asia brought new Iron Curtains around civil societies in the Greater Middle East. The contrast between events in Eastern Europe and events in the Arab world and some parts of the Muslim world is staggering.

After the rise of transitional democracies in the former European members of the Warsaw Pact and the USSR, and as multiparty elections (regardless of their successes and failures) were held in the Caucasus and Central Asia, other authoritarian governments began feeling pressure from within, as well as from the international community. Official Western discourse and the UN narrative on antidemocratic regimes and suppression of liberties grew bolder. International conferences and legislation on women's and minorities' rights confirmed the trend. There was no longer a Cold War to impede the advancement of fundamental rights of national, ethnic, and gender communities. However, this leap into the future didn't register in the Greater Middle East. As if a black hole covered a large chunk of the planet, a number of countries went missing in democracy and human rights development.

In Iraq, Saddam Hussein sent his forces to crush the Shia rebellion in the south. Thousands were killed and dumped in mass graves. Iraqi Baath oppression against its own population was among the most brutal in the world. In Sudan, the National Islamic Front of Hassan Turabi and the Islamist regime of Colonel Omar Bashir waged organized ethnic cleansing campaigns against the southern black population. The number of massacred Africans climbed to hundreds of thousands. In addition, the regime's *Difaa Shaabi* militias spread across the southern provinces, creating mayhem and taking thousands of slaves. In Algeria, the Kabyle Berbers were subjected to persecution by the regime while the Salafi Islamists were committing atrocities against the larger civil society. In Egypt, the Christian

Copts were targeted by the Jemaa Islamiya amid government ignorance of their plight. In Lebanon, the Syrian occupation widened its suppression of liberties, jailing, torturing, and transferring thousands of dissidents to Syria. In Iran, Syria, and Libya, reformers and opposition were arrested, imprisoned, and executed. In Afghanistan, the Taliban established a reign of terror, particularly against women and minorities.

Across the region, democratic rights and basic freedoms were further dissolved. The rise of fundamentalism and the escalation of oppression converged to create one of the largest human prisons in the history of mankind. While the rest of the planet was moving gradually toward increased freedoms or at least maintaining a status quo in the most oppressed places, the Greater Middle East was falling deep into brutal suppression. Making matters worse, the West declined to act in support of freedoms in the Middle East as it did with the Soviet Bloc, Latin America, and Africa.

Western Lobotomy

During the 1990s, when you read headlines like "Mideast Conflict" or "Mideast Crisis" in the news in America or the West in general, your immediate expectation was that the news item was about the Arab-Israeli conflict, particularly the Palestinian-Israeli dispute. The suffering of hundreds of millions of individuals in other parts of the region and their lack of basic rights weren't reported in the West. The American and European public were denied the right to be informed about the abuse of human rights in a region stretching from the Atlantic to the Indian Ocean.

The public ignorance of what was taking place in the Arab world was not lack of interest, as some have argued. Rather, the many causes of democracy and freedom in the Greater Middle East were intentionally "killed" in Western academia, media, and foreign policy circles. During the Cold War and into the 1990s, U.S. and European students, NGOs, legislators, artists, and opinion makers, as well as most citizens, followed with great interest the developments related to Soviet dissidents, Latin American democracy activists, South African militants, and scores of other democratic causes. Scrolling through the bookstores and libraries of America, one could find many books on heroes and stories of struggles against oppression from around the world, but not the Middle East. Numerous movies were produced about insurrections and resistances, from the popular Rambo, fighting with the mujahideen against the Soviets in Afghanistan, to dramas in the former Yugoslavia, to antidictatorship movies in Latin America, but still not one film dedicated to freedom's struggle against authoritarian regimes in the Middle East was ever made. Hollywood, a major cultural educator of Americans and Westerners, has failed to touch on the issue for more than a decade after the Soviet collapse.

More important was the total absence of media coverage of Middle Eastern dissent and resistance to authoritarianism. While every incident in the West Bank and Gaza was covered extensively by cable networks and newspapers, almost no news was reported about the genocide taking place in Sudan. The gassing of Kurds in Halabja in Iraq in the late eighties was poorly investigated. Syria's invasion of Lebanon and its continuous occupation was presented as a "stabilization role." Student protests in Iran were barely mentioned. Op-ed pieces by dissidents almost never appeared in the *Washington Post* or *New York Times*. CNN's famous reporter on crises, Christiane Amanpour, for example, rarely interviewed Berber, Kurdish, Lebanese Christian, Coptic, or Assyrian leaders. Britain's *Guardian* ignored Saudi women's plight and underreported the Salafists' assaults on the secular community in Algeria.

This was also the case with the segment of the human rights community that was focused on helping to free Sudan's slaves. Dr. Charles Jacobs, the founder of the Boston-based American Anti Slavery Group, which advocated the liberation of south Sudanese slaves, asserted that his pieces and press releases, "although liberal to the core," were systematically rejected by the so-called mainstream press. Keith Roderick, the secretary general of the Coalition for the Defense of Human Rights in the Muslim world, repeated the same story: "As of the early 1990s, we tried several times to invite national media to meetings where victims of persecution were testifying, Copts, Sudanese, Lebanese, Assyrians, Arab dissidents, and later on Darfur refugees, but to no avail. Not one TV network showed up, not one reporter from the major papers wrote a piece. We were raising the most pressing aggressions against human dignity since the Holocaust, in the most open and capable society on the planet, yet we were acting in a black hole." Roderick added: "Ironically, the only

TV network that showed up and insisted on filming the whole event was the official state television of the Islamic Republic of Iran."

And the Iranians weren't interested in covering the meetings but in documenting the identities of participants, particularly the Iranians among them, in order to wage punitive actions against them later. This boycott of dissidence messages in the West was systematic, as reported by leaders of ethnic groups, human rights workers, and writers. The Lebanese opposition to Syrian occupation was rarely mentioned in U.S. or European outlets. Tom Harb, who was the secretary of a Diaspora-based NGO, the World Lebanese Organization, when speaking before a conference of exiled activists in 1998, asked, "Critics of Israeli occupation from Palestine and opposition figures from Burma or Haiti would have a full hour on C-Span and were often interviewed on National Public Radio, but critics of the Syrian occupation of Lebanon or reformers in Syria were never given that access. Why?"

The media ban on discussing Middle Eastern dissidence was not restricted to NGOs and exiles, but also applied to public people, including legislators. Throughout the executive branch in the United States under the first Bush and the Clinton administrations, the issue was actually not on the table. In many hearings and briefings, State Department officials were asked by congressional leaders about the state of affairs regarding persecuted minorities. The traditional answer was that things were being monitored. Pressed by Congressman Frank Wolf of Virginia to answer specifically why the United States wasn't raising the issue of religious persecution of the Christian Copts of Egypt, a high-ranking State Department official said the American government must wait to see improvement of rights for all Egyptians and not focus on one particular group. That would have been the equivalent of stating, when Germany's Jews were rounded up in the late 1930s, that one should wait till the general situation of all German citizens regarding political rights was improving. In fact, there was a consensus across the U.S. executive branch that minorities' issues and fundamental democratic questions were not to be raised when it came to the Arab world.

This was a very strange attitude in the 1990s, in a post-Soviet world, at a time when the democracy crises in South Africa, Haiti, and the Philippines were widely debated in the West, yet none of the Middle East's sister causes were discussed, other than the obligatory "Palestinian question."

Even those courageous legislators who broke the wall of silence in the mid-1990s and held hearings and briefings about the voiceless populations of the region weren't covered by the media as much as their colleagues who championed much less pressing issues.

Senator Sam Brownback from Kansas was among the very first members of the U.S. Senate to actually hold hearings on persecution of religious minorities in the Muslim world in general, and the Middle East in particular. Representative Frank Wolf of Virginia led the charge in the House. Representative Michael Forbes from New York brought the issues to the floor of the U.S. Congress, but the American media ignored their actions. Even when these initiatives led to important legislation such as the International Religious Freedom Act, the congressional leaders who raised the issue and fought for it were rarely in the limelight.

In Britain and other Western European countries, similar phenomena were taking place. Baroness Caroline Cox distinguished herself during the first post–Cold War decade by visiting Sudan eight times and, according to her office, liberated more than two thousand slaves. She pushed for a new Sudan policy in the UK, yet the British press was either negative or passive regarding the cause she advocated.

These are just a few examples in a much larger stream of leaders who worked on shifting the struggle from backing Soviet dissidents to assisting the dissidents of the Middle East. In short, there was a tangible resistance in Washington and most European capitals to accepting the new struggle. It was simply ignored.

Why?

Academia and Oil

Decades before 9/11, the Arab and Muslim world's authoritarian elites understood that if you can shape the minds of Western students regarding a particular region of the world, or rather remove any real knowledge of the dramas plaguing that region, you basically paralyze the public's understanding of that part of the world. From the American classroom come the educators of the following generations. If you influence this group, you affect everything in society, including the making of foreign policy.

Since the late 1970s, with the effects of the 1973 oil shock[3] still in place, and Western democracies very much intimidated by the potential of petropower to slow or bring down their economies, a stream of funds gradually began to make its way into American and Western European universities. Throughout the 1980s, while the free world was still containing the Soviet menace, and even as Gorbachev was launching his reforms, Gulf petrodollars landed on U.S. campuses to create centers of learning regarding the Middle East. The new programs created by these donors were aimed at making sure that future decision-makers, journalists, and analysts graduating from these classrooms would be friendly to the status quo in the region. Backed by the full power of OPEC's hard-core members, the Arab League, and the Organization of the Islamic Conference, a stealth lobby was formed within the West focusing almost exclusively on ensuring a "correct teaching of Middle East Studies" on campuses.[4] Resources were mobilized to ensure that "pressure groups" were created in Washington, Paris, London, and beyond to "defend Arab causes," particularly the "holy Palestinian cause." Naturally, the goal of the investors was more ominous: As each year showed signs that the USSR was weakening, the authoritarian Middle Eastern elites, anticommunists and self-described progressive alike, acted together to ensure the next superpower would give them peace. They did not want any scrutiny of the state of democracy in their countries.

Even as the Cold War was still going on, the regimes of the region were meticulously planning on taking out, preemptively, any future Western action in favor of human rights. This made sense in sheer strategic terms. The Cold War granted cover to authoritarian camps in the region, the conservatives and the progressives, Islamists and Baathists, to relentlessly pursue policies of suppression against their own societies and, when possible, their neighbors. As in a jungle, the beasts of oppression began running in one direction as they detected a potential firestorm. The closer they felt international change was, or that foreign powers might support such a change, the more urgent it was to act in unison (even as they continued to hate each other) to ensure that their worst nightmare wouldn't happen. They could not allow an unchallenged West to turn its attention to the horrendous state of human rights in the region. Indeed, as Eastern Europe and some parts of the Soviet Union started to tremble and the Reagan administration seemed to be winning its bet on freedom, the amounts of petrodollars heading toward Western academia escalated at a dizzying rate.

In fall 1990 a significant force was blocking the discussion of Middle Eastern minorities in American academia. Later, by mid-decade, not only were issues of the non-Muslim "ethnic minorities" being excluded from discussion, but Muslim minorities such as the Kurds, Berbers, and later on the black Muslims of Sudan were also being ignored by many.

By decade's end the debate about Middle Eastern democracy at large was selectively stifled by the power of certain lobbies. Challenging any of the regimes in the region, particularly the major oil producers, wouldn't end up as a "legitimate" cause in academia, and thus in the public sphere of debate. No dissident research into the Wahabis, Assad, Saddam, Qaddafi, or even the anti-American Khomeinists was given the visibility required to have the public take notice.

A cause that is not seen is a cause that is not understood. Without the necessary public support, or even public knowledge of their existence, the causes of minorities, human rights, and democracy weren't even on the table to be considered for diplomatic action. Millions of southern Sudanese, Berbers, Kurds, Lebanese, Iranians, Syrians, and other oppressed peoples could be massacred, become victims of ethnic cleansing, or be persecuted and tortured without any Western government lifting a finger, simply because Western public opinion wasn't aware of the problem.

Simply put, the jihadophile network was sending significant financial grants to major educational institutions in the West. The "donors" targeted those programs in academia that shape Americans' vision of international relations, and particularly of the Arab and Muslim world.

The grants didn't land in medical, engineering, or other relevant developmental studies on American and European campuses. One would think that public health and agriculture in the oil-producing countries in the region needed dramatic improvement. But no, the regimes in the Middle East had a more important priority for the use of their divinely obtained dollars: making sure the West didn't realize how bad human rights violations were under these regimes. The grants established Middle Eastern studies and Islamic studies and funded parts of international relations course study. The instructors and the material used were at the mercy of the donors. Middle Eastern programs funded and established by these donors lost their ability to raise human rights issues and discuss democratization. Middle

Eastern studies paid for or influenced by Gulf funding prohibited research in the field of women's liberation, minorities, and pluralism. Textbooks and articles funded by Qaddafi, Saddam, Assad, and the mullahs would in no way challenge totalitarian regimes.[5] The rest of the chain is easy to guess. Classrooms produced the journalists who wrote articles about the region, the producers who created segments on TV, the researchers, and the anchors, but also the defense and intelligence analysts, diplomats, advisors, and all those who, in the end, determined how the public would read, perceive, and respond to Middle Eastern crises. This was the factory, planted in our midst, that was essentially blocking American and Western knowledge of the problem and molding its reaction, or nonreaction, to it. Those scholars and activists who tried to raise these heavy issues in front of the American public were faced with a wall obstructing their message. Coming together like a hydra, the "graduates" of the oil-influenced Middle Eastern studies programs blocked any attempt to influence public opinion. A war of ideas was being waged in the West with clear instructions: Block the messengers from reaching the American people, at any cost. From the classroom to the publishing houses, from media to the entertainment industry, an "intellectual massacre" of the causes of freedom was taking place in America and the West in concert with the real suppression of freedom in the Greater Middle East. Some could make the case that as long as the southern Sudan issue was blocked by the petrodollars lobbies in the West, the real suffering on the ground inside Sudan was expanding. Every disaster in human rights in the Greater Middle East corresponded with an obstruction of truth in the free world.

A year after leaving Lebanon for my newly adopted country, I witnessed the U.S. liberation of Kuwait from my home base in Florida and saw how enthusiastic individual citizens were about this effort. I had already been sought out by the media to explain the bigger picture in the region. At every opportunity, I tried to mention the invasion of Lebanon by Syria as comparison, although it occurred two months after Saddam's takeover of Kuwait. I often saw eyes open wide when I mentioned this, signaling that my interviewer or audience had no idea that another country in the Middle East had been militarily invaded by the Baath regime.

I went back to visit the archives of the mainstream media to see how Lebanon's invasion was portrayed, and I found that the description was very different from the description of events in Kuwait. Syria was portrayed as "stabilizing" its neighbor, not "conquering" it. There were few references to the hundreds, if not thousands of killings and kidnappings that accompanied the Assad blitzkrieg in East Beirut. Evidently, Lebanon had no oil and thus presented no economic interest to the multinational companies, whose coffers funded Middle Eastern expertise in America.

During that first year in America, I came to realize that the elite Middle Eastern studies programs were efficiently blocking knowledge about other tragedies. Southern Sudan's massacres weren't reported as such, nor were other minority struggles. Even the Kurdish resistance in northern Iraq, which rose in response to the call by an American president, George H. W. Bush, was not considered a legitimate resistance movement like the Palestinian Liberation Organization. The list of overlooked causes grew very long during the early 1990s, to the point where I realized, during the fall meeting of a prominent Middle Eastern studies program, that a countereducation process was going on in the largest democracy on earth.

My first encounter with the "war" on Middle Eastern freedom in America was in October 1991 during my first participation in the annual Conference of the Middle East Institute in Washington, D.C. When I saw no event dedicated to human rights and minorities I decided to raise the issue during the last and most prestigious panel of distinguished Middle Eastern studies scholars and former U.S. diplomats. I posed my question to the panel: "Why is it that an important conference on Middle Eastern studies in Washington, D.C., the winner of the Cold War and the maker of the new world order, particularly in this region, didn't cover the fundamental questions of ethnic and national minorities, women under Islamist regimes, and more particularly the rights of southern Sudanese, Berbers, Assyro-Chaldeans, Kurds, and Lebanese Christians?" The chair of the panel read the question and looked at the participants for an answer. Long seconds passed before any of the scholars uttered a word. A heavy silence floated in the room. The moderator finally addressed the most senior scholar on the panel. "Professor, someone in the audience is waiting for an answer: Why aren't we raising the issues of minorities in the Middle East?" The scholar answered that these were issues that needed to be reviewed, but right now the central matter was the question of Palestine only. I was stunned by that answer, which remained a benchmark of my perception of Middle Eastern studies in America. The senior scholar's name was John Esposito, who later became the chair of the Georgetown University Center on "Christian-Muslim Understanding," heavily funded by Prince Talal Ibn al Waleed, a main Saudi donor to a number of American Universities.[6]

For almost a decade I faithfully attended the annual meetings of the Middle East Studies Association of America (MESA). Rarely were panels dedicated to discussing issues that Pan Arabists, Islamists, or authoritarian regimes would have opposed. I knew of dozens of candidates whose papers were systematically rejected because they focused on forbidden topics and contained criticism from inside the Arab world of the dominant political or religious elite. There were two red lines no one could cross: exposing jihadism and exploring human rights of minorities and women.

While the Islamist insurrections and terrorist groups were wreaking havoc across the region, attacking civil societies, seculars, humanists, and intellectuals in Algeria, Egypt, and Sudan, MESA's academic pontiffs produced strange concepts to explain these phenomena. In the mid-1990s, when asked about the roots of Salafist bloodshed in Algeria, Professor John Entelis (whom I met and had discussions with years later) claimed there were two types, the NVIs and the bad guys.[7] NVIs stood for "Non Violent Islamists"; the bad guys were those "frustrated by Western foreign policy." Hence the conclusion was that both types weren't really a fundamental problem, since violence can be stopped if U.S. foreign policy changes.

The lengths to which American and European academia (with notable exceptions) went in its coverup for the jihadist ideology and its suppression of human rights investigation in the region bordered on association with the radical and oppressive regimes of the Middle East. By the end of the decade, apology reached its zenith when a Harvard group extended an invitation to a Taliban delegation to lecture students about their good achievements in Afghanistan, one month before the 9/11 attacks.

The Middle Eastern studies community in America, and throughout the West, was like an impenetrable fortress. If you weren't a rabid supporter of its theses you were an outcast, cut off from the mainstream teaching body.

Another stunning experience I had in the 1990s, in addition to the hundreds of similar experiments by colleagues, occurred when I was on a search committee for a new professor in history at my university in Florida. As we were reviewing files of applicants, I was assigned to contact professors who were cited as references by one of the candidates, who happened to be a black southern Sudanese. The position was in Middle Eastern and North African history. One of the professors, from an Ivy League university, who was cited as a mentor to the young candidate, told me on the phone: "I wouldn't suggest adding him to the faculty." When I asked why, the white professor told me: "Because he is from southern Sudan; he is black." Assuming that because of my Arabic name I must somehow ethnically favor his position, he added: "Well, you know these guys are in rebellion against the Arab government in Khartoum. He is critical of Arabs!"

Here is an American-born professor, neither Arab nor African, telling me that I shouldn't hire a bright scholar from southern Sudan, because as a black he would upset the regime in Khartoum. Obviously, he was acting in concert with the consensus of Middle Eastern studies, fully favorable to its sources of funding, the mighty petrodollar. I now realized, firsthand, how the petrodollar's penetration had corrupted segments of higher education in this dream country, where freedom and equal opportunity are supposed to be available to all.

In order to test this theory, in the mid-1990s, I sent a proposal to the Middle East Studies Association for a paper focusing on Lebanese Christian ethnic identity and the behavior of the community in modern times. As I expected, the proposal was rejected immediately. As I counterargued with the conference committee, the "supreme priests" attempted to defend their position. The following year, to test my theory, I sent another proposal somewhat critical of Lebanese Christians for their "isolationism," a concept cherished by the Arabists. As expected, it was wholeheartedly accepted by MESA.

My theory was confirmed: The more closely you subscribed to the dominant "regime" in academia, and to the narrative of their funders, the more you were encouraged and elevated; the more you expressed concern about oppressed ethnicities or raised criticism of the region's regimes, the more you were suppressed.

War of Ideas against Middle Eastern Democracy

This discrimination extended from academia into other realms of opinion-making and information. Because what you read affects what you think and how you view the world, and how you will act or not act on issues, the selection process of the publishing industry regarding the Greater Middle East was crucial to authoritarian and radical forces in the region. If you can affect what Americans and Europeans read, or do not read, you win a phenomenal victory in the war of ideas. The funders of Middle Eastern studies understood the game and managed to beat democracies at it.

Parallel to the rise of MESA as the forum of ideas regarding the Middle East, with the authority to allow debate on some issues and not on others, rose the "reviewers" who were able to influence which manuscripts dealing with the Arab and Muslim world would make the final cut. Graduates from the compromised American and European classrooms influenced the publishing industry, blocking any project that didn't fit their parameters and serving the interests of the region's dominant elite. Perhaps with the narrow exception of the Israeli narrative on the Arab-Israeli conflict, all works and research critical of the Islamists or other Pan Arabists were killed before they reached the final cut. Across the board, manuscripts addressing the struggle of women under Islamist regimes, slavery in Sudan and Mauritania, non-Arab and non-Muslim minorities, and books advocating the idea that the Arab world needs a profound systemic revolution were thrown in the trash can.

Dozens of authors, Western-born or originating in the Arab and Muslim world, have seen their proposals turned down by academic presses throughout the 1990s. Bat Yeor, the Egyptian-born leading scholar on minorities in the Muslim world; Ibn Warraq, a Muslim-born scholar who criticized the Caliphate rule; Coptic scholar Shawki Karas; and dozens of other professors, Ph.D. candidates, and independent researchers were rejected as they worked hard to convince publishing boards to accept their proposals. The editors weren't responsible for that obstruction; rather, they sent manuscripts to their academic advisors. These "reviewers," members of Middle Eastern studies associations, taught to reject freedom movements against the dominant elite of the region, buried them before they had the chance to go to a publisher, and the circle was complete.

Funding had a ripple effect deep inside the educational and publishing system. Editors were at the mercy of their own "reviewers," who were defending the interests of those who funded them, or the beliefs they had acquired during their years studying under the senior educators—the pillars of the Middle Eastern studies community.

The 1990s witnessed publication of the greatest number of volumes dealing with Middle Eastern wars, Islam as a religion, colonialism, imperialism, and all sorts of subjects except the core of the democracy struggle. Certainly there were books with "democracy" in the titles, but their substance involved how things will evolve toward a future state of democracy—but not now, not against Islamism and Baathism, and not against the will of the oil-producing elites.

In the early 1990s, I sent a manuscript to several academic publishers concerning the ethnic conflict in Lebanon, with an emphasis on the rise and fall of the Lebanese Christian nationalist movement through history. It was a typical case of ethnic strife involving a minority in the Middle East. There was no competitive book on the subject, which should have helped the selection. Indeed, the manuscript invariably made the first cut when publishers recognized its novelty. But once the project was sent for review to the so-called experts, obviously members of the MESA network, it was rejected, forcing me to submit it to nonacademic presses. There, too, the "network" of reviewers, all professors of Middle Eastern studies espousing the party line, continued their obstruction. Ironically, the evaluation reports, which were sometimes sent back to me, had the hallmarks of the MESA network. The book was critical of what they termed the "Arab identity of the region" and the "stabilizing role of Syria in Lebanon." Some reviews added that the research reopened "the question of minorities in the region, shifting attention from the central cause in Palestine."

The culture of suppression of Middle Eastern democracy was breeding in America's holiest space: freedom of thought. There was no debate about the Muslim world's real revolutions: You could get published only if you'd criticize the West, Israel, and those seeking revolt against Arab nationalism or jihadism.

Antidissidents Inquisition

Above and beyond the obstructive power the antidemocracy "mafia" wielded in the West, the apologist networks waged a systematic inquisition against democracy promoters. Kurdish, Berber, south Sudanese, Lebanese, and other intellectuals who challenged the Arabist-jihadist order established within the American and Western intelligentsia were demonized, including feminist activists and researchers on women's rights.

The 1990s were the ultimate decade of activist-bashing at the hands of the jihadist oil lobbies. Authoritarian regimes in the Middle East and the militant Islamist networks in the West had a prime target within democracies. They were intent on destroying the witnesses and eliminating the messengers of the underdogs as soon as they reached the shores of freedom.

For years there was a witch hunt in the United States and the West by the jihadophile zealots, directed against writers, scholars, and journalists who warned about the rise of extremism, including jihadism, but also those who decried the mass abuse of human rights in the southern Sudan, Lebanon, Syria, Iran, and the rest of the region. Lumped together, these dissidents were accused of being "Zionist agents," or "facilitators of American, Western, and imperialist policies and designs." If you asked about the fate of Lebanese detainees in Syrian jails, the persecution of Copts along the Nile Valley, Berber activists who had vanished in Algeria, or Iranian students beaten to death, you were categorized as an Israeli operative. Should you be more sophisticated and challenge the status of women under Islamist regimes such as those in Saudi Arabia or Iran, or the most notorious sexual apartheid regime, the Taliban, you were still portrayed as "pro-Western bourgeois," notwithstanding that Muslim women are savagely treated in many areas of the Greater Middle East.

While the Western-born pro–Middle East democracy activists or scholars were attacked for being "Westerners" and advocating Israel's interests, the harshest attacks were leveled against the Middle East–born intellectuals, Muslims and non-Muslims alike.

Oil-producing regimes such as Sudan, Iraq, Iran, Libya, and to a certain degree Saudi Arabia and Qatar provided funding to lobbies and counterdissident entities with the sole goal of damaging their opponents' credibility within liberal democracies. The Sudanese regime funded a London-based lobby that severely attacked British and American legislators for helping the cause of the southern Sudanese blacks and unleashed a smear campaign against the southern Sudanese rebellion.[8] Tehran, Damascus, and Hezbollah's propaganda forces focused on the exiles, the opposition, and their literature in a systematic effort to cripple their image.

Operatives, acting as academics, investigative journalists, and consultants, wreaked havoc in the ranks of the messengers from the Arab and Muslim world who were trying to inform and mobilize Western public opinion about the forgotten people of the region, years after the end of the Cold War and the liberation of Eastern Europe. Not one among those who made it to these shores with the goal of mobilizing audiences and informing legislators about the efforts against democracy in the region dodged the vicious attacks and isolation campaigns led by the regimes' networks and the Western-based jihadist lobbies.

As with all my colleagues in academia, human rights advocacy, and community outreach who took part in this effort to raise awareness about the battle for freedom taking place in the Arab and Muslim world, I, too, was attacked in the media and online. As of the mid-1990s, with the rise of email and the internet, and as I began briefing legislators and pushing for U.S. action on the issue of Middle Eastern minorities, militant groups and operatives began their criticism of my work, often attacking me personally. The same arguments used against any challenger of the authoritarian order were applied against me; I was "a Zionist, an agent of Israel," and so on. If you raise the issue of southern Sudan or southern Lebanon you are always portrayed as "Zionist." The overarching goal of the antidemocracy movement in the Middle East is to protect the dominant political and social order of the Arab world. The demonization of dissidents and their advocates became an integral part of their daily lives throughout the 1990s.

In 1999, for example, an operative from the Islamist-aligned Council on American Islamic Relations (CAIR), Ismael Royer, started a campaign against my work by writing an article in which he reduced all my research and educational efforts to my "being a member of the Lebanese Forces allied to Israel."[9] Royer filled the internet with attacks against me and human rights workers, as well as against Middle Eastern dissidents in exile. Ironically, Royer, a convert to Islam whose first name was Randall, had joined CAIR and claimed he was working on civil rights while he in fact was forming one of America's most highly trained jihadi terror cells. Uncovered by the FBI and arrested for forming an armed terror unit in Virginia, he was sentenced to prison in 2002. It was troubling to realize that the operatives tasked with targeting scholars and intellectuals were in reality terrorists training to kill their enemies.

The U.S. government, which broke a number of cells, including Royer's Virginia jihad network, after 9/11, never actually investigated the network and the jihadophile NGOs with which he was connected for allowing him to operate under their name. It is evident that writers and dissidents living in America and Europe do not feel safe with the knowledge that jihadists have been charged with their demonization while training as terrorists.[10]

The case of a Dutch MP, the Somali-born Ayaan Hirsi Ali, who had to leave the Netherlands after the assassination of filmmaker Theo Van Gogh, is typical of the witch hunt against the messengers of freedom. Ali and Van Gogh had coproduced a short film on women in Islamic countries that was deemed "offensive" by the jihadists.

Despite acerbic verbal and written attacks during the 1990s, my colleagues and I persevered in the campaign to bring awareness to Americans and Europeans.

Suppressing Voices Eliminates the Cause

Following the Soviet Union's demise, the overwhelming pressures applied by the lobbies of the jihadists and authoritarian regimes within the West bore unfortunate results. Not only were Americans and Europeans denied access to information about what was happening deep inside Arab and Muslim societies, especially the mass abuse of human rights, persecutions, sexual discrimination, and minorities' abuses, but they were blocked from seeing the rise of the jihadi terror threat.

Indeed, once the dissidents, scholars, former diplomats, and other "witnesses" to the post-Soviet Middle East were prevented from informing the public, the opportunity for Westerners to learn, understand, and support the appropriate policies was lost. What Americans and Europeans saw on their TV screens in the evening, received in their classrooms during the day, listened to on NPR and the BBC while they were driving, or read about in their morning newspapers at breakfast determined their vision of the Greater Middle East. And in that vision, a big chunk was missing. There were no reports that most of the civil societies in that part of the world were suppressed, that all ethnic and religious minorities were oppressed, and that radical ideologies were on the rise, supported by oil-producing regimes. What the public also missed in the 1990s was that the Arab-Israeli conflict wasn't the only Middle Eastern crisis, that genocide was taking place in Sudan, ethnocide in Algeria and Iraq, sexual apartheid in Afghanistan, Iran, and Saudi Arabia, that torture was widespread across the region, and that the number of political prisoners in the Arab and Muslim world exceeded the entire population of Gaza. Millions had fled the Greater Middle East because of religious and political persecution, lucky enough to settle in the West. Ironically, the voices of Middle Eastern refugees complaining about the root causes of their resettlement weren't even heard in their new homelands. Surreally, the victims of oppression who reached European and American shores were prevented from delivering their message, unlike the dissidents fleeing communist regimes. Scores of Islamist "political refugees" resettled in the West and became stars of academic and media debates. Salafist or Pan Arabist militants who were repressed by authoritarian regimes, particularly pro-Western governments, were hailed as heroes by Western intelligentsia. But Christians, liberals, or women persecuted by Islamist or any other regimes in the region were not given the microphone, or worse, were demonized by the Western elite.

During the 1990s I served many times as an expert witness in U.S. immigration courts on behalf of those seeking political asylum. As a professor of international relations I offered my reading of the conditions of the countries from which these applicants came. I was asked to testify in cases representing individuals from all religious and ethnic backgrounds. I discovered during these tough sessions at immigration courts that judges and government representatives had insufficient information regarding human rights abuses in the Middle East. Some of the questions I had to answer left me flabbergasted. Neither the judge nor the service representatives had any knowledge of the Syrian occupation of Lebanon, the suppression by the Baath regime of Syrian opposition, the status of minorities in many Arab countries, or which countries abandoned political refugees. State Department reports weren't always helpful, even if they were rigorously written. This is why political refugees often had to hire a professor to testify as an expert witness.

In some of these court cases I noticed something even more perturbing. Not only were the persecuted victims' "causes" questioned, not only did they have to be proven case by case, but the jihadists were able to transform their ideological agendas into "persecution causes." The surreal messages and distorted opinions were ramping up during the 1990s. During one hearing, I was asked about the conditions of the Christian Copts in Egypt, as a young female applicant filed for asylum in the United States for fear of being kidnapped by the Jemaa Islamiya, a terrorist group that later joined the al Qaeda–led federation. The judge leaned in to me and said, "It is strange, Professor Phares, after your testimony I feel I got it wrong in a previous case." I asked him how. He said, "I granted asylum to a member of this group who claimed he was persecuted by the Egyptian government on religious grounds." I told the judge that Egypt is a Muslim state and that the Jemaa wanted to overthrow the regime and establish a jihadist state. "They want to replace an authoritarian government, true, but with a totalitarian regime, Your Honor." The judge was perplexed as he realized that due to poor information, he might have granted asylum to an individual whose group was in the business of persecution against Copts and potentially against Egyptian women.

God knows how many similar "asylum seekers" have entered the United States and become citizens just because judicial and bureaucratic decision-makers or lawyers had no knowledge of the region's realities.[11]

As dissident voices were suppressed, their causes were never really heard by the wider public. Their struggles were condemned to be limited to internal conferences held by democracy advocates, a few human rights associations, some legislators, and the ethnic or religious communities from the region living in the Diaspora. Without identifiable and recognizable "causes," the defenders of liberty and pluralism efforts in the Arab and Muslim world were unable to develop in the West, and therefore in the international community. As a result of this absence of "causes," governments in the West left their foreign policy bureaucracies in full control of the policy agendas regarding the region. This led to a general Western abandonment of human rights and democracy in the Greater Middle East.

Western Abandonment

When the causes of Middle Eastern human rights and democracy vanished from the Western debate and public opinion couldn't identify more than the "sole" crisis—the Arab-Israeli conflict—it was evident that the region's regimes and political forces had successfully influenced Western governments in their policies regarding the Arab and Muslim world. In short, despite the intra-Arab struggles and regimes' tensions, a line was drawn around a significant part of the globe where the promotion of democracy was forbidden.

Even as Saddam invaded Kuwait, Egypt resented Sudan, Iran traded threats with Saudi Arabia, Tunisia and Libya had disagreements, Morocco and Algeria were at odds, and Palestinian factions fought relentless civil wars, the region's elite kept the international community at bay when an intervention loomed on the horizon. I call this solidarity of the region's elite a "Brotherhood against Democracy"—Qatar's rulers, Sudan's regime, the Muslim Brotherhood, hard-core Wahabis, and Lebanon's Hezbollah. They could be at each other's throats in factional and interest-driven confrontations, but when one of the "brothers" is targeted by the outside world as an offender against freedom, the issue became an "*Umma* [relative to the entire community of Muslims] matter." Leaders and commentators would rush to portray it as an aggression against the entire regional community.

Obviously, this was about the fear of political change hitting one regime or ideology, potentially crumbling the entire system in the whole region. The images from the domino-effect Soviet collapse were too fresh in the minds of rulers and totalitarian ideologues.

With this mechanism in place in the Middle East since the end of the Cold War, and the "freedom causes" being killed before they reached the hearts and minds of international public opinion, the United States and the West were in a bind. If executive branches raised human rights issues, leading to incrimination of authoritarian forces in the Middle East, the oil lobbies would blast them at home, using the significant influence they'd acquired with academia and the media. So, national leaders in the West refrained from raising the question of democracy in the Arab and Muslim world for fear of being accused of meddling in domestic issues and exercising "postcolonialism." This retreat by Western governments unleashed the power of oil-linked interest groups in the United States, Great Britain, and other European countries in determining where the West could intervene. The winners of the Cold War became unable and unwilling to pursue policies leading to the liberation of millions of people in that part of the world, because their decision-making systems regarding foreign policy were fully compromised by the influence of the "brotherhood against democracy."

The retreat debuted at the onset of the decade when Saddam invaded Kuwait in August 1990 and committed atrocities against Kuwaiti citizens. The United States, Europe, and the industrialized world rushed to intervene, amassing half a million military personnel in Operation Desert Shield. The strategic goals were clear: stop Saddam from further conquests, protect Saudi Arabia's oil, and push the Iraqi forces back into Iraq to bring Kuwaiti oil back into free markets. On these objectives, the OPEC regimes and the authoritarians in the region were in agreement. This one massive Western intervention against an "Arab-Islamic" army was profoundly blessed by the leaders of the *Umma*, the regional elite, including Iran, Syria, and the moderate Arab governments. The window for international intervention was small but clear. Saddam had to get out of Kuwait.

Stunningly, another Baath regime invaded its small neighbor two months later and no coalition emerged in reaction. On October 13, 1990, Hafez Assad ordered his troops into the last free enclave of Lebanon and, after hours of battling, the Lebanese army surrendered. There was no Western reaction, no American mobilization of units, and no meeting of the UN Security Council. Both Kuwait's and Lebanon's civil societies were subjected to excessive human rights abuses and military occupation, but apparently only Kuwait merited the liberation forces' intervention. The difference? Lebanon has no oil.

With the final crumbling of Soviet power in 1991, the time for reshaping international humanitarian intervention had come. As long as the Soviets blocked NATO from intervening south of its traditional zone of influence, oppressed populations in those areas had no hope of receiving significant help. But when Boris Yeltsin ordered that Russian missiles no longer be aimed at American and European cities, the window for a new Western liberty-based policy was wide open.

The decade's developments confirmed that the power of petrodollars was more of an obstruction to the West than was the balance of power with the Soviets. Moscow blocked Washington and its allies from rescuing southern Sudan, Biafra, Lebanon, and other endangered populations in the region during the Cold War, but U.S. decision-makers were in control of their own strategies in confronting the Soviet challenge.

Incredibly, after 1990, Western leadership, although in a disproportionate balance of power with the authoritarians of the Middle East, was in full submission to their will when it came to democracy policies. Soviet ICBMs and oil power blocked Western aid to the underdogs of the Arab and Muslim world for decades. When the first opposition force collapsed, the free world was left with the increasing influence of the second force, the petropowers.

Consider how the West, or the "international community," intervened significantly and consistently on behalf of human rights and freedom around the world in the last decade of the twentieth century and how it didn't touch the human tragedies taking place in the Middle East. For four years, while the West and the rest of the world community put systematic pressure on South Africa to end apartheid, judged contradictory to the international declaration of human rights, other apartheid regimes were thriving under the eyes of the international community without reaction. Saudi Arabia's sexual apartheid was untouched, and the discrimination against the Copts of Egypt and the blacks of Sudan was never officially debated in the UN General Assembly. In the Caribbean, the United States rushed its navy to bring down a military junta that had removed a democratically elected president. Colonel Cedras and his generals left Haiti, but the generals and colonels of the Arab world were received in chanceries with all the honors due legitimate heads of states. Haiti's human rights abuses were addressed, but the same rights violated in dozens of countries in the Middle East were never restored.

A more powerful example of how the West betrayed endangered people, while rescuing others, bowing to the wishes of the oil financial partners, was Yugoslavia. In 1994 a U.S.-led NATO force waged a military campaign in Bosnia to defend its Muslim-dominated government against attacks from the Serbian provinces. Atrocities were committed, mostly against the Muslim civilian population, and the international community responded. The West conducted strikes against the Bosnian Serbs to push them away from Muslim (and Croatian) areas of the seceding republic. Politically, the United States and the European Union secured Bosnian Muslim independence from mostly Serbian Yugoslavia and at the same time rejected Serbian secession from Bosnia. This policy was encouraged by the Organization of the Islamic Conference (OIC) and endorsed by the oil-producing regimes in the region.

Regardless of ethnic fairness in the end of the process, the outcome was that the West saw ethnic cleansing in Bosnia and acted accordingly. However, during those same years, while NATO jets were striking in the mostly Muslim republic against Serbian militias backed by Slobodan Milosevic, Islamist militias known as the *Difaa Shaabi* were sent by the jihadi regime in Khartoum to fight a rebellion in the south. Hundreds of thousands of blacks were already exterminated in Sudan, yet no U.S. or European planes appeared in the skies of the African country.

This dual standard repeated itself in 1999 when NATO bombed Serbia and forced its troops to evacuate the mostly ethnic Albanian province of Kosovo, while in Sudan massacres had reached genocidal dimensions, yet no one showed up to help.

Western abandonment of human rights causes in the Greater Middle East was systematic. Washington and Brussels were eager to condemn abuses in Latin America, South Africa, and Asia, and even the abuses of the Chinese government, but with Arab and Muslim world governments, they were silent.

I often wondered in the 1990s why American and European bureaucrats were swift in criticizing the suppression of rights in the four corners of the world but dodged this responsibility when it came to Middle Earth. A book by Robert Kaplan, titled *The Arabists: The Romance of an American Elite*,[12] gave me a first taste of the answer. In it the well-known writer exposes how the U.S. State Department catered to the oil-producing regimes and demonstrates how the foreign policy establishment in America was almost "at the service" of the Arab and Middle Eastern rulers. Diplomats, according to Kaplan's research, sought the friendship of these powerful princes of the East, so that after their careers were over, they would be offered financial or career opportunities by these regimes. Former Western diplomats are the real advocates of the petro establishment and the authoritarians who sought influence overseas to quash any real change at home.

I expanded my own learning process as I testified to legislators on both sides of the Atlantic and briefed officials on the region's crises. Many of the offices in foreign policy chanceries I visited had photos of absolute monarchs and dictators proudly displayed on desks and walls. That alone was very telling.

More important was the attitude of diplomats who turned a deaf ear when I raised issues dealing with freedoms, liberation, and counterfundamentalism. From Washington to London, from Stockholm to Rome, the same story repeated itself: High-ranking officials consistently affirmed there should be no meddling in the regimes' "internal business." The use of the word "business" was literal in many cases, as, for example, in the case of French president Jacques Chirac, who was, according to sources, too involved in business relationships in the Arab world to intervene on behalf of France's traditional friends the Lebanese, and to protect them from Syrian oppression. French diplomacy didn't escape the fate of other Western nations, where oil funding penetrated the elites. To be fair, many diplomats, particularly those in charge of human rights, were very frustrated with the general policies of their governments. They knew they couldn't do much, and they realized just how large and powerful the interests involved in policymaking are.

During several meetings with Thomas Farr, who headed the office of religious liberties at the U.S. State Department in the late 1990s, I saw firsthand that expertise and knowledge were not missing throughout the bureaucracy. It was political will that was lacking. Farr, who later published a book on the importance of religious freedom in U.S. foreign policy, was aware of the horrors taking place in Sudan, Iran, and the rest of the region, but his actions were blocked by the powerful decision-makers on Middle Eastern affairs in other bureaus.[13]

In the mid-1990s, many U.S. and British legislators began to exert pressure, and hold hearings, to force their governments to "meddle" in human rights abuses, particularly in Sudan and later on in Afghanistan. Congressman Wolf and Senator Brownback led the charge in the U.S. Congress while Baroness Cox pushed for involvement in the House of Lords in Britain. By 2000, Congress had enacted legislation known as the "International Religious Freedom Act."

In June 2000, I was able (along with other freedom advocates) to organize a forum on "Middle East persecuted minorities" in the U.S. Senate. Keith Roderick, Charles Jacobs, and Nina Shea, veterans of the struggle to bring awareness to the American public on these issues, helped encourage the participation of legislators. Among the participants were representatives of exiled communities, the late Illinois state senator John Nimrod, who headed the Assyrian Universal Alliance, Tom Harb, the secretary general of the World Lebanese Organization, delegates from minorities in Pakistan, Iran, Syria, Iraq, and Sudan, a number of U.S.-based NGOs, and others. The discussion focused on elevating the debate in America to the level of the debates regarding the issues of support for dissidents during the Cold

War. We spoke of a freedom forward policy, hoping the U.S. Congress would push for it.

The meeting was attended by Elliott Abrams, a former diplomat and national security deputy chief for the Middle East and for democracy affairs under the Bush administration. Years later, Abrams played a central role when the time to push for active democratic activities had already come and gone.

The forum was immediately criticized by Pan Arabist press.[14]

The Abandoned Communities

Throughout the 1990s, I followed closely the trail of abandoned nations, communities, minorities, and democracy movements in the Greater Middle East under both the first Bush administration and the Clinton administration. While it should be left to U.S. foreign policy historians to determine if the top leaders were aware of the cascade of horrors unfolding in the region and whether they had the ability to do something for these underdogs, a number of these struggles can be examined.

Perhaps the most horrific crisis was taking place in Sudan. As U.S. war planes were pounding Serbian tanks in Bosnia and Kosovo in order to save Muslim lives, Sudan's Islamist regime sent its Soviet-made Antonov bombers to shower entire tribes with napalm, killing tens of thousands of blacks in the south. In Iraq, the Kurds to the north and the Shia to the south were left to survive under the so-called no-fly zones. While the Kurds realized that they should defend themselves with arms, the Shia were butchered by Saddam's fedayeen and other Baathist militias.

In Lebanon, the Christian community was abandoned to the Syrian occupation, a present to Hafez Assad granted in 1990. Political suppression targeting the community and all anti-Syrian factions lasted for another fifteen years. The abandoning of Lebanon as a country to Syria's Baath, a real blow to democracy, was accompanied by insult: Western diplomats praised the "stabilizing role of Syria in Lebanon."

In Algeria, the oppression of the Berber, particularly the Kabyle communities, was increasing at a time when U.S. and European interest focused only on the fate of the Palestinians in the West Bank and Gaza, which is a worthy cause but not the only crisis to address. In

Egypt, 15 million Copts were increasingly harassed, but support for their quest was not on any Western government's agenda. There were more Copts in one neighborhood in Cairo than Palestinians in the entire Gaza Strip. Both had claims, but only one group received the attention of the international community.

In Iran, minorities were as mistreated as they were under other Islamist regimes in the region. The Kurds to the west were crushed; the Azeris to the northwest saw their cultural rights shrinking; the Balush in the east were marginalized; and last but not least the Arabic-speaking minority in Ahwaz on the Persian Gulf was harshly oppressed. Unlike the response to what happened in Yugoslavia, the cause of Iranian minorities was nowhere to be seen, even though Iran and the United States have had no diplomatic relations since the Khomeinist revolution.

In my quest in Washington and other capitals during the 1990s, I tried hard to understand why diplomats sitting at their desks at the various foreign policy bureaucracies on both sides of the Atlantic disliked raising the issue of clearly persecuted populations. In his revealing book *The Arabists*, Kaplan quoted a junior diplomat at the State Department saying the Foreign Service disliked Middle Eastern minorities. Alberto Fernandez detailed how his colleagues systematically rejected claims by struggling groups in the region. Despite his criticism, Fernandez was appointed as a spokesperson under the Bush administration for the Arab world. Later he was appointed U.S. ambassador to Khartoum, which was the ultimate irony.

Beyond the systematic oppression of the region's minorities, another systematic suppression blocked the rise of democratic culture. The various elements of the "brotherhood against democracy," although at times in dire conflict against each other, acted in concert against all human rights advances. Women in Saudi Arabia, Iran, and Afghanistan, students and youth across the region, political parties calling for pluralism, liberal intellectuals in Egypt, reformists in almost every country, and human rights activists were all to be contained, repressed, and disallowed from joining the international community of democratization. There were reports by Western-based human rights groups and by North American and European foreign service bureaus on exactions, but again none of the essential conclusions encouraged or even sought public support for significant political, let alone regime, change.

In the mid-1990s, the Clinton administration sent aircraft carriers preceded by former president Jimmy Carter to "convince" General Cedras to leave Haiti and allow President Aristide to come back. But no vessels showed up in Tripoli asking Qaddafi to stop the killing of his own opposition. No real Western action, either on the ground or at the United Nations, came to the rescue of hundreds of millions of men and women trapped in Middle Earth, even though the Cold War was over and advancements in human rights policy were bragged about in the West.

These years were lost for freedom in the Greater Middle East, and the brotherhood against democracy won the decade, until Bin Laden decided to attack democracy at its heart.

3.

Lights from the Window: Post-9/11 Western Interventions

On the morning of September 11, 2001, as hijacked passenger jets slammed into the Twin Towers in New York and the Pentagon building in Washington, D.C., and crashed into a field in Pennsylvania, killing more than three thousand innocent individuals, history took another twist for hundreds of millions of people in the Greater Middle East. This mass tragedy, ordered by the leader of the most barbaric jihadists of all time, was a jolt to the feelings and perceptions of many citizens living in democracies, and would cause an uproar with unexpected consequences for those seeking freedom in Middle Earth. Like a meteor hitting the surface of an ocean, the ripple effects of these attacks would touch the destinies of millions half the globe away.

Bin Laden's *Ghazwas*[1] on "infidel" America, revealing the existence of unknown and horrendous intentions by a worldwide jihadist movement against the free world, shattered the dominant worldview that after the Cold War, no real threat could menace the international community. Francis Fukuyama's theory of the "end of history" was dead.[2] As the towers were crumbling, with thousands of men and women buried in the rubble, Americans and other nations watching the horror unfolding in real time questioned what they believed or had been made to believe. Many were taught that with the collapse of the Soviet Union, democracies could now see to the well-being of their own nations, and perhaps assist populations in need around the globe.

Shockingly, though, the free world came to realize on that morning that forces emerging seemingly from nowhere had decided to wage a global war, which they called "jihad." Many believed this kind of battle had ended with the crumbling of the Caliphate in the beginning of the past century, but it clearly had not. By striking hard at the political and financial capitals of the post–Cold War era, al Qaeda pushed America and some of its allies to rise and strike back.

From Afghanistan to Iraq, U.S.-led troops thrust into totalitarian forces and removed two dictatorships from power: the Taliban and the Iraqi Baath. The invasions were quick and decisive, but the ensuing wars, insurgencies, and terror attacks never ended. The liberation of these formerly oppressed countries has not resulted in flourishing democracy and security, at least not yet. But were the Western U.S.-led counteroffensives against al Qaeda, the Taliban, and their allies in the Greater Middle East aimed at liberating the region's peoples from oppression? Were Western diplomats really planning strategically to remove the totalitarian regimes in Afghanistan and Iraq, replace them with elected democracies, and then move to help other populations in their quest for freedom from oppression? Was the plan that clear, that focused, and above all was it successful?

A decade after the September 2001 onslaught and after all the terror attacks that followed in Europe and in the Middle East, and years after battlefields in Central Asia and the Middle East have experienced bloody confrontations, two answers are clear: One, many in the West, particularly in the United States, believed that bringing freedom to the birthplace of the terror forces would somehow roll them back into defeat. That was a bet made in Washington, D.C., and in a few other capitals by decision-makers and their advisors who had a vision during the early fall of 2001 that military intervention and regime change in some parts of the region would eventually spread democracy in the entire area.

The other answer, though, was that millions in the Greater Middle East, Muslims and non-Muslims alike, believed firmly that the West was awakening from its lethargic state of mind, realizing the size of the threat, and deciding that a full-fledged liberation of the peoples of the Middle East must be achieved. Decades from now, historians will have a better grip on how this took place. For even at this stage in the confrontation between the U.S.-led coalition and the various forces of jihadism, the jury is still out as to the commitment of the Western efforts to spread democracy as of 2002 and the efficiency of the methods employed.

More important than the campaigns waged by the United States at the time, the perception of the peoples of the region remains the crucial matter to investigate. Was the Greater Middle East, including the Arab world and large segments of the Muslim countries, ready for that push? Many will be surprised at this question—who is not ready for freedom when it appears? The critical element at these moments is not the need of the human soul, which unquestionably is always for more freedom, but the alignment of circumstances between the liberator, the liberated, and the opponent of liberation. That was and remains the crux of the matter in the future Middle Eastern democratic revolution.

Pre-9/11 Hopelessness

As I've already discussed, between August 1991, when the Moscow coup brought about the real end of the Soviet Union, and August 2001, when antidemocracy militants hijacked the UN-sponsored Durban Anti-Racism Conference, ten years of drama and horrors consumed the lives of many civil societies in the Greater Middle East. Liberty movements inside most Arab and Muslim countries on the one hand and dissidents and committed human rights groups based in the West on the other did not believe in the capacity of the "international community" to intervene to defend human rights and promote democracy in the region. Other than the unending debate about the Israeli-Palestinian quarrel and its ramifications, Western governments and mainstream NGOs had displayed a disheartening disregard for the suffering of tens of millions of men and women, children and elderly from North Africa to Afghanistan.

In the United States and Europe, NGOs representing the causes of democracy or particular ethnic communities had become hopeless. A common frustration was growing among all advocacy groups: The West was not reacting, not even registering these conflicts as part of the international human rights agenda. The "resistance" to this heavy silence was small, unfunded, not recognized, and harshly demonized by the regimes' agents in every capital of the Western world. The critics of Middle Eastern dissidents roamed proudly on campuses, in the media, in foreign policy chanceries, and in the halls of legislatures. The abundance of their cash, provided by the oil-producing regimes, made them extremely powerful. Even more ironic was the invasion by authoritarians of the debate space within the West. To discuss the

Middle East or the Arab world, you'd have to either be associated with the regimes, praising their achievements, or with their opposition, mostly the Islamists. Indeed, even inside the last square of freedom, inside liberal democracies, the true victims of oppression who struggled to inform public opinion about the horrors taking place in their countries of origin were overwhelmed by the oppressors from both camps: sitting regimes and those who wanted to replace them with worse authoritarianism.

The treatment of the Islamists, mostly the Muslim Brotherhood and other Salafists, as a viable alternative to secular and authoritarian regimes was stunning. Hosni Mubarak of Egypt was criticized by liberals in the West, who suggested engagement with the Muslim Brotherhood in order to eventually replace the president-for-life. Ironically, the Muslim Brotherhood's agenda was to cripple liberal democracy for life. In Lebanon, Hezbollah was praised by many in the West as a force of "change," a change that would transform Lebanon into a theocracy, à la Khomeini.

In sum, by spring 2001, the state of affairs of the democracy movement in the Greater Middle East was deplorable. There was no hope on the horizon. Westerners in general, and Americans in particular, were systematically brainwashed about the region. The public's ability to fathom the rising threat of jihadism and the oppression of millions of individuals that it practiced was almost nil.

Several months before the shock of 9/11, while hundreds of thousands of women were brutally dealt with by the medieval Taliban in Afghanistan and millions of females were removed from the country's workforce, a mind-boggling development was taking place on America's golden campuses: A propaganda machine was pushing for an engagement with the fascist militia that had blown up religious sites, shut down movie theaters, and executed artists. Despite this behavior, a delegation of Taliban "scholars" was invited to Harvard to address students and faculty in Boston and other cities. One would imagine that perhaps these turbaned ideologues wanted to learn about the benefit of liberal democracy. But that was not the case. The Taliban were supposed to lecture American and international students on the positive achievements of their regime! It was the equivalent of inviting a delegation of Nazi scholars in October 1941 to U.S. campuses to lecture about the great achievements of Nazism in Germany and the rest of Europe. America had gone totally blind.

This was the state of mind in the United States in the year the Taliban's protégés, al Qaeda, were preparing their Pearl Harbor attack against America.

The Durban Fallacy

There were many ominous cultural indicators of the suppression of the Middle Eastern democracy movement shortly before the savage jihadi attack against the world's most powerful democracy. During August 2001, I monitored the so-called UN-sponsored Conference on Racism and Discrimination taking place in Durban, South Africa. Many Western-based NGOs representing Middle Eastern dissidents were extremely concerned that the main body of the United Nations dealing with minorities' rights was hijacked by sympathizers of oil-producing regimes and groups preaching jihadism and other totalitarian doctrines. The fact that there were no representatives present in Durban from southern Sudan, Darfur, Kurds, Berbers, Copts, Assyro-Chaldeans, Mauritanian blacks, Arabs in Iran, or other persecuted groups in the Arab and Muslim world was a troubling matter. How could a conference claiming to tackle racism and discrimination, and particularly a conference taking place on the African continent, fail to invite escaped slaves from Sudan and Mauritania? These were the actual real slaves, called *Abeed* (meaning blacks) by their masters in two countries, members of the Arab League and the African Union.

Aside from this horrendous sin of sidelining the black slaves at a conference dedicated to antiracism, there were other noticeable absences. Discrimination against ethnic groups within the Arab and Muslim world wasn't even on the agenda. Organizers detailed past historical, and of course Western, racism, but didn't utter a single word on the present-day sufferings of hundreds of millions of disenfranchised peoples from the Atlas Mountains to the Himalayas. Sexual discrimination was addressed, but not sexual apartheid in Afghanistan, Iran, and Saudi Arabia.

In short, the entire Durban process was nothing but a charade to shield the oppressive ideological regimes in the Arab and Muslim world, particularly the oil-producing elites, the propagators of discriminatory ideologies. As expected, the Durban conference hysterically blasted Zionism as the chief abuser of human rights. Jewish nationalism was blamed for all Palestinian miseries, not the Israeli-Arab wars. While Israelis and Palestinians can debate the responsibility of stretching the war for decades, and potentially come to resolve their differences, the hotheaded jihadists, Salafists and pro-Iranians alike, are interested only in stretching the conflicts, regardless of the population's suffering. Durban's crowd went ballistic on the subject of Zionism, but not a word was said about jihadism, Khomeinism, Baathism, and similar ideologies. Zionism demands that all or parts of Palestine become a Jewish homeland, but most Israelis have accepted the partition of the land since 1993, while Baathism, for example, wants all the lands between Spain and Iran as one Arab *Umma*, with no national rights for non-Arab nations living there centuries before the Arab conquest.

In addition, another hatefest was specifically directed at the United States, portrayed as the "mother of all problems in the world" by the organizers of and the participants in that reunion of radicals in Durban. Oddly, the vicious attacks against everything American were endorsed by some American academics, sympathizers of the region's regimes. This rambling party, paid for by the international organization, went mute on all the horrors practiced by the oppressive regimes in Afghanistan, Sudan, Iran, and other parts of the area.[3]

The first Durban conference in August 2001 was the height of insult not against the usual targets of criticism by the jihado-totalitarians, Israel and America, but against the real underdogs of the Arab and Muslim world. Not only was the message of Durban reprehensible, but it consolidated the grip of the authoritarians—via their radical subcontractors—on the international institutions mandated to address racism and discrimination. By seizing control of the main international tool that raised the issue of mass human rights abuse in the Greater Middle East and using it against the West, the brotherhood against democracy reached the apex of its power worldwide. It was able to silence its peoples as long as no one cited these injustices worldwide. The ceiling was firmly closed.

Post-9/11 Windows

I knew on the morning of September 11, 2001, that the earthquake that hit my adopted country and killed thousands of Americans and citizens of the world in less than an hour would create a hole in the wall of silence surrounding Middle Eastern oppression. The attack, formulated by the supreme commander of modern-day jihadism, Osama Bin Laden, was destined to produce such a change, regardless of its success or failure.

That morning, I was attending a faculty meeting of my Department of Political Science at Florida Atlantic University. After the planes hit the towers, as professors and students watched in disbelief, I pondered their initial reactions. A colleague, an instructor of world politics, rushed to criticize how media will "frame it as international terrorism." Although he was teaching U.S. foreign policy and conflicts, my esteemed colleague wasn't able to fathom that indeed there was an international jihadist threat, let alone the link that threat had with Middle Eastern oppression. His reaction was an indication of how international relations studies in the United States have been affected by oil lobbying for years.

Across campuses nationwide, similar attitudes were being expressed in the media and online. Instructors on world affairs couldn't identify the aggressors, explain their ideology, or even in many cases conclude that the United States was under attack from an international terrorist organization. American and to some degree all Western academia was filled with twisted versions of Middle Eastern affairs, to the extent that scholars couldn't figure out what was happening. Of course, with time and as information was gathered about al Qaeda and the Taliban, the academic elite adapted to the post-9/11 realities.

However, in those crucial minutes following the attacks, most of the students gathered around me concluded faster than their professors that the country was under attack and that this was going to be a long war. A librarian whispered in my ear: "I have been reading about these *Islamic extremists* (*sic*) and I know what is on their minds." He wasn't under the influence of "mainstream" Middle Eastern studies and had his own access to original sources. Thus he survived the brainwashing administered to most classroom teachers.

In this moment, the shock of al Qaeda's barbaric attacks triggered the survival instinct in many Americans. They were asking a genuine question: Why were we attacked like this? The first logical answer to come to their minds was: because there is an enemy out there. The next question was: Who is that enemy and what does it want? Piece by piece, the response was like the return from a coma, and it pushed a greater number of Americans, and later Europeans, to investigate this lethal foe coming from "nowhere." Ultimately, the main consequence of the *Ghazwa* of al Qaeda was to open a window onto events in the Greater Middle East, even though in very small increments and often through the dense fog of counterpropaganda. The authoritarian regimes and jihadist networks (other than al Qaeda's rabid Salafists) were terrified by the idea that the American public would eventually discover the realities shaping the politics and societies of the Arab world and large Muslim communities worldwide. Wahabis and Muslim Brotherhood sympathizers maintained in debates on al Jazeera TV that Bin Laden's actions did more harm to the interests of the "Brotherhood against Democracy" than to the West. His main sin, according to the traditional Islamists—those who were banking on obtaining endless influence inside the West—was to awaken the infidels too early. "They were dormant and we were making progress inside their countries," said the advocates of the long-term jihad, accusing al Qaeda of being a hotheaded group. To which al Qaeda's supporters replied that the "blessed strikes" would cause the collapse of the *kuffars* and their democratic systems.

The chain of reactions was rapid. The U.S. president declared war on terrorism and vowed to bring down the Taliban, the protectors of al Qaeda, which was responsible for the massacre. The wheels of regime change were in motion as of October 7, 2001. But as the military prepared to bring retribution to Central Asia's builders of the violent Caliphate, voices surged inside America criticizing other regimes for tolerating terrorism and extremist ideologies, and for funding indoctrination. Among the political establishments accused of complicity were the Saudis, the Iraqi and Syrian Baathists, and the ayatollahs of Iran. The backlash against all radicals was nonspecific and often chaotic. The anti–al Qaeda sentiments exploded in all directions, and writers, commentators, and frustrated dissidents erupted like volcanoes—sometimes excessively—against anything and everything that sounded suspicious on the other side of the world.

Not all debates about Islam were necessarily focused on the most relevant things such as identifying an ideology, jihadism, and linking it to human rights abuse. As someone who had been following the rise of totalitarian ideologies in the Greater Middle East and saw—firsthand—the widespread suppression of liberties across the region since the early 1970s, I was frustrated to see the first massive Western reaction to these evil forces, taking place erratically and without clear strategies. But who was to blame? The United States and other democracies weren't prepared by their own intellectuals to resist and rise against the threat, let alone reach out intelligently to the peoples of the region who were the West's real allies in this expanding confrontation. But during the fall of 2001, the fact that America was waking up was more than enough progress for those who had been warning of the jihadi threat and its human rights abuses for decades. Finally, the greatest power on Earth, the one that had saved Europe twice and had sent its forces to stop ethnic cleansing several times—although very selectively during the twentieth century—had opened its eyes.

However, a U.S. awakening wasn't the only sure path to actually winning the confrontation and extending help to the hopeless communities in that part of the world. Everything would depend on how the U.S. leadership saw the map after it opened its eyes, how it would be influenced by the forces still in control of the Middle East, how it framed the issues, set the agendas, and much more. At the end of 2001, the United States and parts of the West began changing direction in international relations, giving hope to the underdogs across Middle Earth, but the journey was only at its beginning, full of difficulties, obstructions, and uncertainties.

Bin Laden's own speeches and videotapes aired by al Jazeera during that fall added to the stress felt by most Americans. The 9/11 attacks weren't some sort of reaction to frustration or an adventure by crazy people. The sheikh of al Qaeda spoke of a world divided into "two abodes, the *Dar al Islam* and *Dar al Harb*," literally Zone of Islam and Zone of War. Without deep knowledge of the initial meaning of this historical concept, many Americans concluded—and were perhaps not so far off base—that the man who ordered the bloodshed was in the forefront of a gigantic war zone, intent on engulfing the entire world.

Bin Laden didn't ease up on the message. Within a few weeks he and his spokesmen appeared on al Jazeera several times and threatened the American people with an edict to kill up to four million citizens, including women and children.[4] These statements unleashed a wave of questions, inevitably leading to an investigation of the region's problems. Hence, as of the attacks, and while policymakers within the Bush administration waged the Afghanistan campaign and pushed farther into Iraq two years later, a large segment within the American public was ready to accept the idea that the United States could and should push for change in the Arab and Muslim world. To the dismay and fury of the dominant elites, and as democracy activists were excited by this shift in mood, the United States led two wars to bring down two totalitarian regimes, opening two breaches in the wall.

This war continues in 2010, but the window that opened on events in the Greater Middle East was a miracle for all those who are suppressed in that region. Ironically, the outgrowth of the ideologies that took the liberties of millions of people in the Arab and Muslim world was the reason for a change that brought freedom close to the shores of these suffering nations.

The Removal of the Taliban

When President George Bush delivered his first speech to the U.S. Congress after the September attacks, Britain's prime minister, Tony Blair, was in the room. President Jacques Chirac, who two years later would fiercely oppose Bush's campaign in Iraq, paid a quick and symbolic visit to Washington weeks after the massacres. French daily *Le Monde* illustrated Western and international solidarity with America in the wake of the slaughters: "We are all Americans," stated its leading editorial.[5] World leaders and public figures, with the exception of the Taliban and al Qaeda, decried these horrors as "terrorism." An American response was accepted, authorized, and legitimated thousands of miles away.

The necessity of removing the Taliban wasn't questioned. The United States had to retaliate after the horrendous loss of its own people and such a slap in the face to the international community. Besides, Bin Laden's bold statements didn't help in saving the Taliban's skin. Washington's war room was in full swing and ready to wage a complete military campaign. Afghanistan's Northern Alliance would be backed all the way; B-52s and daisy-cutter bombs would pound the medieval Islamist militia to rubble. NATO allies would join enthusiastically and neighboring countries would not oppose. That was the picture, but below the surface there was much nervousness in the palaces and headquarters of authoritarian regimes. From Riyadh to Tehran, from Baghdad to Khartoum, questions were surfacing.

Should the United States be permitted to remove the Taliban by force? Who would replace them? What would a regime change mean in the region? Each authoritarian player had its own concerns.

The Wahabis in Saudi Arabia and their allies in Pakistan were frustrated that the Taliban was to be removed. The committed Salafi clerics in the Peninsula had been backing a Saudi policy of funding and supporting the Islamists in Afghanistan for decades. With the help of significant segments of Pakistan's intelligence apparatus, "Wahabi Aid" had been funneled to the mujahideen throughout the war against the Soviet occupation, creating a vast network of indoctrinated supporters in the country, particularly in the southern provinces. The collusion between "Wahabi Aid" and Deobandi teachings under the auspices of sympathizers inside Pakistan's intelligence apparatus produced the Taliban. The latter were ultraindoctrinated jihadists who were able to seize power in Kabul by the mid-1990s and establish the first pure *Imara* (Islamist emirate) of modern times. The "Islamist experiment" in Afghanistan, produced by the joint Wahabi-Deobandi venture, was the Salafists' first "baby" in a series of "emirates" to be produced around the world. The hard-core clerics and ideologues in the Peninsula were thinking of expansion in Kashmir, Chechnya, the former Yugoslavia, the southern Philippines, and Xinghiang, and also of the possibility of a domino effect in Central Asia's post-Soviet republics. Afghanistan under the Taliban wasn't just an insignificant emirate in the middle of nowhere. It was the building block for a new constellation of provinces of the forthcoming Caliphate.

The architects of the post–Cold war global jihad were troubled that U.S. efforts, in response to al Qaeda's reckless attacks on America, could jeopardize the future of the Salafi empire. This frustration was reflected in several encounters, debates on al Jazeera, and online between the mainstream Islamists worldwide and the hotheaded al Qaeda supporters in the wake of 9/11. The long-serving jihadists accused Bin Laden of risking the collapse of the entire Taliban enterprise because of his "jihadi excitement." But these rational Islamists were actually more concerned about what would come after the Taliban, rather than the turbaned militiamen themselves. If the U.S. intervention was to end by replacing Mullah Omar and his acolytes with another Islamist leader and Sharia would continue to be strictly applied, then everything would be fine. But the clerics of Arabia and the Muslim Brotherhoods worldwide were worried that the post-Taliban era would bring democracy.

The U.S.-NATO military campaign in Afghanistan lasted a few weeks, the Taliban was defeated and pushed underground, and their last forces gathered at Tora Bora close to the Pakistani border for the final stand. Before the U.S. military launched its strikes and backed up the Northern Alliance's march south into Kabul, a last attempt was made by circles within the Organization of the Islamic Conference (OIC) for a deal that would avoid the removal of an "Islamist" regime in return for chasing al Qaeda "away" from Afghanistan. The OIC negotiators, at the behest of its Secretariat General and discreetly backed by Saudi Arabia, Pakistan, Sudan, Qatar, and the *Ikhwan* international networks, proposed to form a committee from three members of the OIC to mediate between the Taliban and Washington. The OIC's foreign ministers' meeting "rejected targeting any Islamic state under the pretext of fighting terrorism."[6] Placing an "Islamic" player between the two foes was seen as a way to appease both sides, preserving the ideology of the Taliban while offering to remove Bin Laden from the country. This last-minute attempt to save the skin of the Taliban was evidence of the existence of a brotherhood against democracy, transcending borders, governments, and narrow national interests. Neither the Taliban nor al Qaeda believed that Allah would abandon them against the American infidels, but that He would eventually give them victory as He did against the Soviets.

The Taliban was wrong, the OIC's initiative was lost, and the door for political change in Afghanistan and the region was open.

Post–Tora Bora Debate

As the remnants of the Taliban were hurdling through the valleys east of Tora Bora during December 2001 to havens in Pakistan's jihadi enclaves, a regime change was under way in Kabul. Within three months women were freed from the horrors of the previous regime, civil society was liberated, and minorities from other religions and within Islam were emancipated. In the first stages of the rebuilding of Afghanistan, the new power was basically a mixture of the victorious Northern Alliance and those among the Pashtun leaders who were swayed from the Taliban. The rise of Hamid Karzai to leadership and ultimately to the presidency was due to his political shrewdness and his years of activities opposing the hardcore Islamist militia. The march toward a post-Taliban and secular republic wasn't that easy, nor was the political modernization of the country's fledgling institutions. American, European, and NATO investments in infrastructure and security were significant but it will take years of reforms and eventually a democratic revolution to unseat the dominant ideology of "Wahabi-Deobandism" embedded by the Taliban in the country. But the regime change opened the door for democratic change. Without the fall of the lethal militia, no dreams of liberty could have been possible. One country in Middle Earth got an opportunity to move toward pluralism and free civil society. Only developing U.S. strategies will determine if such a remote place, surrounded by powerful Pakistani Taliban to the east, Khomeinist Iran to the west, and Central Asian republics themselves vying for their own pluralism, can survive in its democratic experiment.

Following Tora Bora, the U.S. administration was involved in two campaigns, intertwined but with different goals. The main campaign was to pursue the terrorists wherever they were and under any regime. President Bush affirmed this goal in his famous State of the Union Address in February 2002. In it he declared three organizations terrorists: Hamas, Islamic Jihad, and Hezbollah, although all three were already on the U.S. terrorism list. In fact, this was more of an official confirmation of the principle that a "war on terrorism" was declared beyond the scope of one single organization. Then the president added another list, which he called "the axis of evil." In it, Bush included Iran, Iraq, and North Korea.

At the time, I found the speech odd, but still indicative of his willingness to be on the offensive. President Bush's advisors were creating a new American doctrine against global terrorism, but it should have been based on identifying a particular ideology and arguing that these forces were a threat to human rights, and hence to democracy. However, simply naming regimes, as President Bush did, without identifying the ideology and its goals, wasn't enough. Only six months after 9/11, these were baby steps in the longer march for intellectual change in America.

In early 2002, "lists of bad guys" were all one could find as a strategic basis for U.S. plans. What was odd about the lists was that they named just a few groups. There were dozens of jihadist organizations waging war against democracies, and there were certainly more than three regimes supporting terror and oppressing their own people: Sudan, Syria, and Libya were only the most visible. How the Bush administration proceeded to wage its war on terror in the first years is still a mystery to me, and it certainly wasn't the sophisticated global strategy I yearned to see unfold. Often on NBC, Fox News, and CNN, I was asked about my take on the "war." During these years I was clear on what al Qaeda, the Taliban, and the other "bad guys" wanted, but not so clear on what the Bush teams across all bureaucracies were planning. In short, the general direction, as many of my colleagues striving for freedom in the Middle East believed, was beneficial to the larger cause, but the actual steps to advance that agenda of freedoms weren't really clear.

During the year and a half between the attacks on 9/11 and the invasion of Iraq, Middle Eastern activists for free civil societies, mostly those based in the West, became bolder in calling for action, but were still fearful of American shortsightedness. Two camps commenting on freedom in the Middle East witnessed a sudden growth in America. On the one hand, those known as "neoconservatives" began developing the themes of fighting terrorism worldwide and focusing on the "Islamist" threat, calling it predominantly "radical Islam" or "Islamic terrorism." The neocon intellectual push influenced the narrative of the entire Bush administration, but only where the political appointees were in Defense, such as the Pentagon, the National Security Council, and a few positions at the State Department. The story was still a matter of security and not yet an issue of liberation. Another developing camp included the Middle Eastern dissidents in exile, their supporters, and human rights activists, mostly veterans from the 1990s. They made the case that fighting terrorism would ease pressures on civil societies in the region and vice versa.

The two parallel messages expanded simultaneously, as the foe was identified as jihadism, or in the lingo of the time, "Islamic fundamentalism," or radical Islam and its derivatives. In my own writing and interviews I had identified the threat as "jihadi ideology," while other colleagues and commentators in the field chose different terminology. I drew this narrative from the literature of the Salafist and Khomeinist ideologues and movements since the 1980s. But it took the expert community about five years after 9/11 to begin using the word "jihadists" systematically.

The debate in Washington was about what to do next after defeating the Taliban. Since the attacks I had hoped and pushed for a new U.S. (and ultimately a new Western and international) policy that would create a breach in the walls surrounding civil societies in the Greater Middle East. In my many addresses to forums on Middle Eastern politics, to thousands of senior citizens dedicated to foreign policy interest, to dozens of NGOs focusing on ethnic and religious minorities in the Arab and Muslim world, and to the media, and in my briefings to legislators, I relentlessly argued that by supporting democracy in the region, the battle against the terrorists would be won historically and with international support. I advocated the idea that in the wake of the great consensus in world politics immediately after September 11, the United States should do three things simultaneously: 1) reach out to the international community via its institutions, including the United Nations, to mobilize them "against" the jihadists and "for" democracy; 2) launch a campaign targeting the jihadi terror forces, not just the abstract concept of "terrorism"; and 3) unleash the mother of democracy programs by connecting and partnering with dissidents, NGOs, women's movements, students, artists, and all those willing to rise up against authoritarianism. Had the Bush administration, in conjunction with Congress, chosen that three-tiered strategy in the weeks following the al Qaeda attacks, most likely a democratic revolution would have been under way in the region and, at the very least, pressures for significant reforms would have materialized.

UN Obsolescence?

As a body representing governments, the United Nations wouldn't have been pleased about pressuring the authoritarian regimes in the Greater Middle East, simply because of the sheer number of oppressive regimes that have seats in the General Assembly. Since the 1970s, a bloc of states (mostly OPEC, the OIC, and the Arab League) had controlled the General Assembly by numbers and by the influence of petrodollars. But after the collapse of the Soviet Bloc and particularly since 9/11 new coalitions were possible even at the United Nations.[7]

In 2004, I proved to the most skeptical minds in Washington that specific actions could be successfully mobilized against these oppressive regimes. The examples of UN resolutions issued by the Security Council to free Lebanon from Syria and to assist Darfur against the Khartoum regime are examples of what could be done.

As an observer of the international community and particularly of the United Nations since the mid-1970s, I knew two things: that the international organization needed radical reforms to meet the obligations embedded in its charter, and that at the same time liberal democracies should use this forum to its utmost limits, as a way to advance coalition building. In the battle for freedom and democracy for the Middle East, all tools at the disposal of the free world have to be used. The UN, even as it became increasingly dominated by the oil regimes and its bureaucracies were seized by apologists, was still an important institution capable of affecting the liberation of oppressed populations. Unfortunately the West in general and the neoconservative intellectuals in particular were still traumatized by the overwhelming influence of petrodollars in the General Assembly and by the obstructionist power Russia and China had in the Security Council. The constant assault on Israel and the repeated demonization of the United States at the UN and its various councils and agencies led to an almost irreversible trend within the conservative circles in America. There was nothing to obtain from an institution at the service of dictators and corrupt regimes.

While this accusation stood, there was still room for action in the UN. The Security Council's permanent members were three liberal democracies (the United States, the United Kingdom, and France), one transitional democracy (Russia), and communist China. What the UN critics overlooked, especially after 9/11, was that all five permanent members were affected by, and had tremendous problems with, terrorism inspired by jihadism. This was the first window of opportunity. The other window was the fact that when Western democracies partner with underdogs, it would be embarrassing for the regimes to not take action as popular movements of discontent backed by the United States grow inside their region. The UN could have been used much more effectively in fostering democratic change in the Greater Middle East. It would have been smarter to fight the authoritarians and their jihadist allies in the UN rather than to surrender the organization altogether to the oppressive regimes.

Washington Not Yet Ready

After 9/11, a wind of change was blowing favorably around the globe so that the free world, led by the United States, could seize the opportunity and partner with the oppressed people in the Arab and Muslim world. But such a partnership would need grand visionaries in Washington who were able to understand the nature of the jihadist threat, comprehend its strategies, create the necessary coalitions to isolate it, mobilize public opinion, and win wars of ideas. Success would require a coalition to lead multiple strategic campaigns simultaneously, use the UN to the extent of its powers, reach out to governments that are not part of the "war on terror" but that could be partnered with on specific campaigns against particular terror forces, and even work with moderate governments in the region to help them combat threats emanating from within their own borders.

Unfortunately, the sitting administration at the time wasn't ready for such an undertaking. Bush advisors were slowly moving in that direction, but the bulk of the bureaucracy was resistant. By the time the top officials reached a decision to invade Iraq, the underpinning philosophy for the move wasn't based on human rights abuse or democracy promotion, but strictly on national security. The decision-makers ignored their initial freedom forward strategy until the latter part of 2004. Part of the explanation may lie in the fact that the policymakers in the administration were unsure of the state of mind of the people in the Middle East. Some of these advisors were veterans of the Cold War and thus knew more about communism and how Eastern Europe felt about the Soviets than they knew about the Middle East. Other advisors had the knowledge about the region but didn't have enough "trust" in the ability of Arab Muslim culture to produce democratic alternatives.

At a dinner attended by senators during fall 2001, Professor Bernard Lewis, a seasoned scholar who wrote volumes on Middle Eastern history and was respected by many in the Bush administration, particularly in neocon circles, said it was possible that Islamic political culture could produce some form of democracy. Although he praised the Kemalist secular institutions in Turkey, he didn't have the same hopes for the Arab world and Iran for speedy progress in that regard.[8]

From the perspective of Middle Eastern dissidents, the inability of Washington to produce a coherent strategy on democracy promotion was forgivable as long as the Bush administration was pushing back against the jihadists and waging a counterwar against "all terrorists," even though the majority of terror regimes and networks hadn't yet been put on notice. To desperate opposition groups and underdogs buried under layers of oppression, the primary matter was that America was waking up and rising against the bad guys. Iranian, Syrian, and Saudi reformers hoped the United States would learn about the region's web of authoritarians while it moved forward. Lebanese opposition in exile hoped American foreign policy would eventually correct past mistakes and begin questioning Syria on its occupation of Lebanon. Southern Sudanese and Darfur activists felt things could get better for their cause. Across the region fervor was spreading among the hard-core opposition movements and intellectuals. A long time before Bush strategists figured out their own plans, the feeling on the substreets of the region (meaning the nonvisible dissident forces, unlike the so-called Arab street that moves with and not against the dominant ideologies) was that lights had been seen through the tiny windows of a gigantic jail. They hoped freedom was on its way, even though the power beaming that light didn't quite see where it was going.

In several interviews during that period, I answered firmly, when asked about the next step in the so-called war on terror, that wherever the United States wished to start would be good, because the situation of human rights in the region was bleak. This view reflected the feelings of all those NGOs I saw getting energized, post-9/11. My call to action was based on making sure the focus was on people's liberation first, achieved with as many allies as possible. I know that freeing people from oppression is the assured way to defeat terrorists. There is no other alternative. The jihadists' Achilles' heel is in their own societies. Free the population and the forces of terror will be defeated. Even if Washington wasn't ready for the monumental journey of Middle Eastern liberation, there was no other option but to support its efforts to counter the jihadists and weaken the totalitarians.

There were some not completely accurate analogies made with World War II. America waged a war against fascism after being attacked, and the war efforts and titanic sacrifices resulted in the liberation of millions of people. There was no way to win that war without defeating Nazism and its allies. Once this was done, most areas freed by the Allies turned toward democracy. Even the enemy, the Axis, saw its countries transformed into working democracies in the end. The legitimacy of defeating terrorist forces, particularly those constituting a direct threat, wasn't conditioned by the rise of democracy.

But if the result of a confrontation was the possibility, however remote, that entire societies would have a shot at breaking away from
the Taliban or Baath, would prodemocracy individuals oppose it?

Events that followed the offensive at Tora Bora didn't exactly
unfold in the direction I had hoped for, simply because the United
States and its allies didn't choose the appropriate agenda to comple-
ment the enormous effort in military personnel and resources it
committed to the conflict. A perfect platform would have focused
U.S.-led efforts on liberation from terror regimes and ideologies.
Fighting back against terror regimes was legitimate, but helping
populations endangered by terror regimes was actually a principle
embedded in the United Nations charter and reaffirmed in the Universal Declaration of Human Rights. This principle had already been
applied in Yugoslavia twice in one decade, in Haiti, and in different
forms against military regimes.

The United States and its coalition of the willing had the golden
opportunity to correct past mistakes, reach out to the international
community with already applied principles, and launch an international campaign. That campaign would be a "war on terror" and also
a campaign to assist populations in danger of genocide, oppression,
and human rights abuse. It would be fought case by case, to the extent that international law could absorb. In short, the strategy could
have consisted of the same efforts, the same financial burden, and the
same energy, but with revolutionary results. In the case of Lebanon's
liberation and, to an extent, that of Darfur, oppressed people were
freed without direct military intervention. The Greater Middle East
had suffered longer than Central and Eastern Europe and was more
eager than any other part of the world to be helped. The only difference was that the forces of oppression were older, wealthier, and had
a greater grip on Western policy processes.

The lights were beaming, but the windows weren't wide enough
for liberation to knock down the walls.

The Case of Iraq

Much has been said and written about the Iraq War as a whole, the
U.S. invasion, the alleged weapons of mass destruction, and the removal of Saddam. The ensuing chaos, the march to democratic institutions, the sectarian violence, and the terrorist strikes continue as

of the printing of this book. However, there was little debate on the significance of the regime change in Iraq and the actual rise of democracy in that country and beyond. The al Qaeda strikes in America triggered a U.S. retaliation that crumbled the Taliban in Afghanistan. The "license" provided by the international community for American military action did not include approval to bring democracy to that oppressed people, particularly women and minorities. The Taliban could have brutalized its own society for another two to three decades, no questions asked. The world cartel of oil interests, significantly influenced by the Wahabis, the Khomeinists, and the authoritarians in general, wouldn't have allowed a regime change in a Central Asian Muslim country under any circumstances, even if genocide was taking place. The lessons from Sudan are clear: More than a million people were massacred within that country, a member of the Arab League and the OIC. No international intervention was allowed by the OPEC-OIC bloc. But in Afghanistan there was an exception, as the Taliban made a major mistake by allowing al Qaeda, which is organically linked to the regime, to strike deep inside the West, behead its economic symbols, and wound its military command. Such an open, insulting attack had to be paid for. With frustration, the "world Islamist bloc" accepted that they had to pay the consequences. The Taliban would be sacrificed and a regime change would take place. The license was only for Afghanistan and against the Taliban, nothing more. This is how the quid pro quo between the Bush administration and the brotherhood against democracy began.

In Washington, a number of intellectuals and strategists close to the Bush-Cheney teams theorized that the United States still had enough goodwill from 9/11 to crumble another rogue regime in the region. This basic but incorrect assumption led to the decision to go to war with Iraq, and multiple justifications for waging the campaign were developed. The mistaken assessment was that the forces that would block any U.S. or international intervention for any reason in any "Muslim country" had made an exception for Afghanistan, and had changed their attitudes toward regime change. As bad and bloody as the Saddam regime was, that alone wouldn't have granted an OIC-OPEC authorization to remove him from power and install a democracy in his place. Unfortunately, the Washingtonian power establishment misunderstood the situation. They thought Americans were still mobilized because of the effects of 9/11 and that U.S. allies would not oppose a second offensive in the region, particularly since Saddam was an offender against oil countries such as Saudi Arabia and Kuwait. Indeed, Americans at large were still nervous about a jihadi threat, especially since Bin Laden's videos were still appearing on al Jazeera with more threats and revelations about the global goals of this totalitarian ideology.

However, the Bush administration and its intellectual elite failed to educate the public about the link between jihadism or Baathism and oppression of the region's peoples, thus not readying Americans for what was to come. Another failure was the inability of Washington political architects to build a case for liberation as a basis for its antiterrorism action in the region. Yes, Saddam Hussein's regime deserved to be removed on the grounds of massive abuse of human rights of Iraqis, massacres of Kurds, and possibly genocide against Shia. For much lesser evil, other regimes were bombed into submission under international auspices. The military campaigns in Bosnia and Kosovo and the intervention in East Timor were clear examples of situations in which the use of force was legitimate in order to save lives.

I argued forcefully for a strong, unequivocal, and clear human rights platform as a basis for any intervention anywhere in the region. Anything short of that would severely affect the success of intervention. My frustration grew as the administration developed its arguments for the war in Iraq. The op-ed pieces and media statements made by commentators, especially from the neoconservative camp in the defense of the case against Saddam, were factual in their description of his past bloodshed but were extremely risky in terms of legitimizing an action against his regime only on the basis of the threat factor. In my analysis, he had committed enough abuse to justify a U.S.-led campaign to remove him. There was no need to play the WMD card. I had argued in 1991 that the United States and the coalition had made a strategic mistake by not marching all the way to Baghdad and removing Saddam Hussein on the grounds of his invading another country and ethnic cleansing of Kurds.[9] It was a viable option at that time because Europeans and Arabs were part of the coalition to liberate Kuwait, and the Soviet Union was weak and in no position to stand by its former client. Saddam should have been removed and replaced with a democratic government.

The problem hadn't been with a lack of arguments to bring the

Baathist regime down or with the capacity of General Schwarzkopf to deliver militarily. Rather, the opposition to removing Saddam in 1991 was coming from our allies in the region, including the Saudis, Egyptians, partners such as Hafez Assad, and of course the Islamic Republic of Iran. Then and now, there was nothing to expect from the region's authoritarians when it came to promoting democracy. The "license to kill" a regime would be granted if the government was a direct threat to another regime, not to its own people. Now in 2004, the Bush advisors and strategists thought they could still convince the world that action against Saddam was necessary because he had developed weapons of mass destruction.

I, too, believed that if evidence existed that WMDs were being produced and deployed and were a threat to the United States or any other neighbor in the region, Saddam was done. But if no evidence was produced, any intervention, even one predicated on human rights grounds, would be condemned. Why risk the more important mission for a complicated and unproven assumption? Yet when the administration made the case for the existence of such weapons, I (and many advocates for human rights intervention) thought that if a legitimate intervention on the grounds of WMD could result in dislodging the Baath and establishing the basis for a future pluralist democracy, then of course we should support such action.

Washington was strongly in favor of a national security intervention, but not on the grounds of human rights. The "intervene-in-Iraq" lobby had other reasons than just WMD concerns or the human rights violations. There was a very active group of anti-Saddam exiles, such as Shiite businessman Ahmad Chalabi and others who pressed for rapid military action against the Baathist dictator. Naturally, Shiite exiles who fled Iraq's brutal repression of their community in the 1990s lobbied hard to remove the bloody leader. The 9/11 attacks and the psychological readiness of the American public offered a major opportunity for them to seek direct U.S. military action against their own country and enemy. Yet their plans for a post-Saddam regime were unclear. In fact, their ties to the Iranian mullahs were known, and many of the Iraqi Shiite opposition figures were based in Iran.

In the final analysis the choice boiled down to the fact that the Bush administration was fully determined to invade Iraq and remove Saddam. There were no plans to focus on other human rights crises at the time, neither in Sudan nor in Lebanon. When faced with a choice between removing a dictator involved in genocide against his own people and no action at all, the obvious decision for anyone working in the field of human rights was to support the removal. The representatives of suffering communities such as the Kurds, Assyro-Chaldeans, and others in the north, the Shia in the south, and many anti-Baathist Sunnis in the center were all in favor of military action against Saddam. Supporting the campaign to overthrow him was easy; what remained to be seen was if the U.S. government had it right in terms of WMDs, and if it was prepared to help Iraqis cross soundly to a transitional democracy.

The Removal of Saddam

When Secretary of State Colin Powell made his case against the Baghdad regime at the United Nations, the evidence presented for the presence of WMD was convincing, but not of the caliber we've seen before, as when the Soviet Union deployed missiles in Cuba in the early 1960s. Saddam's ownership of such weapons was known for years. He had ordered the gassing of Iranian forces during his war with Khomeini in the 1980s and unleashed chemicals on Kurdish villages, including Halabja in 1988. During the Gulf War of 1991 the Baathists fired Scud missiles on Saudi Arabia and Israel. Missiles and chemical WMDs indicated a clear threat for which he should have been removed years ago. Powell established three parameters to justify U.S. action, by order of importance: WMDs, support of terrorism (al Qaeda), and last, abuse of human rights.

I believed that the United States should have shuffled the order: first, human rights abuse; second, the existence of WMDs that have been used in the past; last, the involvement of the regime in terrorism. Unfortunately, the administration chose the WMD factor first, probably because many of its lobbyists weren't especially excited about the democracy issue or were unsure of how to tackle it. Certainly the weapons existed, because we saw them in action; most likely some of them were transferred to Syria, just as Iraqi fighter jets were transferred to Iran in 1991. The transfer to Syria was for a price. The Assad regime would try to block the invasion of Iraq by holding an Arab Summit in Beirut in 2002. If they could not hold back the invasion, the Syrians would host the fleeing Baathist cadres and would also unleash terror against any new government that was put in place.[10]

The case for invading Iraq was a complicated labyrinth of facts and justifications, but the reality was that Iraq was being liberated from a tyrant. U.S. Marines and soldiers marched through the desert and Rangers and Special Forces parachuted into the north. The bottom line was that Kurds, other ethnic minorities, and Arabs from Shia and Sunni backgrounds were all freed from terror, torture, and oppression.[11] The downfall of the Saddam Hussein Baathist regime was imminent.

A window for freedom was opened. After decades of massacres and oppression, the Kurds and other minorities in the north were free from Pan Arabism and the firepower of the regime. From Baghdad to Basra, 12 million Shiites rose again after the terror regime was overturned. In the capital and in the Sunni provinces, the opponents of Saddam, including those from his own party, became free men and women. The TV footage showing smiling children running in front of the advancing Marines said it all. Those who will become the future of Iraq, the youngest of the population, the souls who had little to hide, were erupting in joy. This was the equivalent of the popular demonstrations in Paris, Prague, or Rome on liberation day in World War II.

In Iraq, the joyfulness lasted mere hours before the "adults" from all political parties took over, and the complexities of political business began. The liberation of Iraq could have been conducted with different strategies, coalitions, timing, and under strong human rights slogans, but in the end, the Baathists were removed, Saddam was gone, and the country's skies were wide open for a new future.

Will freedom ultimately win, or will Iraqis and Americans reach the end of the process without achieving true democracy in Iraq?

The Syrian Pullout from Lebanon

After the invasions in Afghanistan and Iraq, U.S. military offensives in the region stopped and the battle for democracy began. Had these two countries been the equivalent of Nazi Germany and militaristic Japan after World War II, one would have projected a slow and successful march toward stabilization and democratization. Policy planners in the Bush administration kept referring to the former foes of the United States in World War II and how the old enemies' new constitutions came along nicely. However, the comparison wasn't perfect—the Nazis and other fascists were completely overwhelmed, not partially. In 1945 there were no other Nazi regimes across the borders of the former Reich, nor were there other Asian totalitarian regimes still in support of the former Japanese power.

After the fall of the Taliban and the Iraqi Baath, plenty of other regimes and terror networks were still up and running, and fighting. One of these forces still engaged in the fight against democracy was the Baathist regime of Bashar Assad in Syria. The Alawi elite controlling the government, party, and army has been in power since Hafez Assad (the father) took over via a coup d'état in 1970. After invading Lebanon in June 1976 and ending its occupation in the 1990s, the Syrian regime can be included in an axis with Iran's regime, Hezbollah in Lebanon, and Hamas in Gaza. The Assad faction reigned through sheer terror inside Syria and in occupied Lebanon. During the decade preceding 9/11 Lebanese activists in exile and inside the country tried tirelessly to draw the attention of the world community to Syria's crimes against the citizens of its occupied neighbors, but to no avail.

No Western government was willing to lift a finger, even if from time to time a legislative branch in the United States or France issued a declaration or resolution, or held hearings and briefings. Strangely, while the U.S. Congress pressed for a Syrian withdrawal from Lebanon, no administration—Bush the first, Clinton, and the first year of the Bush II Administration—took action. The State Department and other agencies influential in foreign policy decision-making, such as the CIA, constantly blocked any serious move to push Assad's forces out of Lebanon. The oil lobbying powers were keen on maintaining Syrian control over that little country. In addition, the opposition to Syria was reduced mainly to the Christians, and they were deeply divided. The stars were not aligned in favor of a free Lebanon.

However, as of 2000, groups within the Lebanese Diaspora began focusing on the international dimension of the Lebanese crisis. In the aftermath of the 9/11 attacks, the NGOs commenced a campaign to align allies in the international community who would be ready to pressure the Syrians out of Lebanon. The Iraq invasion and the bloody Syrian reaction to the collapse of the Iraqi Baath cleared a path in international relations so that a significant push was possible for the liberation of Lebanon. However, unlike the situation in Afghanistan and Iraq, military intervention wasn't necessary. The United States and its allies didn't have to shoot one bullet or spend one dollar to see democracy rise in the country of the Cedars. Lebanon's civil society was more than ready to rise, despite the divisiveness of its politicians. Almost like magic, by the end of April 2005, the Syrian tanks, trucks, and artillery hurdled out of the Lebanese territories toward their bases in Syria. After almost thirty years of brutal occupation, Lebanon's population became free from military Baathist domination.

The story of the removal of the Syrian occupation of that little country deserves a book of its own. The process of evacuation, similar to the Soviet pullout from Eastern Europe, was too fast to be absorbed by many in Lebanon. Only those who followed up the lobbying efforts in the West, and coordinated the pressures from inside with the demonstrations that took place in February 2005, understood the big picture, and yet they barely believed that it really happened. The story is not over yet, as the remnants of the Syrian influence, Iranian penetration, and Hezbollah's presence are still plaguing Lebanon.

In short, it was 9/11 that led to the removal of the Taliban and opened the path for U.S. intervention in Iraq. The Syro-Iranian reaction to the toppling of Saddam constituted the second chapter, leading to the Lebanese episode and the Cedars Revolution. When U.S. forces reached Baghdad and Mesopotamia seemed freed from the Iraqi Baath, panic spread in the ruling body of the other Baath, in Syria. The Assad clan feared two things: first, that somehow U.S. and coalition forces would find a reason to cross the borders and unseat the dictator in Damascus; second, that Syrian reformers and opposition groups would be emboldened by events in Iraq and, as in Eastern Europe, would rise against the regime.

Assad was wrong about a potential American march from Iraq into Syria. In Washington, there were no such plans. The Syrian dictator was closer to reality on the second concern. Syrian dissidents and opposition, even within the regime, began moving, encouraged by the winds of change in the region. Syria's vice president, Abdel Halim Khaddam, for example, began criticizing the regime, and soon enough, after events took a wrong turn in Lebanon, went into exile. "These were all ominous developments of what was yet to happen," a former high-ranking Baathist from the older generations of the party who also left his country and moved outside Syria explained to me.

Nouhad Ghadri, publisher and editor of the weekly Pan Arab *Al Muharer al Arabi,* published in Beirut and London, was a comrade of the founders of the Syrian Baath and knew Hafez the father. "The Bashar clique was trembling from fear of a revolution inside Syria. Remember that this country has a Sunni majority and ruled with an iron fist by an Alawite minority not exceeding 9 percent via six intelligence and security services," Ghadri explained. "When they saw the crumbling of the most powerful Baath party in the region, under the shock and awe of American military power, they imagined a similar scenario happening in Syria, just by instincts. But such a disaster for the Assad elite couldn't happen unless the Syrian opposition would be supported by outside forces, including a future Iraqi government or even the West, with the Americans stepping up pressures."

Ghadri, an expert on the Damascus regime, told me that "Assad's acolytes decided to strike preemptively at the U.S. role in Iraq before it transforms the country into a working democracy. See, Syria's regime is made of Levantine conspiratorial minds. They unleashed a war against the United States in Iraq, even before being targeted by Washington. They have accumulated so much wealth to protect, both inside Syria and in occupied Lebanon. They would do anything to keep their regime and privileges under control." Indeed, by the end of April and early May 2003, the Syrian Baathist war on liberated Iraq and U.S.-led coalition forces had been escalated by the opening of its borders to a collection of jihadists and Iraqi Baathists in order to conduct terror operations. These, added to al Qaeda's cells, formed what was known later as the insurgency in Iraq.

Washington knew of Syria's involvement and warned the regime several times. By early 2004, Assad had escalated the undeclared war against the United States in Iraq, and the Lebanese Diaspora groups met with officials in the Bush administration and congressional leaders from both parties. Similar meetings took place with French officials. The Lebanese advocacy groups wanted the United States and France to take action against Syrian occupation in the UN Security Council, an action never tried before. The stars were aligning again, but this time against Assad's designs.

In September 2004, UN Resolution 1559 was ratified, calling on Syria to withdraw from Lebanon and on the militias, including

Hezbollah, to disarm. This was an unexpected success by the Bush administration—oddly allied with French president Chirac, who was not supportive of the American invasion of Iraq. The Bashar regime became unbalanced and overreacted by unleashing a string of terrorist attacks in Lebanon in order to prevent the rise of an internationally backed Lebanese opposition. After a failed assassination attempt against Druse former minister Marwan Hamade, a powerful bomb killed the former Sunni prime minister of Lebanon, Rafiq Hariri, a member of Parliament, and their staff and bodyguards.

Tens of thousands of Lebanese took to the streets between February and March, culminating in what was termed by the Bush administration and confirmed by the Lebanese Diaspora as a "Cedars Revolution." This was the single most powerful and nonviolent prodemocracy march in the modern history of the Middle East. One and a half million gathered in downtown Beirut, and a huge hole in the wall of authoritarianism was opened. Uniquely, though, there were no boots on the ground, or no-fly zones, no jets pounding, and no millions of dollars spent. It was the first native, self-propelled, peaceful revolution in the region in post-Soviet times.

Gebran Tueni, publisher and editor of the daily *Al Nahar*, and one of the leaders of the Cedars Revolution, observed, "It was like we saw a light from a narrow hole and suddenly the whole window opened wide and we were submerged with light. It was beyond what we were hoping for." Tueni's words were almost prophetic. In June he and a majority of anti-Syrian politicians were elected to the first post-Syrian-withdrawal Lebanese Parliament. Indeed it was perhaps too much light, as the Syrians and Hezbollah rushed to cripple the newly elected legislative assembly.

In December 2005, after a series of assassinations targeting journalists and activists, Gebran Tueni was killed when a car bomb detonated as he drove from his home to his office in Beirut.

The third free space to open, after Afghanistan and Iraq, was indeed Lebanon. And as on the first two battlefields, the enemy's response was terror. Lebanon's recovered freedom was partial, as the occupier didn't really quit the country. But liberty had shown its face to the world. It found a way to emerge from the abyss and has been struggling since to survive and expand.

The Darfur Campaign

Of all the conflicts in the Middle East and North Africa, and perhaps in the entire Arab and Muslim world, it was the drama of Sudan that attained biblical proportion in its horrors and bloodshed. If I was to decide where the United States and the international community must begin its campaign to save peoples of the region from oppression, I would undoubtedly choose Sudan. Ravaged by internal wars since its creation by British colonial power in the mid-1950s, this half-African, half-Arab country hasn't witnessed a lasting period of peace or prosperity in its history.

The two-decades-long cycles of northern offensives against the animist and Christian south stretched from 1956 to 1972 and from 1983 till 2005. The number of massacred Africans in the south was abysmal and exceeded the number of victims of any jihadi force, including those in Algeria, Lebanon, and Afghanistan combined. More than a million and a half people were killed in three decades. Only the genocide in Biafra in the 1960s comes close to that scale.

Just as shocking as the number of victims and the types of human rights abuses, including abject slavery at the hands of jihadist militias sponsored by Khartoum, was the heavy and inexplicable silence of the West and its liberal democracies. According to Jimmy Mulla, a representative of southern Sudan, one of the most painful policies his group had to endure wasn't a particular policy of the United States or of European governments; rather it was no policies at all. Mulla said one of the main concerns of John Garang, leader of the Sudanese People's Liberation Movement, was the web of oil lobbies operating in the West that worked to block aid and support to the African rebellion in southern Sudan.

It wasn't only the south that suffered from international silence; soon enough, the western provinces of Darfur, inhabited by black Muslim tribes, joined the legions of oppressed populations of Sudan. In 2004 the chairman of the "Damanga Coalition for Freedom and Democracy" (Darfur community in the United States), Mohammed Yahia, stated that his people "were in disbelief that Americans and Europeans waited that long before they declared what has happened in Sudan to be genocide." Yahia indicated that he expected African-Americans to "relate directly to the suffering of the black Sudanese, those Christians and animists in the south and those like us, black

Muslims in Darfur." Mulla and Yahia, and before them a roster of very active representatives of Sudan's underdogs in the West, finally saw with astonishment the "cause of freedom" of their ancestral lands being recognized.

Indeed, as of 2004, the West, followed by the United Nations, began condemning the killings in Darfur, describing them as "genocide." First Pope John Paul II acknowledged the atrocities, then many Western legislators, the U.S. administration, and finally the secretary general of the United Nations, Kofi Annan. Within a few months, the genocide in Darfur became a cause célèbre. Hollywood and other groups joined in a "Campaign to Save Darfur." How could the most ignored struggle in the Arab Islamic world suddenly rise to the top?

When the Taliban, brothers in ideology to Khartoum's Islamist regime, collapsed in Kabul, the Sudanese regime started to have second thoughts about pursuing the war against Africans in the southern Sudan. Pragmatism obliged the Bashir regime to negotiate with the southern rebellion, resulting in a peace agreement. The Sudanese Khartoum elite feared an international intervention on the grounds of human rights violations. But the western parts of Sudan were not covered by the agreement. The Janjaweed militia armed and backed by Sudan's jihadi establishment continued to ravage the extremely poor provinces of Darfur. By 2004 the Bashir regime backed off and accepted the principle of negotiations with the liberation movement in Darfur.

The fall of the Taliban and Saddam had their effect deep in Africa as well. Another suppressed population was finally put on the international radar screen. The light had penetrated the thick walls of Sudan's horrendous mass prison. But again, the jury was still out on whether real freedom would be achieved. Sudan's regime took a few steps backward, until the U.S.-led campaigns in the region and international pressures on Khartoum receded. The future is still uncertain.

The planes of Bin Laden brought down two buildings, damaged one military headquarters, and killed innocent passengers in one hour. The response, in three short years U.S.-led Western and international forces, initially set to retaliate against al Qaeda, thrust through Middle Earth, removing two absurdly violent regimes from Afghanistan and Iraq, freeing millions of people, planting the seeds of potential democracies, and opening free spaces in four nations. The ripple effect was the withdrawal of Syrian occupation forces from Lebanon and the Sudanese regime's suspension of its genocidal enterprises against the black peoples of the south and Darfur. The race between the rise of a violent Caliphate and the expansion of freedom has no parallel in the region's modern history. Would the United States and other democracies develop comprehensive freedom forward strategies to spread democracy? Would the dissidents rise and counter the jihadists? And would the brotherhood against democracy accept this fait accompli, or would it unleash its own counteroffensive?

4.

Democracy Sabotaged

By 2004, the Bush administration felt it was time to use the narrative of freedom promotion as U.S. policy in the Greater Middle East. In less than one year, and for the first time in decades, the most powerful democracy on the planet was gearing up to support the democracy struggle in the region. This stance in foreign policy hadn't taken since the United States openly supported the dissidents in the Soviet Bloc in the early eighties. In opposition to very influential ideologies, the Bush administration's agenda was unintentionally daring, as it challenged the interests of a very powerful bloc of regimes. Calling for the spread of democracy overnight in the Arab and Muslim world was in fact a call for revolution. The ruling elites in that region perceived this as an attempted coup d'état against their interests. This is why the difference between the war of ideas against the Soviets and the one against the jihadists is significant. During the Cold War, successive U.S. administrations knew a good deal about their foe, while in the war against terrorism, Washington's policy architects know little about the jihadists. Let's explore how the U.S. government waged its war of ideas for democracy, how it managed it, and how the opposing forces responded.

Freedom Forward and the Spread of Democracy

In the months that followed the 9/11 attacks, I hoped for a quick strategic response from the entire U.S. government—a campaign for democracy and human rights. I made the link clearly between the rise of jihadism and the democratic struggle, just as many of my colleagues involved in combating persecution and oppression had

over the previous decade. I believed a rapid shift in U.S. policy from
ignoring the plight of oppressed in the region to a full-blown campaign to support those suppressed people was necessary. But what
seemed crystal clear to me was not yet on the minds of policymakers
in Washington, let alone those in Europe.

Ironically, the "idea" of unleashing unlimited support for the
struggle of civil societies in the region was crossing the minds of two
opposing camps in the Arab world and Muslim countries. On one
hand, the dissidents were hoping for America to see the light and
engage feverishly in the only strategy that can eventually reverse terror ideologies, and on the other hand, the authoritarian regimes and
organizations were fearful that the United States would indeed apply
such a strategy fully. In the Greater Middle East, oppressed and oppressors knew instantly what could happen if the American giant
woke up and tipped the scale. The only party that was unaware of
this precarious balance and of its own role in it was the U.S. decision-
makers in the executive and the legislative branches, both Republicans and Democrats.

As I explained earlier, a systematic war of ideas, funded by petrodollars, was able to take out the ability of Western nations to
comprehend the real situation in the Middle East's tightly controlled
societies. When al Qaeda hit, the West wasn't ready psychologically
to respond, other than to physically strike back. And that physical
attack is what the U.S.-led coalition performed in Afghanistan. But
soon enough, Washington and its allies learned pragmatically that a
change had to happen so that the actions on the ground made sense.
It was a sort of empirical discovery that democracy had to be pursued
as the end to justify the means. Indeed, as the Taliban was rooted out,
the question in Afghanistan was: now what? What kind of government to establish instead? The answer to that question between 2001
and 2003 led to the first battle for democracy in Middle Earth in the
post-Soviet era. To the horror of the jihadists in the region, Washington chose to establish a pluralist democracy after the Taliban was
expelled. In fact the Bush administration had little room to maneuver.
If Afghanistan did not achieve a democratic system with elections,
then it would revert to the Taliban.

The first window into free political culture in the Middle East was
forced open by practical necessity. Some in the United States began
to endorse the idea that this type of system should be applied across

the region. Many among the workers for freedom and dissidents in the Soviet Bloc during the Reagan years adapted their old methods to fit the situation in the Middle East. However, while the situations were comparable in terms of fighting totalitarianism, the political and cultural identity of the people in these two regions was dramatically different. In Eastern Europe, multiparty systems had existed before the Soviet domination. The collapse of Soviet rule brought back what had been there before. In the Muslim regions, there was no democratic model to go back to. With very few exceptions, liberal democracy had never taken root after the collapse of the Sultanate. Moreover, the jihadist and ultra-authoritarian ideologies were not rolled back with the collapse of the Taliban, and later on the Iraqi Baath. Since the U.S. bureaucrats never factored in a war of ideas, or an ideological renaissance, they weren't able to sweep societies swiftly into the realm of democratic pluralism.

Despite these systemic difficulties, the Bush administration decided to walk in an unprecedented direction: away from the traditional ideologies of the region and toward a simple implementation of democratic institutions—freedom, political parties, and elections. At the time, I projected that while the direction was good enough, the implementation would be terribly difficult, long, and messy. Three problems faced the Bush administration: the vision, the architects, and the execution of the campaign to promote democracy in that vast part of the world.

The grand vision promoted by presidential speeches and the statements made by senior officials of the administration were too simplistic. They posited that as soon as U.S. efforts crumbled a bad regime, freedom-loving people would rise up and rush toward democratization. The idea defended by the president and many of his advisors was that people are naturally inclined to freedom, and as soon as the possibility of freedom presents itself, they will embrace it.

The essence of the idea isn't wrong. By basic instincts, it is true that all human beings are naturally inclined to freedom. But freedom will come through security. You may have the freedom to fly, but you can do so only if you have wings to lift you up. Those among us who lived in the region and studied its political cultures in depth knew all too well that between the people's ability and its decision to rise is a huge valley of fear, historical experiences, and suspicion. Even with these impediments, the deep nature would eventually prevail, and revolutions would in the end explode. U.S. policy architects who were tasked by the administration with exploring these possibilities failed to understand and then to explain to the administration, Congress, and the public what it would take to get from point A (Middle Eastern realities) to point B (Middle Eastern freedom). The American military invasion of Afghanistan would not lead automatically to sound multiparty elections and liberal democracy, as had been the case with the Allied invasion of Italy and Germany, let alone France and the rest of Nazi-occupied Europe. In those European countries, the masses erupted enthusiastically at the sight of American troops, and within months reestablished normally functioning democracies. It took only a few years before thriving democratic cultures reemerged in Bonn and Rome. We saw the same reaction when the crumbling of the Soviet domination in Eastern Europe led to joy and liberation. And within one decade, regardless of snags and shortcomings, from Warsaw to Prague, normal democracies emerged. It all had to do with what was there "before" authoritarianism, what was there in the political cultures and the psychological readiness of Europeans to engage in rapid democratization.

Similar scenarios were not to be expected in liberated societies within the Arab world. The weight of centuries of Caliphate and decades of brutal dictatorships was too heavy to be lifted overnight by mere military intervention. The crafting of political change requires a deep shift in education, regardless of Western intervention. The Western military could deal with the material power of the authoritarians, but Middle Eastern societies also need the rise of a profound wave of change of intellectual, social, and ideological dimensions. The vision in Washington was aimed in the right direction but wasn't clear in its perception. The architects of this so-called democracy promotion weren't up to the challenge.

One major reason for the failure of the Bush architects in the war of ideas was their narrow experience in Islamist politics, in Arab affairs, and in the labyrinth of the power structure in the Middle East. Most of the scholars and commentators who covered the war on terror were brave, moral, and courageous men and women who had built their careers and specialization fighting Soviet influence and backing the works of dissidents against communism. But very few among them knew the Islamist threat directly or understood the lives of Muslims who were struggling on the inside of their sphere.

Even the few who had a good grip on Middle Eastern history and Islam had little understanding of the sociology of those who were candidates to rise for freedom. Most of the think tanks formed after 9/11 to push for democracy focused on the theology of Islam, or on the abstract notion of freedom. Only a handful of voices actually focused on the men and women who were to lead the movement in the region. Indeed, until about 2005 or so, the pro–Middle East democracy circles in Washington were generous in their writings and in their spending on the cause but did little to engage and support the people. No Muslim reformers were invited to the White House, while Islamist-American lobbies backed by the Wahabis, such as CAIR, were received there and in prominent Washington circles. Iranian dissidents, Syrian reformers, and Darfur activists were not on short lists to be promoted by the U.S. government as Soviet-era dissidents had been.

Simply put, in the first two years after 9/11, the civilian generals leading the campaign for democracy were running things in the media and within government without the soldiers of change—the actual people who would have to produce this new Middle Eastern democracy.

Then came the decision to invade Iraq. As I argued earlier, the opportunity to dismantle Saddam's regime was missed more than ten years earlier when he invaded Kuwait. But this time around, in thirty days or so, American and coalition forces defeated the Iraqi army and reached Baghdad. Iraq became the second country in the Middle East to fall under U.S. occupation in less than two years. Unlike the invasion of Afghanistan, the invasion of Iraq didn't attain vast international endorsement. Most of the Arab League, with the exception of Kuwait, the core of the Organization of Islamic Conference, and a number of traditional European allies, including France and Germany, opposed it. Furthermore, Syria and Iran aided a terror campaign against the U.S. presence via a variety of allies: Baathists, Salafists, al Qaeda, special groups, and so on. More important, the brotherhood against democracy mobilized Arab, Muslim, and international opinion against the "forced occupation of Iraq." Many extreme left-wing networks within the West and in America joined the anti-American campaign.

By early 2004, a crucial election year in the States, the "antiwar" movement had grown bolder and stronger. With the support of petrodollars and a very efficient al Jazeera campaign against U.S. actions, the legitimacy of the effort to bring down Saddam would be questioned. The administration's top political appointees and its supporters in Congress began initiating programs for democracy promotion in the Greater Middle East, including foreign policy, public diplomacy, foreign aid, cultural advising, and outreach to civil society. The White House's narrative focused on "freedom forward," and the constellation of U.S. agencies followed this mandate. The message at the top was taking shape and causing headaches in the regimes around the region. "First America wanted to fight what it calls terrorism," said Sheikh Yussuf al Qardawi on al Jazeera, "now she is claiming a war for democracy."[1] The Bush administration spent tens of millions of dollars on what it thought was an all-out campaign to sway the hearts and minds of Arabs and Muslims. In one year, "strategic communications" offices were set up throughout the military, defense, and national security layers, and a division dealing with "outreach" was set up within the State Department. The U.S. government was gearing up to become a moral and logistical force behind democratic change in the region.

The decision to wage a third war, after Afghanistan and Iraq, that was a "war of ideas" grew out of two necessities: One was the need to combat the massive efforts deployed by the petroregimes and their propaganda networks against U.S. military campaigns, and the second was a genuine belief among neoconservatives and classical liberals that a change is possible among peoples of the region. Bernard Lewis summarized this intellectual rush a few years later by linking Middle Eastern change to Western security.[2] Neoconservative intellectuals such as William Kristol, John R. Bolton, former speaker Newt Gingrich, and others converged with liberal figures such as Senator Joe Lieberman, politician Donna Brazile, and African-American journalist Clarence Page to denounce human rights abuses in the Greater Middle East and encourage the idea of assisting its underdogs. In Europe, a number of public figures, such as Spanish prime minister José Maria Aznar and Czech president Vaclav Havel, also pushed for a new Western policy on human rights in the region.

Two years into what was baptized a "war on terror," the preference in Washington's dominant circles and among many Europeans who had the experience of opposing totalitarian ideologies was to breach the wall of oppression south and east of the Mediterranean. To the delight of thousands of political activists and human rights workers in the region (unlike their counterparts in the West), in contrast with his father, George H. W. Bush, the second Bush at the White House seemed to have broken ties with the oil cartel, or at least the political constraints imposed by "jihadi petro imperialism" and had gone on a "crusade for democracy" in the most hostile region in the world.

As I observed the tide turning, at least in the official narrative, toward backing freedom over oppression in the Greater Middle East, I contemplated two pressing realities. On one hand the opportunity was a historic one. For the first time since the collapse of the Ottoman Empire there was a chance to get these people out of the pit into which the authoritarians had thrown them. A wounded America was awakening to the danger, and by a rare convergence of circumstances, the resources and the moral weight of the most powerful democracy in history were helping to free millions of struggling souls, from the savannahs of Africa to the mountains of Lebanon. Or so we thought, as we listened to the powerful words crafted by Bush speechwriters and the editorials of his supporters in the media. I, and many of those involved in the daunting task of freeing nations in Middle Earth, became hopeful and excited.

On the other hand, among the mobilized human rights activists, scholars, and politicians who came together to share the exhilarating energy of this opportunity, some of us were concerned about the lasting effect of this new announced policy. While we were thrilled that the region might get a chance to gain freedom, we were extremely worried that the opening would be narrow and the experience short-lived. This was the main difference in attitude between those who knew the forces at work in the Arab and Muslim world and the interests that represented them in the West, and those who were excited in America and Europe and assumed that the breach in the wall would last forever. This was where I differed with the neoconservatives and with classical liberals alike, who backed the freedom forward doctrine promulgated by George Bush. Very few workers involved in the cause of Middle Eastern freedom know how deeply rooted is the bond between the power of oil, the wealthiest bloc of economic interest in history, and the forces that obstruct democracy.

Unfortunately, in the following years my concerns prevailed over my hopes. While the intentions of the United States, from the president to key policymakers and their supporters in Congress, were clear in terms of willingness to see democracy spreading across the region, and while the hope of the underdogs in the region escalated, the march toward a democratic revolution was impeded by two dramatic developments. One was the failure of Western strategic communications, and the second was the obstructive power of the authoritarian forces in the region. Nevertheless, dissidents and forces of change leaped to a new stage in their struggle. Once they saw the light of freedom shining, they committed to pursue freedom regardless of Western commitment and jihadist obstruction.

Rise and Fall of Freedom Outreach

The United States and its allies needed to relay the message to the people in the region that the new coalition supported democracy initiatives. During the first two years of the so-called war on terror, activists and NGOs from the 1990s struggle for Middle Eastern freedom, such as the Coalition for the Defense of Human Rights in the Muslim world, led by Keith Roderick; the Mechric Committee, representing Middle Eastern minorities; Freedom House's Center for Religious Freedom; and a web of U.S.- and Western-based Christian, Jewish, Hindu, and humanist Muslim groups, in addition to Sudan's advocacy groups, such as the American Anti Slavery Group led by Charles Jacobs and the late African-American activist Samuel Cotton, all pushed hard for a new U.S. policy favoring freedom and democracy in the region. The number of congressional hearings and briefings focusing on human rights and terrorism in the region increased. As Washington fought the Taliban in Afghanistan and attempted to stabilize Iraq, the stars were aligning for an internationalization of human rights.

At some point one would have expected to see a link between U.S. interest in spreading democracy as a weapon against the radicals and attaining success on the battlefield. At least that is what the United States' foes in the region claimed was taking place. But U.S. strategic interests, as projected by the administration, coincided with the democracy needs of these societies, though the U.S. intervention did not trigger them. Many propaganda campaigns geared against American efforts in the region accused Washington of unleashing the so-called freedom forward policy as a tool to defeat its adversaries on the battlefield. While this may well have been the case in the minds of policymakers such as Vice President Dick Cheney and U.S.

strategists such as Paul Wolfowitz, Douglas Feith, and Richard Perle at the Pentagon, the freedom fight was high on the agenda of liberation movements in the region years before the election of Bush in 2000 and decades before al Qaeda's attacks on America. As in World War II and the Cold War, many nations profited from U.S. resistance against fascism and totalitarianism. American campaigns against terror forces and regimes and a U.S. push for democracy was the news of a lifetime for the oppressed. Fortunately for the victimized societies, the United States mounted a full-fledged operation, involving both public and private sectors, aimed at reaching out to them via diplomacy, democracy programs, and liberty broadcasts, and by putting pressure on their oppressors.

As mentioned earlier, in the wake of the fierce reaction and pressure by regimes as well as jihadist propaganda against the toppling of Saddam, the administration produced a new rhetoric about the conflict. On November 6, 2003, President George Bush delivered a speech on freedom forward at the twentieth anniversary of the National Endowment for Democracy. In it he said:

> This is a massive and difficult undertaking—it is worth our effort, it is worth our sacrifice, because we know the stakes. The failure of Iraqi democracy would embolden terrorists around the world, increase dangers to the American people, and extinguish the hopes of millions in the region. Iraqi democracy will succeed—and that success will send forth the news, from Damascus to Teheran—that freedom can be the future of every nation. The establishment of a free Iraq at the heart of the Middle East will be a watershed event in the global democratic revolution.[3]

Clearly the message was that the change that hit Iraq will reach Iran and Syria. The message from the speech was that a "democratic revolution" was underway. As I heard the president deliver this speech, I told leaders in the NGO network, who also listened in disbelief, that I was not sure if the White House knew how cataclysmic these words were. Obviously, I meant this in a positive sense. At MSNBC headquarters, where I served as a terrorism analyst, I tried to communicate how grave the shift in policy really was.

But mainstream media in America weren't absorbing the new

narrative with the same lenses I and those with similar backgrounds were. With a decade of analysis and observation behind me, I projected instantly that the U.S. administration was declaring war against enormous powers, way beyond Afghanistan and Iraq. Did George Bush and his aides know the titanic force they were heading against, when his speechwriters penned words such as "global democratic revolution"? Not that I was against this mission, in fact just the opposite. I had dedicated the best years of my life to seeing this mission fulfilled. But my concern was that America wasn't ready to handle it. If the United States wouldn't push for comprehensive change in the region, the jihadists would spread out and the only counterbalance to them would be the good old autocrats. However, if we did nothing, the people of the region would continue to be oppressed. If America and liberal democracies went on the offensive, not only in terms of managing two battlefields, but in rolling back the authoritarian powers and opening up spaces for democracy, they would face the entire coalition of the brotherhood against democracy—from petro-regimes, to the Muslim Brotherhood, to the Baath, to the Iranian regime, to Hezbollah, and to al Qaeda and the Salafists around the world. Add to that force the partners of these folks in the West, and particularly in America.

Was the Bush administration aware of the daunting magnitude of the task? And the more troubling question: Was the entire bureaucracy under the Bush presidency on board? In fact, as I will argue throughout the book, entire layers of the U.S. bureaucracies either opposed the project or in some cases were penetrated by the brotherhood against democracy. The distance between the presidential speeches and the bureaucrats and diplomats who were supposed to carry out the policies was vast.

Bush later said, in the same speech, that "the advance of freedom is the calling of our time; it is the calling of our country. From the Fourteen Points to the Four Freedoms, to the speech at Westminster, America has put our power at the service of principle. We believe that liberty is the design of nature; we believe that liberty is the direction of history. We believe that human fulfillment and excellence come in the responsible exercise of liberty. And we believe that freedom—the freedom we prize—is not for us alone, it is the right and the capacity of all mankind." Few would oppose his words, but realists would think this is too abstract and almost poetry.

He added the following: "Our nation is strong; we're strong of heart. And we're not alone. Freedom is finding allies in every country; freedom finds allies in every culture. And as we meet the terror and violence of the world, we can be certain the author of freedom is not indifferent to the fate of freedom." It is precisely the mention of "allies in every culture" that would trigger the wrath of the region's authoritarian elites. While Bush wanted to be seen as another Reagan for the Muslim world, he was seen awkwardly as a "Lenin" by the trembling regimes and dictators.

Later in November 2003, Bush delivered a speech in Whitehall, Great Britain, saying, "Women of Afghanistan, imprisoned in their homes and beaten in the streets and executed in public spectacles, did not reproach us for routing the Taliban. Inhabitants of Iraq's Baathist hell, with his lavish palaces and his torture chambers, with his massive statues and its mass graves, do not miss their fugitive dictator; they rejoiced at his fall."[4]

Where were the Western feminists applauding this speech? There were none to be found. Many, but not all, were busy opposing the "invasion of foreign lands." American and European radical feminists had little to say about the suffering of their sisters in the struggle, brutalized and murdered in the high mountains of Afghanistan or the marshes of southern Iraq, let alone those in Iran.

During the late 1990s, I organized several events on my south Florida campus to address the persecution of Afghan women under the Taliban. Many female students attended, and I saw tears in their eyes after we showed the scant footage we had concerning the stoning, execution, and torture of women by the jihadi militia. Female faculty members were also upset, yet little informed about these acts taking place half a world away. Their most common question was: What is our government doing about it? Well, at the time, not much, as the Organization of the Islamic Conference (OIC) would raise hell if liberal democracies dared speak about Muslim women's issues. However, during these events on campus, well before 9/11, I noted that the more mature female professors were struggling between the feminist "party line" encouraged by their leaders nationwide and what they were seeing. One day we had a feminist speaker from an Ivy League institution. An expert on Afghanistan, she argued, to the surprise of the audience, that the Taliban had "protected" women by stopping rape on the street, prevalent under the regimes of the warlords. A young faculty member shouted back: "Yes, the Taliban organized a holocaust for women; they raped their rights and essence. They wiped them out from the streets and jailed them in houses."

That exchange showed me that the younger generation of American women was moved by the horrors inflicted on their "sisters" under the jihadi curtain. But at the time, the leadership narrative was missing. The 1990s were too selfish. By 2003, I was expecting fiery feminist leaders in America to blast the turbaned fundamentalist men who slaughtered women's souls in Middle Earth. Why must it be a conservative president who would elevate the issue to the international stage and not a progressive leader?

In that same November speech at Whitehall, Bush added: "The third pillar of security is our commitment to the global expansion of democracy and the hope and progress it brings as the alternative to instability and hatred and terror. We cannot rely exclusively on military power to assure our long-term security. Lasting peace is gained as justice and democracy advance. And by advancing freedom in the Greater Middle East, we help end a cycle of dictatorship and radicalism that brings millions of people to misery and brings danger to our own people."

Bush's speechwriters were crafting miraculous words, by the standards of those who had been suffering from oppression and violence in the region. The talk of freedom reverberated throughout the administration as policy officials at the Pentagon, National Security Council, and State Department echoed the White House on democracy commitment in the Arab and Muslim world. Soon enough, "democracy promotion" agencies within government, which hadn't done much in the past in taking on the causes of the oppressed in the region, hurried to claim bureaucratic leadership on these matters, and, of course, claim the immense budgets that had been earmarked for the effort. The National Endowment for Democracy, the various projects at the State Department, and a constellation of subagencies and other contractors rushed to get a slice of the pie.

Oddly, the traditional agencies responsible for new U.S. policy on freedom promotion in the region were the ones that delivered the least, and potentially blocked the "revolution" Bush spoke about. The presidential freedom campaign was soon accompanied by a chorus of parallel speeches by congressional leaders, articles by notable journalists, and statements by well-known commentators. The narrative about liberation and democracy was so compelling at the time that it was rarely criticized by the political foes of the administration, though it was often railed against by the bureaucrats within. On the top levels, the leaders of the executive branch pushed for the project, while most public servants in the middle layers worked on derailing it.

Academics

The first group that should have acclaimed the new U.S. policy of extending a freedom forward program to the region's underdogs, one would think, was academics and scholars. Historians, social scientists, philosophers, and political scientists based in liberal democracies have been known to be the frontline advocates for liberty in the world. From the nineteenth century on, it was professors and scholars who pressed their governments to stand by oppressed nations around the world. After World War II, Western and particularly American academia was dedicated to awakening its flock regarding the injustices committed in many regions around the world. It was the Ph.D. elites who spoke on the issues of dictatorships in Latin America, South Africa's majority's cause, and the Balkans' bloodshed, and who raised the bar for respect for human rights worldwide. One would think that when the political leaders of the most powerful democracy on earth rose to help the weak and disenfranchised in the Middle East—such as the Kurds, black Sudanese, Lebanese, Syrian reformers, Iraqi democrats, Copts, Berbers, women, students, gays, writers, seculars, and humanists—academics at Harvard, Georgetown, Berkeley, and Yale would rise in turn to support the move and ask for more, and faster. Yet reality was different.

The academic elite, especially a majority of the Middle Eastern studies experts of the Ivy League establishment, blasted the Bush administration for making that choice. In fact, the negative reaction by the Middle Eastern studies community to the democracy promotion program didn't come as a surprise to me. The members of that group, well funded by Wahabi and other authoritarian money, were not expected to turn against their donors and lose their privileges. As I mentioned earlier, the regimes and Islamist networks had penetrated American academia to the core with their petrodollars. The design was precisely to stop any U.S. administration, Democratic or Republican, from undertaking any sort of freedom movement support policy in the region. The al Qaeda attacks on 9/11 were the toughest challenge Middle Eastern studies barons had had to face.

The American public had its eyes open, the administration and Congress were determined to do something, and the idea that Middle Eastern democracy was the real answer struck a chord with policymakers. To the authoritarians and jihadists, this was a nightmare. Their academic "militia" in the West was their first line of defense against a massive U.S. push for democratization, which explains quite clearly why prominent scholars (who were supposed to stand by liberty and the underdogs) were defending the regimes and the Islamists against the interests of the masses in the Arab and Muslim world. In fact, the Middle Eastern studies elite fought for its funding and privileges. For if the U.S. government succeeded in unleashing dissidents and human rights advocates in the region, the first people in the West to be embarrassed would have been the Western-based experts in Middle Eastern affairs. The question would be asked, Why hadn't they informed the public via classrooms and writings that hundreds of millions of people were suffering from oppressive regimes and barbaric terrorists in the Arab world? Why did they frame jihadism as if it were yoga and claim women were happy with their status under fundamentalist systems of government?

In fact, the core of Middle Eastern studies in the West and in the United States has misled its students, the public, and the government by teaching, publishing, and testifying while being supported by petrodollars. A revolution in foreign policy would expose this conflict of interest and would create an intellectual backlash in the educational sphere. Inevitably, the success of democratic revolutions in the Middle East would strip Middle Eastern studies in America of every vestige of credibility. Over time, the link between the oil-producing regimes and the intelligentsia on campuses and beyond would be exposed and dealt with. Hence, the "funded" had to fight the revolution to save the skin of the "funders," just to maintain the status quo. Historians may find in this unnatural equation one of the most unethical situations in world history: Those who were trusted with truth and science were the ones who were slaughtering both.[5]

Middle Eastern studies scholars had a tremendous influence over their colleagues in the more senior departments of political science, international relations and other social sciences, history, and literature. The "experts" on the region were sought for advice on U.S. policy inside their higher-education institutions. I was often asked, as a professor of Middle Eastern studies, what I thought of the government's position on the region's crises. My opinion obviously was in the minority nationwide, as the overwhelming majority in my field toed the apologist line.

A big window opened suddenly after 9/11, as scholars in mainstream social sciences rushed to obtain the expert opinion of their Middle Eastern studies colleagues on al Qaeda, the Taliban, and the meaning of jihadist doctrine. The Arabist-jihadophile lobby in our educational system had to fight an uphill battle for at least two years. It was hard for the apologists in academia to swim against the immense stream of American anger against the terrorists. It was not easy to blame the United States for Bin Laden's actions and threats, although some radical professors went to the extreme position of wishing worse on Americans after the massacres. The incredible examples of professors Nicholas de Genova, who in 2003 wished a "million Mogadishus on Americans" and Ward Churchill, who in 2001 compared the "victims in the twin towers to Nazis," are among the most publicized, but are not the only ones.[6] The apologists seized the opportunity of the Iraq War, waged "unilaterally" by the United States, to score significant victories for its old theses. The Marxist left in general, and the so-called antiwar far left (Trotskyite, Maoist, and anarchist, as well as their mutations) in particular were against any war based on patriotism or security claims. The only military clashes they usually endorsed were those waged in defense or in expansion of "Marxist revolutions" or against "capitalist" powers, when possible. A smartly crafted coalition was established on campuses between the jihadophiles, the apologists for oil powers, and the extreme left. This bloc, the core of the antiwar movement, argued that U.S. intervention in Iraq was illegal, illegitimate, and against the will of Iraqis, Arabs, and the peoples of the Muslim world. With al Jazeera and dozens of websites amplifying the arguments in Arabic, the opposition to the war declared that the Bush administration was waging a "neocolonial war" for oil and power.

As I stated earlier, the administration had no real plans for alliances with the dissidents, democrats, and civil forces in the region or in Iraq, at least not until the White House decided to move seriously on the issue after 2004. So, while the U.S. government had no allies in the war of ideas to oppose the antiwar camp, consisting of Islamists, petro-regimes, and the extreme left, it appeared to sensible liberals across academia, and later on throughout the country and within the West, that indeed there was no basis for the intervention in Iraq. The U.S. administration was losing the communications war because of a lack of either outside support or willingness to strike back at the jihadists and the authoritarians.

During the first three years of the post-9/11 ideological confrontation, which I call the "third war of ideas,"[7] I witnessed the rise of the U.S. doctrine on freedom forward, which was garnering the support of millions of underdogs in the region, but had no opportunity to connect with them. At the same time I watched the other camp counterattacking and eventually winning the battle. In short, the hard-core apologist scholars in Middle Eastern studies, in alliance with the antiwar far left, were able to mobilize the wider liberal majority of professors in social science against the aims of the United States. The administration lost the battle in academia very quickly, yet it continued to fight it in other realms, late in the process and with an unhelpful bureaucracy.

Western Media

While U.S. bureaucracies stalled in implementing the administration's policy to push for a democratic revolution, and as most of academia turned against the liberty program, the private sector seemed to better understand what the White House was advocating, sometimes even more than the White House or American government. It was basically the literature published in neoconservative media such as the *Washington Times, Wall Street Journal, Weekly Standard, National Review*, and *Human Events*, as well as the rising TV channel Fox News, which pushed the winds of change for the region. It was about winning a war of ideas at home, in liberal democracies, before even waging it overseas, as British prime minister Tony Blair often argued.[8]

As an analyst of the war on terror with NBC and then Fox, I saw the battle of ideas clearly being waged on the American airwaves and in print as our troops were fighting the Taliban in Afghanistan and the jihadists in Iraq. At first, I assumed that most media, with the exception of jihadophile websites and a few radical intellectuals, would be supportive of at least two goals of the war: defeating the jihadists wherever they were and liberating oppressed peoples around the region. This was the minimum one could expect from the media, and it mirrored the broad goals of World War II, pushing back against the fascists, freeing oppressed nations, and saving communities from genocide.

But I learned that there was no consensus in the West among its intellectual elites and the media over these basic goals. Spanish prime minister José Maria Aznar told me the battle of ideas within liberal democracies was just a precursor, and would determine who would win the war of ideas internationally. Aznar, a leading figure behind the democracy promotion movement worldwide, along with other European leaders who had experienced oppression during Soviet times, such as Czech president Vaclav Havel, told me that left-leaning media were busier unseating right-of-center governments than extending support to the liberals in the Middle East. The Spanish leader was accurate in his description of the real battle of ideas. In a sense, it was a domestic confrontation in the West between those who wanted to help the oppressed in the Arab world and those who did not.

Before 9/11, the overwhelming majority of the international media, which included Western Europe, North America, and Australia, rarely shed light on persecution under either Islamists regimes or Arab nationalist governments. I thought that after the terrorist jihadists made their intentions known, as of 2001 and beyond, the mainstream media would mobilize for the confrontation against the plague that had struck the international community. At a minimum I assumed the liberal media would defend the defenseless in the region. Surely such a professional body of trained journalists, producers, and anchors would accurately report human rights violations. Sadly, the once most valued arm of liberal democracies, their free press and media, failed in its most fundamental task: telling the truth. It failed to stand by the oppressed, ignoring the tragedies that befell entire societies. Not reporting, or worse, poor reporting, becomes deceit. However, the failure is not systemic. A majority of decent people, bottom-up—workers, technicians, writers, anchors, and producers of nonpolitical and of international and national news—are to be praised for their efforts.

From the beginning, the mainstream media stunningly ignored the jihadi threat's doctrine and the plight of the oppressed in the vast Middle East. Most of the reporting was about the mistakes, mishaps, and troubles of the U.S. and coalition forces advancing in Afghanistan and Iraq. While sixty years later, media and Hollywood are still making movies about the Nazis, the same body of the so-called liberal press has ignored the present-day aggressors, and the struggles of the oppressed. Prominent publications such as the *New York Times, Washington Post, Newsweek,* the *Los Angeles Times,* the *Boston Herald*, and many other dailies and weeklies across America, as well as public media such as PBS and NPR, demonstrate a fierce opposition to the U.S. push for democracy in the Greater Middle East. While scrutinizing the potential missteps of the U.S. government, the giant body of mainstream media ignored the mass abuse of human rights of millions of people around the world. Not only American, but also European, Canadian, and Australian mainstream press were serving as shields for the regimes in the region by directing their fire on their own governments. In this war of ideas, the oil powers and authoritarian forces were able to use Western media against a democracy's potential liberating power to free the underdogs of the Middle East.

It is ironic that the Bush administration was calling for a democratic revolution in the Middle East, making a public appeal perhaps once every three months, while NPR anchors were blasting that policy 24/7 for years, as the so-called war on terror was evolving. Never in history has a government struggling to grant freedom to others around the world been so subverted by its own publicly funded media as was the Bush administration by NPR and PBS.

As I listened to public broadcast shows and compared them with the supposed policy of the government, I realized that the White House and its communications advisors as well as those offices in Congress that were tasked with overseeing public media were either oblivious to or didn't comprehend what was happening. Their citizens were indoctrinated, or at the very least woefully misinformed, as the leaders were calling for support in efforts to confront the enemy. You could enjoy NPR programs discussing "yellow chicken in Alabama" for one full hour but not have an author analyzing the jihadi threat looming on the horizon; or you'd have PBS airing apologist literature about Baathist and Khomeinist dictators while excluding writers who could discuss prodemocracy revolts in the Middle East. The American public and other democratic societies were systematically denied the right to learn about persecution and struggles inside the Arab and Muslim world.

It should come as no surprise, then, if over one decade the Western public was made to believe that all people in the region had the same feelings and aspirations, that all they had on their minds was hate for America and the West, and that they would not rest until Palestine had replaced the "usurper" state of Israel. Mainstream media acted, aired, and printed its stories as if the peoples of the region were satisfied with their fate and their only "problem" was the actions of the United States. In a sense, the Western media were expressing the concerns and interests of the oppressive regimes and projecting them falsely as the public's sentiments.

Luckily, Americans had an opportunity to hear another voice coming from an alternative world of media: radio talk shows and bloggers. Dozens of broadcast journalists took to the airwaves on their own, using private funds and private radio studios, using talk shows to shed a different light on the way Middle Eastern issues were framed by the mainstream media. Predominantly conservative, scores of talking heads raised the issue of terrorism, the war of ideas, and the anti-jihadist opposition in the region.

During the 1990s, I was interviewed by just a handful of shows in the United States. After 9/11, however, I was requested by dozens of talk shows around the nation and internationally. Unlike NPR's stiff rejection of the issue of democratization in the Middle East, the "free talk shows" had no limits on shedding light on the jihadi threat and oppression in the region. It was clear that, in contrast to public broadcasts, private talk shows—regardless of their style—were actually providing a free service in democracy advancement to the public. The public was served "yellow chicken" by NPR while dozens of small but determined radio stations were educating that same public about the deep conflicts in the Arab and Muslim world. At some point I thought of comparing public broadcasting to the Soviet propaganda networks that are constantly challenged by underground broadcasts of dissidents. The incredible difference was that the U.S. government funds the propaganda arm that was killing its own message, while private citizens were helping their own government to educate the public. Surely, this was a surreal tableau of American chaos.

The Blogosphere

Beyond the talk shows was another layer of Middle Eastern democracy supporters who challenged mainstream media about oppression in the Middle East: the army of bloggers. With the expansion of the internet in the 1990s, blogs and news sites mushroomed throughout cyberspace. The uncontrolled web gave an unexpected opportunity to a new electronic media. Interestingly, in the early years of the internet, in the mid-1990s, the jihadists were quick to take advantage, first of mass email capacity, and then of the ability to create web pages and sites. The counterjihadists, particularly the opposition inside the region, had almost no access to the web. A few sites belonging to Western-based dissidents shyly emerged by the end of the decade, but the cyber balance of power remained with the jihadists and the apologist forces. The events of 9/11 changed everything. Scores of web pages and blogs were spawned with the counterjihadists and pro–human rights writers taking the lead.

The Islamist and apologist blogs multiplied as well, but the sheer rise of alternative blogs posting on the persecution and reforms shifted the cyber ground. Online it's not the number of outlets that is important, but the number of ideas. If one dissident blog emerges, even while attacked by ten apologist pages, the dissident wins, because while there is one blog versus ten, there are in fact only two ideas. As in real life, all the dissidents need is to emerge; they will worry later about how many follow. First the new idea must appear, and history will take care of its public relations over time. And that is what happened in the prodemocracy blogosphere as of the early twenty-first century. It is a phenomenon not yet understood by most researchers.

The dissidents and reformers from the Middle East posted significant material online regarding the horrors perpetrated by jihadists and authoritarian regimes in the region against their own people. This material was picked up by Western bloggers unsatisfied by the way their mainstream media were handling the informing and education of the public. What goes around comes around. Since the big boys of the press and audiovisual media were cozying up to the oil powers, like lava, the flow of information coming from the region had to find its way out a different path to the international community.

Within a few years after 9/11 the blogosphere became the main source of information about human rights abuses in the region, forcing the mainstream media to pick up stories as they appeared on the web. Instead of leading, the traditional press was lagging behind. The blogosphere, in all languages, became the pioneering area where dissidents and freedom activists met and mobilized. It was there where the Sudan genocide first appeared, with pictures and reports. There, too, emerged the protests of Lebanon leading to the Cedars Revolution. Bloggers debunked jihadi propagandists and exposed regimes' denials of revolts.

As with similar social movements, the blogosphere revolution began sporadically, but soon enough mutated into a dense, organized, and effective force bypassing the mainstream media and forging ahead in democracy promotion. The June 2009 demonstrations in Tehran and other Iranian cities, protesting stolen elections, were brought to the world thanks to the most advanced and simplest of all cyber tools, the famous Twitter.

The blogger resistance uses a variety of systems to express itself, from the oldest forms to the most advanced; from interactive websites and classical blogs, to sites with massive reach like YouTube and Facebook. Obviously, with the unlimited and uncharted terrain in cyberspace come problems. One disadvantage is the chaos that can explode as dissidents post material, not always relevant or serious. Information cannot always be verified. Another disadvantage is the ease with which the regimes and the apologists can discredit dissidents and democracy seekers.

The blogosphere is the space where the final battle in the war of ideas will be fought and decided. Regimes in the region and their allies in the West understand this and are bracing for the major confrontation over "cyber Middle Earth."

Democracy Programs

Logically, when a government wants to pursue a policy it uses the tools at its disposal, particularly institutions that are already funded and operating. The Bush administration instructed its bureaucracies to move forward with democracy promotion in the Greater Middle East. With the resources it had, the United States government could have generated momentum around the globe and helped millions in their struggle for freedom.

In early 2002, I had urged my contacts in the U.S. Congress to work with the president on unleashing a mass campaign of outreach to segments in Middle Eastern societies already engaged in efforts and struggles. I told legislators that inroads already existed; all we had to do was to start a partnership with the democracy workers. In several interviews during the early years of the confrontation I advocated an alliance with those who had made the choice for freedom and democracy, before we tried to sway the hearts and minds of all others. Let's reach out to those freedom fighters who have been in the resistance for decades, I told legislators and NGO leaders in multiple briefings. My idea was to strategically connect with several beachheads in Lebanon, Algeria, Syria, Iran, Sudan, Iraq, Egypt, the Gulf, and wherever possible, in addition to mobilizing the dissidents based in the Diaspora. I advocated the creation of several regional centers for democracy promotion, which would direct aid and assist local NGOs, dissidents, and human rights groups. U.S. task forces for freedom were the concept, and linking with civil societies' activists was the strategy. In short, we needed to learn from the Eastern European experience and adapt it to the Middle Eastern reality. This was how democracy programs were supposed to materialize.

In fact, had the Bush administration established a real war room or a hub with leaders aware of the challenges, a strategic process could have made a tremendous difference. The mobilization of existing democracy programs unfortunately failed, and the informational and ideological battle in the first years of the confrontation floundered. Yet the web of democracy-promoting government funded institutions was enormous. From the various State Department agencies promoting democracy and human rights, to the offices in the Pentagon and other agencies, to the U.S.-funded organizations such as the National Endowment on Democracy, the National Democratic Institute for International Affairs (NDI) and the International Republican Institute (IRI), we're talking about mammoth entities with hundreds of millions of dollars in budgets to promote democracy worldwide. Add to those groups the gigantic nongovernmental institutions receiving huge amounts of funding from public sources or private donations, such as the U.S. Institute of Peace, the Guggenheim Foundation, and the Carnegie Endowment.

The institutional and financial power under U.S. auspices to push for engagement with civil societies in the Greater Middle East is overwhelming. There is a huge constellation of grants provided by the administration or authorized by Congress to universities, NGOs, associations, public libraries, and research entities that are also supposed to be part of the democracy-promoting program. I would even add the immense resources available under USAID and its multiple outreach programs, since humanitarian assistance is yet another tool for promoting democratic values. Some would argue that it may well be *the* single greatest means to achieve interaction with the weak and needy and to empower them culturally and intellectually. In addition, there are Europe's counterparts in human rights promotion, both in national governments and in the European Union and Parliament. One would have to conclude that in a post-Soviet world, the West had ample means to reach out to and connect with the underdogs and empower them to perform the change.

Why didn't that change happen, or at least some engagement occur? A rational argument that I advanced in my previous books was that the political will to use Western resources to help oppressed peoples in the region was lacking in the 1990s. There was no clear vision that democratization is the strategic response to the rise of jihadism and the violence it produces. After 9/11 it was demonstrated, by presidential speeches, administration and congressional narrative, and the launching of so-called programs to promote democracy in the Greater Middle East, that this was the strategy, so why didn't things move in that direction? From all the findings that we have, the efforts to promote democracy by the U.S. government—aside from organizing national elections in occupied Afghanistan and Iraq—didn't produce a mass democracy movement in the region. Or at least citizens in the West didn't see it, hear it, or connect with it. I have argued many times in my briefings to executive and legislative branches in America and Europe that the West failed. But efforts to liberate the Greater Middle East didn't fail by themselves; they were destined to fail from the inside of Western institutions.

One of the main networks that caused this shortcoming, by ignorance or by political intention, was the organization, funded by taxpayers that were supposed to promote democracy in the Arab and Muslim world. Indeed, this is a dangerous but crucial finding. The ensemble of agencies and institutions—government-linked or not, national or international, created before or after 9/11—were compromised in this particular mission. The so-called democracy programs within the United States and Europe failed decision-makers and the public by refusing to engage the real dissidents, failing to support the right NGOs, and cozying up to the regimes. This statement may be too broad, as hundreds of workers and officials in these agencies and programs have been very efficient in trying to promote democracy and human rights, but the bottom line is that the decision-making elite across the board blocked the development of an energetic strategy. They opposed the concept of ideological confrontation with the jihadists and the totalitarians and preferred to act within the status quo, which meant to do nothing about mobilizing—to just spend the budgets and wait.

And of course, behind the decision-makers you had the advisors and the experts, who exercised tremendous influence. So, while the president, senior administration officials, and congressional leaders (often from both parties) decided to support the democratic forces, the core expert group and the bureaucrats it influences blocked the policy, or weakened and eventually killed it. Many of my colleagues in academia and the NGO world who were involved in consulting on democracy with governments, including the dissident and reformer organizations that tried to obtain necessary support to mobilize within their own societies, told me that their experience with the bureaucracy in charge of democracy promotion was not successful.

Reformers of the Arabian Peninsula, Egypt, Libya, Saudi Arabia, the Cedars Revolution of Lebanon, the dissidents of Syria, civil groups in Iraq, and the Iranian democracy groups were all failed by the United States, not on principles but by the agencies and entities tasked to back them up and fuel democracy. According to Manda Zand Ervin, leader of the Alliance of Iranian Women, the U.S. Congress voted millions of dollars in aid to support female democracy activism, but the budgets were spent by universities to "study women's issues in Iran." Tom Harb, the chief executive of a Lebanese NGO, the World Council of the Cedars Revolution, told me that the "democracy chiefs at the State Department promised me several times that they will use the funds allocated to Lebanon's democracy to back up civil society activists struggling against Hezbollah, but they never kept their promises, dodging our NGOs for three years." A seasoned Syrian, Nouhad Ghadri, a publisher and writer exiled to Beirut, told me he was heard "many times by officials at State, USAID, and the Pentagon, and at U.S.-funded agencies and organizations all promoting democracy. They had no plans and they had no strategy to partner with Syrian or any other Arab civil resistance movement."

I wondered where all the democracy dollars went. If you read reports by the grantees and by bureaucrats who dispense them, you'd think U.S. and Western efforts were making miracles. Yet no strategic achievements were actually registered. The question is not raised in terms of corruption and who profited. The inquiry is about the policies implemented. We have spent hundreds of millions of dollars, if not billions in the final count, promoting democracy, but we don't have results. Ironically, the research, mostly funded by these grants, came up with an astonishing conclusion: The United States is not successful in promoting democracy and shouldn't be doing so!

The experts who misled the government and the bureaucrats who didn't deliver what policymakers and a majority of citizens wanted were in fact the core group that derailed America's will to provoke change in the Greater Middle East.

During this same time period, a number of privately funded organizations rose in the United States and the West to advocate direct contact with the dissident population in the Arab and Muslim world and engage in direct democracy activism. Among these groups are the Foundation for Defense of Democracies in Washington and its sister organization out of Brussels, the European Foundation for Democracy. Older private-sector institutions that were active in the war of ideas during the Soviet era also shifted interest to democracy support. Among these entities were Freedom House, the Hudson Institute, the American Enterprise Institute, and the Heritage Foundation. Most of these NGOs are on the conservative side of the spectrum in American politics, while most of the progressive entities that should have taken the lead on human rights worldwide displayed a critical and hesitant attitude toward "freeing civil societies" in the region.

As of 2002 a flurry of smaller private-sector initiatives were mushrooming around America and even across Europe, aiming to raise the profile of the democratic battle in the region. While the gigantic institutions of the U.S. government, endowed with dizzying amounts of money, were sabotaging the campaign for real democratization, a small contingent of volunteer groups were awkwardly reaching out to the dissidents and reformers in the region. The official democracy programs failed their government and the democracy forces in the region, while a mini-industry of freedom activism took the lead to try to save the day.

Strategic Communications

At the same time that it activated its democracy-promotion organizations, the Bush administration scrambled to design what was known as "strategic communications," a more moderate wording of its mission, politically stated, a "war of ideas." The central goal of these communications was to gain support among the local populations in the Middle East for countering extremism and choosing democracy. The concept of trying to win hearts and minds of Arabs and Muslims found its way to the halls of government immediately after the September 11, 2001, attacks, as Osama Bin Laden revealed his radical ideology through videos in which he claimed he was inspired by Islam. Following al Qaeda's declarations against the United States and *kuffars* in general, al Jazeera's panels and commentators revealed an anti-American sentiment never seen before by the Western public. The incitements grew more frequent after the invasion of Iraq, and acts of violence including kidnappings, slaughter, and attacks on civilians signaled a growing hatred of America and its Western partners.

However, the issue in the so-called war on terror isn't to sway the hearts and minds of Arabs and Muslims from anti-Americanism to pro-Americanism. Rather, it is about informing the West that jihadism is, and must be treated as, an ideology, not a religion. The war of ideas was poised to reach out to democracy activists in the region and empower them so that they could educate their own people about the values of pluralism and human rights.

The strategy that I advocated was to find allies and empower them to reform within their societies, regardless of their immediate attitude toward the United States, while the strategy in the administration was to just find ways to assuage anger and "convince" the public in the region that the United States means no harm. During the years following 9/11 and particularly since 2004, I strongly argued in my briefings to Congress and meetings with U.S. officials that Washington must not corner itself in a defensive posture as many advisors advocated. We must be on the offensive on the democracy issue, because the oppressed in the region were already struggling, with hundreds of thousands of civilians having been slaughtered in Algeria, jailed in Lebanon and Syria, tortured in Iran, and massacred in Sudan.

In interviews with media outlets, including al Jazeera, in 2004 and 2005, I told my interviewers that "there are one million political prisoners in Arab and Middle Eastern prisons from the Atlantic Ocean to the Indian Ocean, as many as the entire population of Gaza. Are we in need of a public relations campaign to convince the oppressed that we're extending our arm to help them? Of course they understand; of course they are waiting to be helped. They have been waiting for too long." I never got a clear counterargument to this point on al Jazeera, because there wasn't one. Understandably, the network's invitations to me grew less frequent. What was not comprehensible, though, was the lethargy of those leading the war of ideas within the U.S. government and in Europe. While I attended numerous meetings with clever and strategic minds at the White House, such as Elliott Abrams, the deputy national security advisor, and Juan Zarate, deputy assistant to the president and deputy national security advisor for combating terrorism, who were in full agreement with these ideas, the majority of the bureaucracy was moving in a different direction—away from the dissidents and native democracy forces.

In my meetings with the National Security Council between 2005 and 2007, I was surprised that the top echelon of the administration wasn't yet clear on their strategy. Among the participants in these meetings, both resident and invited experts, there were a number of advisors who insisted that the U.S. government must engage in talks with the Islamists and authoritarian regimes as a way to sway hearts and minds! Other experts insisted that the president must not meddle in democracy promotion and that the United States must instead talk about humanitarian assistance.

In one of these meetings, an academic summarized the crisis naïvely: "All we need to do is to send assistance to the population as we did successfully after the tsunami. That will change the image of America in the Muslim world." I was stunned by this naïveté. This expert was arguing that with foreign aid only—or principally—Washington could win the war of ideas. Apparently, he hadn't studied the immediate aftermath of the U.S. humanitarian operations in Indonesia and how the jihadi propaganda machine, only a few days after, had turned the story upside down. As U.S. helicopters were rescuing stranded civilians, the Salafist clerics argued that "they caused the tsunami to come with their aid and exert influence over Muslims." The Salafist clerics used all the airtime and cyberspace available to get out their message.

I counterargued at that meeting in the White House that it is not just action that counts but how you present your ideas, and how your allies interpret them. Ironically, most experts who were pressing the Bush administration not to engage with the democrats of the region quickly joined the Obama administration in 2009 and advised the president to engage the Islamist regimes. My instincts were correct: The Bush administration was filled with experts who derailed its policies.

At meetings organized by USAID in 2004 to study Middle Eastern outreach, where officials invited representatives from Muslim-American, Arab-American, and Middle Eastern American NGOs and intellectuals to help shape strategies to enhance the U.S. image in the Arab and Muslim world, I was surprised to see participants who had appeared on al Jazeera blasting U.S. policies. I had no idea how the person in charge of that "strategic communications" bureau at MEPI's Middle Eastern division was operating or what he was thinking. To succeed in backing a democracy campaign you have to gather people who believe in it and want it to move forward and succeed. While many of the guests were representatives of democratic struggles in the Middle East, many others were either plants for Arab regimes or apologists for the oil interests. It was clear that there was going to be a fight to stop change from going forward. While U.S. and allied soldiers were sacrificing their lives on the ground in the Middle East and while the indigenous population was suffering and hoping help was on its way, another war was taking place across U.S. bureaucracies—a fierce resistance against the American push for Middle Eastern democracy. I saw the evidence of that obstruction in almost every meeting and seminar I attended inside the Beltway, and beyond.

The USAID battlefront was especially lethal, since it would decide how hundreds of millions of dollars were to be spent on recipients around the region. Properly targeted, this stream of aid would have filled the veins of popular resistance with energy and enabled civil society to take the struggle upon its own shoulders. But the "other camp" was infiltrating the machinery of the American AID. There were bureaucrats who were unwilling to act consistently with regard to the vision of top policymakers, experts who derailed the analysis, and local political activists who blocked the process from reaching the right entities in the region. When assistance was finally extended, in many cases the recipients were NGOs formed by apologists or penetrated by the Islamists (Salafists or Khomeinists). There was no way America's financial aid would secure a change in attitudes. That path was closed.

The issue wasn't, as many have thought for years, that the U.S. administration didn't understand the importance of "strategic communications" with the Arab and Muslim world. Rather, my own observation and experience, across the layers of bureaucracies and decision-making process, show that the tools for outreach were hijacked, or at least paralyzed, by apology politics.

One central organ for outreach was the Office of Strategic Communications and Planning at the State Department, which, according to its description, "provides short- and long-range strategic planning to support the Secretary's effort to bring foreign policy issues to the American people. The office develops strategies to advance the Administration's priority policy issues, shape effective messages explaining U.S. policies in new and ongoing issues and enhance communication with the American people. It coordinates with bureaus throughout the Department, the White House, and other agencies dealing with foreign affairs, and it works with State Department public diplomacy offices to coordinate strategic planning for both domestic and international audiences." This office falls under a senior position known as the undersecretary for public diplomacy and public affairs, which, according to its description, "leads America's public diplomacy outreach, which includes communications with international audiences, cultural programming, academic grants, educational exchanges, international visitor programs, and U.S. Government efforts to confront ideological support for terrorism. The Under Secretary oversees the bureaus of Educational and Cultural Affairs, Public Affairs and International Information Programs, and participates in foreign policy development."[9] In short, this is the equivalent of a "czar of the war of ideas," the person who is in charge of the war room battling the ideologies and political strategies of jihadist forces around the world. One would assume that such a position and its teams would be able to go up against the web of entities involved in counterdemocracy movements in the region. Instead, this strategic communications war room was effectively nothing more than an office for public relations.

The issue isn't with the personal qualifications of the people in charge, who are always selected from a pool of top achievers in professional life, but rather with the policies chosen and the advice offered by experts. For example, after the Iraq invasion, the top person in U.S. strategic communications, Charlotte Beers, a Madison Avenue executive, produced and broadcast throughout the Middle East a series of video clips called "Muslim Life in America."[10] I have repeatedly excoriated this strategy, questioning the link between these DVDs and the confrontation with the jihadists, or better yet, the rationale for producing them when the president was calling for democratization in the region. Muslims in the United States lived well. The issue was not about them, however, but about those who were oppressed in Arab and Muslim majority countries.

Then came what I considered the major blunder in American strategic outreach since 9/11. It occurred within the team that worked for Undersecretary Karen Hughes, who was in charge of these activities from 2005 to 2007. Hughes, a close friend of President Bush, was politically astute but unfortunately wasn't successful in selecting the right team of advisors. Under her auspices, financing for public diplomacy increased to $845 million in 2008, from $616 million in 2004. Incredible amounts of money were spent on producing public relations material and on traveling to countries in the region in order to meet with officials and social groups. Her major achievement was "to reverse decline in the number of visas given to foreigners to study in the U.S."[11]

As I observed the battle between the jihadi propaganda machine and sporadic U.S. public relations efforts, I realized American bureaucracy wasn't even engaged in the right battle. As reports about failures in confronting the doctrinal advances of the jihadists were becoming alarming, my colleagues and I were stunned to learn that advice to Hughes and the State Department in general was being provided by Georgetown professor John Esposito and his associates, leading academics who actually opposed the administration's strategic goals in the region. Professor Esposito, very much respected by his colleagues in Middle Eastern studies, was leading the Saudi-funded center on Muslim-Christian Understanding and was a strong proponent of engagement with the Wahabis and other regimes in the region. Hughes was obviously not getting the necessary advice to engage with democrats in the region, but instead was being advised to reach out to their authoritarian oppressors. Two years later Hughes quit in the midst of an unprecedented rise of jihadi propaganda worldwide.

Even as the civilian branches of the strategic communications campaign were compromised by their own advisors, one would think that the defense institutions would be spared from failed expertise, but in fact they were not. Stunningly, while the military authorities sought help from experts to reach out to civil societies on the battlefield and worldwide, the help they received was the actual problem. Slowly but gradually most positions designed to engage in and win the war of ideas, or more precisely the ideological battle, came under the influence of apologists, and in some cases Islamists. Even as the leadership rank and file desperately needed to see successes in reaching out to moderates and antiterrorist elements in Arab and Muslim societies, the entire strategic communications apparatus from top to bottom was penetrated and disabled from delivering successful strategic plans.[12]

The coalition of interests embodied by oil-producing regimes, the authoritarian ruling elites in the Arab and Muslim world, and the Islamist movements, despite their internal struggles, wanted to make sure the defense institutions in the free world—and U.S. defense in particular—would not engage in efforts triggering a democratic revolution in the Greater Middle East. The Pentagon, even under the Bush administration, never planned to back up democratic revolutions, uprisings, or political reforms in the region with the U.S. military. Such activities are in the realm of political planning, and under the auspices of the State Department and the White House. As far as we know, there was no U.S. policy to instigate democratic uprisings. There may have been pushes encouraging democratic movements, but these uncoordinated campaigns were quickly derailed by the apologist and Islamist lobbies. The defense institutions barely contemplated plans and strategies to mitigate the psychological actions of al Qaeda and in some cases merely flirted with the idea of counterideology.

The reality was, as I saw firsthand, from the top military chain of command to the regional and arms commands, there was no clarity regarding the purpose of the so-called strategic communications. Was it to fight the radical ideologies, in this case obviously jihadism? Or was it to engage with the dissidents, who would in turn fight extremism? Or was it only to mitigate the actions of terrorists, such as by finding ways to stop suicide bombers? God knows how much was spent on conferences, studies, grants, and consulting on behalf of defense contractors to figure this out, and how many related conferences I attended or addressed on the subject between 2002 and 2009.

I observed dozens of baffling cases as I was consulting or lecturing at defense and national security organizations. For example, during my participation in seminars at CENTCOM over several years, I noted that some foreign militaries were in fact advocating jihadism and rejecting the calls for democratic change in the countries they were representing. Ironically, they were invited to take part in U.S. meetings to explore what should be done to counter the jihadists in the region. Obviously many of these military leaders from Pakistan, Saudi Arabia, Egypt, and the Gulf—who were not reformers or liberals—strongly advised against backing civil societies in the region against authoritarianism. Even if they weren't radical themselves, one can easily imagine that they were monitored closely by the intelligence operatives of their own regimes. Officers from Lebanon couldn't say a word about how to counter Hezbollah's ideology and reach out to communities that the organization dominates. I have heard military leaders from Pakistan, even when their forces were battling the Taliban in Waziristan, defending jihadism in Tampa, and I have watched officers from Saudi Arabia and Egypt arguing against supporting democracies as their governments were fighting jihadi terror in their home countries.

These surreal experiences were topped when I was invited to participate in a Defense Department–sponsored seminar in Texas to explore the jihadist propaganda leveled against the United States in the region, along with the CEO of al Jazeera and representatives from other media sympathetic to the jihadists. It seems the higher echelons were advised by their experts to "engage" with the forces that have an impact on the public in the region. Hence al Jazeera was "helping" the U.S. military figure out how to face jihadism while its programs were hosting the most radical Islamist ideologues on the planet blasting human rights activists in the region.

To be fair, the overwhelming majority of U.S. Defense officers in charge of planning strategic communications are smart, educated, determined men and women who understand the importance of civil society's role in the resistance against radicalism. All the people I met and worked with deeply wanted to win that battle. Their problem was the body of cultural advisors they had to deal with. In my estimation, more than 90 percent of the contracted experts who were tasked with winning the war of ideas vehemently opposed the spread of democracy. An army whose advisors don't want it to win can be easily derailed.

In 2005, I was invited to a Washington, D.C., conference sponsored by CENTCOM's commander, General John Abizaid, to study suicide bombers. A hundred or so of the top experts in the field from both the private and public sectors attended, in what seemed to be the largest meeting addressing a vital matter for the defense of America. Abizaid wanted to find strategic answers to the ideological force behind the *Istishaad* (jihadi martyrdom) issue. In our brief chat just before the conference began, I realized how crucial the battle of ideas is in the long-term confrontation in the region, even from a military perspective. I anticipated a focused discussion on how to develop democratic forces inside the civil societies where the suicide bombers lived.

Instead I was surprised to see a majority of academics and consulting representatives testing multiple sterile theories about the psychology of individual suicide bombers. The Washington consulting establishment, often handsomely funded by the government, had already ruled out any venture in democracy-backing as a defense against these bombers, even for national security needs. The regimes in the region had their arms deep inside the industry of ideas surrounding Washington and, as noted earlier, across campuses. Military planners were always surprised when they were told that dissidents from the region were ready to act and to spread a culture of human rights and pluralism. "That is not what we heard from expert so-and-so and professor so-and-so" was their most common answer.

In late 2008, Pentagon officials asked me to organize a panel at the National Defense University that would include Muslim dissidents. Participants on that panel included former Islamist Dr. Tawfik Hamid, now a Washington-based expert on Islamic reform, and Omran Salman, the director of Arab Reformers, a group of writers posting on the internet. The participants, all from various military agencies dealing with strategic communications, had a hard time believing that Muslim intellectuals who opposed the jihadists even existed, let alone had developed a powerful message. When asked by the audience why their voice wasn't heard within the U.S. military or the greater national audience, the panelists were quick to answer: "You never heard us because you never invited us before."

This was the heart of the matter. It was really about a war to convince decision-makers in America and the West that the battle for democracy was possible, but only if you reach out to the democrats of the region. The other camp understood this much earlier. They were able to better position themselves to block U.S. institutions from moving toward the dissidents.

During the winter of 2009, I was invited to participate in a lunch meeting with General David Petraeus and some of his aides, along with three other experts on the Middle East, to discuss the best ways to influence Iran and Syria to desist from their radical attitudes. During that session I found myself the only one advocating a strategic outreach to the dissidents and reformers in both countries. I felt my suggestions had the ear of the new commander of CENTCOM, himself a professor of political science. But the three other scholars strongly advocated a dialogue with Damascus and Tehran, along the lines of President Obama's "new direction" already declared during his presidential campaign and reaffirmed in the Cairo speech "to the Muslim world" delivered in June, after our meeting. In my remarks I recommended building bridges with Middle Eastern reformers in general and Iranian and Syrian opposition groups in particular because, as I argued to General Petraeus, their day is coming anyway, and we need to be ready to meet them halfway. I argued that engaging the reformers may spare us future military confrontations in the Middle East.

My feeling at the time was that the top U.S. military commander for Middle Earth was receptive to my ideas, as he asked me to elaborate later. However, due to the heavy rhetoric coming from the other side using the "deal cutting" position of the president, there was no follow-up. Ironically, a few months later a formidable series of demonstrations exploded in Tehran and other Iranian cities with millions on the streets. Had the United States and the international community been ready to reach out to those Iranian reformers, that country could now have shifted toward freedom.

I have drawn one general conclusion from this decade-long journey inside the defense discussions: the experts hired by the U.S. defense establishment to advise on civil societies in the region killed the prodemocracy option. The U.S. military had the capacity to reach out to segments in civil societies that were ready to promote democratic change while protected by America and its allies, so it was crucial for the brotherhood against democracy to ensure that U.S. defense projects dealing with counterideology would fail.

5.

Freedom and Its Obstructors

T he campaign waged by the U.S. administration after 9/11 to spread democracy in the Greater Middle East was resisted fiercely by opposing forces in the region. The American effort to produce a change of hearts and minds in the Middle East was not a singular outflow of policies and resources. Rather, it was a confrontation between freedom and its obstructors. This formidable battle, not always understood or followed by the public, pertained to international diplomacy, which involved engagement with dissidents, and broadcast, which was hindered by the grand alignment of obstructing forces.

Prodemocracy Diplomacy

Before 9/11 the United States didn't have a grand strategy to counter the radicals in the Middle East or their infiltration of America. In addition, U.S. foreign policy was not focused on strategic promotion of freedom and democracy in the region. During my many visits and briefings in Congress and at the State Department in the 1990s, I was stunned to see the wall erected around the issues of human rights in the Arab and Muslim world. Despite some steps taken by legislators, including hearings and legislation pertaining to religious persecution in the region, the United States wasn't pushing for a strategic change.

The State Department, following a directive by President Bill Clinton, established an entity to monitor persecution of religious minorities. At the invitation of the U.S. Senate, the Clinton administration unveiled its new "proactive" policy in congressional hearings in spring 1997. In an unprecedented hearing before the Near East and South Asia Subcommittee of the Senate Committee on Foreign Relations on May 1, 1997, five witnesses, including Representative Frank Wolf (Republican of Virginia) and three specialists, Bat Yeor, Nina Shea, and I spoke on the subject of religious persecution in the Middle East. Congressman Wolf, whom I had briefed and advised on his legislation regarding international religious freedom, advocated at the hearing that a strong change of U.S. policy toward the oppression of minorities and persecuted groups would have a significant impact in the international community. Steven J. Coffey, principal deputy assistant secretary of state in the Bureau of Democracy, Human Rights, and Labor, was the fifth person to speak to the subcommittee. Coffey made sweeping claims about U.S. policy: "In February, we convened the first session of the Secretary of State's Advisory Committee on Religious Freedom abroad. This new committee brings together twenty of America's most prominent religious leaders, activists, and thinkers to help us forge new policy directions on religious freedom."[1] I felt this was a historic moment when America was finally going to rise to the occasion.

Coffey's testimony seemed to signal a U.S. policy that had never existed before. Indeed, Washington had been insensitive to minorities' persecution in general and to religious oppression in particular for many decades. I witnessed this nonchalance from the Middle East years before I emigrated. The genocide in Biafra and southern Sudan and the persecution of Copts, Assyrians, and Baha'is were largely ignored. Almost one decade after the collapse of the Soviet Union and after years of pressures by the U.S. Congress, the Clinton administration began to show some signs of life in this area. I felt the bureaucrats were wasting time. The obstacles created by the deep reach of the oil regimes inside the U.S. government was insurmountable. The achievements claimed by the State Department, in launching new offices and programs, didn't seem to go far enough in confronting the authoritarians, the regimes, or the jihadists. The notion that all will be fine as soon as the Arab-Israeli conflict is solved was still at the center of the U.S. diplomacy narrative.

Mr. Coffey testified: "I've spoken, for example, about how the Arab-Israeli conflict has given rise to extremist groups such as Hamas, and has exacerbated religious tensions and intolerance in the region. I have pointed out that our chief policy emphasis is on the Middle East peace process." When I heard this conclusion, I realized that the cause of the oppressed in the region was hopeless in the 1990s. I whispered to my friend Bat Yeor that unless some earthquake hit the free world, the people we were advocating for wouldn't get any help. She replied, *"Dhimmis, they have become Dhimmis."*

The term, from the Arabic *Ahl al Dhimma,* refers to the populations in the Greater Middle East who were invaded by the Caliphate in the seventh century and occupied for centuries after that. Caliph Omar, who conquered Jerusalem and Syria, devised a code for the occupied and "protected peoples," which included a special tax and second-class status for Jews and Christians who wished to stay in the "land of Islam." The *Dhimmis* were in fact the Jews and Christians who lived under the Caliphate. Initially the term meant the oppressed nations living under the yoke of the Islamic empire. But in the last few decades, particularly since a number of non-Muslim minorities against modern-day jihadist or Pan Arabist regimes, as in Lebanon and Sudan, historians and intellectuals from Middle Eastern Christian and Jewish minorities started to use the term in a derogatory manner. Currently, the word *Dhimmis* refers to those in the free world who had the liberty to reject the label "nonacceptable status," but preferred to tolerate the jihadists for financial reasons. Bat Yeor in Europe and myself in the States began using it as a charge against Westerners who bowed to OPEC and the OIC and allowed human rights of minorities to be abused to protect the interests of the petro-states.

The question among Western governments was whether leaders and bureaucrats would act as free men and women, or as *Dhimmis* when confronting Arab and Islamic regimes on human rights issues. Throughout the 1990s, despite pushes by the U.S. Congress to liberalize and grant more freedoms to minorities in the region, the apparatus of government remained in the realm of political "Dhimmitude." This attitude was severe in Western Europe, but it was also prevalent in Canada and the United States. At the aforementioned benchmark congressional hearing in 1997, headed by Senator Sam Brownback, we realized the wall built with petrodollars was too strong to be destroyed. The entities and commissions dedicated to freedom and religious liberty grew, and their budgets expanded. Prominent scholars and politicians sat on boards under the direction of the White House and the State Department and looked into the issues of "tolerance," but no real policy was shaped.

Soon enough, representatives from Islamist groups, with endorsement from the regimes in the region, sat at these meetings and succeeded in causing a complete paralysis of policies aimed at freeing actual communities and people in the region. They could not allow rights to be granted to religious minorities because of Western pressure. That would lead only to granting even more rights to other suppressed populations and the eventual collapse of ruling elites. Nothing had really changed since the end of the Cold War; the Iron Curtain was now surrounding the entire Greater Middle East, and U.S. and Western diplomacy was unable and in most cases unwilling to challenge the region's wealthy elites.

However, with the Twin Towers falling in the barbaric strikes by al Qaeda in 2001, U.S. foreign policy began shifting gears. As previously noted, the Western-based advocates for human rights in the Middle East, myself included, were pleased to hear the Bush administration talking about the freedom forward doctrine. We were satisfied to see a widening group of neoconservatives and classic liberals supporting this new direction. But most of us were still watching for the actual steps to be taken by the United States.

A series of strategic decisions to support the struggles in Darfur, Lebanon, and Iran were early signs that change was on its way regarding a new direction in assisting oppressed people in the region. Aside from the regime changes in Afghanistan and Iraq provoked by military means, U.S. diplomacy was activated from the top tiers to engage in democracy promotion and outreach to other governments.

Early in the process we realized that the only significant push was practiced by the president's political appointees, not by career diplomats. I had the opportunity to see this dichotomy firsthand. When the NGO delegation I accompanied met with the bureaucrats of the State Department in 2002 to propose ideas to liberate Lebanon from Syrian occupation, the faces were somber, the words unsupportive, and the attitude unhelpful. When we met with Bush appointees, the encounters were warm, the discussion focused, and the outcome fruitful. At the United Nations Security Council in 2004, we had several meeting with U.S. Ambassador John Negroponte, whose actions were instrumental in pushing for a UN resolution calling on the Assad regime to pull out of Lebanon, a step that had not been taken since Syria's invasion in June 1976.

That same year we also met with Ambassador John Bolton, who

headed a policy bureau at the State Department to get support for the idea. There, too, Bolton was enthusiastic and carried out the guidelines of the White House. Regardless of the debates about Iraq's invasion, American policy on Lebanon signaled a revolutionary change. That move was as real as one could hope for.

The other indication of a change from traditional U.S. policy was the new attitude toward Sudan's regime. After years, if not decades, of diplomatic nonchalance regarding what was becoming the largest genocide since the Jewish Holocaust, serious American pressure was at last applied on Khartoum and international organizations to address the horrors in Darfur. Also as of 2004, we witnessed U.S. efforts through the United Nations and other entities to identify the massacres in Darfur as genocide and to call for sanctions and legal actions against the regime. This revolutionary move was made by political allies of the president across the foreign policy establishment. Coincidentally, the two secretaries of state under Bush were African-American—Colin Powell and Condoleezza Rice. It was inspiring to watch descendants of African ethnicities leading U.S. diplomacy in support of liberation of African populations on the old continent. It offered an ironic parallel to watching an American of Lebanese descent, General John Abizaid, overseeing the military campaigns in the Middle East. I thought of it as retribution—the descendants of the oppressed nations coming back to render justice, or at least be its vehicle. By 2005, the diplomatic revolution was under way, and more dissidents were hopeful that the most powerful democracy on Earth was coming to rescue the most oppressed peoples on the planet, while confronting the widest spectrum of authoritarian regimes in history.

This diplomatic outburst for democracy in the Greater Middle East would soon be confronted by a formidable convergence of forces. There were U.S. bureaucrats opposed to weakening the oil elites in the region, the authoritarian regimes, and their powerful lobbies worldwide. Then there was the shift in the majority of the U.S. Congress that occurred in 2006. By early 2007, the new diplomatic initiative in support of freedom movements was already over. Secretary Rice still delivered speeches about promotion of democracy in the region, but the corresponding policies had vanished. The last two years of the Bush administration looked very awkward in the eyes of reformer groups in the region, those opposed to the jihadists. The president and his assistants still preached freedom and democracy, especially to the region's people, but U.S. diplomacy abruptly stopped assisting with real action.

The last supporters still trying to fight that battle were the U.S. mission at the UN Security Council headed by Ambassador Bolton, and a few policy advisors at the Pentagon. During meetings I had with Bolton at the Security Council in 2006, I found that he was deeply convinced that assisting democracy forces in the region would eventually reduce the influence of the jihadists and their allies. No wonder the brotherhood against democracy hated him, maybe more than any other living U.S. diplomat. Bolton was a nightmare for entrenched totalitarian regimes and jihadist strategists and ideologues. He transformed the U.S. mission at the UN Security Council into the highest international resistance against terrorism.[2]

First under Negroponte, then under Bolton, America was raising the profile of causes previously untouched; Darfur's genocide, Lebanon's Cedars Revolution, Syria's and Iran's reformers, human rights throughout the region, and the fight against radical ideologies. Eliminating these freedom advocates at the UN became a priority for the "political Caliphate." As soon as the Bush administration lost a supportive majority in Congress in November 2006, Bolton was removed. Critics said, "Bush should alter course now and nominate someone less hard-charging, with greater finesse in handling sensitive diplomatic matters." These in fact were the requests by the OPEC-OIC bloc to begin the "engagement" with the new leadership of Congress at that time. "There are a lot of competent people. Send someone new up, Mr. President," then senator Joe Biden said after the elections.[3]

Indeed, after Bolton, American diplomacy at the UN stalled. Ambassador Zalmai Khalilzad, with whom I also met at the Security Council to discuss issues pertaining to Syria, Lebanon, and the pending UN Resolution 1559, is a shrewd and very well-informed U.S. diplomat. He knows what's happening on the ground and has his own network of contacts. But he knew the wind wasn't blowing in favor of democracy promotion anymore. His concern was to protect the "advances already made." After meeting with the main players, French, British, Russian, and other missions interested in Middle Eastern priorities, I understood that the international backing for democracy causes in the region was over, as of January 2007. The changing of the guard at the UN Security Council was a pivotal moment signaling the decline of legitimacy in freedom advocacy. This is something that freedom activists, human rights workers, NGOs, and lawmakers on both sides of the Atlantic didn't really understand.

In the years between 2002 and 2006, almost every time I participated in a media debate on Arab TV or radio shows, the jihadophile side raged against America's "use of the United Nations Security Council to impose its will." I always returned fire by showing that it was the authoritarian regimes and totalitarian organizations in the region that were brutalizing their people, and thanks to a "new direction" in U.S. diplomacy, the United Nations was acting at last to serve the principles upon which it was founded and the universal declaration of human rights. I was among the very few (actually just two or three) commentators in the Arab media who blasted the oppressive nature of the authoritarians and jihadists in the region. However, with time, I found it odd that I—an independent analyst and writer—was doing the job of explaining and promoting the freedom forward doctrine in the Arab world while the U.S. and Western media weren't. Even though U.S. diplomacy was fighting for the rights of the underdogs in the Greater Middle East, American outlets funded by taxpayer dollars were reluctant to follow through with reporting on these issues, and in many cases, failed their government and the struggle for freedom in the region.

With the election of Barack Obama as president of the United States in November 2008, one could have projected a cataclysmic change regarding the interests and aspirations of democracy movements in the region. With millions of Americans voting for the "candidate of change," it was hard for activists and NGOs to believe that change would be *against* democracy in the Middle East. I was surprised that most freedom advocates, those based in the West and those operating out of the region, took so long to realize that the "new direction" advanced by the Obama campaign was in fact a return to the old direction prevalent in the 1990s. It was devised by advisors who had published in the field and have been among the most outspoken critics of the Bush promotion of democracy. The new administration would abandon the push for democracy in the region and "engage" the regimes and the Islamists in discussion. U.S. diplomacy in 2009 was expected to take a dramatic turn away from a democracy agenda, which, as I will detail in later chapters, it has now done at a dizzying pace, particularly regarding Iran and Sudan, but also with regard to the support of dissidents in the region, which was cut off completely.

Liberty Broadcast

One of the most important decisions made by the United States in its efforts to promote democracy was undoubtedly the launching of a broadcast media campaign aimed at the Arab world, and at many other cultural regions in the Muslim majority countries. The "liberty broadcast" included all TV channels, radio networks, publications, websites, and other media funded by taxpayers and geared at encouraging pluralism, freedom, and antiterrorism in the Greater Middle East and beyond. The idea was brewing in parallel to the concept of a global war of ideas in which America and its allies would vie for the hearts and minds of Arabs and Muslims.

There were multiple roots to this "front." First, you had those seasoned experts who had worked on the battle of ideas during the Cold War and claimed that the success of Radio Free Europe in influencing listeners behind the Iron Curtain and the success of the Marshall Plan after World War II could be repeated in the twenty-first century with those populations living under fear and oppression in the Levant. Second, and probably more pragmatically, there was the need to counteract the profound impact that al Jazeera broadcasts in the region had in impeding U.S. efforts against al Qaeda and the Taliban.

Al Jazeera Syndrome

Since fall 2001, the Qatari-funded channel al Jazeera had systematically challenged war efforts and public relations of U.S. and allied campaigns in the region. It played a tremendous role in arousing sentiment and mobilizing large segments in the Arab and Muslim world against America. Amazingly, despite the savage attack against the United States, al Jazeera was able to turn the tables against Washington by portraying the United States as waging war against Islam, and not in defense of its own security. I followed the network closely and saw clearly that the ideological and political line, from editorial to talk shows, was without a doubt that of the Muslim Brotherhood. It was barely even camouflaged. The network was fully funded by the Qatari energy industry, and thus had the full endorsement of the government and the emir, but management and editorial control were predominantly in the hands of Muslim Brotherhood supporters and members, many of whom had been professionally trained by the BBC.

Volumes could be dedicated to the immense success of al Jazeera in promoting not just jihadism as an ideology, but also the actions by jihadi forces in countries around the world. The doctrinal identity of the network is not a secret in the Arab world—it is open, clear, and unapologetic. Its opinion shows, such as *Al Sharia wal Hayat* (*Sharia and Life*), hosted by a leading Islamist ideologue, Egyptian sheikh Yussuf al Qardawi, or *Al Ittijah al Muakess* (*Opposite Directions*), moderated by Syrian Dr. Faysal al Qassem, openly support jihadi agendas. Even its editorial and news line is in favor of Pan Arabism and Islamism with no hesitation. The network definitely represents the inclination of millions of viewers and sympathizers with such ideologies as Salafism, the Muslim Brotherhood, Baathism, and even the platforms of Khomeinist Hezbollah, although many of these movements contradict each other in nuanced ways.[4]

The debate about al Jazeera's message doesn't take place in the region but rather in the West, and more particularly in the United States. Stunningly, the majority of elite media and academia perceived the network as a sort of Arabian CNN and not what it really is—a force of mobilization of the masses against the West. In 2003, I wrote an article in *National Review* in response to many misguided interpretations of al Jazeera's mission. My intention wasn't to criticize the network, because I know they firmly believe in their reporting.[5] Rather, I wanted to respond to Western misrepresentation of the debate. I often went on al Jazeera and praised their very efficient delivery while expressing my opposite opinion when confronted with the views of their commentators. The debate continued in the West with one side claiming the network was neutral and critics arguing that it was disseminating a projihadist message.[6]

It was only after Arab voices rose in criticism against al Jazeera that the picture became clearer. Iraqi officials and NGOs accused it of supporting the radicals, as did the Palestinian Authority when it charged that al Jazeera supported Hamas. Dissidents also voiced criticism of the network by writing on liberal Elaph.com and reformer website Aafaq.com, accusing the station of an antidemocracy attitude. The defenders of al Jazeera replied that the network is independent from regimes. Critics also charge that al Jazeera is entirely funded by the oil industry of Qatar, thus run by a regime, and that it comes to the defense of oppressive regimes such as those of Iran and Sudan.

Regardless of the debate over al Jazeera's role in the ideological battle, it was clear that U.S. diplomacy and public relations were taking a beating on the network. While the network gave access to jihadi commentators to blast U.S. actions, from military and political to humanitarian assistance, their commentators "massacred" U.S. officials when they were invited to air their opinion on al Jazeera. I remember watching the charade every time a spokesperson from the State Department or other agencies came on. From the shrewd questions to the subsequent commentary, the U.S. message was completely distorted.

Al Hurra TV's drama

After experiencing the heavy pounding of al Jazeera and other militant media in the region, particularly after the Iraq invasion, ideas were brewing inside the Bush administration to launch U.S.-funded media to balance the other side's propaganda efforts. As early as 2002 I briefed a number of congressional offices on the necessity of "talking" to the Arab and Muslim public worldwide and reaching out to like-minded people in the Greater Middle East. My plan was to achieve two goals. One was to link with the oppressed, who were conscious of the threat in the region, including ethnic and religious minorities as well as the liberal element within the majority, thus establishing a partnership with millions of individuals in the Arab world who had been waiting for that change in U.S. policy to occur. The second goal was to engage those in the popular majority who were getting only one voice, representing the views of either the authoritarian regimes or the jihadists.

The initial idea I proposed in 2000 to my Senate and House contacts was to launch an Arabic media network comprising a TV channel, radio stations, publications, and websites, all manned by native-language journalists and commentators committed to the battle for democracy. Since petrodollars back the jihadi propaganda machine, U.S. dollars, and perhaps euros, should in turn back democracy media. The original plan I hoped for wasn't official U.S. media in Arabic, like the Voice of America, but an independent institution funded fully or partially by Congress to stand as the free voice of dissidents, democrats, and liberals in the region and in exile.

In my government briefings, I described the war of ideas as an area in which to gain ground. If the United States doesn't support the anti-jihadists and the democrats in the region, the other side will fill the gap and win the entire space. It is an issue of being proactive, I argued. I hoped that the U.S. administration would call for a strategic planning meeting in order to quickly launch such a project. In fact, these ideas (which I and others in Washington pushed for) were taken, reworked, and intercepted by the apologist "lobbies."

It was critical to the brotherhood against democracy to ensure that America didn't empower dissidents in the region by providing them with a world podium. Intercepting, manipulating, and paralyzing U.S.-backed media became a high priority to radical and authoritarian decision centers in the region and their partners in the West. This opposition caused strategic communication unleashed by the U.S. government to fail in its goals. In short, almost all projects funded and managed by the U.S. government were penetrated and their central mission disabled. I observed the rise and disappointing decline of that communications project firsthand both by being on air and by learning directly from people who worked inside these organizations.

By summer 2003, my contacts in Congress were informing me that a new channel called al Hurra TV (translated as "the Free") would soon be launched with U.S. funding in response to al Jazeera. Congress also added a radio network called SAWA to the package. Both channels fell under the government's Broadcasting Board of Governors, which oversees Voice of America and Radio Free Europe. At first I was pleased to see Washington finally moving in the right direction. Likewise, all those who complained about the losses incurred by the United States in the war of ideas were supportive and anxious to see the new channel launched.

Toward the end of 2003, Arab media mentioned that a U.S.-backed broadcast was soon to be launched and that the first director of the channel would be Muaffaq Harb, who was then a popular columnist with the Pan Arab Saudi-funded *al Hayat*. Harb, a U.S. citizen, was from a Lebanese Shia background, and thus would have played an important role in countering Iranian-inspired propaganda. Interviewed on al Jazeera's show *Min Washington* just before the launching of the station, Harb was asked if he would call Hamas a terrorist group or promote "pro-American ideas." The newly appointed director for al Hurra, to avoid the clash, asserted that al Hurra would be "neutral," reporting facts, and would not commit to any ideological direction.

From that moment I realized that the enterprise would not put battling jihadist propaganda or raising the profile of democrats and dissidents in the region high on its agenda. These very first statements by its director revealed the editorial direction for the years to come; al Hurra wouldn't engage forcefully in democracy struggle as Radio Free Europe did during the Cold War, even though it defended the positions of the administration. The hybrid attitude taken by the network was in fact a half measure. It aired the statements of the U.S. government, the president, and his secretaries, but in fact did not push for spreading democracy.

After the channel was launched in February 2004, jihadi ideologues didn't wait long before blasting it as "infidel." A senior Saudi judge condemned al Hurra, saying it was "waging a war against Islam and Americanizing the world."[7] One year into its broadcast, al Hurra was criticized harshly by a number of anchors and journalists. One of them, Magdi Khalil, an Egyptian intellectual who appears in the Arab media and leads the Middle East Freedom Forum in Cairo, published acerbic pieces accusing the network of not fulfilling its mandate. Khalil, who had once worked at the station, claimed the station was not following President Bush's guidelines on advocating freedom and democracy in the region.

In 2007 Tom Harb, a Lebanese-American activist, briefed members of Congress about what he called a "takeover of al Hurra by apologists for friends of Hezbollah." According to Harb and other Lebanese-American activists, including a number of journalists fired from al Hurra, a number of officials at the station were apologists for Hezbollah in Lebanon. They claimed this pressure group ensured that the station wouldn't criticize Iran, Syria, or Hezbollah. To me, it was hard to believe that a media institution funded by the U.S. Congress had been neutralized by Hezbollah apologists and its Iranian masters. But the Lebanese exiles were adamant about this assertion.

The battle over al Hurra was not only between democracy

advocates and regime interests. It turned into a battle between regional influences: Whom not to criticize, Iran or the Muslim Brotherhood? Which of the lobbies close to the brotherhood against democracy would influence the channel—those close to Iran or those close to Saudi Arabia and the *Ikhwan*? According to former journalists at al Hurra, the atmosphere was tense, with different camps vying for influence, much like the Middle East itself. In November 2006, Harb resigned and Larry Register, a former CNN journalist backed by the State Department and (according to insiders) liked by the Wahabi-Muslim Brotherhood lobbies, took over. According to his critics, Register opened the airwaves to statements by "terror organizations such as Hamas and stopped criticizing regimes in the region."[8] The scene at al Hurra was surreal: A channel funded by the United States to take the battle for democracy to the airwaves had mutated into a battlefield between the two streams of jihadism and their apologists in Washington.

A few months later Larry Register resigned and the deputy under Harb, Daniel Nassif, took over. Of Lebanese Christian descent, Nassif was profoundly critical of the Wahabi influence and has written against Syria's occupation of Lebanon in the 1990s, but because of his support for General Aoun, a Lebanese politician allied to Hezbollah, he was accused by his opponents, the "March 14 coalition," of cozying up to the Syro-Iranian influence as a result of internal politics in his homeland of Lebanon. The critics said the station aired the full speeches by Hassan Nasrallah, Hezbollah's leader, to which Nassif, who had extensively and strongly published against the Syrian occupation of Lebanon in the 1990s, replied he was adopting a "no-propaganda attitude."[9] The only channel dedicated originally to speaking on behalf of the voiceless was impacted by the region's authoritarian infighting, and with it went the hope of the dissident community worldwide that an alternative podium to the oil-funded media could ever help promote democracy.

I had the opportunity to witness these tribulations, as I was invited occasionally to take part in interviews and panel discussions on al Hurra. It was the first time I saw dissidents and reformers from Libya, the Gulf, Lebanon, Syria, Iraq, and other countries mingling and producing the first Pan Arab democracy narrative, or at least trying to. The station had talented journalists, producers, and writers from across the Arab world. It could have played and could still play a pioneering role in triggering a regionwide debate on fundamental issues, but Middle Earth's rulers knew all too well that al Hurra would be lethal to their interests, so they struck pre-emptively, trying to marginalize the primary outlet America had in the war of ideas. In short, the project was revolutionary, but it was paralyzed intellectually.

Al Hurra wasn't the only program targeted by the other side.

U.S. and Western Broadcast Disabled

Radio SAWA was also influenced by political pressures. "We tried hard to press for a prodemocracy and antiterrorism line," a seasoned journalist who worked at the radio station told me. "We are in Washington, D.C., two blocks away from the U.S. Congress, but we feel we are located psychologically in downtown Tehran or in Damascus because of the political environment we live under." Readers may find it impossible that the long arm of jihadi political influence could reach that deep inside Western capitals, but the reality is that both Iranian and Wahabi-*Ikhwan* influences were prevalent within the layers of almost all institutions that can affect their interests in the Middle East. The Caliphate's virtual arm is very long, thanks to endless petrodollars.

As with democracy-promotion institutions based in the United States and other Western countries, freedom-promoting media funded by taxpayers were also penetrated by these regimes. Not only were al Hurra and SAWA significantly compromised, but American broadcast programs directed to the Muslim world were influenced, and in most cases subverted. According to many Iranian-American activists, the Voice of America Farsi language service, financed by Congress, was infiltrated by the Khomeinist regime from day one. Voice of America's gigantic web of channels, in multiple languages, that reached as far as Central Asia, Indonesia, and the Sahel of Africa, were also taken out by the influence of the regimes and Islamist networks.[10] A *Washington Times* editorial stated: "The Voice of America is becoming the Voice of the Islamic Republic of Iran. Recent programming choices have revealed a creeping bias toward opponents of the pro-democracy movement." The *Times* cites interviews by Hooshang Amir-Ahmadi and Trita Parsi, described as close to the Iranian regime.[11]

In Prague, where I visited the impressive buildings of Radio Free Europe, also funded by Congress and airing in dozens of languages, such as Pashtun, Arabic, and Turkic, the same situation prevailed. "U.S. forces are bombing the terrorists overseas and we are bombing these populations with anti-American and anti-Western narrative," whispered workers in the cafeteria. For years I could not get the thought out of my head that American taxpayers were funding propaganda encouraging the defeat of the United States and democracy around the world. The jihadi and authoritarian forces had indirectly seized control of our own systems and were using them against us. Worse was the fact that this couldn't be explained to the lawmakers in Washington or anywhere else, because the bureaucracies in charge of assessing the progress of democracy promotion were the ones delaying it. I, a few colleagues, and those brave workers inside these institutions saw the battle happening, and we weren't able to do anything about it.

With time I also realized that the other camp had already penetrated every single Arabic and Middle Eastern broadcast funded by other Western countries. France 24 Arabic, BBC Arabic, and even Russia Today in Arabic were following, at times, editorial lines barely distinguishable from al Jazeera's. As I appeared on these networks and engaged in debates, I quickly realized that the very distinctive and sophisticated methods of the Muslim Brotherhood dominated the newsrooms. "It's all over," concluded Sue Myrick, the cochair of the U.S. House Caucus on Counter Terrorism, at the conclusion of a session. "If the jihadists, regimes, or networks can direct the editorial line of American broadcast into the Arab and Muslim world, how can we help promote democracy and moderation, let alone reformism?" The congresswoman and her colleagues were right: The battle for spreading democracy was lost at the outset. The foes had seized America's most formidable weapons—its own messages. In 2010, U.S. lawmakers at last formed a caucus to investigate the massive failures in strategic communications, but the Obama administration had changed strategic direction: no more support to democracy but "engagement" with the regimes and the Islamists instead.

6

The Taliban's Nightmare:
Women against Their Oppressors

The Harvard professor visiting our Florida campus at my invitation was very excited that night in 1999. The title of her presentation was "What are the Taliban's achievements in Afghanistan?" She delivered an hour-long lecture on the turbaned and bearded men who had ruled Afghanistan since 1996 with an iron fist, hoping to become the cornerstone of the renewed Caliphate.

"Women are happier under the Taliban?" asked a student of mine.

The speaker fired back, "Women are certainly happier for not being raped on the roads. At least there is some stability under these revivalist militias."

I knew that the narrative used to apologize for the Taliban was Wahabi-inspired, but I listened in disbelief to the lecturer. She was a female, a scholar from an Ivy League University. I had a hard time absorbing her attitude. How could an expert on the region, who promotes feminism at home, defend the archenemies of her own sex? That scene was a benchmark. It sealed my conviction that the debate on human rights alone is not going to undo the stubborn lobbying by apologists who seek favor with the petro-powers. Middle Eastern studies in America and in the West were too subdued by the oil influence to be reasoned with. The conflict isn't about liberalism, it is about jihadophile elites seizing the microphone within the academic world. It is a war of ideas. Who among the educated Western elite could stand by the Taliban—a brute force straight out of the dark ages—against the rights of women in civil society? The defense of the Taliban inside the West shows how deeply rooted and entrenched the forces of authoritarianism and their supporters are in the free world.

How ironic that out of an entire region suffering under barbaric regimes and militant organizations, it was the Taliban that, via al Qaeda, shocked the West out of lethargy. Despite the layers of oppression and scores of powers fighting for dominance across the region throughout the 1990s, one of these forces, thriving in the margins of the region in a poor country with no oil and an unending civil war, blew up the status quo. By launching his men against the financial and political heart of the West, Osama Bin Laden unknowingly came to the aid of the most oppressed societies on the face of the earth by triggering a U.S.-backed campaign for freedom in the entire region. The Taliban had become a nightmare to its people, and archives left from their time in power show clearly how brutal their reign was toward women.

But will the liberation survive when the West later backs away from supporting democracy in Middle Earth? That is the most dramatic question for Afghanistan's fate in the decades to come.[1]

Pre-Taliban Discoveries

I learned about the Taliban nightmare through a decade of research about Islamist movements and jihadi organizations that migrated to Afghanistan to fight the Soviets. Since my years in Beirut in the 1980s, we've known them as the "Arab Afghans." They are Salafists who left their original countries in the Middle East and beyond and headed to fight the Soviet occupation of Afghanistan in the 1980s. While a majority of mujahideen were basically Afghan warriors who happened to be Muslims, a portion of this fighting force was gradually indoctrinated by Wahabis dispatched from Saudi Arabia and other Islamist networks, with the support of the Pakistani intelligence service.

As I read about their ideology and strategies, and engaged in debates with some of their supporters out of Beirut, I came to the conclusion that the jihadi network that penetrated the Afghani resistance against the Soviets had a greater agenda than simply kicking the Russians out of that rugged country. From their literature, the jihadists who supported the "Islamization" of the struggle in Afghanistan intended to use the clash with the communists to establish what they had dreamed of for decades—a building block for the Caliphate, an entity they would call an *Imara* or emirate. I wrote about how bad this development was for international security, religious freedom, minority rights, and the status of women. In the midst of a Western (mostly American) confrontation with the Soviets, no one was interested or concerned about future jihad, including those at the French Quai d'Orsay in Paris and the British Foreign Affairs Ministry in London, and ambassadors and diplomats representing the United States and several other countries.

The ambassador of the United Kingdom in Lebanon at the time, Sir John Grey, understood my apprehension regarding Khomeinist and Wahabi ideological expansion in the 1980s. In one of our meetings in 1987 in Beirut, he told me: "Walid, we British have one of the greatest historical experiences in that part of the world. We fought the Pashtun for years and lost and we helped the Saud clan and the Wahabis to control the Arabian Peninsula. We know these places, but today's priorities are defeating the Soviets and ensuring the flow of oil. After the Soviets, we will always need that flow of oil to stay put. As long as the mujahideen aren't aiming at our capitals, why should we be concerned? What they'll do to their own people is their own business."

Grey's dose of realpolitik was one of my first encounters with the higher priorities of Western governments. In my meetings with U.S. diplomats, I had more sobering experiences. During an encounter with diplomats of the U.S. embassy in that same year, I asked one of them if Washington had any concern about the rise of Islamism in its jihadi form, particularly among fighters in Afghanistan. He said, "Why would we?" I replied, because of the threat they pose to human rights, women, non-Muslim minorities, and secular Muslims. He smiled and replied, "Do you really think American policy is about values, especially these universal values?" I paused and reflected upon my answer. In fact I had none, as I was stunned that the last democracy I thought would back down from human rights values would be America. I knew from French, British, and other Western powers that oil influence has dominated their international politics, particularly since 1973. But I struggled with the notion that the United States, the soon-to-be victor of the Cold War, would accept abuse by Islamist radicals. This conversation took place three years before I discovered firsthand the dependence of U.S. foreign policy on petrodollar influence, even at the expense of freedom.

The U.S. attitude before 1990 was odd to me, as one type of jihadism had already wreaked havoc among Americans. Hezbollah blew up an American embassy twice and was behind the hostage crisis in Lebanon, while the Iranian Islamist regime was still involved in conflicts with America. It seemed at the time that the issue wasn't framed as conflict with jihadism but with "Shia extremism." The Salafists in Afghanistan and the region, who were technically "Sunni extremists," were perceived as allies against the Soviets. So Khomeinist suppression of liberties was condemned, but Salafi rejection of human rights wasn't. That explained the lack of interest of the West in general and of the United States in particular in analyzing the antidemocracy nature of those among the mujahideen who would eventually become al Qaeda and the Taliban. Diplomats and intelligence agencies either didn't know or didn't want to know about the extreme fascist identity of Salafi jihadism.

In my frequent discussions with French ambassador René Ala, the mood was different. The French diplomat, who had socialist inclinations himself, seemed to appreciate the mounting threat of the Islamists in the region. From Algeria to Egypt, their agenda was gaining ground. We both understood it, but Ala was pessimistic about Europe's handling of that threat. "Europe will hear from these extremists," he told me. French concerns were logical, as their diplomats had been killed in Beirut and terrorist bombs rocked Paris during the 1980s. Their guard was already up.

Diplomats representing smaller Western countries were more open to discussing the menace. The ambassador of Spain, Pedro Manuel de Aristegui, with whom I had similar conversations, and whose wife is Lebanese, had a deep knowledge of what a rise in jihadism could lead to in the region and in his country. Sadly, and almost as an omen, de Aristegui was killed by a shell fired from areas controlled by terrorist organizations and under Syrian domination.[2]

I came to learn the importance of the Taliban's objectives to the rank and file of the Salafi Islamists in personal encounters, both online and in the real world. The power structure being built in Kabul was a dream come true to hard-core jihadists worldwide: a true, real, and pure "Islamic state." During the 1980s I traded articles in the press with intellectuals who defended the historical views of the Islamists. Later in the decade, I had few face-to-face debates with Islamist cadres during my trips to Europe. The ideas they advanced were an early version of what would become the Taliban and eventually al Qaeda. They spoke of Afghanistan's jihad as the new path ultimately leading to the return of the Caliphate. Since the late 1970s and throughout the 1980s I had learned most of what there was to learn about jihadism—its history, strategies, and future projects—and realized the fate of humanity if Islamism as an ideology ruled. There were instances during the 1990s where I grasped the determination of the individuals committed to the Afghan jihad. I read the minutes of the Khartoum conferences of 1993[3] and the Taliban declaration in 1996 and followed the literature emanating from Kabul under the new regime.

Personal encounters were vital in showing me the perceptions of regular supporters of the new Caliphate. In fall 1998, I invited a self-declared "imam" to give a lecture to my graduate seminar in Islamic politics in Florida. He asked for the title to be "True Islamic State." Along with a female convert, who also preached the Caliphate, the guest speaker lectured about theology but also about the geopolitics of Islamic causes. When asked about the best model for the Islamic state in current times, he replied that it is "only in one country." A student said: "Iran?" The speaker said: "Not at all. They aren't even real Muslims." Another student said: "Then is it Saudi Arabia?" The Salafi imam answered with a grin: "Saudi Arabia follows the true teaching in its laws, but its rulers aren't good." Then I asked: "Where *is* that promised land?" He snapped back: "It is Afghanistan. The Taliban are really the true embodiment of Islam, of the Caliphate to come, *inshallah*."

Taliban Oppression

However, as we were learning more about the ideological nature of the internationalist jihadists who had penetrated the mujahideen as of the late 1980s and rose to power to become the Taliban regime in 1996, the totalitarian essence of the movement was confirmed by many of its victims, particularly women. In the years leading up to 9/11 and the subsequent U.S. intervention in Afghanistan, women's groups sent SOS messages throughout the West about the gender oppression taking place in the country. I interacted with a number of exiled female groups and underground women's movements in Afghanistan and saw the breadth of the problem. The Taliban was a nightmare to every woman in Afghan society. It removed working women from their jobs and virtually jailed them in their homes.

Detention, harassment, torture, and execution of women who didn't comply or were accused of not complying with the Taliban's self-described Sharia rules were prevalent.

One feminist organization, not fond of the West or of America, described the jihadists' rule of the country as of 1992 as follows:

> The domination of the criminal fundamentalists in 1992 in Kabul and other provinces completely shattered their hope. Our people realized that they became the victims of a more painful and disastrous invasion, wrapped with the religious slogans. The fundamentalists' record is so horrible which is not comparable to any other war-ridden land in the world. The killings of thousands of people; the destruction of Kabul and other cities; the raping and "disappearance" of women and young girls and boys . . . the gifts of the ominous entrance of the criminal Islamic parties in our land. And the emergence of the Taliban was another dagger in the heart of our people. . . . They have established their own fundamentalist dictatorship which is thoroughly anti-women, anti-democracy, anti-culture and science. In the last analysis, Taliban are the brothers-in-faith of the "jehadis," trampling women's rights and antagonism towards freedom and democracy.[4]

Established in Kabul in 1977 as an independent political and social organization of Afghan women "fighting for human rights and social injustice," the Revolutionary Association of the Women of Afghanistan (RAWA) was the first independent women's movement in the country. Its first leader, Meena, was assassinated in 1987 by Afghan agents of the KGB. Under the Taliban, RAWA and other feminist movements were banned and persecuted. The jihadi oppression widened to systematically crush any non-Islamist movement, group, or non-Muslim entity. The destruction of the Buddhist statues in Bamiyan Province in March 2001, when explosives, tanks, and anti-aircraft weapons blew apart two colossal images of the Buddha,[5] sent a message to the world about the totalitarian regime of the turbaned men in Kabul. Their rage against the "other" or "*Kafir*" revealed the deep anti–human rights sentiments of the Taliban. In the years preceding 9/11 and the American invasion, Taliban leaders weren't much concerned with international perceptions of the nature of their regime. They constantly boasted about their purity as jihadists. Years later, after their defeat, they finally understood how far from international norms they were and saw a change in the youngest element of their society, so they began a counterpropaganda campaign. Mullah Omar, leader and supreme Emir of the Taliban, declared: "We would like to say we are victims of the black propaganda of the enemy media. They have wrongly depicted us as a force being against education and women's rights. They also accuse us of our being a threat to the countries of the world."[6]

"Brotherhood" with the Taliban

The battle to remove the Taliban as a ruling regime uncovered signs of a "brotherhood" between the Taliban in a number of Muslim countries. Although supporters such as Saudi Arabia and Pakistan funded the medieval militia, they weren't ready to adopt its methods and interpretation of Sharia. The Taliban was seen by the Wahabis in Arabia and the Deobandis of the Indian subcontinent as an experiment in Islamism.

How far could the Taliban go in its implementation of its version of Sharia without attracting international reaction? Pakistan's institutions were secular, but the Islamists had penetrated its intelligence and defense apparatus. Those sympathizers in Pakistan protected the Afghan regime. Eventually, Mullah Omar and his allies in secular Pakistan would coordinate a massive "Islamization" of the region. Had al Qaeda not attacked the United States in 2001, the ultrajihadist regime in Kabul would have moved its operations into Pakistan, linking with the Taliban of Pakistan and other jihadists. As for the Saudi support, it was initially provided to contain the Soviets, and later became part of the universal embracing of Wahabism in many regions of the world. The radical circles in the Kingdom were pushing to spread Salafi indoctrination from Central Asia to the Sahel of Africa.

Afghanistan under the Taliban was an ideological success story for the Wahabis. Even when al Qaeda declared war against the United States and the "infidels" in 1996 and 1998, then launched two terrorist attacks in East Africa against U.S. embassies, the Saudis, the Pakistanis, and their allies within the Organization of the Islamic Conference (OIC) convinced Washington under the Clinton administration not to support a regime change in Afghanistan. In other words, the "brotherhood" protected the Taliban up till 9/11, first because they were Islamists and second because a removal of the Taliban would bring a swell of democracy, in contradiction of jihadi ideology. But Bin Laden shattered that shield by massacring thousands of Americans in New York and Washington, D.C., on September 11, 2001.

Interestingly, for a few weeks reports in the Arab media floated the idea that the OIC would initiate a mediation by three Islamic countries to convince the Taliban to shut down al Qaeda's operation inside Afghanistan, capture Bin Laden and his supporters, and hand them over to the OIC, or at least kick al Qaeda out of the country. The Taliban "ambassador" in Pakistan, Abdul Salam Zaeef, in his defiant news conferences after 9/11, said the Islamist regime in Kabul would never surrender Osama Bin Laden and his organization.

The inclusion of the Taliban in the OIC was an issue of concern to begin with. How could an international organization that has the largest voting bloc in the UN General Assembly recognize an extremely oppressive militia as representing Afghanistan? A statement by RAWA from the 1990s shows the frustration of Afghan women:

> It is five years that our people have been burning in the ever higher flames of the fundamentalist tyranny. However not a single member state of OIC took notice of this situation as if nothing has happened in Afghanistan. The policy of forging unity among the different fundamentalist parties is nothing but a brazen act of enmity against Afghans. Should the religious criminals be united to kill and ruin physically and spiritually more and more freely and brutally our bereaved people? The real reason of the current disaster in Afghanistan is the domination of the so-called "jehadi" and the Taliban parties. As long as these arch enemies of democracy and women's rights are ruling the country, the suffering of our people will never end. . . . The presence of the Taliban delegation in the OIC summit would be counted as a sharp blow to the dignity and reputation of the OIC and is also ridiculing the people of Afghanistan. The religious fascists should not be regarded as the "leaders" of our country just because they have tanks, guns and dollars.[7]

Eventually, the American reaction to 9/11 derailed all OIC attempts to absorb the shock and protect the Taliban. The Islamist regimes of the OIC watched their extremist "brothers" falling from power and fleeing the advancing U.S. and alliance forces. The sinister solidarity with the Taliban seemed to be more with their doctrinal outlook than anything else. Since the opponents of the jihadi militia were also Muslims and had even been part of the mujahideen resistance against the Soviets, one would presume that the fall of the terrorist regime and the rise of an alternative Muslim government in Kabul would be acceptable. In fact the brotherhood against democracy cared less about the Muslim identity of the post-Taliban government and more about with the disbanding of an "Islamist" regime and the rise of democratic institutions, even though those elected would be Muslims.

As soon as al Qaeda and the Taliban crossed the border after the Tora Bora battle to take refuge in Pakistan's northwestern enclaves, the jihadi propaganda machine concentrated its fire on what it termed the "Crusader-Infidel takeover of Muslim Afghanistan." Leading the charge, the Qatar-funded al Jazeera unleashed a world campaign against the legitimacy of post-Taliban Afghan governments and elections. The Salafi web around the world followed through with similar claims.

Jihad against Any Alternative to the Taliban

In several panels on Arab TV, and on al Jazeera in particular, I asked my interviewers, who were emphatic in charging America with waging "a war against Islam," if those ruling Afghanistan after the Taliban, particularly elected officials, weren't Muslim enough. Answers varied from "No elections, as long as there is an infidel occupation," to "You can't impose democracy from the outside." These were "politically correct" answers, but there were no answers to what happens after the withdrawal of NATO forces from the country. Will women and minorities keep their post-Taliban acquired rights? Again, no answers. Strangely, many commentators were also unable to answer a comparative rebuttal when I mentioned the cases of Bosnia and Kosovo, Muslim populations who voted under the presence of "infidel" forces (NATO) while no one from the OIC complained. The projihadists argued that the Muslim people of Afghanistan didn't call on U.S. forces to help them as was the case with the Balkans' Muslims. So, according to many voices on al Jazeera and other Salafi-influenced media, women, minorities, and youth were "exhilarated" about their unelected rulers until the *kuffar* (infidel) forces showed up, which obviously wasn't the case.

The issue with the Taliban was the nature of the regime they erected. If we put aside the jihadi terror unleashed by al Qaeda worldwide under Taliban patronage, the ideology and system of the Taliban were in flagrant abuse of international law, human rights, and natural humanitarian rights. Regardless of the 9/11 attacks, the most extreme jihadists in Middle Earth were devastating to women and other powerless segments of Afghan society.

The scandal started before 2001, with the recognition given by the OIC to the medieval militia and the heavy silence of world democracies regarding its abuses. It took massive bloodshed on U.S. soil to instigate the removal of the thuggish force and to replace it with the only institution the international community could establish: a democratically elected government. The United Nations, NATO, and the United States could not remove a criminal totalitarian regime and replace it with an ideologically similar one. That is what the OIC didn't understand and what jihadi sympathizers in the region couldn't tolerate. The brotherhood against democracy was frustrated with Mullah Omar for having allowed Bin Laden to strike at the infidels' heart and causing uproar worldwide. Many ideologues of contemporary Islamism—Egyptian sheikh Yussuf al Qardawi on al Jazeera, or Saudi sheikhs Safar Al-Hawali and Salman Al-Auda—criticized al Qaeda's decision to attack, not because it was ideologically wrong, but because it led to the collapse of an experiment of an authentic "Islamist" regime.[8]

Beyond purist clerics, the authoritarian regimes, whether Islamist or not, were more concerned about what came "after" the Taliban than about the fate of the jihadi organization. For nine years, Salafi networks, the jihadi propaganda machine, radical clerics, and regimes frustrated with a possible rise of democracy in Afghanistan converged in an effort to defeat the U.S.-backed project in that Central Asian country. The common goal was, and still is, to derail efforts to defeat the Taliban, stop the spread of democratic culture, and undermine women's rapid rise in participation.

The Taliban Antidemocratic Ideology

In both Afghanistan and Pakistan, Taliban leaders have been clear in their ferocious opposition to democracy and women's rights. In Afghanistan, the jihadi militia showed the world in bloody fashion how they went about this apartheid.[9] But since their regrouping in Waziristan and the Swat Valley in Pakistan, the Taliban has made further statements about their anti–human rights worldview. The leader of the movement to implement Sharia in Pakistan, Sufi Mohammed, told his followers in Mingora, in February 2009: "We hate democracy; we want the occupation of Islam in the entire world. Islam does not permit democracy or election. From the very beginning, I have viewed democracy as a system imposed on us by the infidels. Islam does not allow democracy or elections; I believe the Taliban government formed a complete Islamic state, which was an ideal example for other Muslim countries."[10]

Going further in rejecting pluralism, Mulla Nazeer Ahmad, emir of the mujahideen in South Waziristan, said: "No, no, we do not accept Democracy. It is a code of law formulated by kufr. [I]t is a system in which people are merely counted, not weighed. And this counting can include Shiites, Christians and drunkards alike . . . and then they elect an emir (ruler) for us! What suffices is that it has been devised by kufr and we can never ever accept it. I have never casted a vote myself. In our own region too, I have made it clear that vote-casting is unlawful and it will remain so in future, may the candidate be a religious scholar or someone else. We utterly reject Democracy."[11]

On women's rights, the Taliban has shown radical hostility. For example, Ahmad Mukhtar, spokesman from the Afghan Taliban media wing, declared: "The role of women in Afghanistan is to raise the Jihadi generations and sacrifice them against the occupation and invasion. We do not forbid the Afghani woman from education, but we have restrictions that must come first before her education and work in the community. The callers of human rights are killing our women, children and elderly and accuse us that we forbid women from education . . . it is all lies."[12]

Mixed Results of the United States

The U.S. campaign to dislodge the Taliban was successful on the military level. Unlike what jihadi propaganda claimed, the country didn't rise against the marching infidels when American and coalition forces removed the regime. Instead, the northern areas marched against the Taliban, while the southern provinces failed to offer hundreds of thousands of fighters and suicide bombers to salvage the regime, as Mullah Omar, Osama Bin Laden, and Ayman Zawahiri had hoped.

By the end of 2001 and early 2002, as the space occupied by the jihadi forces was cleared, the United States and its allies had a historic opportunity to help launch a cultural revolution in the country, so a new generation of Afghans and a sea of women could transform the archaic social structures of the country into a transitional civil society. However, the challenge facing American strategic management of the country is imposing and the options are limited. U.S. and NATO efforts could lead to the rise of a new country able to defend itself against the Taliban and move forward like the rest of postcolonial and post–civil war countries, or the country could revert to an emirate of the dark ages. There was one direction to follow if re-Talibanization was to be prevented—defeat the jihadi militias so that an empowerment of civil society could be accelerated. The equation seemed simple: Fight the remnant of the Taliban and al Qaeda, train Afghan armed forces to take over, and engage in partnership with local and national social entities eager to trigger change.

Nine years later, the debate on Afghanistan is still raging. What to do about the U.S. presence? And in the last years the question became even more dramatic, especially under the Obama administration: Should the United States engage the Taliban politically? Why couldn't the United States, with all its human and financial investments, succeed in winning the battle of ideas in Afghanistan?

The Push against Bush's Democracy

From 2001 through late 2006, the Bush administration had the opportunity to engage in an all-out campaign to energize Afghanistan's progressive forces and empower those who fought for freedom and democratic culture. Surely, the challenges were enormous. Afghanistan's many years of devastating wars and trauma from a decade of

Taliban oppression, a strong tribal and clan system, weak liberal elements, and rampant corruption are still huge hurdles. It was one thing to bring down the Taliban; building a liberal democracy was quite another. The Taliban's shadow and operations were haunting the country.

The removal of the Taliban alone wasn't the sole condition for success. It was necessary to provide a free space for a moment, but it was only the first step. The essential question of the battle in Afghanistan was what to do during those first pivotal years. Human rights and democracy groups connected with secular and progressive elements in Afghanistan knew all too well that the removal of the Taliban didn't mean the vanishing of the jihadi forces from the country. Years of radicalization and indoctrination had created a vast web of Islamist networks, embedded within tribal clusters, mostly in the Pashtun south. There were many knots to unravel.

The Taliban was still omnipresent in the country and across the borders in Pakistan. These jihadi militias were kept in check by the presence of NATO forces but couldn't be isolated and reduced in size unless the democracy forces could spread across the country. But those forces were too weak to move forward, especially since the United States needed to use them to contain the Taliban. Obviously, the tribal and bureaucratic leadership weren't enthusiastic about the growth of democracy and secular forces. Washington had to give priority to traditional forces over the much more modest progress of democracy groups. So, the mostly corrupt political elite stayed in power for eight more years, standing against the Taliban but blocking the liberal element.

It has been clear to me since 2002 that unless the United States moves beyond the status quo and aggressively backs the Afghan democrats, the Taliban will gradually erode the balance and threaten the country again.

I conducted several briefings with lawmakers both in Washington and in Paris about focusing support on NGOs, starting with a massive campaign to empower teachers across the United States. As of 2004, I began helping in forming a coalition of Middle Eastern American groups supportive of a cultural revolution in the region, particularly in Afghanistan. I argued forcefully that a democracy movement must be the strategic response to jihadism. The Bush administration was derailed by many in its own bureaucracy who advised otherwise. In 2007 and 2008 I attended two meetings at the White House sponsored by the National Security Council. The meetings were dedicated to brainstorming with outside experts and intellectuals, and I found myself in a tiny minority calling for a proactive prodemocracy engagement, while the majority of participants opposed this idea. A partnership with democracy advocates was what the president initially called for, and very few in his own government followed or even understood this strategy. The bureaucracy's advisors, particularly those at the State Department, objected to a push for democratic changes. These academics argued that it would be seen as American involvement in Muslim affairs. This was exactly the argument of the Taliban, often aired on al Jazeera. It was disturbing to hear the Taliban's stance adopted by U.S. advisors.

Something was utterly wrong in Washington. The real battle for Afghanistan's democracy was in fact fought within the Beltway between the aides of the president and his supporters on the one hand, and the mass of apologists festering in government bureaucracies on the other. The United States handed victory to the Taliban by not extending support to the anti-Taliban, prodemocracy, progressive elements in Afghan society, instead heeding the advice of the oil-producing regimes.

It was clear that while U.S. forces have militarily defeated the Taliban regime and maintained a space for freedom for over eight years, little was strategically done to back the rise of democracy forces in the country. Religious liberties groups such as Freedom House's Religious Freedom Center[13] criticized the post-Taliban government of President Hamid Karzai for not defending secular rights and for allowing Sharia courts to survive. The case of Abdul Rahman was a serious warning. An Afghan citizen who converted to Christianity and was charged with rejecting Islam, Rahman faced execution under Sharia law unless he reconverted.[14] Because the political changes essential to counter jihadism were not seriously implemented by the Bush administration, democratic culture in Afghanistan didn't move forward at the pace needed to confront the fundamentalists.

Afghan Human Rights Entities

Afghanistan's capacity to absorb democracy has been questioned by apologist lobbies in the West criticizing U.S. and allied efforts to spread democracy. In fact, these lobbies were acting on behalf of the interest of the Islamists and the authoritarian regimes in the region that feared that an Afghan success in democratization would eventually shatter their own bastions. Because I witnessed the rise of a democracy-seeking group in Afghan society, I am convinced, not just theoretically but also practically, that the advance of democratic culture is a matter of education and is a war of ideas. If we support those who wish to advance it, they can expand; and of course if we do not support them, ignore them, or worse, cut deals with the totalitarians, Afghan society will lose the opportunity to move toward liberty and pluralism. There are continuing human rights efforts in Afghanistan. Some are efficient and others are not, but they exist and need to be reinforced. More important are the democracy activists and movements. They are the hope for democracy in that part of Middle Earth, and they should be considered the prime allies of the free world in Afghanistan. Their mission is difficult but unavoidable, and their message is clear: It is either us or the Taliban.

In a conference on democracy, human rights, and terrorism organized in Prague in 2007 for worldwide dissidents, I heard Afghan participants urging the international community to hasten the support to their NGOs. Many women attended the conference. They are at the heart of the freedom movement in Afghanistan and are also the prime targets of the Taliban. The United Nations Assistance Mission in Afghanistan (UNAMA) was established in March 2002 by UN Security Council Resolution 1401 following the Bonn Agreement of December 2001 to coordinate international efforts in supporting elections. But the Taliban tried to discourage popular participation in presidential and provincial council elections, including those in August 2009. Threats of violence were accompanied by publications in several languages questioning the legitimacy of elections. The jihadists organized attacks by rocket and mortar fire.[15]

In addition, the Afghanistan Independent Human Rights Commission (AIHRC) worked to promote respect for and understanding of human rights, prevent systematic violations of human rights, strengthen civil society activists and human rights defenders, and encourage law enforcement organizations to implement human rights international rules and standards in Afghanistan.[16] Amnesty International's 2009 report referred to "terrorism by Taliban of millions of inhabitants, mostly in the south," while Human Rights Watch in its

2008 report summarized the "threats facing human rights defenders, women, children, journalists, and civilians in Afghanistan." Women's rights groups such as RAWA and Afghan Women's Network (AWN) and the NGO Rights in Practice, which are battling the menacing Taliban, fear not only the return of the Islamist militia but the deeply rooted antiwomen practices in the ruling Afghan institutions. Individual human rights leaders such as Sima Samar are struggling within society to keep schools and clinics for Afghan women and girls open in response to the Taliban's laws prohibiting education for girls for more than eight years.

Obama's Retreat from Democracy in Afghanistan

With the election of Barack Obama in 2008, a new American approach to the battlefield of Afghanistan may constitute a severe setback to democratization efforts in that country, including greater challenges to the cautious rise of women's movements.

While the Bush administration supported democratization and saw its efforts sunk by its own bureaucracy, the Obama administration reshaped the previous policies altogether. By 2009, the policy of standing with and supporting democracy groups as they struggle against jihadists and authoritarian regimes was abandoned. The change was described as "distinguishing between Taliban and al Qaeda," meaning the fight against the "terrorists," led by Bin Laden, remains a U.S. policy, but the struggle against the Taliban can be amended.[17] In his speech at West Point on December 1, 2009, outlining America's new strategy in Afghanistan, President Obama rejected the idea of "decade-long nation building" and suggested the notion of partnering with those in the Taliban who would "accept human rights."[18] However, jihadists who accept equal rights of women and minorities aren't Taliban anymore. The Obama administration is seeking to find sympathizers among the Taliban to settle the crisis in the country, and believes in the potential of engaging the jihadi militia in negotiations to join the government, or form a government. The removal of General Stanley McChrystal in 2010 and his replacement by General David Petraeus won't change the Obama administration's determination to eventually engage the Islamists, and the Taliban in particular.

Under the current administration there is a real possibility of a strategic defeat for democracy forces in Afghanistan. The current attitude in the U.S. government may lead to an unprecedented oppression of Afghan civil society if the Taliban are re-empowered. Although the general retreat of the Obama administration from supporting democracy in Middle Earth is not exclusive to Afghanistan, the strategy used to defeat the menace hovering over the heads of women, youth, artists, minorities, intellectuals, and liberals in that country will make or break that country's future.

Taliban Strategic Threat to Democracy in the Region

Currently out of power in Afghanistan, the Taliban is still a threat to that country and to its neighbors, starting with Pakistan. If this radical Islamist militia seizes the country, either partially or fully, it would crush the nascent democratic movement. Not only would Afghan females and youth be brutalized, but their sisters and brothers in Pakistan would also feel the wrath of terror and oppression. As I stated in briefings to the majority party at the European Parliament in December 2009 and testified to the U.S. Congress in November 2009 and March 2010, the Taliban nightmare in Middle Earth is at a crossroads. Either the international community empowers the democratic resistance in Afghanistan to confront and reverse the jihadi threat, or a new dark age will engulf that part of the world.

The confrontation between freedom and the Caliphate will be decided in many places, but Afghanistan's battle will be one of the most decisive.

7.

Mesopotamia Rises

In my appearances on NBC, Fox News, CNN, and Arab TV during the fiery media debates surrounding the U.S. invasion of Iraq and the deposing of Saddam Hussein, I argued that the United States and the international community not only had the right to bring down the Baath regime in Baghdad, but had the duty to do so. My position was definitely different from that of most commentators. I argued forcefully that by the principles of international humanitarian law we were wrong not to intervene, and that we were very late in recognizing that obligation. Evidently, this position didn't register in the minds of either camp involved in the debates. The Bush administration's core argument for action was that Saddam's regime had built weapons of mass destruction that were a threat to U.S. national security. Bush's critics, a sea of domestic, European, and Arab detractors, responded that America didn't have the right to unilaterally wage war against a sovereign country and bring down its legitimate government without a direct threat.

I rejected both arguments, one as too weak and the other as too irresponsible. The Saddam Hussein regime had to be removed on the grounds of mass abuse of human rights, ethnic cleansing, and genocide. Democracies had the moral obligation to assist civil society in Iraq. It became the international community's duty to step in after the Baathist regime gassed its own Kurdish citizens in Halabja, massacred its own Shia citizens in the south, and invaded a neighboring country and tortured its population. In my view Saddam should have been taken down in 1991, or at least in the early 1990s. The advocates of regime change in 2003 were late and those who criticized them were morally wrong. The essence of the battle for Iraq is about basic

freedoms, and Iraq's future will be decided by the success or failure
of democratic forces in its own society.

Having grown up in Beirut, I had an early understanding of the
brutality of the Baath regime in Iraq and the need of Iraqis to free
themselves from the tyranny of Saddam Hussein. The oppression in
Iraq was not unique in the region, but it was singular in its nightmarish, violent assault on millions of individuals. The Assyro-Chaldeans
are the descendants of the oldest population of Mesopotamia and
today, the oldest Iraqis. Reduced to minorities living mostly in the
mountainous region north of Kurdistan, and in some neighborhoods
of Baghdad, these Iraqi Christians were suppressed by the Caliphate
for centuries until the British arrived in 1919.

Ironically, with the eventual departure of the colonial power, the
Assyro-Chaldeans suffered from even worse Pan Arabist brutality
before the advent of the Baath regime in the mid-1960s. These native
populations were the victims of ethnic cleansing for decades and were
eventually reduced to only a few villages and streets. Even worse,
Iraq's ruling class was robbing them of their own history in the twentieth century. "The Baath Party, which claims to uphold Arabism,
has the audacity to assert that they are the descendants of Ninive,
Babylon, Kings Ashurbanipal and Hammurabi, and that great civilization which was destroyed by the Arab conquest they boast about,"
declared the survivors of these ethnic communities, dispersed across
the world, all the way to Chicago and Detroit.[1]

While still in my ancestral homeland, I met Iraqi political refugees
who had fled the brutality of the Baath Gestapo in the late 1960s.
Arab Sunnis and Shia, many of them writers, journalists, and activists, fled to Beirut, the Paris of the Middle East, and at the time a
haven for all opposition in the Arab world and beyond. Many of
these Iraqi refugees were the precursors of generations of citizens
who reached the West decades later to tell the story of a "Republic
of Fear."[2] The tales of horrors recounted by the Iraqi exiles in Beirut
preceded what Americans and Europeans would learn many years
later. The weight of their testimony piled up with the sea of reports
on abuse by refugees from Egypt, Syria, the Arabian Peninsula,
Libya, and other areas in the region.

I discovered details of Saddam Hussein's killing machine from two
peculiar sources during the 1980s. A number of Lebanese journalists
worked for or with Iraqi state media both in Baghdad and in various

other capitals. Their knowledge of how the intelligence services went after the regime's opponents was extensive. These journalists, whose position between the Arab world and the free West allowed room for maneuver and travel, had saved a number of people pursued by the Iraqi Mukhabarat. But the most sophisticated look inside the Saddam machine came through a number of Lebanese politicians and diplomats who traveled to Saddam's palaces and spent time with the dictator and his aides before coming back home to Beirut to share their incredible stories.

The Unachieved Symphony

Desert Shield, the buildup of U.S.-led forces to expel Iraqi troops from Kuwait during the fall of 1990, took place as I was leaving Beirut. Eastern Europe's revolutions were shattering totalitarian regimes, but authoritarian powers were expanding in the Middle East. Saddam's tanks stormed through Kuwait, triggering one of the largest mobilizations in modern history to liberate the Kuwaitis. Assad's tanks invaded Lebanon's last free enclave, and not only did the international community not attempt to stop the invasion or even condemn it, but U.S. diplomats actually praised it. It was odd to see how the Lebanese were ignored as they were invaded while the Kuwaitis were rescued by forces from all over the world. Well, it was all about oil, wasn't it? I watched Desert Storm unfolding on CNN, a phenomenon never seen before: an instant war on cable. The most powerful dictatorship in the region faltered as the coalition moved forward, thrusting through lines of Soviet-built armor.

More important in historical terms was the silence of Moscow, even as its ally was being defeated. In previous wars in 1967, 1973, and 1982, the Soviets had always condemned the aggressor against their customers, then quickly replenished the arms reserves of Egypt, Syria, or the PLO. By spring 1991, times had changed and the dictatorships of the region couldn't count on the unconditional support of the USSR, which was plagued with its own domestic issues. This was the window of opportunity eagerly anticipated by millions of people in the region.

The symphony of liberation could have begun in Iraq and spread across the region. It should have started with the downfall of the Baath regime in Baghdad, and with the establishment of a democracy.

As Stormin' Norman Schwarzkopf was battling through the southern desert of Iraq, the vision of Europe's liberation in World War II came to mind. One of the worst dictators of the region, who, by breaking international laws, had invited a regime change, was being toppled. Could this be the gate from which democratic change would come to the oppressed people of Iraq and beyond? The Nazis' horrors, followed by the crumbling of Hitler, eventually brought democracy to Germany; the aggressive militaristic regime of Japan triggered the saga that ended in a pluralist system in Tokyo; and last but not least, Mussolini's fascist rule ended with democracy over the Tiber. Would the bloody Baath regime in Baghdad invite the free world to do the same and install a democracy in the middle of the Arab world? Had the international community, led by the United States, reacted against the gross human rights violations by helping democracy take root on the Tigris and Euphrates, coalition forces would have moved forward from south to north in 1991, all the way to Baghdad, and toppled the dictatorship.

Saddam shattered international law by abruptly invading Kuwait and torturing its citizens, after having abused Iraq's people for years. On the grounds of Halabja's gassing and the mass killing of Shia, the regime was due for removal. The Kuwait invasion gave liberal democracies an unexpected opportunity to save a population longing for freedom in Iraq, and the regional and international context couldn't have been more appropriate for it. France, Britain, and many other Western partners were fighting on the ground. Saudi Arabia and other Arabs initially called on Washington for help to push Saddam back, and the United Nations authorized the action. Moscow was busy on its own path of reforms, and Israel acquiesced to U.S. demands for nonretaliation despite missile attacks on Tel Aviv. And to top it all off, Syria's Assad pledged to help against Saddam, and Tehran wouldn't have rushed to help just a few years after Saddam's forces had massacred half a million Iranians.

History couldn't have offered a better alignment for democracy to take root in one of the darkest places in the region: Iraq. All it would have taken were two things: a push by coalition forces along the highways across southern and central Iraq to reach Baghdad, and a call by the free world on the peoples of Iraq to rise up.

A U.S.-led march to Saddam's bunker in spring 1991 would have been unstoppable. However, the hope that the United States and its allies would finish the job in a few weeks and open a breach in the dark ages of Iraq was quickly shattered. Had the coalition removed Saddam as a natural and legitimate response to his regime's invasion of Kuwait and the massacres against Iraqis, under UN auspices, the start of Middle Eastern democracy would have been possible ten years before 9/11 and in the wake of the Soviet collapse and Eastern European democratic revolutions. The opportunity of the century was within our reach, but it was missed. Why?

It was missed because of the first manifestation of the brotherhood against democracy in the post-Soviet era. While the rest of the Arabs urged the United States to intervene against the Iraqi invasion and liberate Kuwait, the Arab League wasn't ready to accept a regime change in an Arab capital. The reason they opposed the legitimate removal of an aggressive dictator was a fear of democracy. The idea of toppling Saddam and replacing him with another authoritarian figure was rejected by the West. Liberal democracies couldn't install a dictator to replace a dictator. Stunningly, both the Sunni Arab leaders, with the exception of Kuwait, and their competitors from the Shia axis, including Iran and Syria, came together to dissuade Washington from pursuing Saddam all the way to his bunker. Once out of Kuwait, the Arab leader was again one of them. He was indeed brutal against his own people, but so were most of his colleagues in Middle Earth. To be fair, the Iraqi Baathist leader was at least open in his ambitions, unlike many around him. Saddam was a beast, but his peers were hyenas.

Iraq in the 1990s

Left to the revenge of Saddam, Iraqi populations entered the ultimate stage of oppression for more than a decade. President Bush and Prime Minister John Major decided to enforce two no-fly zones, in the north above the Kurdish population and in the south over the Shia populations. Both groups heeded the call to rise against the regime as coalition forces were pushing Iraqi forces out of Kuwait and pounding the Republican Guard from the air. Kurds and Shia believed that their D-Day was imminent. A majority of Iraqis, including many Sunnis opposed to the Baath, were readying themselves for a new dawn in the country, but that hope was stolen from them on the day of the cease-fire in 1991.[3]

Luckily for the Kurds, they established their own military force in the north and were able to survive under the allied-enforced no-fly zone. The Kurdish areas were not exactly a democratic haven yet, but they'd obtained their basic liberty from the totalitarian Pan Arabist power in Baghdad. The Baathist forces couldn't deploy in their enclave anymore. In the south the Shia were out of luck. Living on flatlands and unable to reach out to the outside world, they were quickly subdued by Saddam's helicopter assaults.

Iran, Prepare for Iraq

The strategic mistake in 1991, made under pressure from oil interests, would lead to ten more years of oppression against Iraqis. Saddam's survival gave him the opportunity to strike back against the Shia in the south, and in the following years, tens of thousands of Iraqi Shia were massacred by the Baathist agencies while thousands fled into exile, many into Iran. The Iranian regime hosted them, organized them, and readied them for a return to their country when circumstances allowed, trained to install a similar Islamic Republic in Iraq. The Iranian infiltration of Iraq continues to this day. Even when the Baath collapsed in 2003 the oppression continued.

The most important single political party in the Iraqi Parliament was created in Tehran in 1982, by a fatwa from Ayatollah Khomeini. The SCIRI—Superior Council for the Islamic Revolution in Iraq—was rebranded in 2008 as SIIC, the Superior Islamic Iraqi Council. Initially, like Hezbollah of Lebanon, SCIRI was organically linked to the Iranian regime. The military wing of SCIRI/SIIC became the so-called Ninth Badr Brigade, and later entered Iraq as a Shia militia before it transformed itself as a distinct political force in the current Iraqi Parliament. "Badr" was created within the Iranian regime's Revolutionary Guard, the Pasdaran, as an armed wing of both the SCIRI and the Dawa Party, one of the oldest and most radical Islamist organizations of Shia background. The ideological force behind all Shia jihadi networks in the region was indeed the Dawa Party, a Shia equivalent of the Sunni Muslim Brotherhood, Hezbul Tahrir, and the Wahabis. From its original birthplace in southern Iraq it spread to Iran and Lebanon. After the Khomeinist revolution in Tehran in 1979, Shia jihadism's center was based in the Iranian regime, but naturally the ayatollahs wanted to conquer the launching pads of the ideological movement in Mesopotamia. Iran's plan for Iraq was as old as Iran's revolution, which was inspired by ideologues from southern Iraq. In short, while Saddam's Baath represented fascism as produced by Pan Arab Sunni leaders who claimed secularism, Khomeinism in Iran and Iraq represented a jihadi type of fascism.

Since its inception, the Iranian regime has worked tirelessly to seize the parts of Iraq with a Shia majority, which in fact was one of the reasons Saddam preemptively invaded Iran in 1980. Khomeini wanted to remove Saddam and impose a jihadi Shia regime on Iraq. The unfortunate Iraqi citizens were subjected to Baathist Sunni authoritarianism under Saddam before being targeted by Salafists in the Sunni areas and Khomeinists in the Shia areas, both with a totalitarian outlook. The democracy groups in Iraqi civil society after 1991 didn't have an opportunity to free themselves from either dragon.

Iran's regime proceeded in the 1990s to prepare SCIRI, Badr, and other groups and train them in the Ahwaz region, the predominantly Arab province of Iran, for the day of their "return" to Iraq. Since the 1980s, Iran's regime had hosted Iraqi and Lebanese Shia Islamist groups and equipped them to redeploy inside their countries for future takeover. The Hezbollah and SCIRI "admission test" consisted of suicidal terrorist attacks on Western military forces in 1982 in Lebanon and 1983 in Kuwait. In the international terrorist arena, the IRGC (Iranian Revolutionary Guard Corps) assigned military operations in Iraq and the Gulf to SCIRI, and Hezbollah was assigned global terrorist operations, as Lebanese are far more ubiquitous than Iraqis.

The Bush Decision on Iraq

As in 1991, removing the oppressive regime was the key to liberating the people of Iraq and paving the way for freedom and reform in the region. But the brotherhood against democracy—Qatar's rulers, Sudan's regime, the Muslim Brotherhood, hard-core Wahabis, and Lebanon's Hezbollah—was still protecting its "virtual Caliphate" and immense interests. After defeating al Qaeda in Tora Bora, the United States and its allies needed to continue to press on with counterjihadism and push for democratization. As I stated earlier, the battle for freedom in Middle Earth didn't have to be a result of the collapse of one specific regime; it was an issue of principle. After 9/11 and the removal of the Taliban, the free world should have developed a doctrine on freedom and acted upon these principles.

I briefed lawmakers on the necessity of winning a war of ideas first, or at least as long as the fight against terror was being waged. It was crucial that the public in free countries understand the big picture and support it. Forces for democracy in the region needed to be in full partnership before Washington could jump into action anywhere in the region. It would have been advisable to spend more time and resources after the removal of the Taliban on a worldwide mobilization targeting two goals: a mass campaign against al Qaeda and the jihadists from all backgrounds, Salafists, and Khomeinists and a massive outreach to the democracy forces in the region before engaging in the battlefield, including Iraq.

A better plan than a full-fledged invasion of Iraq or the removal of any other regime was to develop support for all resistance movements against the oppressive regimes. It was more legitimate and strategically better to move in horizontally instead of vertically, to engage with and support the populations already resisting and ready to escalate their opposition. I called for supporting the Darfur resistance, the Lebanese opposition against Syrian occupation, the Iranian reformers and minorities, and last but not least the Kurds and Shia of Iraq, as long as they sought help and wished to use it benevolently. It would have been more effective to side with the democracy and resistance movements instead of entering the fray and fighting for full regime change based on uncertain claims of WMDs and in the absence of a clear alliance with the alternative democratic forces.

The Bush administration's advisors on Iraq, as many writings and debates have shown, wanted to invade for many reasons, one of which was a democratic dividend. Attracted by promises made by Iraqi exile Ahmad Chalabi, the Iraq National Council, and others, the Bush strategists hoped the downfall of Saddam would lead to the rise of an alternative democracy, even if it was weak and shy at first. What they failed to realize was that Chalabi and other Shia exiles were aligned with Iran-based Iraqi exiles, and the alternative to Saddam's Baath in the Shia majority areas would be sympathetic to Iran instead of to a new pluralist democracy in Baghdad. To avoid falling into bad alliances that would lead to Iranian and Syrian influence over a post-Saddam Iraq, I suggested that U.S. and international action be limited at first to the established no-fly zones to support the Kurds and empower democracy forces in the Shia south. But the architecture I was advocating was too complex to satisfy the enormous geopolitical designs at work in Washington. My suggestions assumed the existence of a war room in America that understood the nuances of Levantine labyrinths and realized what the United States was about to engage in and engage against. Many analysts discovered years later how unprepared the administration was, not only in strategizing for a war in the region, but also in fighting the ideological battle against the jihadists and authoritarians. It's no wonder that eight years later a majority of Americans still don't understand the threat and the type of confrontation their country has been engaged in since 2001.

In the end, U.S. and British forces thrust through the Iraqi armed forces, making their way to Baghdad, with the American military machine using shock and awe in classic warfare. By the end of April, the Baathist structures of power were destroyed, but the next enemy of a potential democracy was up and running, striking at the coalition and civil society as well.

Iran's Shadow Invasion

A powerful account of the history of Iran's preparation for its own "invasion" of Iraq is outlined in *The Hidden Invasion of Iraq*, by Paulo Casaca, a European Parliament member from the Socialist Party.[4] Casaca was the chairman of the European Parliament delegation to NATO and a leading activist on behalf of democracy in Iraq and the region. According to his findings, the main opposition organization in Iran, the PMOI (known also as Mujahideen Khalq), presented to U.S. authorities comprehensive and exhaustive information on Iran's organization in Iraq, including a list of more than thirty thousand Iraqis on the Iranian payroll. Tehran was able to widely penetrate the Shia areas and with the support of Kurdish militias occupying territory close to Iran, secure limited influence in the north. Tehran and Damascus, fearing the blooming of a democracy between them, were eager from the start of the U.S. invasion to kill the political consequences of the departing one-party rule and a possible multiparty system. Bashar Assad and his Baathist command instinctively feared that the coalition would continue its campaign into Syria. Although policy planners in Washington were barely able to digest what their mighty military machine had achieved in thirty-two days and weren't planning on crossing the border to the east of Iraq, there was a prevalent sentiment in Damascus and in Tehran that this could happen, particularly if uprisings exploded in those countries. The dictatorships surrounding Iraq were extremely nervous about the next stage and moved quickly to preempt what Americans and Europeans had not even contemplated.

The Syro-Iranian axis waged an all-out terror war beginning in late April 2003. While seasoned observers in the region understood the big picture, neither the Bush administration nor Great Britain seemed to comprehend the forthcoming wild counteroffensive waged by the Syro-Iranian axis and al Qaeda in combined, but not coordinated efforts. Once again, the body of experts upon which Western democracies were relying betrayed their decision-makers.

That summer I participated in several meetings called by military and foreign policy offices in Washington to discuss how best to help Iraqis absorb the change and help their country move forward. I was surprised by the relaxed and we-have-all-the-time-in-the-world attitude toward this enormous task. I called it *une cuture de lièvre* in reference to the fable of the tortoise and the hare.[5] Washington obviously seemed to be the hare and all of its enemies were supposed to be turtles. But as I analyzed the rapid moves of the Islamist and jihadist networks, often simply announced on al Jazeera, and the decision by the Syrian regime and the Khomenei circles in Tehran to break the fledgling democracy before it could take off, it seemed to me that the United States had become a tortoise and its foes were acting with the speed of hares. The rest was easy to project. America would deploy huge efforts in Iraq, with many lost lives and billions of dollars spent, but its enemies, particularly the Iranian-Syrian axis, would slow its speed. A fierce race had begun between the American Gulliver and the many jihadist Lilliputians.

The counterinvasion by Syria and Iran had several facets. Scores of Iraqi Baathists and jihadi fighters crossed the borders from Syrian territory into Iraq to wreak havoc on coalition and newly trained Iraqi forces, as well as civilians. Thanks to these porous borders, al Qaeda moved in and installed an emirate, headed at first by Abu Mas'ab al Zarqawi. The terror came mostly from Syria, but the stealthiest attacks, including assassinations and bombings, came from Iran's networks. Tehran was swifter than Syria in penetrating the various layers of Shia politics. Faster than any program backed by the American occupation, the Khomeinist web stretched throughout the land, seizing control and influence among clerics, political parties, and ministries. For five years, Syria maintained a lifeline to Sunni radical groups and Baathists, and Iran took care of penetrating the Shia areas. The intensity of Syro-Iranian efforts against democracy in Iraq was revealed by the fact that despite their distaste for al Qaeda, the two regimes allowed training and support for al Zarqawi, the most important leader of AQI (al Qaeda in Iraq).

In *The Hidden Invasion of Iraq,* Casaca describes behind-the-scenes maneuvering for a misguided U.S. invasion and occupation of Iraq through a very sophisticated set of actions. Among the Iranian manipulations were the stories on Iraq's nuclear plans, Chalabi's double-dealing with Washington and Tehran, insertion of pro-Iranian militias in towns and cities as U.S. troops were marching north, and scores of other activities. In short, under the direct administration of U.S. ambassador Paul Bremer, and later under Iraqi prime ministers Iyad Allawi, Ibrahim Jaafari, and Nuri al Maliki, the Iranian machine continued to expand inside the country. So, did democracy even partially take root inside Iraq at all after the fall of Saddam?

The Rise of Democracy Forces in Iraq

At present, the Iraq War has certainly produced the ferment of democratic culture and ingredients to affect the big picture in Middle Earth. Scholars and researchers will most likely establish that "generation democracy" will take longer to take root than the actual U.S. involvement. I believe it is a matter of time and international support. Had the coalition toppled Saddam in 1991 and begun working on democracy and pluralism then, Iraq's civil society would have been twelve years ahead by now; by 2003 Iraqis would have voted multiple times, Iran would have had less influence, al Qaeda would have been confronted with younger secular generations, and al Jazeera's message wouldn't have been influential. But the United States was pressured not to move forward in the early 1990s, so when it was forced to act in 2003, thirteen years had passed, and the obstructionist power had gained influence. In those years Iran's influence increased, Iraq's youth weren't being educated on democratic culture, and al Jazeera had been up and running since 1996.

The rise of democracy as a social phenomenon in Iraq, and in the region, for that matter, has been limited by the time available and by what was done to help it rise. The Obama administration's intellectuals, who led the opposition against Bush's freedom forward policy, claim that such movements grow by themselves. While it is true that ultimately they decide their own future, on the other hand their very existence at a particular time is the product of how much support they receive. Over the years, I've argued that democratic revolutions will happen eventually; the only question is when. If they are helped by circumstances or other societies, they will win faster. If not, the task may take a few more generations. The forces of obstruction want to delay these revolutions, but supporters of democracy in the free world can make a difference by supporting freedom.

In 2004, I was invited to join the team of the Foundation for the Defense of Democracies, based in Washington, D.C. It was a young NGO launched just a few weeks before 9/11 by former officials and public figures from both parties and independents, committed to counterterrorism and supporting democratic struggles around the world, particularly in the Greater Middle East. The group worked on reaching out to Iraqi voices to rapidly engage in democratization of the society from within. Although a small private-sector entity, FDD launched experimental democracy programs for Iraqi women, youth, and journalists. It was during that intense period of mobilization that I met a large number of Iraqi activists and intellectuals engaged in the long-term education of civil society in Iraq. The immediate goal was to use the precious space where U.S. and coalition forces defeated the Baathist military force and were containing the jihadists to link up with liberal and progressive elements in Iraq, so that a new generation of Iraqi democrats could form and expand on its own.

The U.S. government used its enormous resources—military, financial, and administrative—to maintain Iraq's infrastructure as best it could while attempting to find a consensus among the existing political forces, which, unfortunately, weren't completely devoted to pluralist democracy. There needed to be a new wave of younger elements capable of gradually moving up the sociopolitical ladder to become the bureaucrats, politicians, and new intellectuals—all committed to democracy. However, there was no war room within the Beltway dedicated to this specific mission. Billions of dollars were spent managing Iraq's political life and running it from election to election, from one constitutional draft to the next, but not a dollar was spent to produce a new Iraqi political culture.

The new democratic culture was being built by Iraqis inside the country and in the Diaspora, and by the small NGOs backing them. These were a very small piece of a complex machine of human rights activists, democracy educators, and journalists dispersed from Kurdistan to Basra, from Brussels to New York, all working to provide literature and support to those willing to educate Iraqis on democratic ideals. Most U.S. (and one might say Western) involvement in democracy building while confronting jihadi forces worldwide was heavily funded and poorly guided. Private-sector initiatives were generally better focused but extremely limited in resources. In Washington, for example, our foundation and similar entities counted on private donors to help fund a publishing program focusing on freedom in Iraq. Grants from the State Department to promote democracy were sometimes available, but a global strategy for a democratic revolution wasn't on the agenda. So, the battle for spreading democracy in Iraq was waged in a dispersed manner by a number of Iraqi NGOs operating in Iraq, a few NGOs in the West backing them, and a number of bureaucrats in Washington and Brussels who signed grants and reviewed reports but never designed an effort parallel to the military, economic, and diplomatic campaigns. Much will be written in the future about this phase in the post-Saddam era and the struggle for democracy, but today it is hard to see the whole picture and determine who the real activists and political leaders who are pushing for a true democracy are.

To be fair, a number of officials at the State Department, including Liz Cheney, the late Peter Rodman, and Mary Beth Long at the Pentagon, and Elliott Abrams and Juan Zarate at the National Security Council, understood the importance of a mass movement in favor of democracy as a long-term guarantee for success in Iraq and in the region. Among the many activists I met working on promoting democracy in Iraq were Zeinab Sueij, a Shia Iraqi woman leader who later ran for and won a seat in the Basra municipal elections; Tania Gilly, a Kurdish-American woman who ran for and won a seat in Iraq's first legislative elections in 2005; Kathrin Mikhail, an Assyrian who fought in the resistance against the Baath, and who is active in human rights causes; and Dr. Najmaldin Karim, president of the Washington Kurdish Institute, who was elected MP for Kirkuk in 2010. Interacting with dozens of veteran activists, young politicians, and exiles enlightened me about the real future of the sociopolitical map in Iraq.

Western-style democracy was not the immediate next step after liberation from an oppressive regime. The antidemocracy forces in Iraq were very powerful and were determined to sink the political process or take control of it. Unlike the situation in Afghanistan, there were various groups in Iraq ready to move on their own to establish democratic institutions and a free civil society. A larger educated and secular population made all the difference.

The political landscape in Iraq is complex. In the north, the Kurdish communities practiced some measure of representative democracy, by consensus between the Barzani and Talebani factions. Kurdish political forces pushed to build their own "ethnic democracy," not without significant problems, including marginalizing smaller minorities such as Assyrians, Turks, and Zaidis. The Kurds, however, wanted to participate in the greater Iraqi democracy that was being encouraged and shepherded by the United States. In the south, the Shia political forces also rushed to participate in the process. Most groups, including those returning from Iran, were quick to form parties, seek seats in the legislative branch, and grab as much power in the executive branch as possible. Shia political forces were diverse, as some smaller factions were genuinely looking toward a secular system, while others wanted to use the available structure to insert more Islamist policies. On the edges, a web of forces such as the Mahdi Army presented candidates and won seats but vowed to change the regime into a Khomeinist-type republic after the withdrawal of the "occupier." In the center, the Sunni communities were striving to adjust after having the upper hand under Saddam. Small factions joined the Baathist and jihadi insurgencies; larger groups formed Islamist parties; other traditionalist Pan Arabists joined the political process even though they were resentful of the Iranian backing of main Shia forces; and last but not least, a significant number of Sunni liberal groups started to form but were too small yet to affect the political culture. In addition to the three giants, Assyro-Chaldeans and other Christians formed their own multitude of parties, as did the Muslim Turkmen and Mazdeans.

After several years of both monitoring and participating in panels and debates on Arab media in the years following the invasion of Iraq, my global conclusions were clear: There are all sorts of Iraqi attitudes toward democracy, but the majority of the political players, including those who might turn against it later, have chosen the multiparty system. There is no way to return to the one-party system if Iraq is to remain a united country.

Additionally, among the political forces vying for power within the democratic context, there are those who are hard-core liberals and those who accept a minimal version of democracy. For example, the model for a hard-core democratic politician is elected legislator Mithal Allusi, who has been and continues to be persecuted for his rejection of all forms of authoritarianism and for his call for peace with Israel. He has suffered enormously for his views; his two sons were assassinated as he was traveling with them in Iraq. Allusi is the liberal figure of future Iraq. Among the Shia, former prime minister Iyad Allawi and Sayed Ayad Jamal Al-din are among the secular and democratic leaders. Prime Minister Nuri al Maliki, despite all the Iranian pressure, has developed an Iraqi Shia political identity, between Iran's rigid ideology and a real liberal democracy. In Sunni politics, liberals are forming pressure groups and expanding their influence, but they are far from tipping the scales in favor of pluralist culture. However, some politicians, including Vice President Tarik Al-Hashemi, defend the post-Saddam status quo. Ethnoreligious minorities such as Christians and Zoroastrians have a keen interest in promoting the widest democracy possible so that they can be part of it. Despite the small size of their voting bloc, it's better than nothing.[6]

Prodemocracy forces in Iraq face several combined challenges. First, Arabs, both Shia and Sunnis, have to accept the idea that Kurds are another ethnic group and have the right to develop autonomy and control over their resources. Second, Kurds have to accept the same idea when applied to the ethnic minorities living among them, such as Assyrians, Turkmen, and Zaidis, and grant them the same autonomy they received for Kurdistan. Shiites, who are about 60 percent of the population, will have to accept basic rights for the rest of the country's communities, and Sunnis will have to accept that the country is multiethnic and multireligious and cannot be absorbed by Sunni-inspired Pan Arabism or Salafism. These are only a few of the concessions that Iraqis will have to make to one another for democracy to defeat authoritarianism in the country. Some concessions are essential, as the foes of the Iraqi democratic revolution are numerous and still very strong.

Obstruction Forces

In Mesopotamia, in order for democracy to rise irreversibly, it will have to overcome the many forces obstructing its path. First and foremost is Iran's regime. Paulo Casaca, the leading MEP expert on Tehran's strategies in Iraq, argues that "the Khomeinists are betting on the takeover of the country after the complete withdrawal of U.S. forces: They are actively reorganizing its Shia followers, trying to convince them to gather into a single alliance." Casaca believes Prime Minister Maliki wants an Iraq aligned with Tehran, "but with a certain degree of autonomy, not quite an Islamist state, a somewhat different version of present-day Syria. Iran will certainly try to get a working arrangement with the most important Sunni confessional organization, the Islamic Party, and will do its best to crush both the independent-minded and prodemocratic Kurds and the democratic secular pro-Western forces gathered under the Iyad Allawi coalition."[7] In the Sunni areas, al Qaeda and the Salafi combat networks remain the most ferocious opponents to any form of democratic institution, on ideological grounds. The Saddam Baathists have mutated into two types: those who remain against democracy and those who have slowly accepted a pluralist country.

Outside Iraq, in addition to Iran's regime, other governing elites in the region aren't satisfied with the political process in Mesopotamia. Baathist Syria has pledged to kill the process via terrorism, and Baghdad's government has been accusing Assad's regime of backing the suicide bombers crossing the borders.[8]

Surprisingly, many in the West who are influenced by the region's authoritarian elites lend a hand to the obstructors of pluralism in post-Saddam Iraq. As a number of Iranian dissidents have affirmed, and according to Casaca, "Organizations like Human Rights Watch have been consistently and strategically biased in favor of Iran and against democratic forces in the region, like Israel or the Kurds, and were thus fundamental in justifying the Iranian control."

Post-Withdrawal

With the withdrawal of U.S. combat troops from Iraq in 2010, al Qaeda and Iran's regime resumed their terror assault on Iraq's government and civil society. Iraqi military loyal to the notion of an independent country and political forces opposed to jihadism and Baathism are now the bulk of the "resistance."

How to Help Iraqi Democracy?

Saddam's nightmare is behind the Iraqi people, but other nightmares are still hovering around this and the next generation. Iran's regime and its allies, Syria's regime, al Qaeda, and the remainder of Iraq's irreconcilable Baath remain imminent threats. General Petraeus's strategy is on the right course, but is four years too late to be effective. To help Iraqi democracy survive, the international community needs to shield the nascent political process from the two major threats—Iran from the east and Syria from the west. In June 2006, I presented a plan titled "Freedom Borders" to the U.S. Caucus on Counter Terrorism. In it, I proposed a redeployment of U.S. and coalition forces from urban areas to the countryside and to Iraq's eastern and western borders in order to block Iranian and Syrian intervention.

In addition, the international community must support the political process in Iraq, despite its failings, until a younger and newer generation of Iraqis can climb the ladder of sociopolitical power and move the country from the current transitional status to a functioning liberal democracy. Such a process won't be successful before a democratic revolution of ideas takes place in the country, within each community, and then across all communities. Iraq has liberated itself from just one layer of nightmarish dictatorship, but it still faces the danger of falling under at least two worse options: an Iranian Khomeinist province in the south and a Talibanlike power in the center. Freedom will be difficult to achieve, and what lie ahead are enormous sacrifices and terrors. During the legislative elections of 2010, the centrist, more secular coalition led by Iyad Allawi obtained the highest number of votes. Regardless of who will lead the country for the following decade, the forces of democratic change are on the rise in Mesopotamia. The future is wide open.

8.

The Cedars Revolution: The Battle over Free Lebanon

While the West was watching Afghans and Iraqis head to the polls after the fall of the Taliban and the Baath, many American and European critics of the freedom forward policy, obviously influenced by the antifreedom cartel in the region, claimed that the Bush administration was forcing democracy on nations that didn't want it. Fighting the rise of pluralist political processes with all their power, the brotherhood against democracy promoted the notion that America and its allies were imposing a political culture that was not accepted by Afghans and Iraqis. They omitted the point, of course, that it was the dominant elites who rejected the rise of liberal democracy, not the popular majorities. The "cartel" and its allies in the West argued that without military intervention in Iraq and Afghanistan, such elections wouldn't have taken place.

It was clear that without the removal of the oppressive Baath and Taliban by force, the two societies underneath would have been unable to access freedom. But they would have risen against the horrors of the totalitarian Pan Arabists and jihadists at some point in the future. However, other societies have demonstrated their readiness to rise and fight for liberty, even without the presence of foreign boots on the ground. All that was needed was a clear, unequivocal, steady position by the West regarding the right of these populations to liberate themselves and a moral commitment to help at some time when conditions called for it. That promise alone can fuel the deep forces of nations under oppression, and an unexpected leap of courage could happen. An example of such a nation, which was part of my younger life, embodied this reality: Lebanon.

The impact Lebanon's "Cedars Revolution" had on the psyches of many Americans and Europeans is by itself a major benchmark in U.S. and Western perception of the region's political culture. I personally witnessed this psychological shock from Washington to Brussels as I was shuttling between capitals to advocate the liberation of that little country from its occupiers between 2003 and 2005.

One scene I will always remember took place at the headquarters of MSNBC in Secaucus, New Jersey, where I served as one of the network's analysts on terrorism and Middle Eastern affairs. On February 15, 2005, the day after the assassination of former prime minister Rafiq Hariri, American and Western media were focused on the unusual images coming through satellites to newsrooms on both sides of the Atlantic. Thousands, then tens of thousands, and then hundreds of thousands of Lebanese citizens, mostly young boys and girls, had taken to the streets and were chanting anti-Syrian-occupation slogans with a passion unseen before. My colleagues were stunned. "Who are these people, who are these young men and women? There are thousands of them challenging the Syrian army and Hezbollah in chanting. They are so young, so energetic, and so colorful. Where did they come from?" Retired colonel Ken Allard, former dean of the War College, was in disbelief. He and retired colonel Jack Jacobs and retired lieutenant colonel Rick Francona, specialists in world conflicts and NBC correspondents for terrorism and military affairs, were in awe at seeing up to a million and a half people in a peaceful march through downtown Beirut, with signs in almost all languages, demanding the end of occupation and oppression and the rise of democracy and freedom. Jacobs raved about the beauty and energy of the demonstrations' younger women. "I bet you these girls of the revolution are the Taliban's nightmare and Hezbollah's real competitors," the Medal of Honor winner observed.

On Fox News, CNN, the BBC, and elsewhere the newsrooms seemed to be very much surprised. Our media elite, particularly since 9/11, and especially since the Iraq War, were convinced that the people in the region were averse to Western democracy, or to democracy, period. For years our foreign policy establishment claimed everything was fine in Lebanon and there was no need to remove the Syrian forces as long as the country's civil society was not demanding it. Then here we were in 2005 watching these events unfold in real time. A revolution was taking place in Beirut, more than one-third of the population was in the streets, and they were telling the world that they had had enough of oppression. In fact, this was a revolution in how revolutions were carried out. Alone and forgotten for more than a quarter-century, the Lebanese people were rising. Without a no-fly zone to protect them, like the Iraqi Kurds, or a military invasion to remove the oppressive ruling power, like Afghanistan and Iraq, finally a nation, small in size but culturally vibrant, showed the international community that revolt in Middle Earth was brewing. That revolt would explode on March 14, 2005.

Of all the Middle Eastern countries, Lebanon is the most complex in terms of socioethnic and political composition. Aside from Israel and to some extent Turkey, modern Lebanon has experienced significant levels of democracy in its political system since before the 1975 war, and its civil society has tasted and tested the democratic culture at various times and in different circumstances. It would take volumes to describe and analyze Lebanon's experience with the democratic phenomenon, but among all members of the Arab League, this country witnessed one of the earliest democratic revolutions, though the outcome of the uprising has not yet been decided. The highly publicized Cedars Revolution of 2005, which surprised the world and drew the attention of the international community in general and the United Nations in particular, has been fighting for survival since 2008.

The surge of a peaceful revolt in the midst of one of the most violent and prolonged wars in the region deserves to be considered the most advanced movement for freedom in the Middle East, even as the combined forces of jihadism and authoritarianism are currently circling this free enclave of democratic culture. This wasn't the first time in its history that Lebanon had produced a resistance to occupation and suppression. The scourge of invasions and revolts has plagued the country since antiquity.

Historical Background

Growing up in Beirut, I developed a keen interest in Lebanon's history. The unending war that ravaged the country compelled me to understand what it was in the country's genome that produced such a dizzying level of violence and intolerance between the warring factions. Syria's refusal to acknowledge the legitimacy of an independent "Lebanese Republic" since its inception in 1943 puzzled me.

Lebanon's special democracy in an Arab world mostly ruled by dictatorships and authoritarian regimes was unique. Unlike most Arab countries, Lebanon had known political campaigns, elections, parliamentary negotiations, government coalitions, and a vibrant free press—all unparalleled in the region. As with other oases of democracy, Lebanon's experiment with pluralism and liberties collapsed under the pressure of the regional authoritarian "Caliphate." However, major challenges to the brotherhood against democracy emerged. As assassinated Lebanese president Bashir Gemayel once claimed in a speech, "The Lebanese are at the same time the devils and the angels of this Orient." Probably a better description would have been that this was a land where hell and heaven met and fought: Oppression and liberty—this was the fault line between them.

Lebanese nationalists always consider their ancestors the first population having a recorded living history and civilization on the coasts of the eastern Mediterranean, mostly in the ancient Phoenician cities of Byblos, Tyr, Sidon, and Ugarit. The country's historians are proud to claim a Phoenician heritage, which has produced the alphabet, the earliest laws of the sea, and—some assert—the first consultative democracy, preceding those of Greece, in the senates of the city-states along the Lebanese coasts. Regardless of the historical debates, evidence tells us that for millennia the early inhabitants of Phoenicia, mostly from Aramaic, Amorite, and Canaanite ethnicities, adopted different forms of predemocracy institutions. Christianity spread very early on and by the fifth century, Christians inhabited the entire territory of today's Lebanon.

Over the following centuries, a mosaic of eastern Christian communities, including Maronites and Melkites, spread throughout the littoral and mountains. In the seventh century the forces of the Caliphate invaded from the south, conquering the coastal cities and the Bekaa plateau, and Arab populations began to settle these areas. Since the eighth century, the configuration of Lebanon has remained almost unchanged, consisting mostly of Christians in Mount Lebanon and Muslims in the lowlands. For seven centuries the *Marada*, a fighting force of the Maronites, resisted the armies of the Caliphate, maintaining a free enclave at the edge of the vast empire.[1]

After the fall of the Christian state of Mount Lebanon in the fourteenth century and the occupation by the Ottomans beginning in the sixteenth century, an autonomous principality survived in the mountains and valleys of Lebanon until European intervention formally established protection for Mount Lebanon's state in the nineteenth century. The new entity was called *Petit Liban* or Smaller Lebanon, as it predominantly covered the Christian majority of the mountain plus a minority of Druses. During World War I, the inhabitants of that small autonomous country were severely suppressed by the Turks; one-third of Mount Lebanon perished, one-third emigrated, and the last third formed the nucleus for a modern republic.

With the defeat of the Ottoman Empire in 1919, France was mandated to administer the area and proposed a gradual full independence for *Le Petit Liban*. The Christian politicians asked for more lands to be added to Mount Lebanon, and a Greater Lebanon was created in September 1920. It became a multiethnic and somewhat binational state, with Christian Lebanese looking toward the Mediterranean and Muslim Lebanese affiliated with the Arab world. After French rule ended in 1943, the new republic knew a golden age economically but was hit with a major crisis over its national identity, until the explosion of the 1975 war.

Lebanon's Peculiar Democracy

By 1943 Lebanon's precarious balance between Christians and Muslims and the quasidemocratic system that existed under Mount Lebanon's autonomy while an Ottoman Caliphate ruled the rest of the region had helped shape a constitutional democracy with sectarian representation. The president was a Maronite, the prime minister a Sunni, and the Speaker of the House a Shiite with the seats of the Parliament and all bureaucratic positions divided between religious communities. This undeclared "federal system" was unique in an Arab Muslim Middle East where countries were ruled by either Pan Arabist or Islamist authoritarians.

In 1945, Arab nationalists pressured the country into adhering to the Arab League, putting its international relations under the control of the organization of authoritarian regimes. In 1948 the Arab League dragged Lebanon into an unnecessary, decades-long war with Israel by forcing Lebanon to take hundreds of thousands of Palestinians fleeing the fight and instructing Beirut to keep this refugee population in a miserable state of limbo for many decades. "We had no reason to be in a war between the Arab regimes and Israel," the founder of the Lebanese University, erudite thinker Fuad Afram Bustany, told me in 1982.[2] Former president Charles Helou told me that in 1974 most Lebanese didn't want to be part of the Arab League or to enter the Arab-Israeli conflict. "It would give the regimes in the region a say over how we manage our democracy in Lebanon," said the former president, who had faced the first armed insurrection by Palestinian forces in 1968.[3]

In the Lebanon of the late 1960s and early 1970s, many criticized the "confessional regime," claiming it favored the Maronites and the Christians against the growing number of Muslims. The reality was that the republic was ruled by a gathering of political and economic elites from all communities, profiting immensely from Lebanon's free market and booming economy. Regardless of the debates about its uniqueness, the fact was that citizens voted freely for their municipal and legislative representatives, and liberty of expression was more or less protected. Had it not been for the decades-long campaigns by the Pan Arab and Islamist movements to shrink the precarious democracy, Lebanon might have gradually joined the club of Mediterranean democracies, an exception in the Arab-speaking world. Instead of becoming a half-Khomeinist country, the small republic could have fostered the democratic revolution in the region decades later. But the brotherhood against democracy since the late 1940s had been nervous about the emergence of the "Switzerland of the Middle East." Early on, the authoritarian regimes in Egypt, Iraq, and particularly Syria, as well as a horde of radical organizations in the region, pushed back against Beirut's pluralist model; after the Iranian revolution, Khomeinism crumbled the Lebanese democracy.

In 1958, Egypt's dictator, Gamal Abdel Nasser, backed an armed insurrection against the pro-Western government of Camille Chamoun, triggering the first short civil war. Lebanon's democracy survived, but the ability of the country to call for international help diminished and the influence of the surrounding authoritarian regimes in Lebanese affairs grew exponentially. Attacks by Palestinian organizations, later armed by the Syrian Baath and other regimes, including Libya and Iraq, against the Lebanese army and civilians escalated throughout the 1960s and early 1970s. Entire areas were swept from under the rule of law, citizens were kidnapped, and Lebanese democracy was gradually paralyzed. The institutions and the democratic culture of the country were crushed following several clashes with the armed terror groups funded by radical Arab regimes. The breakdown of the government led to the rise of militias in Christian and Muslim areas, leading the country to its second, longer, destructive civil war with massive foreign intervention.

On April 13, 1975, the unique democratic experiment of the republic of Greater Lebanon collapsed. The country was divided among warlords and militias and split into two major zones. One was under the control of the PLO and a combination of Islamist, Marxist, and Pan Arabist forces. In that part of the country democracy and freedom vanished and the dominant militias aiming at destroying the liberal Lebanese system took over. In the other part of the wartorn country, the Christian forces clung to multiparty democracy in theory, but in reality armed militias practiced authoritarian control. Liberal and moderate Muslims were crushed by layers of Islamist and Pan Arabist forces, while their counterparts in the Christian zones were ruled by right-wing warlords, setting the stage perfectly for action by Hafez Assad, the dictator of Syria.[4]

Syrian Invasion: 1976–90

After having armed multiple militias to overrun the Lebanese state and crumble the constitutional institutions, Syria's dictator sent in his regular troops in June 1976. In a speech a few weeks later, Assad openly admitted his regime backed the radical forces and that he considered Syria and Lebanon as "one people in two states."[5] No international coalition stepped in to resist the invasion, which would not be the case when the other Baathist dictator, Saddam Hussein, invaded Kuwait two decades later.

I witnessed the Syrian tanks deploy into my mother country and noted the checkpoints placed at crossroads. Not only had Lebanon's civil war shattered the country's unique democracy, but the Syrian forces crushed any possibility for freedom to reemerge before the Cedars Revolution thirty-five years later. The Baathists dominated the mostly Muslim areas and a few conquered Christian districts, creating an oppressive layer cake topped by the Syrians, including all types of radical forces, such as Palestinian, Lebanese, and, as of 1980, the Iranian-backed Hezbollah. Democracy in Syrian-controlled Lebanon had virtually no chance of survival.

There was hope, though, in the rhetoric of what became known

as East Beirut: promise of a future return of freedom once the Syrian and other occupations were lifted. The Christian forces would
be unified by Phalangist military commander Bashir Gemayel and
rebranded the "Lebanese Forces." This "Christian resistance" had its
authoritarians, mostly among the Phalangists, and its liberals, such as
the followers of President Chamoun, and a number of intellectuals,
including former president of the UN General Assembly Charles
Malek and intellectual Fuad Bustany. These forces were supported
by a coalition of political parties whose agenda included the formation of a federal and pluralist Lebanon. In short, authoritarians ruled
East Beirut but its official narrative remained attached to liberal
democratic principles, while Baathist, Pan Arabist, and jihadist forces
dominated West Beirut, leaving no space for pluralism.

During Syria's partial occupation of Lebanon between 1976 and
1990, I had the opportunity of working with many politicians and
intellectuals and then forming my own school of thought within the
limits of the freedom that I could enjoy. The question during the
Lebanon war was, with which side do you stand? Many argued that
democracy was crushed in both camps, so if you favored freedom on
either side you were marginalized. It is true that the dominant forces
in West and East Beirut prevented the rise of democracy, but individuals and groups fought diligently from within their communities
to expand the struggle for liberty. If you were born and raised in the
Christian communities, you would naturally be inclined to defend the
ethnic survival of that group. The difference was that while in East
Beirut, the long-term goal of most political forces was to free Lebanon from Syrian, Iranian, and PLO forces and return to a pluralist
democracy, the long-term goal of dominant forces in West Beirut was
to replace the liberal republic of 1943 with ominous ideologies such as
Baathism, Pan Arabism, communism, or later, jihadi Islamism.

In the darkest days of the Lebanese conflict, defenders of democracy faced a tough path: resisting the Syrian-controlled and Iran-
backed forces from East Beirut, only to struggle within the "free
areas" against authoritarianism and fascism. This was what many prodemocracy groups based in the free Christian areas chose to do, while
liberals caught under PLO and Syrian domination in the rest of Lebanon had to wait for many years before a national revolution against the
Syrian occupation would open the door for them to rise again.

In 1977 a number of villages in southern Lebanon formed a local force opposed to the Palestinian militias and the pro-Syrian forces. Isolated from the free areas and the rest of the world, the southern enclave had no choice but to seek help from bordering Israel. As a result, the Free Lebanon Army, led by Major Saad Haddad, which was later renamed the South Lebanon Army (SLA), was branded by the pro-Syrian forces and Hezbollah as the "agents of Israel." Between 1978 and 1982 a raging war took place between the Syrian forces and their allies and the Lebanese forces under the command of Bashir Gemayel. The latter was pro-West and sought an alliance with Israel, which invaded from the south in 1982 all the way to Beirut. At one point the Syrians were on the verge of being ejected from Lebanon, but President Assad, a shrewd strategist, defeated his enemies.

In September 1982, days after having been elected president, Gemayel was killed and replaced by his brother Amine, who was more conciliatory toward Syria. One year later Hezbollah bombed U.S. Marine and French barracks, forcing the multinational force to leave the country. Gradually, the Syrians led offensives and pushed the East Beirut Christian forces back, cornering them in a small enclave. Incredibly, the last pocket of resistance split during 1990 in a devastating civil war between the Christian militia led by Samir Geagea and the Lebanese army led by General Michel Aoun.

While the free enclave fought internally and the West worried about Saddam's invasion of Kuwait, Assad proposed a Machiavellian deal to Washington: I'll side with you to kick Iraq out of Kuwait but my prize is Lebanon. He indicated his terms to Secretary of State James Baker in September 1990. The United States, under pressure from the oil-producing regimes in the region, nodded, and on October 13 of that year the T-62 tanks of Assad rolled through the free enclave of Lebanon, ending a fifteen-year-old war. But his invasion also ended the chances for democratic resurgence in both East and West Beirut. The entire country fell under the Baathist yoke. I left Lebanon on October 24, 1990, only a few days after the assassination of liberal politician Danny Chamoun and his wife. The trail of terror began then, and it would last another fifteen years.

Syrian Occupation: 1990–2005

In a matter of weeks the Syrian Mukhabarat took control of the entire country with the exception of the southern enclave of the SLA under Israel's control. It would take another ten years for the patient Assad and his Iranian allies to complete their full domination of Lebanon by forcing Israel to withdraw to the international border and dismantling the SLA. The first ten years of the complete Syrian occupation of Lebanon (1990–2000) are known as the darkest age in Lebanon's modern history. The republic's officials, from top to bottom, from president to bureaucrats to officers, were controlled by Damascus. A Vichylike state was established in Beirut under the tight control of Syria's "Gestapo," headed for many years by General Ghazi Kanaan. During this dark decade all-out oppression struck all those who opposed Syria's occupation. Within the Christian communities, defeated militarily in 1990, the level of suppression was the highest, with hundreds of activists and ordinary civilians arrested, beaten, and tortured. Many were imprisoned in Syria.[6] Young men and women frequently disappeared from their homes without a trace, and all media were closely monitored. The democracy movement was crushed across all the diverse communities in Lebanon. The resistance to the occupation, however, never really died.

In the 1990s, the followers of Lebanese army general Michel Aoun and supporters of various ex–Lebanese Front groups, such as the Guardians of the Cedars, were forced underground or into exile. In 1991, the Syrian regime imposed a Soviet-style "Cooperation and Brotherhood Treaty" on Beirut, which granted Syrian intelligence and Hezbollah the freedom to operate in Lebanese territories. That year all militias, with the exception of Iranian-backed forces and the radical Palestinian organizations, were disarmed. The entire country was at the mercy of a Syro-Iranian regime. In 1994, Samir Geagea was accused of several crimes and jailed, and his movement, the "Lebanese Forces Party," was disbanded.

By mid-decade, all real opposition to the Syrian-controlled regime had been dismantled. Some student demonstrations took place sporadically with little or no national support. In the Diaspora, supporters of exiled leader Michel Aoun and jailed commander Samir Geagea, as well as many independent activists, organized a core opposition, but had little effect on the international community. In southern Lebanon, the Israelis maintained a so-called security zone under the South Lebanon Army (SLA) led by General Antoine Lahad. The SLA controlled 10 percent of Lebanon's territories and was faced by the full force of Hezbollah and its allies.

Gradually, the Syro-Iranian alliance pushed back against the southern enclave, until Israeli prime minister Ehud Barak decided in 2000 to withdraw from the security zone and dismantle the South Lebanon Army. On May 23 of that year, Hezbollah forces reached the international borders, and Syria obtained full and unchallenged control of Lebanon. The oppression of the Lebanese increased exponentially, as no force challenged the occupiers. But from extreme suppression arose a movement of protest that developed into a revolt.

The Road to the Revolt: 2000–2005

Syria's dictator, Hafez Assad, passed away in June 2000, still at the helm of the domination of Lebanon. The Baath machine immediately replaced him with his son Bashar. The change from father to son gave the anti-Syrian voices in Lebanon a small opening to begin their mild criticism of the Syrian occupation. Among the first to publish opposition articles in the country was Gebran Tueni, the publisher of the daily *Al Nahar*. On September 20, the Council of Maronite Bishops issued a statement calling for withdrawal of Syrian forces and the release of prisoners. Gradually the Maronite patriarch and a number of supporters raised their voices against the Baathist dominance of the country. Student demonstrations escalated and security forces were sent to campuses. In the Diaspora where exiled groups had mobilized since the late 1990s, the lobbying of legislatures and the United Nations increased. Successive Lebanese governments, acting on behalf of Syria internationally, tried unsuccessfully to mitigate the activities of émigrés. A leadership of emigrants met in a conference in Mexico in May 2000 and decided to take the case to the United Nations. They would call on the UN to support a withdrawal of Syrian forces from Lebanon. At the time this seemed like a very long shot.

However energetic these pushes were, had it not been for the attacks of 9/11, events in Lebanon might not have been the same. After al Qaeda's attacks in September 2001, a war on terror was declared by the United States, and Iran and Hezbollah were labeled members of the "Axis of Evil." Lebanese Diaspora leaders, mostly in the United States, moved quickly to support American efforts against terror and initiated a platform to take the case to the UN. A series of meetings took place in Congress, at the State Department, and in the White House. The Lebanese delegation pressed for U.S. action in the UN

Security Council. In one of these meetings in March 2004, Elliott Abrams, who was in charge of the Middle East at the State Department, asked the NGO leaders, "If we move to pressure from the outside, will the Lebanese people support the initiative?"

U.S. leaders weren't sure the masses in Lebanon were ready for a democratic uprising. Inundated by jihadi and apologist propaganda in the wake of the Iraq invasion, the Bush administration was cautious about engaging in any campaign that could backfire. Critics were assaulting Washington about the freedom forward policy. The *New York Times* and American academia argued that people in the Middle East were not prepared for democracy, nor would they choose it freely.

My reply was, "If America and other democracies move forward in helping Lebanon free itself from Syrian occupation, the Lebanese civil society will meet us halfway." I had no data to confirm this, but I based my statement on my trust in human nature and on the basic instinct of people under threat. If the Lebanese longed for freedom, they would rise and seize the opportunity. A few months later I was proven right when, against all odds, the Cedars Revolution burst onto the scene. The Bush administration was on board and the road to the UN Security Council opened before us.

The meeting with U.S. ambassador John Negroponte in March 2004 was the first push at the UN Security Council. The NGO delegation explained its plan and goals and dispatched their memo to the ambassador and his aides. The battle for liberating Lebanon now had a formal beginning. We informed the head of the American mission that the Syrian-controlled Lebanese mission at the UN was blasting the Lebanese-American team as some sort of "renegade." Negroponte dismissed the criticism by the Syrian and Lebanese regimes. The administration was moving forward with its promise to give the Lebanese a diplomatic opportunity. We then visited the French and British delegations, which greeted the project positively, and we even met with the Russian ambassador and Chinese diplomats at the Security Council. After the five permanent members, we met with the nonpermanent members and the representative of the Arab League.

With the Lebanese Diaspora's demand now inside the UN system, the next step was the alignment of diplomatic powers. In Beirut and Damascus the regimes' rulers were informed that something was happening in New York, but they dismissed it. By midsummer, thousands of emails and letters, generated by Lebanese-American citizens and activists, reached the U.S. Congress and administration as well as French embassies around the world. The Lebanese Diaspora was mobilizing to urge the Security Council to issue a resolution. Bashar Assad started to get nervous, his intelligence blaming the UN move unfairly on some Lebanese politicians, including former prime minister Rafiq Hariri, a Sunni, and former minister Marwan Hamade, a Druse. Damascus thought French president Chirac was influenced by Hariri to support Bush on the Lebanon issue, but in reality Lebanon's politicians had nothing to do with it.

The UN initiative was a project propelled exclusively by Lebanese NGOs in exile. Hariri was summoned to Syria, where Assad threatened him, as was reported in the American media.[7] On September 18, 2004, the UN Security Council passed Resolution 1559, calling on Syria to withdraw its troops and on Hezbollah and other militias to disarm. Since June 1976 when Hafez Assad ordered the invasion of Lebanon, and even after the 1982 Hezbollah terror attacks against the multinational peacekeepers in Beirut, this was the first crystal-clear UN-led move to end the Baathist-Khomeinist domination of Lebanon. The regime in Damascus responded furiously with an assassination attempt against Druse liberal politician Marwan Hamade in fall 2004.[8] In January 2005, Lebanese Diaspora leaders called on Lebanon's civil society to rise against Syrian terror.[9] On February 14, 2005, Rafiq Hariri and several other politicians and their security guards were killed by a massive bomb in downtown Beirut. The victims' allies accused Bashar Assad of ordering the killing, while reports years later fingered Hezbollah as the executioner behind the terror attack.[10] Months later the United Nations formed a special tribunal to investigate and try the terrorists. The savage killing of Hariri triggered a series of mass demonstrations in downtown Beirut. Tens of thousands of citizens, mostly Christians, Sunnis, and Druse, chanted and marched against the Syrian occupation for the first time since 1990. Civil society was acting on its own instincts of freedom. My predictions were being realized: The U.S.-led initiative at the UN had been met halfway by the masses in Beirut.

On March 8, 2005, Hezbollah and the pro-Syrian forces organized about three hundred thousand of their supporters to counter the rising revolution. That day a Fox News anchor asked me if it was really true that the majority in Lebanon wanted democracy, since

Hezbollah's gigantic march "in support of Syria" exceeded a quarter of a million people. I told him that this was the maximum strength of three regimes, Iran, Syria, and Lebanon, to keep the dominant elite in power and that this would be a pivotal moment for the silent majority in favor of freedom to speak up. Indeed, one week later a million and a half men, women, and youth marched through the capital calling on "freedom to ring," Syria to withdraw, and Hezbollah to disarm. On March 14, 2005, the Cedars Revolution had arrived.

The Cedars Revolution: 2005–8

As soon as the masses took to the streets of Beirut and the pictures and footage appeared in the media, the international community responded. The Cedars Revolution, a term coined in Washington but not alien to the history of Lebanese resistance against Syrian occupation, was recognized immediately by Western democracies, including the United States, France, and many members of the European Union, as well as being endorsed by moderate Arab governments, such as Saudi Arabia, Jordan, and Egypt. The success of the democratic revolution was stunning to many as it didn't involve armed violence and relied strictly on mass demonstrations and peaceful expression. There was a sharp contrast between the democracy movement of Lebanon, which matured to include many communities, and the Syrian, Iranian, and Hezbollah forces that dominated the country. While in Afghanistan and Iraq elections and democratic manifestations such as the formation of political parties and open debates were brought about by military campaigns, in Lebanon an authoritarian government backed by Baathists and jihadists collapsed under the chants of unarmed civilians and the pressures by émigrés' NGOs.

In the wake of the million-and-a-half-person march in Beirut, Washington and Paris asked Bashar Assad to pull his troops from Lebanon immediately. The Syrian dictator was faced with the choice of either sending more troops to crush the revolution or pulling out. With U.S. forces to his east in Iraq and to his west in the Mediterranean, his military command made the quick assessment that if international action was taken against his forces in Lebanon, he wouldn't stand a chance.

Facing a vast popular revolution from below, and sandwiched strategically by the Western presence, Assad reverted to a third option, pulling out his regular troops but keeping the "second army" in Lebanese territory. That force consisted of Hezbollah, Syrian intelligence, and radical Palestinian groups. By the end of April the Assad plan was in motion; his military quickly withdrew to Syria, leaving behind only a few positions across the long border separating the countries.

The politicians who surfaced to lead the popular revolt baptized their coalition "The March 14 Movement." In addition to the core anti-Syrian opposition, which had been struggling for liberation since the 1990s, Sunni and Druse politicians joined the movement, which now counted members of Lebanon's many different communities as supporters. The Cedars Revolution showed that the majority of Lebanese people had deep aspirations for freedom and democracy and were willing to fight foreign occupation, totalitarian ideologies, and terrorism. They'd accomplished the enormous task of showing the outside world the real will of their society after fifteen years of Syrian occupation and apologist propaganda and media, which praised the "stabilizing" role of Syrian forces in Lebanon.

The "revolution" was in its purest state until politicians took the reins. Instead of completing the acts of the revolution by fully collapsing the pro-Syrian regime and removing the two other symbols of the years of occupation—President Emile Lahoud and Speaker of the House Nabih Berri—the politicians of the opposition preferred to run for legislative elections, and some among them entered a political alliance with Hezbollah. The Cedars Revolution won a large majority in Parliament, but their politicians invited the terror group to join the cabinet.

Those few short weeks of the revolution were comparable to the days Iraqis and Afghans walked to the ballot boxes to exercise their democratic rights. The only difference was that while voters in Mesopotamia and Afghanistan walked to the polls they were protected by the most powerful armed forces in the world. In Beirut, one-third of the population walked in the streets to challenge two of the most repressive regimes in the region without an international presence to protect them.

By July 2005 the most authentic days of the democratic revolution were over. The government was run by March 14 politicians, and as incredible as it may sound, by the pro-Iranians and pro-Syrians, though they were in the minority. The revolution's "politicians" trapped themselves in a half revolution. They couldn't call for more international support for fear of Hezbollah and they couldn't let go of a "national unity" government they had entered into with the terrorists. The Syrian- and Iranian-supported politicians quickly reclaimed the strategic advantage, to the dismay of the population. Before the end of the year, three important leaders of the Cedars Revolution were assassinated by the Syro-Iranian axis operating in Lebanon. George Hawi and Samir Qassir, both of the left, and Gebran Tueni, the liberal editor freshly elected to the Parliament, were killed. During the following year, Hezbollah tricked March 14 politicians into a sterile so-called dialogue process. By July, Hezbollah's Nasrallah had fired the first salvo in a war with Israel aimed at eventually crumbling the weak Fuad Seniora government. Indeed, in the months following the 2006 summer war, Hezbollah retaliated against the cabinet by paralyzing the center of the capital with an urban uprising.

Assad and the ayatollahs had calculated impeccably; with the change of majority in the U.S. Congress, the Bush administration became a sitting duck on the issue of foreign policy. There would be no more strategic pressure on Hezbollah or on Syria's regime as of 2007. The counter-revolution against the democracy movement escalated, with more terror attacks and assassinations targeting legislators, members of government, military officers, politicians, NGO leaders, and ordinary civilians. On May 7, Hezbollah's militias invaded mostly Sunni West Beirut and attacked Druse areas in Mount Lebanon. Despite fierce resistance by armed villagers against Hezbollah, the March 14 politicians were forced to surrender the government and recognize the pro-Iranian militia as "legitimate."

Hezbollah's Takeover: 2008–10

After its takeover of Beirut's main governmental areas, Hezbollah became the central player in the country. Ironically, new legislative elections in June 2009 gave the March 14 politicians another majority in Parliament. Senior leaders of the coalition, fearing another Hezbollah military action, surrendered their political majority once again to the "March 8" forces, tightly allied with Damascus and Tehran. In two years the Cedars Revolution had been marginalized inside government institutions and pushed back to the streets, into the world of powerless NGOs. The new president of the Republic,

Michel Sleiman, accepted the reign of Hezbollah and reactivated the old Syrian-Lebanese "treaties." The newly appointed prime minister, Saad Hariri, son of the slain Sunni leader Rafiq Hariri, also submitted to Syrian and Hezbollah influence in 2010. Swiftly, the Hezbollah pro-Syrian alliance extended its control over a number of ministries, including Foreign Affairs, shaping the political guidelines for embassies around the world, and at the UN, where Lebanon will be at the Security Council beginning in 2010. Throughout the bureaucracies the "axis" has been pushing against the supporters of the Cedars Revolution, purging offices and security positions of sympathizers of the March 14 Movement. By early 2010, the Cedars Revolution's political leadership in Lebanon had all but abandoned the initial struggle of 2005. Druse leader Walid Jumblat met with Hassan Nasrallah of Hezbollah; Sunni prime minister Saad Hariri visited Bashar Assad in Damascus; and Christian leaders have reluctantly recognized Hezbollah as a legitimate "resistance movement."

The return of Hezbollah and Syria's allies to power, although not in full, signals the end of the Cedars Revolution, or at least of the first one. Below the surface and openly in the Diaspora, those forces opposed to the Khomeinist-controlled state and to Baathist influence are bracing for a second Cedars Revolution.

Democracy Forces in Lebanon

I've met with leaders of Lebanon who rose and vanished, who were assassinated, exiled, or jailed. I've learned that the forces of democracy in that small country travel from generation to generation, from community to community, and reemerge like the phoenix. The constant search for freedom is as old as the societies that live on Lebanon's mountains and shores.

The past thirteen centuries have seen a resurgence of resistance against oppression, from empires to neighboring powers. The inhabitants of the deep valleys of Lebanon are among the very few peoples in the region who resisted tirelessly against the Ummayyads, Abbasids, Mameluks, and Ottomans for centuries. Such a struggle is engrained in their history and will continue to resurge. But internal fighting among its leaders caused most of its failures and defeats at the hands of the "Caliphate."

In modern times, the forces of democracy dispersed within the many communities that form contemporary Lebanon. The struggle of freedom movements in each community was not always coordinated with those of like-minded freedom fighters from other ethnic groups. The Christian community chose the path of resisting the Syrian occupation starting in 1975 and continuing for fifteen years before collapsing due to a Christian civil war in 1990. During the war years, liberal elements in the Muslim communities were severely suppressed by the dominant militias and by the Syrian intelligence services. Examples of heroic activists and writers abound, including Muslim liberal author Mustafa Jeha, who was assassinated by jihadists on January 15, 1992. Jeha was outspoken against Ayatollah Khomeini, Hezbollah, and the Syrian occupation.[11] In 1985, I asked him why he didn't fear reprisal from terrorists, particularly since he was a Shia opposing the Iranian Khomeinists. He said, "Those Muslim intellectuals, who, like us, are braving the dominant Islamist forces in the Arab world, and particularly in Lebanon, know all too well that we are walking martyrs for freedom. Some of us will see our societies liberated from here. Others will see it from up there."

In early 2010 *another* Mustafa Jeha sent an email throughout the Lebanese Diaspora announcing the resumption of the struggle via the republishing of the assassinated author's books. It was his son, who had decided to take the banner and resume the struggle. Democrats in the Sunni and Druse communities were starting to rise, especially as the Syrians withdrew their military from Lebanon in 2005. During that crucial year of the uprising a number of Sunni liberal figures were killed.

In East Beirut, those who pushed for democracy and human rights were prestigious personalities such as Dr. Charles Malek, former president of the General Assembly of the UN and one of the writers of the Universal Declaration of Human Rights; the founder of the Lebanese University, Fuad Afram Bustany; the former president of St. Joseph University, Selim Abou; liberal lawyer Musa Prince, and a large number of activists and union leaders. While the democracy advocates supported the struggle of the community for survival, they also kept pressure on politicians to respect pluralism and liberties. Under the direct Syrian occupation of the 1990s, liberal writers and commentators were particularly targeted. But the drama reached a climax in the year of the revolution, with the attempt to assassinate journalist May Chidiac in 2005. Chidiac lost her leg and hand when her car exploded. Leftist writers, such as Samir Cassir, a writer at the *Orient Lejour* daily who was assassinated, were also the victims of attacks. Last but not least, the brutal car-bomb killing of liberal MP Gebran Tueni in December 2005 demonstrated the high price of democratization in Lebanon.

However, from a historical perspective the democracy forces have regained momentum. These voices were at the core of the Cedars Revolution. In the Muslim communities, liberal forces tried hard to rise and break the yoke of totalitarian ideologies. The revolution gave a historic opportunity to the democrats in the Sunni community. As one of their leading young figures told me, "Sunni liberals will surprise the rest of Lebanese, for they are the real counterbalance to the jihadi extremists." Member of Parliament Misbah al Ahdab is one of these promising Sunni leaders for the future. Representing Tripoli, one of the largest Sunni cities in the Levant, Ahdab agrees with the notion that in Lebanon's multiethnic society each community has its own tempo and timing, "but in the end, democrats from all religious sects are the force that can make change happen."

In Washington, the rising young Shia leader Ahmad Asaad told reporters in a briefing cohosted by the Foundation for Defense of Democracies in 2007 that "even in the midst of the Shia community, reformers and democrats are vigorous and ready to rise, never mind the power of Hezbollah." These words, uttered three years before the Green Revolution exploded in Iran, speak volumes about the strength of this revolution. Asaad, who had been critical of Syrian interference in Lebanon even before the Cedars Revolution, told me that the spirit of democracy is omnipresent among Shiites across the Bekaa and southern Lebanon, traditional strongholds of Iran-backed Hezbollah. We must irrigate these souls with recognition and moral support.

As of May 2008, Hezbollah "re-invaded" the country in stages. In 2010 the militia had blocked all attempts to reestablish pluralist democracy. Although possibly indicted by an international court for terror assassinations, Hezbollah threatens renewal of violence to stop the return of the Cedars Revolution.

Prospects for the Future

The battle for democracy in Lebanon is crucial for the Middle East. In an article I published in 2004, based on a memo I sent to the U.S.

administration and members of Congress, I argued that Lebanon is the cultural nerve center of the region. With five major universities, many media outlets, a tradition of democratic elections up until 1975, and a multiethnic society at the crossroads between West and East, any breakthrough for democracy in Beirut will affect the region. The Cedars Revolution was the first step in that direction. The totalitarian forces opposed to liberalization and pluralism crushed this major, peaceful uprising in an attempt to eradicate its effect.

While disagreeing among themselves, the members of the brotherhood against democracy came together to block the rise of a leading liberated society in Lebanon. Authoritarian regimes and jihadist movements in the Middle East view Lebanon's democratic revolution, the success of which will signal a massive shift in the region's political culture, as extremely dangerous for them. More than in any other nondemocratic country in the region, a change in the Cedars land would crumble the "ideological Caliphate" jihadists and other totalitarians wish to erect.

9.

Syria's Reformers:
Opposition against the Baath

Screams from Syria

"The tanks are thrusting through buildings and destroying everything, houses, schools, and even mosques. Security forces are shooting men, women, and children. The artillery is pounding the streets and the air force is pounding the main highways; it is a massacre, it is genocide." The screaming voice was guttural and came through a bad phone line but was broadcast live on the radio. Surrounding the radio, a number of Western journalists were trying to understand what was happening in the city of Hama, in northern Syria. From a listening post in East Beirut, these European and North American foreign correspondents were trying to get information about terrible things happening in the sealed country. International media rushed to Lebanon as they heard about an uprising by Sunni populations against the Baathist regime of Hafez Assad. At the time, I headed an ethnic minorities NGO that helped media representatives understand the messages from that city that were broadcast on a radio station called Voice of Lebanon (VOL).

It was in February 1982, in the midst of a popular uprising spreading from Aleppo to Hama. The Syrian dictator had ordered a full-scale offensive against the mostly Islamic opposition. "The butcher has sent his entire army and security against our defenseless city," said the spokesperson from the opposition on VOL, "land forces, artillery, air force, and everything he could muster against his own people. Had our city been on the coast, he would have ordered the navy, too." He was desperately calling on the world to intervene against the massacre. Deep inside I felt what it was like to be surrounded inside a city while the "Stalin's Organs" were dumping shrieking rockets indiscriminately on neighborhoods. I lived through such a hell in 1978 and 1981 in Beirut when the forces of Assad were smashing through streets, cars, and shelters with Katyushas and the terrible Soviet-made 240 mm cannon. But Hama was a Syrian city, and it was being crushed by its own government. The voice on the phone announced that the special forces had entered the building and that all was lost. The last words were: "Justice will prevail one day followed by Allahu Akbar." The line died out and the anchor at the radio station said, "The last communication with Hama is now cut."

We learned later that month and in the following years that the brutal oppression at Hama in 1982 left more than eighteen thousand dead and leveled large parts of the city. Just as brutal as Saddam's regime, the Baath of Damascus had no room for tolerance. Not only had Syrian forces been occupying neighboring Lebanon since 1976, but an oppression of epic proportions had afflicted the Syrian populations for decades, particularly since the coup d'état by the Assad clan in 1970.

Relentless Oppression

In contrast with adjacent Lebanon, modern Syria had known political oppression almost since the first days of the republic in 1945. As a child I saw families of Syrian origin settled in Beirut's eastern suburbs. Known as Syriac (Siriani), they spoke a form of Aramaic, Jesus' language. They'd fled their ancestral lands, which they'd inhabited since the dawn of history, centuries before the Arab conquest and the establishment of the Caliphate. The Baathist authorities marginalized their culture on the ground that Syriacs didn't claim Arab nationalism. This would be the equivalent of asking Native Americans in the United States to claim they were European. Thousands of these Christians fled to Lebanon, and many among them left in the Diaspora, ending up in Sweden, North America, and Australia. A second group of oppressed people fled Syria and escaped to Lebanon—the Kurds. Muslims but non-Arabs, they, too, were culturally and ethnically suppressed. Our perception of the ruling elite in Damascus was shaped by the flow of refugees reaching our cities and the stories they brought with them. From Beirut we looked out upon the borders with Baathist-controlled Syria as an iron curtain separating a relatively democratic culture from a dark reign of socialist Pan Arabism.

Many politicians, journalists, and students—mostly Arab Sunnis, and in many instances former Baathists—had survived the nightmarish oppression under the one-party regime ruling Damascus since the early sixties. Syrian voices living in free Lebanon before 1975 described life under the Baath as comparable to life behind the Iron Curtain in the Soviet Union.

On a trip I took to Syria in 1974, I had the opportunity to meet with ordinary citizens away from the eyes of the Mukhabarat. Their tales confirmed years of testimony on the state of freedom inside one of the oldest societies of the Middle East. I saw a fully militarized country where kids were already enrolled in ideological services and the motto of the regime was to unite all Arabs in one *Umma*—or Reich—under one party and one leader. It was a country that fell under the rule of a "socialist Caliphate." Months later the soldiers of the "Baathist jihad" crossed the borders into the Bekaa valley of Lebanon and started the gradual occupation of Lebanon that would last more than three decades.

Syria's Heavy History

Syria's history is as rich as Lebanon's, and its geography has played a central role in shaping its various ethnic identities. Invaded by most classical empires of antiquity, Syria's indigenous populations were nevertheless able to form independent kingdoms. Mostly inhabited by Aramaeans in the north and west, Syria was also settled by ancient Arabian tribes in its east, particularly in the city of Palmyre or *Tadmur*. Its ancient coastal cities were Phoenician, and Damascus is identified as one of the oldest inhabited urban centers of early civilizations. In the first two centuries after Christ, Syria's religion was Christianity. In 636 C.E. the armies of the Caliphate, commanded by General Khalid Ibn al Walid, defeated the Byzantines at Yarmuk, at the southern tip of Syria, and quickly conquered Damascus and the rest of the country's flatlands. Gradually, the majority of its population converted to Islam as large Bedouin tribes settled across the country, changing its ethnic makeup from mostly Aramaic to predominantly Arabic. The "Arabization" of Syria affected its history for centuries and later naturally influenced a number of its modern political movements, one of which was the Baath Party.

One of the most significant developments in the Arab history of

Syria was the establishment of the first capital of the Caliphate in Damascus. The Umayyad dynasty, the first bloodline of the caliphs, chose the city as their capital, from which they directed the *Fatah*, or the conquest of infidel lands in the Middle East and North Africa, all the way to Spain. This "golden age" of the Arab Islamic empire left a tremendous legacy of grandeur and assertiveness to the successive elites who ruled the country, and later served as additional ideological motivation for the Baathist agenda. The Abbasids eliminated the Umayyads in 750 C.E. and moved the capital of the empire to Baghdad, leaving Syria as a province, albeit a powerful one, of the Caliphate. During the Crusades, Islamic rulers based in Aleppo and Damascus, including the great Saladin, waged constant warfare against the Latin kingdoms of the Levant. The Mameluks, from Egypt, ruled Syria after the Crusades until they were defeated by the advancing Ottomans in 1516. Damascus served continuously as the capital for the Syrian province, for all Caliphate dynasties. In 1918, the British commander, General Allenby, entered the city on his way to defeat retreating Turkish forces. The following year, and according to an agreement between Paris and London,[1] Syria and Lebanon were turned over to France, which later established a mandate on behalf of the League of Nations.

Modern Syria as designed by the French was multiethnic and multireligious, but its path to pluralism was rocky. Its majority population is Arab Sunni, with significant minorities: Kurds to the northeast, Druse in the southwest, Alawis in the northwest, and Christians in the north and in the capital. A French attempt to create separate Alawi, Druse, and Kurdish states while moving Syrian Christians to join their community in Lebanon was opposed by the Arab nationalists and the Islamists in the 1920s and 1930s. The Damascus elites, mostly Sunni Pan Arabists, wanted all the minorities' areas in Syria under one Arab state, and in addition rejected the formation of a separate Lebanese state on Syria's western frontiers. Arab nationalists would rule Syria uninterruptedly until Hafez Assad took control in a coup in 1970. The "Damascus, capital of the Umayyads," propaganda was used by the ruling elites, both Sunnis and then Alawis, as a catalyst for passionate nationalistic sentiments, a stark reminder of European extremist nationalism leading to World War I.

But extreme Arab nationalism witnessed a radical turn toward entrenchment and hardening with the founding of the Baathist movement in the late 1950s. Without the ability to oppose Lebanon's full separation from Syria when both countries obtained their independence from France in 1943, the ruling elites of Damascus adopted a policy of pressure and boycott for decades against their small neighbor. Since 1945 Syrian governments have not appointed an ambassador in Beirut and have often shut down the borders, creating economic suffocation in Lebanon. Problems with Lebanon aside, tensions between Syria and most of its neighbors grew with the advent of Baathist rule in Damascus in 1963.

Hafez Assad

The Baath Party was founded in the 1950s by ideologues and activists who firmly believed in eliminating borders between all modern Arab countries "created by colonialism" and supported a socialist and powerful Arab *Umma*. These goals would be achieved through two severely oppressive policies: One was to oppose self-determination for any non-Arab minority community in the region, such as Kurds, Aramaean, Copts, southern Sudanese, and Berbers; the second was to maintain a strong grip over domestic politics through a one-party system under which liberties would be curtailed according to the whim of the ruling Baath.[2] The movement's founding ideologues were Michel Aflaq and Salah Bitar, both Pan Arabists and socialists. They laid out the platform for an anticolonialist Arab nationalist movement seeking the collapse of the post-Ottoman state system in the region, the destruction of Israel, and the merging of all existing entities under one Greater Arab Government.[3] In fact, the Baathists were secular jihadists looking to bring back the Caliphate, wrapping it with republican and progressive labels.

The Baath took power in Syria in the early 1960s and banned all liberal and democratic parties, sending droves of Syrians into exile. The first Baathist regime was controlled by Sunni urban elites. Liberties were crushed and a hypermilitarization of the country took place, leading to the 1967 war with Israel on the side of Gamal Abdel Nasser, Egypt's Pan Arabist dictator.

The smashing defeat of Syria and the loss of the Golan Heights to Israel in the Six-Day War created a depression among the Syrian military, opening the door to a coup d'état led by minister of defense Major General Hafez Assad, who was commander of the air force during the 1967 war. Assad came from a small ethnoreligious minority in Syria known as Alawites or Alawi. An offshoot of Shiism, the Alawites are considered heretics by orthodox Sunnis, as they are accused of mixing Koranic teachings with theological beliefs of their own. Fearing reprisals, the community, tightly concentrated in the northwestern mountainous region of the country along the Mediterranean shores, was historically remote from Damascus's politics and intrigues.

Assad found his path to leadership via the army and the party and followed an extremely Arab-nationalist line, pleasing many in the Baathist movement. Rushing with tanks and special forces through the capital, he sent the sitting president, Nur Eddine Atassi, and many other Sunni Baathists either to jail or into exile and installed his own Alawi-controlled Baathist regime. Hafez Assad quickly purged potential enemies from the armed forces, the party, and the bureaucracy and appointed numerous Alawis, creating a de facto Alawi regime with a Sunni face.[4]

The first few years of his rule were marked by systematic suppression of his opposition, the 1973 war against Israel, and arming guerillas inside Lebanon. In 1976 he sent his army into the Bekaa and many Lebanese cities. He subsequently concentrated on consolidating his own regime in Syria with extreme brutality, epitomized by the Hama massacre of 1982, and on crushing anti-Syrian resistance in Lebanon with mass military campaigns in 1978, 1981, and later in 1986, before invading the last enclave in 1990.

"The Assad regime was a mixture of Ceausescu, Papa Doc, and Stalin," Nouhad Ghadri, the editor of *Al Muharer al Arabi*,[5] told me in 2006. Ghadri, an old-timer and a former senior Sunni official in the Baath Party of Syria, knew the entire apparatus of the Assad Alawi elite as well as many of the Sunni officials in the party, such as Syrian vice president Khaddam, who broke away from the regime in 2005 and left for Paris. "Like a serpentine chain the Baath Party controls the bureaucracy and all aspects of public life including municipalities all the way to religious authorities." Nouhad Ghadri sums it up clearly: "Nothing is left to randomness; all is tightly and overwhelmingly controlled, monitored, and suppressed."

This description by a very seasoned observer of the regime has been corroborated by almost all analysts not on the regime's payroll. Over three decades the merciless abuse of human rights in Syria and in Lebanon has been well documented by NGOs and international monitoring entities.[6] During the Cold War, the Assad regime openly acted in brutal fashion, as it felt fully supported by the Soviet Union. The period from 1970 to 1990 saw the worst twenty years of oppression in the country's modern history. In the following decade the ailing Assad concentrated on Lebanon, ordering his apparatus there, commanded by General Ghazi Kanaan, to crush any opposition to Syria's rule and its surrogates. Indeed, this was Lebanon's worst decade under full oppression, a period during which kidnappings, arrests, and transfers to Syria's prisons took place in the midst of international silence. Sadly, segments of the Western media covered up for the brutality of the Assad regime, praising the "wise man" and portraying him as a "needed leader" for peace.[7]

However, even at the apex of his brutal power, Hafez Assad, the Sphinx of Syria, as he was called by many of his critics, was opposed by determined forces. In the early 1980s, Hafez's brother Rifaat, who was his faithful shadow and commander of the Praetorian Guards, "the defense units," was forced out of the country by the dictator, most likely over the issue of succession. Hafez naturally wanted to leave his position to his son, instead of risking a coup orchestrated by his powerful brother. Rifaat began with a nucleus of opposition based in Paris. The Muslim Brotherhood, a Salafi Sunni organization, also went underground, and some of its leadership fled. The liberal elements organized themselves in secrecy while a number among them left in the Diaspora.

A member of Syria's parliament, Ma'moun al Homsi, who later rose against Bashar Assad, explained to me that during the 1990s, "those who dared criticize—let alone openly oppose—Assad were signing their death warrant. He had no tolerance for dissent." As Ma'moun told me in 2007, "Outside the institutions of the ruling Baath, it was simply too risky to organize because the party would detect you and take you out. If you were a Sunni liberal, a Kurd, or a Syriac Christian, the Baathist machine would crush you and your activities before you had a chance to expand. But if you were inside the party and tried to mount an organized opposition to the edicts or policies of the Qa'id (supreme leader), you would be killed instantly. There was no mercy."

The Sunni liberal opposition always tried to operate within established institutions but was extremely limited by the weight of the

Baathist machine. In 2005 Farid Ghadri, the president of the Syrian Reform Party, told me that since Assad took over in 1970, "there was an automatic Sunni majority against him but it had no means to express itself. When the Muslim Brotherhood instigated acts of violence against the regime in the late 1970s and early 1980s the Assad machine crushed them, as was the case in Hama. Since then the violent choice receded among Sunnis, giving way to civil society activism binding Sunnis to other communities such as Kurds, Christians, and even Druse."

Christians had a long history of opposition to the Baath, despite the narrative encouraged by the regime and parroted by apologist Western journalists that the Alawi were more sympathetic to Christian minorities than a Sunni power would have been. This myth was encouraged by the Assad faction in order to consolidate its support among other minorities, allowing it to withstand the pressure of the Sunni majority. In 1997 Joseph Saouk, originally from northeastern Syria and an expert on Aramaic and Syriac communities who teaches at Uppsala University in Sweden, told me that the bulk of Syria's Christians were as oppressed as the rest of the population. "But the regime was able to recruit from the Orthodox families in Damascus and other urban centers, just as much as it recruited from all other communities. Keep in mind that a number of bourgeois Christians in Syria and the Levant have chosen the *Dhimmi* path, collaborating with Pan Arabist regimes in order to maintain financial well-being for their kin." In 1999 Abgar Malul, one of the leaders of *Athurayo*, an identity movement active among Aramaic Christians in northern Syria, told me that "even under the Assad regime, hard-core networks of Aramaic Christians have been in action in the Jazeera province."[8] Malul, who moved to the United States, told me later in September 2004 that "during the peak of Assad's regime in the 1970s and 1980s, minorities, particularly the Syriac Christians and Kurds, kept the movement against Assad going. But with the passing of the father, other opposition entities emerged further and the movement became wide and cross-sectarian." Indeed, as asserted by Nouhad Ghadri in several of his articles and in briefings to the U.S. Congress after 2005, "The forces in Syria's civil society range from Sunni liberals and moderates to Kurds, Christians, and even a minority of Alawi, not satisfied with the brutal methods of the Assad faction."

Even at the peak of Hafez Assad's power and while his forces were occupying Lebanon and his regime was backing Hezbollah and Hamas in remote lands, the fervor for reform and democratic revolution survived and developed deep within Syrian society. Soon, circumstances changed in the reformers' favor.

Bashar Assad

With the death of Hafez Assad in June 2000, a new era began in Syria. Dissidents were still oppressed, but they had more courage and will to organize and express themselves. As in any other totalitarian regime, when the dictator reaches an apex of terror against his own people, civil society adapts to the level of suffering, and thus, any weakening of the system is an opportunity. Assad the father passed away shortly after one of his major goals was achieved: the withdrawal of Israel from southern Lebanon, the dismantling of the SLA, the last militia in Lebanon allied to Israel, and the deployment of Hezbollah and its allies all the way to the border of the Jewish state. The Sphinx had ensured several victories before he left this world. One, he had surrounded his foe Israel with another hundred kilometers of battlefront in southern Lebanon. Two, he gave ultimate victory to his strategic ally, the Iranian regime, by granting Hezbollah power across large areas of Lebanon. Finally, he left not one, but two republics for his son Bashar to rule—Syria and Lebanon.

Bashar was swiftly appointed by the Baath elite as head of the party and installed as president of the country, without free elections. At the peak of Assad power, Bashar greatly enjoyed the benefits of such glory, but at the same time was confronted with the rise of criticism in both countries. Western apologist media painted the new leader as reform-inclined, and some Western academics rushed to present him as a "lion."[9] The reality was far from this flattering portrait. "The regime after Hafez Assad fell into the hands of five security and intelligence agencies, all involved in financial and other interests inside Syria and in Lebanon," said Nouhad Ghadri in his briefing to members of Congress on Syria.[10] "Bashar's regime is a clone to his father's," exiled MP Ma'moun al Homsi told me. "It is the same brutal elite ruling the country with one difference: It benefits from voices in the international media and academia who claim that the man is just an eye doctor who had to replace his father after his older son died in a car accident in the 1990s. He is painted as a reformer while in fact his regime is just as brutal as that of his father."[11]

Indeed, what was described as a brief "Damascus Spring" by observers in Syria and Lebanon before Bashar's appointment during the summer of 2000 was a respite that quickly ended. During those months of reorganization within the regime, the propaganda machine of the Baath Party painted a rosier picture than the harsh political reality. The Syrian government relaxed few political and economic restrictions and allowed some previously unauthorized civil activities, mostly in the scientific and administrative realms. The measures were aimed at addressing widespread discontent as the various wings of the regime struggled to settle the issues of power. Authorities needed calm on the outside for the government to finish its business on the inside. Although it couldn't be compared to Gorbachev's glasnost and perestroika, the attitude of "Hafez is not here anymore" encouraged a number of dissidents to act in public. The "Damascus Spring" opened the path for a short rise and fall of dissident leaders, as the full power of the Baathist machine quickly stomped down on the growing voices for freedom.

Syrian Dissidents

In 2003, Ammar Abdelhamid helped launch an NGO named Dar Emar to raise the standards of civic awareness in the Arab world. He then initiated the Tharwa Project, a program designed to address diversity issues in the region. Advocating pacifism and gradualism, Abdelhamid believed change must come, but it must be peaceful and free of violence.[12] By 2005, he and his family were exiled from Syria.

Another brave dissident is Michel Kilo, who by 2003 had become one of the most prominent democratic supporters in Syria. In 2005, Kilo brought together diverse groups in society, including capitalists, communists, secularists, and fundamentalists, to sign a document calling for democratic reforms. This statement, known as the Damascus Declaration, created a quasiofficial council of opposition leaders (the National Council for the Damascus Declaration—NCDD) to serve as a focal point for opposition unity and planning. Kilo was concerned about the Assad regime's role in oppressing democratic activists in Lebanon. In late 2005, these Lebanese activists installed a prodemocracy government in Beirut, in the Cedars Revolution, and compelled the Syrian regime to remove its military forces from Lebanon. Inspired, Kilo and other like-minded activists wanted to unite with Lebanese democratic forces to achieve similar popularly inspired reforms in Syria. Kilo helped draft another declaration by Syrian and Lebanese activists, calling for an end to the Assad regime's imperialist policy in Lebanon and for functioning democracy in both countries. Three hundred Syrian and Lebanese intellectuals signed the Beirut-Damascus Declaration on May 11, 2006. Three days later, Kilo was arrested by the Syrian authorities along with thirteen other signers of the Beirut-Damascus Declaration. Formal charges were not filed against him until March 2007. He was charged with "weakening national sentiment," "spreading false information," and inciting "religious and racial dissension." Similar charges were filed against lawyer Anwar Al-Bunni and activist Mahmud Issa. In March 2007, Kilo was brought before a military prosecutor in Damascus. He was accused of inciting other inmates in his Adra prison to rebel against the regime. On May 13, 2007, almost a year to the day after his initial arrest, Kilo was formally sentenced to three years in prison.

Kilo adamantly opposes the use of violence for political change. He wants to bring down the Assad regime, but not in the way that the Romanians had executed Ceausescu. He uses substantive, logical arguments to gain supporters and attack his opponents.[13] According to CLIME, a U.S.-based NGO focusing on human rights in the Middle East, a journalist who knows Kilo's work very closely said: "The harder the regime has tried to silence him, the more he's grown into a hero for the repressed liberals of the Arab world, and a cause célèbre on Pan Arab satellite television channels. Some have hailed him as the writer who just might become the Vaclav Havel or Alexander Solzhenitsyn of his country, breaking through the cone of silence that the regime relies on to preserve its rule."

Today, Michel Kilo remains in jail, a victim of Syrian tyranny and an inspiration to democracy activists around the world. To his friends and relatives, Kilo is a quiet and jovial man. The Marxist views of his youth are long gone, replaced by a focus on freedom and democracy.[14]

During the year Bashar came to power, another high-profile dissident, Riad Seif, already at the forefront of the Syrian opposition movement calling for constitutional reforms in favor of liberal democracy in Parliament, started the Social Peace Movement Party. Seif was arrested and sentenced to five years in prison, where he languished as his health deteriorated. But Seif continued his political activities in prison. He routinely smuggled political writings to his supporters, including the "Damascus Declaration." Seif was released seven months early from his five-year prison sentence and resumed his political activities.

Two months after his release from prison, Seif was detained by the Syrian authorities for attending a demonstration supporting Kurdish rights. In August 2007, the Syrian government imposed a travel ban on Seif; he could no longer travel abroad, even to treat his worsening health problems. In January 2008, he was arrested, this time for meetings on the Damascus Declaration he had participated in a year earlier. He was treated poorly in jail; his head was shaved and he was forced to sleep in a cold cell. Seif suffered from prostate cancer and despite pressure from foreign governments, Syria refused to allow him essential treatment in foreign medical facilities.[15]

Regime and Reformers

The rise of reformers in Syria in the post–Hafez Assad era went through multiple stages. First was a short so-called Damascus Spring in 2000 and 2001, during which the dissidents were testing Bashar's willingness to reform. Within the following year the son of the Syrian Sphinx ended any hope that he would initiate openness, but the Syrian dissidents resumed the struggle with the belief that they could mobilize civil society. The state and reformers were on a collision course. The new post-Hafez reality was that the opposition to the Baathist rule was omnipresent in the occupying country, Syria, and in the occupied country, Lebanon. Out of Beirut a number of liberal journalists published pieces calling for change in Syrian policy toward Lebanon and the Syrian people. Reformers in Damascus echoed the calls, and an alliance of prodemocracy voices was established, forming an unprecedented threat against the ruling Baath.

After 9/11, the calculations of the Bashar regime regarding dissidence and democracy movements were ambivalent and erratic. On one hand, some in the halls of power wanted Syria's government to keep a low profile after the United States declared "war on terror." The idea, explained my colleague professor Robert Rabil, an expert on Middle Eastern politics, "is that Washington would be on a collision course with Damascus if the Syrian government would sink in confrontation with its own population and throughout Lebanon." A faction of the Damascus elite advised Bashar to moderate the regime's behavior regarding its opposition as the United States committed itself to fighting terrorism and supporting democracy in the region. "Bashar's realists didn't want a clash with American power after 2001 and preferred to play moderate until times would change," explained Rabil.

The critical period post-9/11 was seen by other advisors, according to Farid Ghadri, as "dangerous and risky." Ghadri told U.S. and European lawmakers in briefings he conducted after the Iraq invasion that "Assad II was also convinced by many of his intelligence deputies that any relaxation of domestic suppression of dissidence would lead to an expansion of the democracy movement."[16] As a result, the regime's policy regarding reforms after 9/11 was schizophrenic. Public statements coming out of Damascus and amplified by the apologist media machine in the West spoke of "cooperation with the United States in the war against terrorism" as well as openness toward civil society; however the suppression, jailing, torturing, and exiling of dissidents continued.

The struggle of Syrian reformers between 2001 and 2003 varied from one field to another but most dissidents felt that regardless of Assad's ambiguous policies, "the regime's time had come to an end," as Farid Ghadri puts it. "The reformers in Syria's society felt that a change was happening." In fact, by basic instinct Syrian dissidents knew that the new positioning of Washington under the Bush administration, regardless of its efficiency and message, was a push in the right direction. "There was a whole shift in Washington," argued Syrian MP Homsi. "We, the reformists, were on the run, persecuted, and singled out, but we had hope just because people in the free world were now mobilizing against terrorism."

It was natural that the underdogs in Syria would take advantage of the shift in power. The Assad regime was on a U.S. list of regimes sponsoring terror. The U.S.-led coalition was mobilizing against the terror facilitators, and eventually the Syrian regime would become a target. Ironically, both the democracy movement and the regime came to the same conclusions after 9/11, and each party tried to adapt to the new circumstances. The dissidents wanted to scream loudly that they were oppressed by a terror regime, and the government wanted to shut them off so that the international community wouldn't begin to pressure Damascus.

Between 2001 and late 2002, I had several briefings in Congress and with NGOs to discuss likely occurrences in the region after the U.S. military moved into Afghanistan. As I pointed out earlier, the idea was that after 9/11, U.S.-led efforts and international institutions would begin a steady, systematic, and relentless campaign to support oppressed peoples in the region. An alternative to a military campaign in Iraq could have been massive assistance to dissidents across the region in conjunction with specific antiterrorist actions. Syria should have been a prime recipient of this democracy-support policy. Iraq absorbed hundreds of billions in spending and is still struggling. In an international conference in support of the dissidents, held in Prague, reformers from the region agreed sarcastically that had Washington helped the Syrian democratic opposition with one or two billion dollars, Syria might have shifted to freedom more quickly than Iraq.

The jury is still out on this assertion. The counterargument was that had the Saddam regime not been removed, it would have continued to present a common front with Assad and the ayatollahs just as U.S. efforts for democratization were getting started. Despite the strategic choices made at the time, the battle between the Assad regime and the reformers escalated after the Iraq invasion. As American forces thrust through Mesopotamia, the Syrian regime got nervous and began preparing for the next stage.

The moment was tense as U.S. Marines entered Saddam's capital. From the direct cable feed that we were receiving at MSNBC headquarters, I looked at the civilians pouring into the streets of Baghdad and celebrating, and I understood what no Middle Eastern studies class could ever have taught me. The majority of the demonstrators and dancing folks in the streets weren't adult males or women or older persons. It was all young people! The very first moments of that regime change were a genome of the revolution that could happen not just in Iraq, but also in Syria and beyond. I told my colleague, military analyst and retired lieutenant colonel Rick Francona, "You're seeing what lies way deeper in these societies. The children's behavior tells it all. They are telling us that they detest the Baath dictatorship and want freedom and fun. They want life." Of course the minute the politicized adults appeared, the spirit was gone. That very short moment told me everything, but it also showed the same to those who were watching in the Damascus Baathist headquarters.

Syria's Baathists understood that the fall of their counterparts in Iraq, and a majority of Iraqis' expressing their elation, was a bad omen. From that moment on, the Assad regime went on a jihad in three directions. One, they would strike to the east at the forthcoming democratic process in Iraq by unleashing terrorists across their common border. Two, they would make a preemptive strike to the west at a potential uprising in Lebanon, and three, they would strike in the center at dissidence within Syria.

The offensive into Iraq unleashed six more years of bloodshed. The repression in Lebanon led to the assassination of Rafiq Hariri, which triggered the Cedars Revolution; and the repression inside Syria dismantled what little progress Syrian dissidents had achieved. In 2005, Bashar went after the signatories of the Damascus Declaration and tightened his alliance with the Iranian regime.

The regime's ultimate nightmare was to see the day young kids in the streets of Damascus brought down the statues of the father and the son dictators—the end of the regime. After being forced to withdraw from Lebanon in April 2005, Assad feared the worst. The international investigation into the Hariri assassination could eventually bring him or his aides to the Hague for prosecution. That would certainly signify the collapse of the regime.[17] Besides, the Cedars Revolution in Beirut was spreading democratic ideals in Lebanon and would soon enough serve as a springboard to inflame a revolution in Syria. To his east, Assad resented the multiple elections taking place in Iraq and the expansion of a multiparty system, the antithesis of his one-party system.

The Baath of Syria were under siege from democracy on the outside and dissidence on the inside. At one point, anti-Syrian Lebanese media and some Arab press projected a collapse of the regime in Damascus. In Washington, liberal Syrian NGOs trained the personnel of civil organizations to educate Syrians on how to adjust to democracy after decades of authoritarianism. Farid Ghadri's Syrian Reform Party called on the U.S. administration and the European Union to apply greater pressure to hasten the collapse. Michael Ledeen, a seasoned Middle East expert in Washington working at the American Enterprise Institute, wrote as early as 2003 about the necessity of extending pressure to Iran and Syria after the Iraq invasion.[18] In Paris, former Syrian vice president Abdel Halim Khaddam spoke out against the Assad faction as much as he could, and with the authority of someone who was a main player inside the Baath regime for many years. He told media, "The security services control power. They have interests and their leaders have their own interests. Therefore, the role of the security services decreases when people are empowered to believe in their ability to confront the mistakes committed so far."[19]

Out of Europe an opposition coalition was formed including Khaddam and other anti-Assad groups, including the Syrian branch of the Muslim Brotherhood. Their participation in the coalition raised questions about the democratic nature of a post-Assad government. As of 2009, the Brotherhood withdrew from the "Salvation Front" and began a "dialogue" with the regime.

Between 2005 and 2008, the long and indecisive "Beirut Spring" gave an opportunity to the Syrian reformers to find breathing space not far from their mother country. Lebanon was to Syria, in the mind of the dissidents, as Poland was to Russia during the Eastern European revolution. Beirut attained a modicum of freedom before Damascus. But Syria couldn't sustain the democracy pressure for too long. It was only a matter of time before the Cedars Revolution would trigger a similar uprising in Syria. Supporters of reform waited for the tide to turn. However, as the Arab proverb says: Winds didn't blow in the ship's preferred direction.

A series of setbacks on the regional and local levels forced the dissident movement to go on the defensive again. The failure of the Cedars Revolution to mobilize the international community in order to disarm Hezbollah and the pro-Syrian militias led to a collapse of the pro-Western Fuad Seniora government, piece by piece. The defeat of the Cedars Revolution in Lebanon translated to a victory for the Assad regime, which was able to gradually erode the international pressure surrounding Damascus. With the decline of U.S. policy in support of democracy in the region as of 2007, due to a change of majority in the U.S. Congress, the Syrian regime was able to come back to international political life. The more elements in Washington circles, encouraged by pro-Syrian academia, spoke of "engaging" Assad, the less isolated he was.[20]

In May 2008, Syria's allies seized the government in Lebanon, paralyzing the Cedars Revolution, preventing the Syrian dissident community in Beirut from assisting its sister in Damascus. On the Iraqi front, Baghdad was accusing the Bashar regime of masterminding bombings in Iraq so that democracy would be delayed, and its influence on Syria's reformers would be weakened.[21] Naturally, Iran's ayatollahs have a convergent interest in rolling back democracy everywhere in the region, and Tehran's operatives were allied with Syria's intelligence in crushing democracy forces in Lebanon, Iraq, and Syria.

By 2008, profreedom forces were defeated in Lebanon and intimidated in Iraq while dissident elements inside Syria were receiving much harsher treatment. With the coming of the Obama administration to the White House, the hope for any American support for democracy in Syria faded away. Instead, U.S. foreign policy was all about "engaging" the Assad regime. The word "engaging," when used of a brutal dictator, has become synonymous with "disengaging" from democracy in the new administration. President Obama's attitude in 2009 regarding the Iranian protests said it all to Assad. America has turned away from its commitment to the reformists. In the past two years, the signatories of the 2005 Damascus Declaration have been further persecuted. By 2010, the reformers in Syria had reentered the dark ages of oppression.

Is everything lost?

Dissidents' Future

Farid Ghadri, the most radical opposition figure to the Assad regime, says otherwise. "This is a setback to the reformers. The United States has caved in to the pressures by the Syrian-Iranian axis and as a result, Lebanon's democracy collapsed and Syria's dissidents are suffering further. But one thing we need to understand: The Syrian people are angrier than ever against the regime. The reformers are in a rough patch, but the Assad dictatorship has lost its legitimacy, let alone its credibility as a governing body," he asserts.[22]

Ghadri's description of the readiness of most Syrians for a massive change contradicts the descriptions by some scholars in the United States who have argued otherwise, including Professor Landis in his writings about the unreadiness of Syrians to absorb democracy.[23] But other scholars, such as Professor Rabil, disagree: "Readiness for democracy in Syria is one thing and the ability to fight for it is something else," he told a conference on Middle Eastern studies in January 2008.[24] The real question is if the Syrian reformers have the capacity to organize and lead that movement in the years ahead. There is no doubt that a majority of Syrians want change, a real radical change toward democracy and freedom. There is no question that a society that was as brutalized as Syria's was by the Baathist dictatorship would be more than ready for change. Actually, as we have learned from the struggle of the Eastern Europeans, it awaits signals from both inside and outside. What remains to be seen is whether the reformers will come together to mount a coordinated effort.

In a speech given in April 2008 at the invitation of the Syrian American Congress, in Los Angeles, Chicago, and Detroit at the celebration of the Syrian Independence Day, exiled human rights activist Haytham Manna said: "Syria's last century has been one of upheaval and political-social disintegration. Colonialism, nationalism, and Islamism have each played a role in this disintegration, which has seen the law of force consistently replace the rule of law. This disintegration has left a political vacuum, with the struggle for human rights and viable civil society the only option if we are to reclaim the political life of Syria and rescue it from this black period of history."[25]

The agenda is clear: dissolution of the police state, abandoning Caliphate-type ambitions, unleashing freedom, multiparty elections, and social justice. The reformers of Syria can do it if they come together, and once they do it, it is evident that the Syrian masses will mobilize for the change to come. When that happens, democracies around the world must stand by Syria's civil society, all the way to a democratic revolution. No doubt about it—it is coming.

10.

The Green Revolution:
Iran's Youth, Women, and Minorities

The sight of tens of thousands of young men and women taking to the streets of Tehran in June 2009 after the botched elections was moving and inspiring. Here were the youngest in society, raising their fists and blasting the most powerful jihadi regime on the planet. It was a vision that was surreal, even though I had expected it to happen ever since the Khomeinist elite took over and expanded its grip on the Iranian people in the mid-1980s.

I always believed that eventually a new generation would reverse the oppression that befell the Iranian people at the hands of the ayatollahs. It is a constant principle in the history of nations. The antidote to suppression always comes from within the societies that are subjected to suffering. The differences are in the context, the players, and above all the time needed to achieve change. But in the end, oppressive regimes have one certainty: They will go down.

Tehran's ruling elites are part of the Khomeinist movement, one of the two world networks of jihadism. They control the resources of an oil-producing government, a highly militarized supporter of terror organizations in many countries in the region, including Iraq, Lebanon, Yemen, and the Palestinian territories. In addition, the Iranian regime has formed a strategic axis with another oppressive military regime in Syria, maintains security and intelligence ties in multiple spots in Africa, and has alliances as far as Venezuela and Bolivia. It maintains a lethal grip over its own population and supports oppression in Syria, Lebanon, and Gaza in the Palestinian territories.

Perhaps the most critical race between totalitarianism and democracy is taking place in Iran, the home base of Khomeinism. After thirty years of Islamic Republic rule, the opposition is slowly emerging. Ethnic minorities such as the Kurds, Azeris, Baluch, and Arabs are already developing tensions with Tehran's mullahs. Even among the Persian ethnic majority, students, women, artists, workers, and other sectors are clashing with the regime, whose central force—known as the Pasdaran—is the most powerful and wealthy Islamist militia in the world; it is the primary tool of Tehran's ruling elite in maintaining power. But all indications are that a revolution is brewing. The 2009 election's aftermath was only one link in a long chain. It is because of the immense ramifications of a potential anti-jihadist revolution in Iran that the stakes there are the highest in the entire Arab Islamic world.

The outcome of the demonstrations that erupted in June 2009 will determine the fate of the struggle for freedom in the entire region. That is why, when the words of President Barack Obama were aired live days after the start of the bloody repression in Tehran, all those whose hopes swelled at the sight of a million people in the street of the Iranian capital were depressed. "It is not productive, given the history of U.S. and Iranian relations, to be seen as meddling in Iranian elections," President Obama said. Unlike the words of President Ronald Reagan in support of the Eastern European demonstrations against communist dictatorships in 1989, the cold statement by President Obama in 2009 was described as "cautious" by his supporters, and clearly signaled a decline in U.S. support for the freedom struggle across the region.

Fortunately, Obama's unwillingness to back the youth in Iran didn't affect the commitment of Iranian reformers. One year after the June 2009 eruption, the "Green Revolution" is still breathing, and perhaps expanding. It is an odd reality that this revolution, which has been abandoned by Washington's decision-makers, is marching forward despite the lack of U.S. support. Of all democratic revolutions to come from Middle Earth, Iran's Green uprising will be the most decisive. If, or rather, when it achieves its goals and the ayatollahs are removed, the region will at last be on its way to democracy.

Iran throughout History

Modern Iran is a mix of ancient Persia and the legacy of the Islamic Caliphate. The Persian Empire was the most powerful of the empires east of the Mediterranean and conquered the widest territory, from

India to Greece. Advanced in sciences and urban organization, the Persians, who are ethnically Indo-Europeans, dominated provinces on three continents (Europe, Asia, and Africa) and produced a classical universal civilization. Just like other empires throughout history, Persia was invaded and conquered by outside forces, led by the Hellenic armies of Alexander of Macedonia in 331 B.C.E. Surviving the Greek domination, the Persian Empire rose again under various dynasties, including that of the Sassanid clan, until Arab Muslim armies invaded the heartland of ancient Persia, transforming its identity profoundly by the seventh century C.E. The Arab *Fatah* of Persia was a benchmark in the history of the Persian nation. After defeating the Persian armies in Mesopotamia at the battles of Qadissiya and Nehavend in 637, the forces of the Caliphate marched through Persia, taking one city after another until the complete dismantling of the empire and the establishment of Islamic governorates were accomplished.[1]

The Arab *Fatah* of Persia led to important developments, particularly a change in religion. The majority of the Persian population was converted to Islam, the religion of the conquerors. Zoroastrianism and Mazdaism, the historical religions of Persia, shrank into small minority faiths. The majority of Persian converts to the new religion opted for Shiism rather than Sunni tradition, as a protest movement against the Caliphate, a chief institution of Sunnis. In the centuries following the conquest, Persia remained a collection of mostly Shia provinces within a vast Caliphate empire. It was ruled directly by the Arabs until Farsi-speaking local dynasties (Farsi is the language of Persia) began to administer areas of the country such as the Tahirid, the Alavid, and the Saffavid.

Independent Persian dynasties rose to power in 1501 with the Safavids, until the rule of the Pahlevi in 1925. Under the Pahlevi a modernized state was established in Persia under the name of Iran. It was a monarchy ruling a majority of Persians in the center and a number of other nationalities who lived on its periphery.

Iran as a multiethnic country is a product of modern times. It is a merging of two identities: ancient pre-Islamic Persia and Shia Islam. Persian nationalism was able to achieve what other pre-Arab nations in the Levant weren't able to accomplish, that is, to resist "Arabization" of their culture and maintain a level of "Persianism." The conversion to Islam created a peculiar situation for the former empire.

Persians entered the Islamic *Umma* under the Caliphate, but not the Arab identity. Besides, the choice of Shiism kept the peculiarity of Persians within the wider *Umma*, with a Sunni majority. In addition, Persian dynasties were able to free themselves from the authority of the caliphs early on (around the time of the Crusades), and by the time the Ottomans invaded the Arab provinces of the Near East, Persian dynasties had secured a geographical independence from the Caliphate. The Sunni Ottoman Empire was denied control east of Mesopotamia, and Persia was able to exit the dominance of the Sunni Caliphate.

Since the 1920s the Pahlevi crown, although authoritarian, has pushed in the direction of Iranian secular nationalism while maintaining Shia Islam as a state religion. Modern Iran witnessed the rise of several ideological forces: As a neighbor to the Soviet Union, the country saw the rise of a powerful communist party, the Tudeh. Liberal elites spread across the educated segments of society while the business community, known as Bazaar, and the moderate Shia clerics supported the shah's regime. Iran under the Pahlevi survived World War II even as the Soviets and British exerted influences from the north and the south.

During the Cold War, the new Shah Reza Pahlevi stood firmly in the pro-American camp as he was severely criticized by the left wing, which was sympathetic to the Soviets, and the liberals, calling for rapid democratization. In 1951, a reformist prime minister, Mohammad Mossadegh, moved to nationalize the oil industry, mostly controlled by British companies. A struggle between Mossadegh and the shah led to a brief exile of the shah, followed by a military coup, backed by the CIA, against the prime minister. The shah's supporters claimed they were liberalizing the country, while their opponents accused them of authoritarian populism. The shah took back power in 1953 and kept Iran under tight control to prevent a countercoup by the communists. In order to contain the left wing, Reza Pahlevi had to proceed with land reforms and alphabetization. In doing so he alienated a large segment of the clerical order, already penetrated by a new brand of Shia Islamists.

The Khomeinist Revolution

On the evening of February 11, 1979, I was in Beirut, listening to the international radio. Suddenly, half the city started firing shots into the air. They were celebrating the fall of the shah's regime in Tehran.

The celebrations stretched from West Beirut, dominated by Syria's allied militias, across Syria itself, through Iraq's south, into Iran's cities, now under control of the Islamic Revolution led by Ayatollah Ruhollah Khomeini, the supreme leader of Shia jihadism. A new empire was born, but it wasn't a renewed Persian Empire. In fact, it was the rise of a Shia form of jihadism, competitive with the Salafi form already entrenched in the Arab and Muslim world.

That evening I witnessed the birth of a power structure that would dominate the politics of the Middle East for three decades. The "other" jihadi dragon was born and would compete with the Salafist dragon for the hearts and minds of Muslims and Arabs. The two groups struggled between the reestablishing of the Caliphate (in the eyes of the Sunni jihadists) and establishing an Imamate (in the eyes of the Shia jihadists). The Iranian Islamic Revolution was an affirmation by the Khomeinist jihadists of their exclusive control of the Shia populations of the Muslim world, while the Salafi movement rushed to establish its own control over Sunni people around the world.

The three-decade-long history of the Khomeinist Republic has three main characteristics: first is the suppression of democracy within Iran as a way to maintain control for the regime; second is the penetration of other Shia communities outside Iran, including Lebanon, Iraq, and Arabia; third is the intention to transform Iran's Khomeinist regime into a world power with a series of alliances and the acquiring of nuclear military power.[2]

As soon as the shah abdicated and went into exile with his family, the Khomeinist forces, acting as the Bolsheviks did in 1917, seized all power in the country by eliminating their revolutionary partners one after another. Liberals, Marxists, and other political forces were swiftly marginalized as the Islamists established the foundation for a new institution they characterized as an "Islamic Republic." The Iranian Communist Party, the main opposition to the shah during the Cold War, was banned, and many of its members were executed. Another partner in the revolt against the shah was the Islamic left-wing organization Mujahideen Khalq (the People's Mujahideen), whose members fought the previous regime so fiercely that they were accused by the United States of terrorism, but nevertheless were suppressed by Khomeini's militias and forced into exile. Toward the end of 1979 a "referendum" was organized by the followers of Ayatollah Khomeini as a base for the launching of an "Islamic Republic."

The Islamic Republic

Global Islamist ideologies as designed by the Wahabis, Muslim Brotherhoods, and other Salafists since the early twentieth century traditionally reject the Western forms of government, including republics and democracy, on two grounds. The first is antisecularism: They believe laws should be derived from Sharia, and only the institutions of a republic should be man-made by the voting process. The second is that as Salafists, they believe that nations—in this case the *Umma*—follow the guidance of Allah through the clerics, and not the elected officials representing the will of the people. But the Khomeinists don't subscribe to all of the Islamist ideas. Since they hail from a Shia background and have been historically persecuted by the Sunni caliphs, they will not seek the "reestablishing" of this same institution. Theologically, their faith calls for the "return of a vanished imam" who would bring justice to the *Umma*. However, the Shia jihadists developed another concept adapted from modern laws but integrated in the nondemocratic notion of religious fundamentalism.

The state the Khomeinists launched has the name "republic," yet derives its ultimate legitimacy from a supreme leader who derives his power from Allah. Therefore the *Jumhuriye* doesn't reflect the will of the people but the will of Khomeini and his elite, who claim they are mandated by the divine. This "mandate," known as *Vilayet*, is granted by Allah and recognized by the religious peers. The wisest and most knowledgeable of these clerics is the one who would lead unquestioned. The *Faqih* is thus the supreme leader, and the untouchable institution is called *Vilayet e Faqih*, the "mandate of the wisest." In short, it is an ideological construction to concentrate power in the hands of the Khomeinist elite. A totalitarian regime with an expansionist agenda is born.[3]

The "revolution" launched by the radical ayatollahs doesn't represent the traditional views of the mainstream Shia clerics; rather, it contradicts those guidelines. The classical Shia position known as *Samita* or "quietist" does not promote a "jihad" or call for a totalitarian republic to prepare for the end of time and the return of the vanished imam. The Shia jihadists, the followers of Khomeini, "innovated" (some say twisted the faith) by adding the necessity of jihad and the suppression of democratic forms of government. With the rise of Iran's regime, the quietist school was suppressed in Iran and Lebanon and marginalized in Iraq's holy cities.

The supreme leader oversees any opportunity to generate more power for himself in the country. He is assisted by a Majliss, his peers and advisors. His office controls the central militia of the country, the Pasdaran, known as the Iranian Revolutionary Islamic Guards. Organized like the SS, the Pasdaran controls every aspect of public life in Iran and has gradually expanded its control in the financial and economic sectors. The nerve center of the regime, the "Islamic Guards," oversees its own popular militias, the Basiji, who tightly control the civilian neighborhoods. The militias and intelligence services, under the supreme leader's control, monitor the army, the police, the justice system, and the rest of the country's institutions. The Islamic constitution "allows" elections of the legislative branch, but only with candidates "authorized" by a ministry of interior under Khomeini's control. It is all severely controlled by an elite group of mullahs and intelligence chiefs.

The regime, with all its tentacles, suffocates the segments of society that are the most prone to reject this political culture: women, youth, and workers. Iran's women are harshly suppressed, almost at the same level of brutality as is practiced by the Taliban. Students were crushed on their campuses for years in any attempt to raise issues of freedom. Workers, artists, and other groups within the society were subjected to unbearable regulations restricting the actions of unions and associations. The regime funded its own supporters graciously from Iran's oil dividends and maintained a web of connections to the countryside, recruiting most of its militiamen from villages with low levels of education.

Iran's Persian majority was coerced into the grip of the Islamic Republic through oppression and control of its citizens, and the enticement of a minority of collaborators. Through the seizure of the ministry of education and the school system, the regime was able to mold teaching curricula to promote the Islamist agenda, unleashing one of the most powerful brainwashing processes in the history of the region. Droves of youth were indoctrinated into the Khomeinist version of jihadism for decades, before they were recruited into the regime's apparatus, a concept reminiscent of national socialist and Bolshevik methods.

Even though the majority of Iranian civil society wasn't enthused by the totalitarian methods, a strong radicalized minority formed the "constituency" of the regime, providing eager men and sometimes women to the militias, bureaucracies, and intelligence services. Just as in the communist systems, the Iranian regime was able to display its "popular basis" whenever politically necessary by gathering hundreds of thousands of demonstrators chanting, "Death to America and death to Israel." The demonstrations created by the Khomeinists served as a catalyst for national mobilization, fuel for their external propaganda and intimidation of potential opposition.

By the early 1980s, Khomeini's power within Iran was completely unchallenged. The path for the "empire" was wide open. Dispersing their message through the region's Shia communities became the next strategic step of the mullahs. The map of expansion had been clear since the inception of the revolution. The central and southern parts of Iraq, the Shia areas of Lebanon, and the Shia enclaves in the Arabian Peninsula were the main targets.

It was clear that Khomeini's priority was to "conquer" as many Shia regions as possible. First, ensure dominance in the Shia sphere, and then move to the Sunni space. It was logical that Iran under the Islamic Republic wanted to bring down Saddam's Baathist regime so that it could link with Assad's Alawi power in Syria, and from there connect with Hezbollah in Lebanon. Just as with similar totalitarian regimes in the twentieth century, the Iranian rulers planned to use outside confrontations to tighten their grip on their civil societies. The more Khomeini engaged in wars outside Iran, the more his apparatus inside the country was able to crush the forces of opposition. Naturally, the main argument used by the ayatollahs to eliminate opposition and dissidence was the alleged link to the enemy. Iran's regional adventures became Khomeini's tool to preempt the rise of democracy among Iranians.

Iran-Iraq War and Domestic Oppression

The Iran-Iraq War of 1980 was initially triggered by a regime change in Tehran, even though it was the regime in Baghdad that first ordered its forces into battle. Under the shah, a balance of power was established between the two countries, with Iraq backed by the Soviets and Iran supported by the United States. Khomeini's agenda of "exporting the revolution"[4] upset the balance of power and sparked a confrontation between the Islamist Iranian movement and the Baathist Pan Arab rulers of Iraq. Saddam knew the Iranians were going to enflame the Shia majority in his country and preempted this by attacking the Islamic Republic.

The devastating Iran-Iraq War, fought between two totalitarian forces, Islamism and Baathism, and based on the historical resentments between Shia and Sunnis, claimed the lives of one million victims. The lethal clash between the two titans devastated civil societies on both sides of the border and allowed both regimes to further crush internal opposition. Inside Iran, the Pasdaran and the Basiji militias wreaked havoc among secular sectors, eliminating intellectuals, students, militaries, and members of other banned groups.[5] Between 1980 and 1987, the Khomeinist regime eliminated the bulk of its opposition, from royalists to communists, including moderate Islamists and liberals. Among the groups repressed were the Mujahideen (PMOI), a left-wing Islamic group that fought the shah during the revolution but opposed the establishment of a theological regime in Iran. The PMOI was exiled and some of its members established an opposition base in Iraq to operate against the Khomeinist regime.

The war with Iraq allowed the mullahs to consolidate their powerful grip in ways that would have been impossible otherwise. During these bloody years hundreds of thousands of citizens were killed, arrested, and tortured by the Pasdaran and Basiji. Millions were forced to serve in the deadly battles against Saddam's military machine. Children as young as twelve were sent to war with a key to heaven around their necks and herded into dangerous areas to clear up minefields.

The slaughter was reminiscent of the horrors of World War I, with tens of thousands massacred each month. In addition to suppressing the majority Persians, the Iranian regime went after almost all minorities. The Kurds were among the most persecuted by the Khomeinists. Secular and seeking their own autonomy, the Kurds of the Mahabad province in the western part of the country demanded cultural and political rights when the Islamic Revolution succeeded. Beginning in 1980, they were met with severe repression as the regime's militias were sent into their towns and villages to quash their protests.[6] South of the Kurds, the Arab population of the Ahwaz province was also subjected to ethnocide, as the regime refused to recognize the Arab cultural identity.

However, the province of Khusistan, known also as Arabstan, is the richest in oil. The Khomeinists used their war with Saddam to accuse their Arab citizens of collaborating with Iraq. The Ahwaz Arab minority accused Tehran of attempting to remove them from their ancestral lands to ensure full control of the oil fields. An Arab separatist movement spread throughout the province in response to the oppression.[7]

To Tehran's east, the Baluchi minority—mostly Sunni—was also a target for persecution by the Islamic regime. Hundreds of citizens and activists were arrested and tortured in the early years of the "revolution," and many were executed.[8] Last but not least, the large Azeri (Turkic-speaking) community living in the northwestern part of Iran and traditionally bound to the Persian power centers in Tehran witnessed tensions as well. Despite the fact that a number of Iranian leaders, including those of the Islamic Republic originally from what was known as southern Azerbaijan (relative to the post-Soviet independent Republic of Azerbaijan), demanded autonomy from Tehran, just as they had hoped for democracy after the shah was deposed, they received none. Mahmud Ali Chereghani, an activist in Tabriz, called for the separation of Azeri provinces from Iran and unification with what he called "North Azerbaijan." His arrest in 1999 was swift and Tehran's response draconian. That year, prodemocracy protests in Tabriz ranked second only to those in Tehran in terms of size and focused on the granting of greater freedom of the press throughout the country.[9]

Khomeini's war on Iran's minorities was parallel to his regime's suppression of the Persian majority in the center. The equation was simple: If the center got more freedom, the periphery would follow, and if the nationalities were granted autonomy, then the democracy opposition in the center would be emboldened. The regime's overwhelming oppression of the Iranian people was simple: freedom to none.

Reform and Reformers

As of the end of the Iran-Iraq War in 1988, the regime focused on consolidating its gains internally. Repression grew systematically against dissidents and potential opposition. Tehran, which considered itself victorious against Saddam, was watching the reforms initiated in the Soviet Union by Gorbachev with great concern. Dangerous precedents were being set in Moscow as perestroika and glasnost were under way. When a totalitarian regime liberalizes, the local totalitarians begin to get nervous. The very idea of "reforms" in an Islamic republic whose legitimacy descends from the discretion of the *Vilayet e Faqih* is equivalent to undermining the divine root of power. The Khomeinist republic is rooted in Allah's will, which is accomplished via the grand ayatollah. Undermining this equation by proposing reforms to the system is like reforming the will of Allah, which is impossible. Khomeini rejected any attempt to conduct reorganization of the republic's basic ideological structure. The Stalinist era of Iran was embodied by the ironclad seal of the founding ayatollah. That era ended with the death of Khomeini in June 1989, but he was quickly replaced by his faithful follower Ayatollah Khamanei, who resumed the work of his predecessor.

The collapse of the Soviet Union transformed the United States into the world's sole superpower. The end of the Cold War signaled to Tehran's elite that "the Greater Satan" was freed from the containment policy and could direct its power against the Islamic Republic. The Desert Shield and Desert Storm operations in response to Iraq's invasion of Kuwait brought U.S. military power to the Gulf and coalition airpower to northern and southern Iraq.

The Iranian regime, which hoped for a renewed offensive in Iraq at some point to link with Syria near the Mediterranean, was indirectly blocked by the American presence in the region. The plans were stalled, but not stopped. Isolated by American containment, Iran's economy was not booming despite the oil dividends. Since the early 1990s, there had been two dynamics within the regime—first, the Khamanei agenda of domestic suppression and regional expansion, and second, attempts by elements within the regime to engage in economic reform reminiscent of the Gorbachev perestroika.

The new mood in the country, particularly after the death of Khomeini and the ascendance of the United States as sole superpower, allowed for the rise of so-called reformers within the system. Backed by religious figures not aligned with Khamanei's orthodoxy, such as Ayatollah Muntazeri and Prime Minister Mir Hossein Mousavi, they paved the way for the election of Mohammad Khatami to the presidency of the republic in 1997. A scholar and a religious figure, Khatami was overwhelmingly supported by women and youth, signaling the real energy that could lead to democratic revolution years later. Khatami projected an image of being willing to reach out to the international community as a way to attract financial investments and business expansion. His supporters within the government were called "reformers," but opponents of the regime rejected that description.[10] "The followers of Khatami wanted the same republic as Khomeini but with economic viability, while the followers of Khamenei would take Iran to its economic downfall to maintain the ideology of Islamism," Mrs. Manda Zand Ervin, founder and president of the Alliance of Iranian Women, told me in 2007. Ervin's reading of the Khatami presidency, which lasted until 2005, seems to be the consensus among all Iranian exiles, from the shah's son Mohammed Reza Pahlevi, based in America, to the left-wing Maryam Rajavi, head of the People's Mujahideen Organization, based in France.

By the end of the 1990s, there were two types of reformers, those within the system who supported Khatami and those outside the system whose leaders were in exile.

The Student Revolution

The reformers had a wide following among students, women, and minorities. More accessible than the other movements because of their presence on campuses, thousands of Iranian students staged vast antiregime demonstrations in their universities in 1999. Reminiscent of the Chinese revolt at Tiananmen Square, the first student uprisings in Iran since 1979 spread throughout Tehran and other cities. Uniquely, there was a large female element in the movement. For the first time since the 1979 Khomeinist revolution, young couples were demonstrating hand in hand, expressing their desire for personal freedoms. Iranian youth were now yearning to live their lives without dark clouds hovering around their heads. The repression of romantic relations, of sexual freedom, and of women's rights were so extreme under the Khomeinist regime that some of the protests looked like a sexual revolution spreading on the street and on the internet.[11] Banafsheh Zand-Bonazzi, a leading New York–based Iranian activist, told me in 2004 that "the youth in Iran consider the ayatollah regime as a whole, not just Khamanei or this or any other president, as an enemy of their personal lives." Zand-Bonazzi, the editor of *Planet Iran*, said the 1999 uprisings on campuses "were the beginning of a revolution that will unfold and will only end with the removal of the Khomeinsts from power completely."

As I observed the students' struggles in Iran in 1999 and compared them with demonstrations in following years, I saw that their dynamics were deep, culturally motivated, and transferred from generation to generation. More important, the mutating leadership of the Iranian students was moving in step with world events. As with the Polish workers of the 1980s, the Iranian students of the 1990s understood that they needed to keep their movement alive until the planets of international relations aligned themselves favorably.

Iranian dissidents based in the West agreed that the Iranian democratic revolution would not happen as rapidly as the Eastern European revolutions of 1989. It will happen gradually and steadily, with many reversals. In Central Europe, changes in world politics affected the speed of revolutions. The Soviet Bloc had Gorbachev's reforms to facilitate protest movements. And those movements were possible only after years of U.S. pressure, particularly during the Reagan years. Iran's student revolts were at the core of any forthcoming democratic revolution, but these protest movements would burst into a wider social movement only when the outside world was sensitive enough to recognize them. It was clear to me that 9/11 was a benchmark even in the evolution of the democracy movement inside Iran, for a simple reason. After terror hit the heart of the free world, public opinion in the West became more interested in the fate of forces of change in the countries that generate terrorism. Iran's reformer intellectuals and students understood the link and maintained their pressure accordingly.

In July 1999, students started to demonstrate in various universities. For one week violent confrontations took place between the regime's forces and the students. It started with a police raid on a university dormitory, a response to demonstrations by a group of students of Tehran University against the closure of a reformist newspaper. The unrest, with no support from the outside world, lasted for days before the Pasdaran could take back the campuses and jail dozens of protesters.[12] Akbar Mohammadi was given a death sentence, later reduced to fifteen years in prison, for his role in the protests. In 2006, he died at Evin prison after a hunger strike protesting the refusal to allow him to seek medical treatment for injuries suffered as a result of torture.

Under the "reformist" rule of Khatami, the state militia was still in charge of protecting the regime and crushing any form of protest. But the student movement didn't die out. Many left the country and formed a younger generation of activists abroad. Iran's democracy developed voices overseas that would be crucial for the future domestic uprising.

Bin Laden's attack on New York and Washington during the summer of 2001 triggered a tsunami of changes worldwide, starting with a rapid regime change in Afghanistan. The fall of the Taliban and their replacement by a gradually developing democracy, even though far from completed and still under threat, sent chills into the veins of the Tehran regime and boosted the revolutionary feelings among youth and women. Many within Iran's underground movement thought that if the jihadi regime of Afghanistan fell, then why not crumble the equally fascist regime in Iran? Iran's Pasdaran, quick to understand the effects of 9/11 and the fall of the Taliban, proceeded to take out those elements that could start the student revolt again.

The demonstrations resumed toward the end of 2002 as students held mass demonstrations protesting the death sentence of reformist lecturer Hashem Aghajari for alleged blasphemy. More than ten thousand students gathered at Tehran University in support of Professor Aghajari, who had dared "question the clerical rule in the Islamic Republic." In June 2003, thousands of students took to the streets of Tehran in antigovernment protests.[13] They promoted associations between terrorist groups and their regime's oppressors. Their slogans were evolving: "No, no to the Taliban, from Kabul to Tehran," was a common mass chant. This was a signal that the student movement wanted the world to realize that the ayatollahs and their Pasdaran were a Khomeinist form of the Salafi Taliban. If the Taliban were removed from Afghanistan, the Pasdaran had to follow in Iran. The revolutionary movement in the country was looking for a complete political change, not just a few reforms that would allow some breathing room inside a dark dungeon.

Emboldened by the collapse of two totalitarian regimes to the east and to the west of their country, Iran's student movement expanded its reach through national coordination, acquiring communication technologies such as cell phones, online access, and satellite dishes. Overseas, exiled student leaders who had left Iran between 1999 and 2005 provided a better understanding of the democracy movement to decision-makers, media, and the public in general. Many young names emerged in the Iranian Diaspora, among them that of Amir Farshad Ebrahimi, who quit the supporters of the regime and joined the dissidents overseas. A former child soldier and political prisoner, he declared that Iran's bloody crackdown on protesters prompted him to expose ex-colleagues in Ansar-e Hezbollah who took part in the beatings.[14] Amir Fakhravar, the former president of Iran's National Students Union, was a prominent student voice. After escaping the Pasdaran, Fakhravar exposed the all-out suppression of freedom in the country.[15]

Civil Society Rises

Between 2003 and 2005, Khamanei's agencies scrambled to contain what could have become an expanding revolt among youth and other sectors of society. Iranian women, the most dangerous segment of the population to the authoritarian elite, were specifically targeted, and a number of feminist activities drew the attention of international observers. On International Women's Day on March 8, 2003, a large gathering of women in Tehran's Laleh Park was the first public female demonstration since the imposition of compulsory hijab and the protests that followed in 1980. Later that year, a Hyde Park–style women's rally was organized at the Shafagh Cultural Center. Then, the first online conference of Iranian feminists around the globe on gendered stereotypes of "good mother," "good daughter," and "good wife" followed. In 2004 about 60 percent of female college students joined the Women's Intellectual Coalition. On June 12, 2005, two thousand women demonstrated in front of Tehran University, demanding equality under the law, chanting the anthem of Iran's women's movement for the first time.

The protest movement of Iran's workers is less well-known. Placed under the control of the "Islamic Labor Councils," explicitly defined in Iran's labor law as ideologically centered entities, the masses of workers were among the most active in their opposition to the jihadi regime since its inception in 1979. Influenced by socialist organizers and independent secular forces, Iranian labor unions never surrendered to Khomeinism. They criticized the regime's Labor Council for not focusing on promoting workers' rights and for being incompatible with the concept of independent unions. Iran's workforce, although silent politically, has been the most consistent and largest bloc of civil society to resist the control of the Islamists. Ironically, left-wing and liberal media in the West have long ignored the workers' opposition to the ayatollah's regime. Teachers, cab and bus drivers, and the crucial oil industry workers organized strikes.[16] Iran's economy wasn't taking off, despite large revenues from the oil industry, precisely because the lower middle and the working classes weren't on board with the Islamic Republic.

However, in the countryside, a small number of jobless youth have been the breeding ground for the regime's Pasdaran. Less-educated and nonpoliticized peasant supporters of the Islamic Republic were shipped from their villages to join the militias of the regime and confront the popular uprisings. These supporters of Khomeinism aren't the largest segment of the villagers; the silent majority in this vast part of Iran isn't satisfied with the opposition by the clergy to the land reforms supported by the shah before 1979.

On the periphery of the Persian population, the forces of secession among ethnic minorities also rose in opposition to Tehran's policies. The rebellion of non-Persian peoples, previously attached to the Pahlevi crown in a symbolic Iranian federation, was the most threatening to the power of the mullahs. After being crushed by the Pasdaran in the 1980s, Kurdish, Arab, Baluchi, and Azeri ethnicities moved to assert their cultural and political rights. Hundreds of activists who were forced into exile organized NGOs and created websites to make the case for their causes to the international community. The global opposition to Khamanei's regime—if aggregated—represents a majority of Iranians. The ethnic minorities alone form around 35 percent of Iran's population. Among Persians, particularly in the urban zones, a majority of women, youth, and workers were also opposed to the Islamist ruling elite. What the outside world ignored, or was made to ignore, was that the majority of Iran's people rejected the jihadi regime. Yet, as in the Soviet Union and in Eastern Europe, there was no way to know exactly how people felt about their government. It took years for students and other opposition groups to signal to the West the presence of a large discontented population in the country.

Media War

The regime was determined to prevent the population's message from reaching the international media. The opposition exposed the

Pasdaran war against satellite dishes. "They used military helicopters to shoot down dishes from afar," Saeed Ghanji, a leading activist from the Iranian opposition in exile, told me. "Tehran's regime was adamant about accusing the outside media of being controlled by the American aggressors," said Alireza Jafarzadeh, an Iranian expert with Fox News, who also revealed the locations of the nuclear program inside Iran. The media war between the regime and the opposition raged on, especially after 2003 and the fall of Saddam. Tehran strengthened its propaganda machine, particularly via its Arab outlet al Aalam TV, and its English satellite channel, Press TV, as well as the sophisticated media arm of Hezbollah in Lebanon.

What Iran's regime couldn't directly achieve in its battle against its own democracy movement, Hezbollah's propagandists could. The Iran-funded militia established out of Beirut a web of media including al Manar TV and a number of newspapers. Hezbollah's major task in support of the Khomeinist elite in its confrontation with the dissidents was a vast propaganda network made of Western journalists, bloggers, websites, and research teams operating between Beirut and the rest of the world's capitals. Veteran journalist Marvin Kalb argued that Hezbollah had been "exercising absolute control over how journalists portrayed its side of the 2006 war in Lebanon."[17] In 2007, military analyst Thomas Smith exposed a network of Western journalists and bloggers who had been groomed by Hezbollah to become attack dogs against any critics of the Iranian agenda in the region. The online artillery was deployed to strike at Iranian dissidents across the world, with no apparent link to Tehran. Similar to the Soviets' stealth propaganda during the Cold War, Iran's web of propagandists unleashed a media war against the Iranian Diaspora. The former dissidents who had fled the regime as well as many allies from the exiled communities developed a significant network of satellite TV stations, internet outlets, and blogs, particularly out of California. Slowly but surely the media counterbattle of the exiles was penetrating the regime's defenses and reaching into civil society within the country.

In 2003, the Bush administration launched Radio Farda, a Farsi-language broadcast aimed at Iranians at home. The following year the United States and France forced Syria—Iran's prime ally—out of Lebanon and demanded the disarming of Hezbollah. A coalition of Middle Eastern dissidents, including a large contingent of Iranians, was formed in Washington to sustain constant support of democratization in the region.[18] American officials and intellectuals pressed for engaging the Iranian reformers and dissidents.[19]

During summer 2004, I held several meetings with Iranian-American activists to evaluate the democracy movement in Iran and find the best ways to educate the U.S. public about the aspirations of that country's civil society. One of our findings was the dichotomy within the U.S. government between the rhetoric of the president and his senior officials, who constantly spoke about freedom for the Iranian people, on the one hand, and the resistance of the traditional foreign policy bureaucracy to any serious action in that direction, on the other. As with all things freedom-related in the Middle East, the post-9/11 era in America was marred by sabotage from inside the political establishment. Iran's democrats were hopeful based on their perception that Washington was moving to meet them halfway, at least, while lobby groups inside the Beltway were maneuvering to kill any initiative that would have led to the success of a democratic revolution in Iran.[20]

The Ahmadinejad Counter-revolution

While President Khatami's government was struggling with the economic viability of the regime, the real powers in Iran were preparing to operate the greatest shift since the advent of Ayatollah Khomeini in 1979. The cataclysmic events in the region—the removal of the Taliban, the crumbling of Saddam, and the pushing back against Assad in Lebanon—added to the unbearable narrative on freedom forward by the United States and its allies, such as British prime minister Tony Blair and Spanish prime minister José Maria Aznar (until the demise of his government in March 2004). These developments were a bad omen for the ruling elite, both clerics and militia lords.

The reelection of George Bush as president of the United States on November 4, 2004, was the last straw. The oil-producing regime saw four more years of pressure for democracy and reforms in Iran by the United States as lethal. So the Islamic Revolutionary Guards and the web of intertwined networks of hard-core mullahs and supporters moved to bring back the presidency of the republic into the fold of radical Khomeinism. To make matters worse, as Khatami's term was ending in August 2005, more catastrophes occurred in the region, indicating that the storm was approaching Tehran. In Syrian-occupied Lebanon, the assassination of Rafiq Hariri led to a series of conflicts for Iranian allies. A popular revolt took to the streets of the capital amid the collapse of the pro-Syrian cabinet of Prime Minister Omar Karami, at the same time that Assad was accused of masterminding the assassination of Hariri and his regime was to be investigated for the terror crime—and finally, the Syrian army evacuated Lebanon.

To counterattack, the hard-liners in Tehran organized a trumped-up presidential election in May, bringing Mahmoud Ahmadinejad, the "Stalinist" of the regime, to power. In Iran, the process of selecting the right president involves undermining the opponents' candidacy. Khamenei and his Pasdaran are in control of the Ministry of Interior and the court system. No reformist candidate can survive the barrage of obstructions, with candidacies controlled and ballot counting manipulated. Ahmadinejad was "elected" in June, and from that day the counter-revolution began in Iran.

The regime change in Baghdad, democratic elections in Afghanistan and Iraq, the call for Syria's withdrawal from Lebanon and the disarming of Hezbollah, and the labeling of Iran and Hezbollah as part of the "Axis of Evil" were all developments that indicated—in the eyes of Tehran's ruling body—that a hurricane was brewing in the region, blown there by the United States. Khamanei's elite, which for half a decade had tolerated the management of a somewhat milder government headed by President Mohammad Khatami, found itself at a critical juncture. If the democracy offensive backed by the Bush administration, as unorganized and erratic as it was, continued, the Iranian regime would eventually be targeted.

The regime's strategists projected a more sophisticated and efficient U.S. policy than that which the Bush administration had actually devised, and they responded as if Washington was moving in these critical directions already. During my briefings and lobbying for democracy efforts in the region during 2004, I realized that while the good intentions and the will to produce democratic advances were omnipresent, strategic visions for implementation were lacking. This episode of the war on terror between Washington and Tehran reminded me of the apex in the Cold War when the Soviets were preparing for strategic moves they expected from the United States that our government hadn't decided on yet. The Khamenei elite thought U.S. efforts in Afghanistan would soon establish a democratic force, which in turn would support Iranian insurrections in the east. Tehran also projected that American activities in Iraq would soon produce a government that would mobilize against the Islamic Republic. The offensive by the Iranian regime against the democracy efforts moved forward on all fronts.

Moving swiftly, the Pasdaran broke the backbone of the reformist movement within the institutions of government, cleansing the Majliss (Parliament) from most pro-Khatami figures. In Iraq, the new direction of Iran's regime invested heavily in breaking up the core of the new democracy. European MEP Paulo Casaca, chairman of the European Delegation at NATO, told me, "Western democracies knew about the massive intervention of Iranian intelligence against the shy advances of Iraqi democracy. To the east, the mullahs allowed ammunition to be sent to the Taliban in Afghanistan to fight the young democracy in Afghanistan, and they sent unlimited support to Hezbollah to break the backbone of the Cedars Revolution." Ahmadinejad's Pasdaran and security services acted as the central force striking back against the region's budding democracy movements in Afghanistan, Iran, Iraq, and Lebanon.

Nukes against Democracy

At the same time, Iran's nuclear program was put on the front burner in order to deter potential aggressors from outside the country. From day one I argued—in the media and in my briefings to Congress—that the first strategic goal of the acceleration of Iran's nuclear program was undoubtedly to send a message of deterrence to the United States and its allies that any support to the democracy forces inside Iran would result in a military escalation, with the nuclear component at center stage. The scenario of nukes against democracy was obvious.[21] The logic is impeccable: Khamenei's worst nightmare was the advance of democratic movements in Lebanon, Syria, Iraq, and Afghanistan that would lead inevitably to a copycat in Iran. The regime in Tehran knew better than anyone how critical the situation was within civil society.

I tested this assessment several times during media encounters on several Arab networks. Put one-on-one with a chief propagandist of the Iranian regime, in charge of inciting the Arab audiences against the West, I battled his agenda twice. As al Husseini ranted against "imperialism, Zionism, and America," I used my time to reach out to millions of listeners, in Iraq and in the Arab areas in Iran. To the unease of my opponent, I exposed the oppression of Iranians and projected that a revolution was coming. Al Husseini said no one can defeat Iran's military and no one can shut down the nukes. I replied, to his surprise, that eventually it may not be the West or the United States, or even Israel, that will stop the military nuclear program, but the masses in Iran. I added that the Ahmadinejad regime's oppression is going to produce a revolt, and millions will march in the streets.

Railed against by my detractors, as often happened on Arab airwaves, I was vindicated five years later when the Green Revolution exploded on a day in June, sending to the world pictures I had imagined and predicted.

The Road to the Green Revolution

During the May 2005 Iranian presidential election, Iran's largest student organization, the Office to Consolidate Unity, advocated a voting boycott. After the election of President Mahmoud Ahmadinejad, student protests against the government continued.

Martin Walker wrote in 2005 that "Iran's Ayatollahs may have the power to stop this whole movement that the Middle East is calling 'the Arab Spring' dead in its tracks. They can throw Iraq and probably Lebanon into chaos at will—and can probably unleash upon Israel a new assault by suicide bombers that could derail any prospect of a settlement with the Palestinians."[22] Iran's Khomeinist leaders thought they'd stop the reformers and the dissidents by hardening their position in foreign policy and waging a terror campaign against Western interests in the region. With the support of what became known as *al Mumana'*, the axis between Iran, Syria, Hezbollah, and Sudan to crush democratic movements, Tehran could break its isolation and break down its own reformist movement.

In 2005, the regime arrested the editor of a student paper after the publication of material deemed insulting to Islam in four reformist papers at a prestigious Teheran university.[23] Ahmad Ghassaban, the editor of *Sahar* (*Dawn*), a student paper in Amir Kabir University, was arrested after caricatures and articles deemed "insulting to Islam" appeared on campus in papers bearing the insignia of *Sahar* and three other student publications. In May 2006, as many as forty police officers were injured in clashes with demonstrating students in Tehran. At the same time, the Iranian regime called for student action in line with its own political agenda. Ahmadinejad urged students to organize campaigns to demand that liberal and secular university teachers be removed. The roots of the 2009 revolution were born.

The first steps of the uprising were missed in Washington, even under the Bush administration. The student movement was not recognized as a legitimate force of change, as the Solidarity Movement of Lech Walesa in Poland in the 1980s had been.[24] Michael Ledeen, a top Iran expert at the American Enterprise Institute (AEI) in Washington, criticized the U.S. administration's failure to boost support of the student movement in those critical years.[25] Ledeen said in 2009 at the Foundation for Defense of Democracies in Washington, "Washington could have and should have invested seriously in backing up the student movement in Iran already since 2001, but certainly as soon as the Ahmadinejad faction took over. We could have gained tremendously by witnessing the reform movement toppling the regime democratically by 2005."

Ledeen, as well as many Iranian-American leaders from across the community's spectrum, such as the shah's supporter Saeed Ghanji, liberal feminist Banafsheh Zand-Bonazzi, and Mujahideen Khalq advocate Alireza Jafarzadeh argue that the Bush administration failed to partner with the student movement opposed to the Iranian regime because of the maneuvers of the Iran lobby, at the center of which is the NIAC, "National Iranian American Committee," headed by Trita Parsi.[26] Anti-Khomeinist spokespersons charge that NIAC and a whole web of Tehran apologists in the United States and the West are being backed by Iran's petrodollars.

During Ahmadinejad's first term, women's uprisings never stopped. In 2005, the regime closed the Presidential Center for Women's Participation and destroyed hundreds of books and pamphlets. On March 8, 2006, on International Women's Day, a gathering in Daneshjoo Park in Tehran was organized, but the women were beaten by police. On June 12, 2006, a women's gathering took place in Hafte Tir Square and was also suppressed. On August 27, a "One Million Signatures" campaign was launched to claim women's rights. On October 31, the "Abolish Stoning Forever" campaign was organized. Iranian women and their feminist struggles were the main fuel leading to the Green Revolution a few years later.[27]

Iran's workers' dissatisfaction with the Khamanei-Ahmadinejad regime and women's alienation were at the core of the deep opposition to the regime. According to a national survey of "values and attitudes" implemented in 2004 by the Ministry of Islamic Guidance, about 71 percent of Iranians were dissatisfied with "the economic situation of the country," while 25 percent were somewhat satisfied and only 5 percent were very satisfied. The survey data showed that about 71 percent of men, 70 percent of women, 72 percent of the employed, and 79 percent of university graduates classified themselves as dissatisfied.[28] The Pasdaran-backed regime suppressed the workers all across the country.[29] Workers' leaders wrote later, after the June 2009 revolt: "The key potential social force that has yet to throw its weight into the balance is one which can expect nothing from either of the two Islamic factions: the 22-million-strong Iranian working class. It has faced heavy repression for decades. As noted earlier, the factory committee (shura) movement was broken in the period 1980–81. The Pasdaran seized militant workers inside the plants and whipped them in front of their coworkers, when they were not simply dragged off to Evin prison and ultimate execution. It took almost a generation to recover."[30]

The Green Revolution

June 12, 2009, would become a benchmark in Iran's modern history. As I observed the masses marching in the streets of Tehran protesting the fraudulent elections, as alleged by the opposition, I noted that something fundamental had changed, something that would irreversibly affect the future of Iran and its Khomeinist regime. Iran's civil society had broken the wall of fear. Indeed, while the previous uprisings since 2003 had been limited to students, this surge in the streets of the capital was of a national dimension.

In a sense, the Green Revolution of Iran is a sister to Lebanon's Cedars Revolution—two arms of the same body of democratic revolution in the Greater Middle East. Hundreds of thousands of Iranians of all ages and walks of life chanted through the main avenue of Tehran, "Where is our vote?" "Ahmadinejad, usurper of power," and the more daring, "Death to the dictator," a slogan chanted exactly thirty years ago by those students who brought down the shah regime. The shocking scene was only to become more unbelievable as the demonstrations stretched over a week. Soon enough the protesters wore green and established the slogan of Green Revolution.

This wasn't a limited outburst on campuses. It had become a full-fledged popular movement lasting for months. Evidently, the mere fact that the main candidates who were defeated unjustly by the regime, Mir Hossein Mousavi and Mehdi Karroubi, were previously leaders of government helped create a political balance of power. The protesters actually used the unfair election to launch a regime change movement. Manda Zand Ervin told a U.S. congressional briefing in July 2010, "This was a revolution bound to happen. The electoral fraud was only the spark."

Iran's presidential elections ended—as predicted by the unapologetic regime's experts and the real opposition groups in exile—with Mahmoud Ahmadinejad, the "pure son" of the Islamic Revolutionary Guards, being elected by a wide margin. For those accustomed to Khomeinist politics, it had been a foreseeable outcome since the beginning of the so-called Iranian presidential elections. There couldn't be any result that would contradict the principles upon which the Islamic Republic was founded. There was not a shred of doubt about the full control the supreme ruler, Ali Khamenei, had over the process and the result.

As detailed by many specialists on the regime's workings, the selection process of a "new" president for the "republic" has multiple security mechanisms, which ensure that the "elected" leader is in line with the Khomeinist ideology, platform, and long-term goals. First, no candidate opposing the Islamist ideology can be granted authorization to run. The institutions regulating elections are solidly in the hands of the ayatollahs. There is no pluralist process. Voters have to select from among those chosen for them by the regime. Democracy is dead in the first stage of the process; citizens can choose only from a carefully cultivated group, and candidates can discuss only what is determined to be permissible. In short, Iran's presidential elections are a charade, a show of colors and sounds, nothing more. However, the international public, particularly in the West, has seen images of "different" candidates, some called more moderate than others, and has watched large numbers of voters rushing to the polls in Iran.

With the rise of political pluralism in the neighborhoods, pressure in Iran from youth, women, labor unions, intellectuals, and many other citizens to move toward a true democracy continues to grow.

Seeing women freely elected in Afghanistan after the Taliban, witnessing the rise of more than a hundred political parties in a multiethnic Iraq after the fall of Saddam, and watching the Cedars Revolution in Lebanon defeat the Iran-backed Hezbollah in elections is creating an epiphany among regular people living under the suppressive rule of the mullahs. The longing for debates and for freedom in the electoral process was getting harder and harder to contain for the ruling elite in Tehran. Even Kuwait and Pakistan are producing slowly mutating democracies. "If you don't give some room to breathe they will explode," advised the regime's architects about their country's citizens.

In addition, the issue of ethnic minorities is already exploding. Arabs in Khusistan, Baluchis in the east, Azeris in the northwest, and Kurds in the west are celebrating over obtaining autonomy. The regime organized this show of a presidential "election" in part as a way to divert national attention from the real ethnic uprisings taking place in many regions of the republic. How ironic to conclude that the Iranian presidential elections have been initially organized as a national show to delay democracy, not to hasten it. How can the real domestic opposition, whose leaders are assassinated, pursued, exiled, tortured, and jailed, claim a lack of freedom if millions of Iranians have been "part" of an election? To preempt a full democracy, the regime placated the public with sham elections before it closed the gates on real change. But this time, the forces of change had a historic opportunity.

A sea of men, women, and young citizens flooded the main arteries of Tehran on June 13, 2009, and started to spread toward other cities. In the words of Amir Taheri, Iran's most seasoned international writer in exile, students, women, workers, and minorities became the core of the resistance against Khomeinism.[31] The youthful and tech-savvy launched a Twitter and YouTube revolution. The world was able to see for the first time since 1979, thanks to the internet, the heart of the Iranian people beating hard for democracy. At the sight of high school kids, boys and girls, singing and chanting, I was convinced that after this revolt there was no going back.[32] Week after week, the Green Revolution was in and out of the streets. The repression was also relentless, creating more "martyrs" for the new revolution.

The killing of Neda Sultani by the Basiji militia on June 22, 2009, inflamed passions throughout the youngest segments of the Iranian population. Her boyfriend described her tale powerfully when he declared that "I realized I couldn't prevent her from going . . . she was only thinking of her goal—democracy and freedom for Iranians."[33] When the regime called in outside terror militias to join the repression, the demonstrators became even more motivated. Hezbollah's security was spotted in Tehran riding the same type of motorcycles used to repress the Cedars Revolution in Beirut.

The determination of the forces of civil society to continue to the end was described by Professor Bahman Baktiari, the director of the Middle East Center at the University of Utah:

> The latest protests have shaken the Iranian establishment, plunging it into the worst political crisis it has ever seen. What has become clear now is that the Iranian regime is facing more than just an intensification of factional warfare within the Iranian political system. It is confronted with an opposition movement that is both exceptionally resilient and spreading. Although Mir Hossein Mousavi and the other leading reformists (former president Mohammad Khatami and Mehdi Karroubi, the second presidential candidate) remain symbols of the opposition, and their refusal to call for an end to popular protests has been a huge irritant to the authorities, their imprisonment and execution will not bring an end to demonstrations against the regime. Hard-core elements and the Revolutionary Guards are scrambling for ways to quell the discontent. They have started a second "cultural revolution" in the universities and are looking at an overhaul of education. They plan to open 6,000 bases for the basij youth militia at primary schools, as well as sending in "political training teachers" and supportive clerics. It has created a new police unit to sweep the Internet for dissident voices, and the Revolutionary Guards plan to open a news agency with print, photo and television components.[34]

The amazing shift by former regime politicians such as Mousavi and Karroubi was the window of opportunity for the real revolutionaries.[35] In a series of radio interviews I compared these leaders to former Communist Party leaders Mikhail Gorbachev and Boris

Yeltsin, who triggered the collapse of the Soviet Union. The Islamic Republic's regime may prove even more resilient then the USSR. Regardless, the march has begun and the clash will continue until one of the two parties collapses. Heshmat Tabarzadi, the leader of the Iran Democratic Front, reported: "The basijis in civilian clothing confronted the students and the people. In Enghelab Square, I saw a woman in her late 20s get kicked so hard in her spine that she flew through the air. On Ghods Street, near Tehran University, I saw another young woman as her head was pounded into a car by the basij. All the while, they screamed disgusting epithets like 'whore' and worse. Yet the movement only became more determined. More than 50 universities throughout the country, both private and government-run, joined in a historical display of resistance."[36]

The confrontation between the jihadist regime and the uprising is creating two republics, one for the oppressors and another for the oppressed. Writing in the midst of the Tehran Green Revolution, activist Arash Sobhi declared, "The bosses of this Islamist supremacy atop of which sits Seyyed Ali Khamenei should be well aware of the fact that his life and that of his sinister regime has come to the twilight of its existence."[37]

Indeed, when the fear factor begins to dissipate from the hearts of the revolutionaries, the revolution is on the road to victory.

The American Abandonment of the Green Revolution

As the demonstrations expanded in Iran, a moment of truth was coming to Washington. Had George Bush, Ronald Reagan, or John F. Kennedy been in the White House, there would have been little doubt about how they would have reacted, putting American democratic values first, transcending all politics and international relations. I knew it would be different with President Barack Obama. Since his speech in Cairo in 2009, and his commitment to "respect" the Arab and Muslim world, which in fact meant a respect for the integrity of its authoritarian regimes as it was lobbied for by the administration's new apologist advisors, there was no escape from an attempt to dodge the democracy commitment. I waited to see how the U.S. president who had committed himself to letting the region fall into the hands of its authoritarians would choose his words.

In the first few days, no statements were made, perhaps with the expectation that the ayatollahs would take back the streets quickly and it wouldn't be necessary. The protests went on and pressure on the White House mounted. French president Nicolas Sarkozy denounced the Iranian government's "brutal" reaction to demonstrators, protesting the disputed election. "Germany is on the side of the Iranian people, who want to exercise their rights of freedom of expression and free assembly," said Chancellor Angela Merkel. The Czech European Union president asked the bloc's members to consider summoning the heads of Iran's missions in Europe to express "deep revulsion" over postelection violence. Many members of the U.S. Congress and the European Union issued statements of condemnation of the Iranian regime.

Finally, the president of the United States spoke, and his words will mark the history of his presidency regarding the battle between democrats and totalitarians in the Middle East. "We refuse to meddle."[38] That statement, very predictable yet disappointing for me, left disturbing effects on the reformers and democratic forces of the region. Leading Middle Eastern studies professor Fuad Ajami described it as "a choice for the regime over the people on the streets."[39]

President Obama's abandonment of Iran's democratic revolution was a blow to the demonstrators in the streets of Tehran. The protestors, well aware of the U.S. political debates, started chanting, "Obama, Obama, you're either with us or with them," making it harder for the "candidate of change" to turn his back on millions of youth who had great hopes for a progressive leader of the free world before they were profoundly disappointed.[40] Realizing that the Iranian revolt wasn't going away, the administration tried to readjust its position by imploring the Iranian regime to behave humanely toward its own citizens. Few symbolic acts were decided, including diplomatic gestures.[41] In those crucial days all friends of a free Iran did their share to keep the flame of the revolution alive internationally.[42]

During the marches in Tehran I was the first to notice and report on international media that the signs being written by Iranian youth were in English, signaling that they wanted the world to read them and intervene. Many legislators and commentators gladly picked up on the finding, particularly after former presidential candidate and popular Fox News commentator Mike Huckabee also noted it. Yet authoritarians around the world, led by the Middle Eastern brotherhood against democracy, stood by the ayatollahs against the people of Iran. Syria, Sudan, Hamas, Hezbollah, and Qatar backed the regime against the demonstrators. Syrian foreign minister Walid al Muallem said, "Anyone betting on the fall of the Iranian regime will be a loser," and warned Europeans against interfering in the internal affairs of Iran.[43] Hezbollah accused the West of "fomenting turmoil in Iran."[44] Hugo Chavez, the populist turned dictator of Venezuela, lashed out against the democracy movement in Iran. The AKP Islamist government in Turkey, which claims to be "Muslim-Democrat," stood by Ahmadinejad against Iran's democrats.[45]

In the United States and other Western countries the apologists for the Iranian regimes argued that the ayatollahs are better suited for American interests than the unpredictable post-Khomeinist movements.[46] Iran's prodemocracy activists accused the so-called Iran lobby of cutting deals with the U.S. administration and warned against stealth maneuvers by regime allies to derail the perception by Americans of Iran's real revolution.[47] Former CIA analyst Clare Lopez asserted that political interests were behind the U.S. administration's decision "not to meddle" in support of Iran's demonstrations.[48] A prevalent theory among foreign policy analysts in Washington asserts that the odd U.S. position regarding what is obviously the most important democracy uprising in the region for decades was a result of a deal that had already been cut between the administration and the Iranian regime before the revolt took place, outlining that the United States wouldn't get involved in return for Iran's cooperation in Iraq, in Afghanistan, and on nuclear issues—an assertion that is unproven but seemingly logical. Reza Pahlevi, the shah's son, told him during the summer of 2010 that the youth on the streets of Tehran are tomorrow's responsible citizens. "With or without the West, the Iranian people will rise. The harm caused by the regime until that day is what we need to avoid."

Time and historians will tell.

Future

The future of Iran's democratic revolution is certain in the long run, but dependent on many factors in the short and medium term. In my own reading, this is an inexorable movement that will continue until its fulfillment regardless of setbacks, defeats, or obstructions. Its speed, expansion, and success will depend on the level of support it receives from the international community, particularly the United States. As with other revolutions, including the Eastern European uprisings, the Iranian people expect to hear from international leaders and would be encouraged to know that the outside world is supporting them, in any way necessary.

First and foremost, democracies should acknowledge it for what it really is: a democratic revolution seeking regime change.49 Second, the international community must exert enough pressure on the Khomeinist regime to enable the masses in the country to rise and achieve their goals of change by nonviolent means. Third, once the free world stands firmly by the Iranian people, they will choose the form of government they wish to establish after the totalitarian regime is crumbled. Fourth, the Iranian forces struggling for democracy must create the widest coalition ever formed inside the country and in the Diaspora, gathering all movements previously incompatible with one another: the Green Movement, women, students, the left wing, conservatives, ethnic minorities, and intellectuals. The West must talk to all anti-Khomeinist forces, from the constitutional monarchists to Mujahideen Khalq. Any Iranians struggling for freedom against Tehran's terror regime must be recognized and supported.

The stakes of this revolution are very high. The ruling elite in Tehran is seeking nuclear weapons so that it can achieve deterrence against its own people and the international community. The Khomeinists, who have used the enormous resources of petrodollars to build a "Caliphate" at the expense of peace and stability in the region, can be stopped only by their own people, who have chosen to sacrifice for their country's freedom and the world's security.

They must not be abandoned.

Hell in Sudan: Genocide against Africans and the End of the Last Apartheid

I   t was May 1995 and the conference room at Columbia University was packed. The subject of the conference was abolitionism, but it was a century and a half after the scourge of slavery had been eliminated in the United States. Why, then, were all these African-American activists, human rights advocates, and intellectuals who were attending the conference frustrated and calling for the end of slavery? As the late Samuel Cotton described that afternoon, "Blacks are still captured and sold in slavery, they are still serving masters in plantations and farms and their women and children are still abused. But that is not happening here, on our American soil, it is happening in Sudan, in the twentieth century under the eyes of America and the rest of the world."

Cotton, a descendant of African slaves who worked in the cotton fields, and Charles Jacobs, the founder of the Boston-based American Anti Slavery Group, were the principal leaders who organized the event on slavery in Sudan in New York. Attended by southern Sudanese exiles, independent human rights activists, and African-American supporters, the Columbia University abolitionist conference was a benchmark in the launching of the worldwide battle for freedom in Sudan. It was the first open public gathering to expose the scourge of slavery still taking place in Sudan at the hands of the jihadi regime in Khartoum.[1]

The testimony about massacres, rape, and ethnic cleansing sent chills throughout the amphitheater. I observed the Sudanese speakers, often in tears, sharing with their "African brothers" how their tribes and nation were subjected to genocide because of their skin color and their African culture. And I watched the reaction of black men and women who had experienced similar trials and sufferings in this country. Sitting behind me, an African-American woman encouraged the witnesses from Sudan when they hesitated to speak. "We know what you're talking about," "Keep talking, brother, keep talking," she'd exhort. As escapees from Sudan shared their experience as slaves serving Arab masters, the audience became tense and some participants became understandably emotional. Most attendees had tears in their eyes, as did I, as southern Sudanese narrated the horrors of armed militias raiding black villages in the south, burning huts, killing elderly people, and capturing entire families.

"This can't be the twentieth century" shouted Samuel Cotton, who specialized in the study of modern-day slavery, including slavery in Mauritania and Sudan.[2] Cotton, who passed away years later, was the conscience in the African-American community in its outrage over the unbearable idea that black African slavery was still taking place, at the hands of jihadi forces.

Representatives from the brotherhood against democracy showed up to discredit the African liberation meeting. Diplomats from the Sudanese, Mauritanian, and even Egyptian embassies, as well as representatives from local Islamist groups, including the Nation of Islam, erupted in the convention to refute statements that slavery was taking place or that oppression was occurring in Sudan. The men and women from southern Sudan, led by Sabit Ali and Dominic Mohammed, blasted them as "representative of Arab and Islamic imperialism and stooges of masters." African-Americans, including a number of pastors, stood by the Sudanese, as did the representatives of secular, liberal, and church groups. John Eibner from Christian Solidarity International, the oldest NGO to have ever raised the issues of southern Sudan in the West, and Keith Roderick, the secretary general of the Coalition for the Defense of Human Rights, the first alliance of NGOs defending liberties for minorities in Muslim countries that emerged in the United States after the Cold War, attended.

The regimes' operatives and jihadist sympathizers felt the anger of the Africans and left quickly. They witnessed the birth of what would grow into a movement in America in favor of Sudan's liberation that would eventually reach the U.S. Congress and the Clinton and Bush administrations, resulting in the development of legislation and UN action in favor not only of the southern Sudan cause but also the causes of Darfur, the Nuba, and the Beja, other mostly Muslim black communities also brutalized by the Khartoum elite.

Bloody History

Sudan's multiple conflicts are no different from other struggles in the region. In the center of the country's political structure sits the elite class, living off its oppression of the majority of the people. Khartoum's Arab nationalist and Salafi Islamist dominant forces were at the root of the wars to dominate the south, west, and east, where a majority of Africans rejected the central authority's programs of Arabization and Islamization.

Sudan witnessed the longest period of civil war in the region, and also the greatest genocide since the Holocaust. Up to two million people, mostly from the African populations, were murdered or enslaved. Statistics of death and losses are dizzying. The losses to blacks in Sudan are twice the size of the entire population residing in Gaza. The African lands invaded by Khartoum's military against the will of their population are the size of Lebanon and Palestine combined. The black refugee population is almost equivalent to the population of Libya. To top it off, more black slaves have been captured in Sudan by Arab militias than have been enslaved by all enslavers of the world combined since 1956.

War in Sudan between the mostly Muslim north and the mostly Christian and animist south started in 1956 and continued intermittently for over four decades. In the past decade, the total deaths resulting from the genocide in Darfur number from 2.1 to 2.5 million, making this one of the bloodiest conflicts of the post–World War II era.[3]

Despite these horrendous numbers, the war through all these years has taken place in near-obscurity. Only since 9/11 has some international attention been focused on it, as the result of several factors: the ability of human rights groups to prove ethnic cleansing and slavery; the involvement of Sudan's regime in terror activities abroad, including the World Trade Center explosion in New York in 1993; and the interest of multinational companies in exporting oil from Sudan. Beyond the human catastrophe, the fighting in Sudan touches on a number of geostrategic interests. Sudan has 300 million barrels in proven oil reserves and 86 billion cubic meters of natural gas reserves, and this is before the main oil areas of the Red Sea coastal zone and the southern part of the country have been explored.[4] The country also has potentially rich agricultural resources. Sudan is the only source of gum arabic, an ingredient used in such varied products as baked goods, beverages, dairy products, frozen foods, candies, low-fat foods, and pharmaceuticals.

In addition to controlling these rich natural resources, Khartoum's regime has involved itself since the 1990s in terror activities in Eritrea and against Arab neighbors. For example, assassins dispatched from Khartoum nearly murdered President Hosni Mubarak of Egypt in June 1995. In more recent years, and as the regime's head, Omar Bashir, was indicted by the International Criminal Court for geno-cide in Darfur, links to Hezbollah and Iran developed fast.

Historical Background

Sudan means "the blacks" in Arabic. Despite this clear description, the country's single most important crisis concerns its identity: Is it black or Arab? Arabs dominate the central government in Khartoum and blacks are struggling to win autonomy from the central govern-ment. In ancient times, the lands that now constitute Sudan included a number of kingdoms, principally Nubia, a chief competitor to pharaonic Egypt. As of the seventh century successive waves of Ca-liphate armies eroded Upper Nubia, forcing the African peoples to retreat to the south. Further advances over the centuries opened the way for Arabian and Arabized settlers to push the Africans farther south. For twelve centuries, while northern Sudan was steadily Ara-bized, subtropical Sudan escaped Islamization.[5] In 1899, Lord Kitch-ener led Anglo-Egyptian troops in the conquest of both the northern and southern regions, establishing a governorate over the whole. In 1946, the British created a separate governorate in the south, and this served as the basis for decades-long coexistence. According to one scholar, "The British saw it in the best interest of the Sudanese that because they were such a different group ideologically and culturally than the north, they should have had distinct administrations."[6] In particular, Britain's announcement in 1930 of a southern Sudan policy helped to contain the Islamization process in the south.

This insulation was opposed, however, by Arab nationalist elites in the north of Sudan, as well as by the newly sovereign Arab states and the Arab League, all of which supported a unified and independent "Arab" Sudan. Widespread agitation in Khartoum in 1945 calling for a unified Sudan caused the British a year later to reverse the southern Sudan policy and declare that "north and south are bound together."[7] From the beginning, the south suffered political under-representation in Khartoum. With independence imminent, the British confirmed this approach, declaring in 1952 that "the future of the south lay in a united Sudan."[8]

In 1954, as a precursor to full sovereignty, the north set up a provisional government. The south, in contrast, was ill prepared to claim its own state. Further, the bulk of the colonial socioeconomic structures were located in the north under "Arabized" influence, while the south was largely underdeveloped and socially tribal. Empowered by the British and Egyptian colonizers, the Arabs of Sudan controlled their own territories and also those of the Africans of the south, who had never shared their identity or their goals.

First Round of Rebellion and Repression: 1955–72

Troops stationed in the south rebelled against Khartoum on the eve of independence in 1955, beginning a revolt that lasted until February 1972. Independence came in January 1956, and several incidents in the following six months led to civil war. Once freed from British pressure, the Arab Sudanese elite waged an implacable program of Arabization of the south, bolstered by the Pan Arab movement led by Egypt's Gamal Abdel Nasser. Symbolically they imposed Friday as the day of rest and Sunday as a workday.

In 1963, a rebellion exploded with the uprising of military units in Juba in the south. In the same year, the Ananya—a liberation movement for southern Sudanese—rebelled against northern troops stationed in the south. The insurgency escalated over the next two years, peaking in July 1965 with civilian massacres in Juba and Wau, the south's largest cities, and again in 1967, with massacres in the Torit district and massive air strikes by the north.[9]

Between 1963 and 1972, most southern districts followed the Ananya and its allies, Joseph Lagu's Southern Sudan Liberation Movement (SSLM) and Aggrey Jaden and William Deng's Sudan African National Union (SANU). These rebels sought full independence from Khartoum, claiming that black people were never consulted at the time of independence. Successive northern governments responded to their demands with harsh repression and continued efforts to Arabize the south. Member states of the Arab League—primarily Egypt, Iraq, and Syria—backed Khartoum. On the other side, Haile Selassie's government in Ethiopia supported the rebels.[10]

General Ja'far Numayri's successful 1969 coup in Khartoum led to a quick proposal for southern autonomy, but fighting and negotiations continued for another three years, until the two sides signed the Addis Ababa Accord of March 1972. This agreement granted semiautonomy to the south and promised southerners a greater role in the central government. The seventeen-year war had taken a terrible toll. More than half a million southerners died and the region suffered considerable destruction. The north also paid a high economic price for its involvement in the war.[11]

Second Round of Rebellion and Oppression: 1983–96

A number of factors contributed to the failure of the Addis Ababa Accord and the second round of civil war eleven years later. One important element was the central government's decision to divide the south into three provinces, thereby preventing it from becoming a single entity. The most important development, however, was the increased strength of Salafism.

The Numayri government initiated an Islamization campaign in 1983 when it imposed Sharia law on non-Muslim southerners. This campaign also required the use of Arabic in schools to teach the Koran and to impart Islamic culture, the segregation of females and males, and the enforcement of Islamic dress codes. It led to the expropriation of Christian schools and the severance of financial links with foreign Christian donors.[12]

The renewed Islamization effort broke the backbone of the fragile 1972 peace and triggered a second round of fighting in the south. In the appraisal of a southern Sudanese scholar, "The Addis Ababa agreement was the last chance for a historic peace in the Sudan during the Cold War. The Arab north was given a chance to demonstrate its ability to rule the African south with justice and fundamental rights. Instead, the Arab nationalist regime allowed jihadism to destroy African-Arab peace. By attempting to steal our basic liberties as a people, they forced us to reclaim our land, as the only guarantee for our freedom."[13]

The Sudan People's Liberation Army (SPLA), the military branch of the Sudanese People's Liberation Movement (SPLM), led the new uprising. Headed by Colonel John Garang, SPLA included many veterans of the first war and was better organized. It achieved significant successes in the field during the 1980s, gaining control over most of Equatoria province. Garang, a U.S.-educated military officer, won the backing of Ethiopia's leaders and espoused a leftist agenda in which he portrayed his struggle as anti-imperialist. If Ananya had called for the separation of the south, SPLA sought to bring down the ruling power in Khartoum.[14] As explained by the SPLM spokesperson in Washington, Garang believed "all democratic and progressive forces of the Sudan should join the SPLM in its struggle for a better and just country."[15]

This strategy won military and political successes for several years. The landscape changed dramatically in 1989 when General Omar Bashir toppled the elected government in Khartoum and installed a military regime that enjoyed the support of the jihadists led by Hassan Turabi's National Islamic Front (NIF). With this coup d'état, Turabi became the real power broker in an ethnically divided country; and the first-ever jihadist Islamist regime had come to dominate an Arab country, except for Saudi Arabia, which contributed ideologically, but didn't wage military jihads.

The Islamist takeover had tremendous implications for the civil war. Government forces, armed with sophisticated weapons and Islamist morale, waged an unrelenting jihad against the "atheist and infidel" southern rebels. By 1991, the Islamist north was on the offensive, and soon the southern Sudanese resistance movement was almost defeated. By late 1992, the "liberated areas" in the south had split in two as an all-out war flared between the two southern factions. By the end of 1993, the south was militarily crippled and socioeconomically in disarray.[16]

Turabi, who was arguably the leading Sunni Islamist ideologue of the 1990s, found support from foreign Islamist forces. The Popular Arab-Islamic Congress he convened in Khartoum in 1992 brought the Iranian, Lebanese, Palestinian, and Algerian leaders of powerful Islamist and jihadist movements to Sudan. Such foreign backing provided Turabi with a psychological and logistical endorsement that had significant implications inside the country.[17] Turabi's regime also profited from assistance from Iran, Syria, and Libya.[18] These advantages permitted Khartoum's soldiers to recapture many strategic strongholds and march into the southern hinterland.[19] By 1996, the Sudanese army and its auxiliaries from the NIF militia had invaded most of Equatoria province and pushed the southern forces to the borders.

The Southern Counteroffensives

Though repeatedly defeated, the southern guerrilla movement was never annihilated. "The Arab army controlled the towns and the main villages; we controlled the jungle and the bushes," said Steven Wondu, U.S. representative of the Liberation Army.[20] In January and February 1997 the SPLA led a major counteroffensive, winning back lost territory and changing the balance of power. This success resulted from a combination of factors.

First, the SPLA managed to join forces with other Sudanese opposition forces, including those of former prime minister Sadiq al-Mahdi and other secular and moderate Muslim forces under the umbrella of the National Democratic Alliance (NDA). Second, after meeting in Asmara in 1996, they agreed on a common agenda to overthrow the Bashir regime through the "creation of a new Sudan." Garang declared his support for "the formation of a four-year transitional government and for holding a referendum on self-determination."[21]

The insistence on self-determination marks an important shift in Garang's rhetoric. The SPLM's declared objective for years was to replace the regime in Khartoum with a united Sudanese coalition, which would preserve the country's territorial unity; Garang's tilt toward self-determination reflected a growing trend among southerners toward complete separation from the Arab north.

The third factor in the SPLA's momentum was Khartoum's decision to pursue a systematic policy of Arabization and Islamization in the south, prompting a severe backlash. It isolated non-Muslim regions, or regions inhabited by blacks who are Muslim but not Arabic-speaking, notably Nuba, from the outside world.[22] It made schools and churches prime targets. Christians who refused to convert were denied food, others were kidnapped and enslaved.[23] In the north, particularly around Khartoum, the NIF's "peace camps" forced hundreds of thousands of southern refugees to convert to Islam.[24]

The intensity of this repression against the southerners directly benefited SPLA and other opposition forces; thousands of young men and women flocked to those movements. It also prompted Boutros Boutros-Ghali, then United Nations secretary general, to express his deep concern over the "serious deterioration in the humanitarian situation in Sudan, as a result of the unilateral and unjustified obstruction by the government of Sudan of urgently required humanitarian assistance to the affected population in southern Sudan.[25]

Finally, the utter barbarism of the northern regime increased popular revulsion among southern Sudanese against the fundamentalists of Khartoum. Government forces, mostly the NIF's militia and the "Popular Defense Forces," perpetrated terrible atrocities against the people of southern Sudan.[26] The regime's policy of continuous jihad mobilized tens of thousands of peasants and urban dwellers, many attracted by the prospect of acquiring weapons, conquering lands, and collecting booty. The Popular Defense Forces engaged in violent offensives that relied on overpowering force (including air strikes) and employed extreme measures and widespread acts of brutality. Entire villages might be eliminated during one advance.[27]

Perhaps the most characteristic and horrifying aspect of the civil war has been Khartoum's consistent practice of enslaving the black populations of southern Sudan and the Nuba mountains. So extensive is the practice of slavery that it can be used as the symbol of the southern Sudan's tribulations. Armed factions, mostly NIF militiamen, raid villages, kill the elderly and those attempting to protect the population, then round up other adults, mainly women, and children. "Slave trains" carry these abductees to the north, where they are sold to slave merchants who in turn sell them to work on plantations, or for use as domestic servants. Some slaves are shipped to other countries of the Middle East, including Saudi Arabia, Libya, and the Gulf.[28]

Northern Propaganda

Confronted with new geopolitical realities and a growing sympathy for the south abroad, Sudan's government turned to public relations and diplomacy. Of course, the government rejected all allegations of persecution and had its embassies engage in a major campaign, endorsed by the Arabist and Islamist lobbies, to prove that it opposes terrorism, that no slavery exists, and that the governments of Ethiopia, Eritrea, and Uganda are interfering in its internal affairs.[29] It hired public relations firms and lobbyists to counter the impact of the southern Sudanese devastation in Western Europe and North America. These firms engaged in sophisticated efforts to defend the regime's reprehensible practices. Sean Gabb, director of the London-based Sudan Foundation, for example, admits that "there is some religious discrimination in Sudan" but positions everything in the context of the civil war. Gabb even justifies slavery: "It would be surprising if military and tribal prisoners of war were not put to work by their captors."[30]

To isolate Garang's powerful SPLA, the government invited competitive factions to negotiate. The Turabi regime signed peace agreements with a number of southern groups and argued that the "SPLA is preventing [a] peace accord."[31]

Khartoum relied on that old standby of international relations: the need to maintain the status quo because breaking up Sudan would endanger regional stability by having a domino effect on other countries. The regime argued that the population would be worse off, stating, "We all know what happens in African countries when the central authority is dissolved . . . killing and burning, and the long lines of starving, terrified refugees."[32]

Khartoum called for Islamic and African mediation, prompting Iranian and Qatari responses. It dispatched emissaries to the Muslim world, where it found much support. In Tehran, the authorities blessed efforts to "repel the African aggression against the Sudan" and called for a pan-Islamic jihad to defend the Sudan while volunteering to play peace broker. In Beirut, a good barometer of the Arab political mood, many organizations[33] formed the Committee for the Support of the Arab People of Sudan, which proceeded to condemn "the cowardly African attack on the brothers in Sudan, and the United States that backs them."[34] Several governments (Syria, Iraq, and Libya) and the PLO declared their support for Khartoum, while Saudi Arabia expressed its concern for the unity and sovereignty of Sudan. The Arab League declared, "Arab national security was threatened." The rhetorical war escalated against Eritrea, Ethiopia, and Uganda, all three accused by Arab regimes of "staging a conspiracy against the unity of the Sudanese land."[35] Not surprisingly, several Arab governments accused Israel of being behind the events.[36] Others found "Zionism and the hand of Israel" guilty of inciting the African nations against the Arab world.[37]

Even the Egyptian government—already at odds with the Bashir regime over a territorial dispute at Halayib, highly critical of Khartoum's fundamentalist cast, and still seething over a Sudan-backed attempt to assassinate Mubarak in Addis Ababa—stood by the "Arabism" of Sudan. It rejected the military successes of the SPLA and declared itself in favor of "stability and status quo."[38]

Business interests and the Nation of Islam (NOI) are the two major groups that have lobbied on Khartoum's behalf in the United States. Despite legislation restricting trade with Sudan because of terrorist activities, the State Department allowed two American companies to negotiate oil contracts with Khartoum from January to March 1997.[39] Louis Farrakhan defended Khartoum's innocence and held that allegations against Sudan are not just lies but part of a concerted Zionist campaign against an African country.

Southern Sudan Advocacy

The southern Sudanese resistance has also been active internationally to promote its cause. It has had much success in the African states around Sudan, where governments reject the accusation that they were "invading Sudanese lands"[40] and actually increased their assistance to the south. President Isaias Afewerki of Eritrea declared that "what we as Africans are confronting today in Sudan is the continuation of the struggle against colonialism."[41]

Khartoum's aggressiveness in supporting Islamist movements in its region came back to haunt it. The Ugandan and Ethiopian governments presented evidence of NIF involvement in their countries. South African leader Nelson Mandela, although traditionally close to the Arab regimes, signaled his views by receiving John Garang and allowing the SPLA to open an office in Pretoria. Mandela may have stood with Arab allies like Muammar Qaddafi, but when confronted with an Arab-versus-black situation, he offered solidarity to fellow blacks.

In the United States, several developments have given the south a fighting chance in Washington. Indeed, the cause of southern Sudan is now winning the battle for American public opinion. Taking a page from other national movements, one leader notes that the southern Sudanese "learned from the Jews and the Palestinians."[42] The pro–southern Sudan movement has formed coalitions to win support from a wide range of groups.

Christian rights groups: The Middle East Christian Committee (MECHRIC), a coalition of four ethnic organizations[43] launched in 1992, was the first international Christian organization to endorse southern Sudan's quest for self-determination. In 1993 the Geneva-based Christian Solidarity International (CSI) was the first human rights group to organize field visits to southern Sudan, where it investigated the persecution of its population and documented the slave trade. In addition, it mobilized both the British and American legislative branches. In 1994 an alliance of sixty North American grassroots organizations, the Illinois-based Coalition for the Defense of Human Rights Under Islam (CDHRUI), raised the issue of southern Sudan in the context of defending the rights of minorities within the Muslim world. CDHRUI then introduced this issue to human rights groups, the churches, and the U.S. Congress.[44]

Evangelical Christians: The American concern with the "persecution of Christians under Islam"[45] mobilized the Christian right, with southern Sudan as a rallying point. Since early 1997, for example, Pat Robertson's Christian Broadcast Network (CBN) has intensified its coverage of the southern Sudanese plight.[46]

Human rights groups: Atrocities in southern Sudan have attracted the notice of established human rights groups. Human Rights Watch and Amnesty International took the lead in mobilizing world opinion.[47] Human rights activists criticized Arakis, a Canadian oil company exploring in Sudan, for seeking an agreement with the NIF-backed government.

Antislavery groups: The almost unbelievable resurgence of slavery triggered a new antislavery movement in the early 1990s. The Boston-based American Anti Slavery Group (AASG), led by Charles Jacobs, was the first group to systematically denounce black bondage in sub-Saharan Africa.[48] Slavery International also became involved. The "First Abolitionist Convention for Sudan" took place at Columbia University in May 1995 and formed a leadership council, intent on influencing the U.S. government and mobilizing American blacks.[49]

African-Americans: Exiled Sudanese Catholic bishop Makram

Gassis believes that "Christians in America, black Christians particularly, will change the hearts of the American people, and hopefully the minds of the foreign policy establishment vis-à-vis southern Sudan."[50] Indeed, starting in 1995, some African-American activists joined forces with expatriate southern Sudanese leaders, challenging what they perceived as "abandonment by U.S. black leaders of their brethren in Africa."[51] Writers and activists have initiated a movement of support for the southern Sudanese struggle. Heated exchanges take place between these "abolitionists" and Farrakhan's Nation of Islam.[52] The abolitionists accuse NOI of protecting the interests of the fundamentalist Islamic regime in Sudan as a means to suppress the issue in the United States.[53]

The left: Some liberals addressed the issue. The American Friends Service Committee raised the issue of slavery on campuses, journalist Nat Hentoff raised it in the press,[54] and Congressman Barney Frank (D-MA) raised it in the U.S. Congress. Small socialist circles in the New York area actively support the abolitionists. Even some Marxist groups, such as the Sudanese Marxist Front in Exile, stand by the SPLM.

Antiterrorism groups: The emergence of radical Islamism in Khartoum, with links to international terrorism, aroused American concern and facilitated the awareness campaign by the southerners. Sabit Aley, a southern Sudanese leader in the United States, notes that "after the New York bombing [of 1993] we got the ears of both the legislative and executive branches."[55]

U.S. Congress: Congressman Chris Smith (R-NJ) was the first House member to advocate a strong and serious American reaction to the "massacre of the people of south Sudan by the NIF regime."[56] Donald Payne (D-NJ) was the first black representative to openly criticize slavery in southern Sudan. In the Senate, Sam Brownback (R-KS), chairman of the Foreign Relations Committee's Subcommittee on the Near East, stated that "Congress intends to continue the pressure on Sudan until the conditions of the southern Sudanese are improved."[57] Senator Russ Feingold (D-WI) noted that "Sudan continues to serve as refuge, nexus, and training hub for a number of international terrorist organizations. . . . This is not a regime that should be included in the community of nations."[58]

In addition, twenty pieces of legislation touching on southern Sudan have been introduced in Congress, dealing with both

terrorism and human rights issues. The best-known of them, introduced by Representative Frank Wolf (R-VA) and Senator Arlen
Specter (R-PA, turned Democrat in 2009), calls for economic sanctions against the Khartoum regime along with others who engage
in religious persecution.

More broadly, Congress seems determined, as Senator Brownback
put it in his opening remarks at a hearing on the persecution of religious minorities, to wage the battle for "all persecuted groups in the
Middle East."[59]

U.S. Policy

Until mid-1997, the White House and State Department had little
interest in the plight of southern Sudan. After a meeting with senior officials in May 1997, Steven Wondu concluded that "the U.S.
administration had secretly agreed to allow U.S. companies to sign
contracts for oil extraction in Sudan." Nina Shea of Freedom House
added, "Despite an American law which forbids commercial trans-
actions with states sponsoring terrorism—a list established by the
State Department—Occidental was authorized to negotiate with the
butchers of Khartoum."[60]

Over time, however, the north's rogue activities made it an increasingly prominent opponent of the U.S. government. This, plus the
pressure coming from American groups and Congress, along with
the black African states, prompted President Clinton to issue an
executive order on November 3, 1997, severing nearly all economic
dealings with Sudan. It states that the policies and actions of the
government of Sudan, including continued support for international
terrorism, continued efforts to destabilize neighboring governments,
and the prevalence of human rights violations, including slavery and
the denial of religious freedom, constitute an unusual and extraordinary threat to the national security and foreign policy of the United
States and therefore declared a national emergency to deal with that
threat . . . all Sudan properties in the United States were blocked.[61]

Secretary of State Madeleine Albright asserted, "Sudan is a sponsor
of terrorism since 1993. The new [executive] order will cut off trade
[with Sudan] despite the interest by companies to exploit oil."[62]

Southern Sudan in the Post-9/11 Era

With the new millennium, the fighting continued in southern Sudan despite attempts by the Clinton administration to facilitate peace between the regime and the south. The battles between the regime and SPLA between 2000 and 2005 had no decisive winner, even as the fighting escalated. Under the Bush administration, also pushing for Khartoum and the rebels to come to a peace agreement, a resolution was issued on June 13, 2001, in the House of Representatives to provide southern Sudan with $10 million in assistance.

The U.S. government, quick to suggest military action twice against Serbia in 1994 and 1999 to help endangered "populations," resisted using force against the regime in Sudan. The brotherhood against democracy backed by the "oil Caliphate" still had significant influence in Washington regardless of the president's party. However, the attacks of September 11 created a different climate in America and the free world in general. In 2002, I argued that a strong U.S. initiative to help all oppressed in Sudan (south and other areas) would be a legitimate and winning policy. I was glad to witness the Sudan Peace Act introduced by Representative Tom Tancredo, condemning Sudan for genocide. President Bush signed the act into law on October 21, 2002, and it was enacted to facilitate a comprehensive solution to the second Sudanese civil war and condemn violations of human rights, the slave trade, and the use of militia and other forces to support enslavement and slave trading, as well as the aerial bombardment of civilian targets. It authorized the U.S. government to spend $100 million in the years 2003, 2004, and 2005 to assist the population in areas of Sudan outside Sudanese government control.

The regime in Khartoum watched as U.S. forces defeated the Taliban in Afghanistan in 2001 and the American-led coalition toppled Saddam's Baath regime in 2003. They saw the Libyan dictator surrender his nuclear ambitions in 2004, and as U.S.-French diplomacy produced UNSCR 1559 during the same year, Bashir's elite decided to accept the principle of negotiations with the southern resistance after decades of war against the African areas in the south. The peace agreement was signed in Nairobi on January 9, 2005, by Sudan's vice president, Ali Osman Taha, and the Sudanese People's Liberation Movement (SPLA) leader John Garang. President Thabo Mbeki of South Africa committed to provide assistance to Sudan from his country and from the African Union. The regime and the southern resistance agreed to divide political power, share the oil wealth, merge their armies, and hold a referendum in six years to give southerners the right to decide whether they wished to secede from the rest of Sudan.

Tragically, Garang was killed in a helicopter accident on August 3, 2005. His deputy in the SPLM, Salva Kiir, was quickly and unanimously chosen to succeed him. Kiir was a popular military leader and a member of Garang's Dinka tribe, the largest ethnic group in southern Sudan.

The Darfur Genocide

Years before 9/11, I was told by a representative of John Garang during a visit to Washington that the revolt in Sudan was not only the south against the north: "Rather, it is the African majority of the country against the ruling minority in Khartoum." Dominic Mohammed, a veteran of southern Sudan's liberation movement in the United States, explained at a conference in the U.S. Senate in June 2000 dealing with minorities in the region, "People think that the conflict is only between the black Christians and animists in the south and the Arab northern majority. That is not the case. In reality it is between the blacks in the south, the Africans in the west, those in the east and in the Nuba mountains on the one hand, and the 10 percent Arab nationalist and Islamist elite in control of the Greater Khartoum–Omdurman triangle. It is Africans from Christian, Muslim, and animist background versus the National Islamic Front. It is also between the Arab Muslim democratic opposition and the military regime. Those who rule the Sudan are less than 4 percent of the population, but the opposition is made of many groups. When Khartoum settles with one, it moves against the other."

Mohammed was right on target. As soon as the Bashir regime accepted the settlement with the south, his forces attacked another ethnic community in the western part of the country, Darfur. The people of Darfur are Muslim. Surrounding them from the east are militias called the Janjaweed (literally bad spirits on horses), gathered from Arab tribes armed by the regime. Khartoum sent the Janjaweed to terrorize Darfur's villages and push their populations to the edges of the province with the aim of settling tribes linked to the Islamist ruling elites in the center.

The genocide began in February 2003, and hundreds of thousands of black civilians fled into the surrounding deserts. Soon enough the Darfuris formed local groups of resistance, mainly the Sudan Liberation Movement (SLM) and the Justice and Equality Movement (JEM). The largest African-descended community in the region is the "Furs." The second-biggest ethnic group is the Masalit, followed by the Zaghawa, and by a community of Darfuris of Arab descent. Abdul Wahid Mohamed el-Nur, an ethnic Fur, is the main resistance leader in Darfur, along with Minni Minnawi, an ethnic Zaghawa, and Khalil Ibrahim, who also have significant influence.[63] The proregime militias, led by Musa Hilal, are drawn from Arab settlements in the area and backed by the regime's armed forces and security services.

In the post-9/11 environment, the United Nations' Security Council moved swiftly to sanction the Khartoum regime. Resolution 1502 of August 26, 2003, and then Resolution 1547 of June 11, 2004, allowed the establishment of a force of nearly twenty thousand military personnel and more than six thousand police to be stationed in Sudan. The hybrid operation had an initial mandate of twelve months. It incorporated an existing African Union mission in Sudan, which was deployed across Darfur in 2004. Resolution 1769 of August 2, 2007, made it the largest peacekeeping force in the world. The Islamist regime of Khartoum defied the UN decisions and continued to dispatch the Janjaweed against the African villages in Darfur.

During the summer of 2004, Mohammed Yahia, who leads the Massalit community in the United States, told me the regime in Khartoum was moving from one front to another against the black African population in Sudan. "They waged genocide against the south for decades and failed in exterminating them. Hassan Turabi, the ideologue of the Khartoum elite, wanted to thrust into black Africa via the south by fomenting insurgencies in Uganda, Ethiopia, Kenya, and beyond. But when the international community and the United States stopped them from going south, they moved west to ethnic-cleanse Darfur. What they aim at in this huge province is to depopulate the African population and settle Arab tribes that are controlled by their regime. From Darfur, they seek penetration of the Sahel via Chad."

The Darfur-American activists received the support of a large number of churches and NGOs such as the National Council of

Churches and the Genocide Intervention Network. From these activities rose the "Darfur Campaign in the United States," backed by a number of liberal elites and Hollywood celebrities.[64]

It was odd to observe over the decades how the genocide in southern Sudan and Darfur was treated internationally. From 1956 till the late 1990s, the massacres in southern Sudan went unchecked by the West and the international community. A million and a half victims later and after the 9/11 attacks, Washington and other governments began pressing for solutions. The problem of the southern Sudanese, as summarized by a State Department official in the 1990s, is "that the southerners are black and non-Muslims." Asked to clarify, my source said, "U.S. interest sides with oil-producing Arab regimes versus poor black populations; that is a fact. Besides, the southern Sudanese are Christian and animists. We're not going to provoke the Organization of the Islamic Conference (OIC) and its powerful influence on OPEC because of the tribes."

The brotherhood against democracy, which controlled the OIC and OPEC, sided systematically with the "Islamic regime" against the "animist-Christian" secession. The Darfur affair was different. The oppressed population was Muslim and the oppressing regime was Islamist. Thus, divisions were different. All Arab states sided automatically with Khartoum, while a number of African Muslim states refused to endorse genocide of their racial kin.

Once the OIC–Arab League "fraternity" with the Sudan regime was broken, Western players reacted. Pope John Paul II was the first international figure to raise the issue of Darfur, in his Christmas message of 2004. Immediately thereafter, UN secretary general Kofi Annan and other leaders started to address the genocide as an international drama.

It was clear to me at the time that world leaders were afraid of mentioning "genocide" when the massacred were black Christians and Muslims in southern Sudan, as they did not want to offend the OIC. Those same leaders were quicker to level such accusations when the victims' religion was Islam, and there was less risk of alienating the oil-producing regimes. Only after African Muslim countries such as Chad, Mali, and Eritrea backed the resistance of Darfur was it possible to internationalize the crisis. The accusation in jihadi propaganda of being Islamophobic was the ultimate nightmare for international leaders. Southern Sudan lost 1.5 million victims to massacres without its being labeled genocide, while Darfur's losses—equally disturbing—were about 250,000 but were cited as genocide simply because they were black Muslims and the OIC couldn't play the "war on Islam" card. Nevertheless, I found that charging Khartoum's military junta with serious breaches of international law was a major achievement of the new U.S. policies.

Darfur was a signal that justice was moving forward to sanction the most genocidal members of the brotherhood against democracy.

Bashir Indictment and the Regional "Brotherhood"

After years of investigations by international bodies, the regime was finally designated a perpetrator of mass human rights abuse. On Monday July 14, 2009, the International Criminal Court indicted Sudan's president, Omar Bashir, for crimes against humanity for having ordered and facilitated Darfur's genocide. ICC prosecutors, led by Luis Moreno-Ocampo of Argentina, a courageous legal expert, made a direct challenge to the regional order. Although solid on legal grounds, the decision was to be severely attacked by the "virtual Caliphate" in the region.

I warned that Moreno-Ocampo's powerful initiative would be obstructed by the gathering of regional ruling elites, who would see it as a prelude to the targeting of their own regimes. If one leader were indicted for genocide, massacre, or assassination, it would cause a domino effect and the other regimes would crumble as well.

This projection was confirmed by the events of 2009 and 2010. The International Criminal Court issued demands that Omar Bashir be arrested and remitted to the tribunal, as had been the case with Yugoslav leader Slobodan Milosevic. The African victims of Khartoum's regime hoped the arrest, investigation, and eventual trial of the dictator would signal the ushering in of a new era in Sudan. The oppressed were hopeful but discounted the regional support the jihadi elite would receive from its "brothers" in the Greater Middle East.[65]

The ICC indictment can be attributed in part to the post-9/11 environment and the fact that U.S. and European policies raised the bar against the terror regimes in the region. The Assad regime came close to being indicted on the Hariri assassination in Beirut, and Iran was sanctioned on the nuclear issue. International courts, like other justice systems, operate in an environment in which they examine the possibilities for the carrying out of their sentences. Before 2009, the U.S.-led effort at the UN encouraged legal action against abusers of human rights. But the new U.S. policy toward the region announced by the Obama administration in January 2009 contradicted the Bush agenda. The new president spoke of engagement with the so-called Muslim world, which in fact translates into "Islamic regimes." The perception by the Sudan regime shifted quickly and the value of the ICC indictment was lessened by Obama's statement that the United States would not "meddle" in another nation's "affairs." In short, the indictment by the ICC came just as American policy shifted again, away from human rights and back toward "respect" for the interests of oppressive regimes.

This new approach unleashed a realignment of the Arab League members and other regimes in the region. Shamelessly, all Arab governments sided as one bloc with Omar Bashir against the International Criminal Court. Some, like Syria and Libya, supported him with enthusiasm, while others coalesced under pressure from jihadi propaganda. Iran's regime stood firmly by Sudan's president, and the region's oil-funded media lashed out against international justice as "another form of war against Islam."[66]

Shockingly, Turkey, a NATO member, ruled by the Islamist AKP government, rushed to the rescue of "brother" Bashir. Turkish prime minister Recep Tayyip Erdogan continued his government's denial of the genocide in Darfur, questioning ICC charges against Sudanese president Omar Bashir on the grounds that "no Muslim could perpetrate genocide."[67] Playing a game of good cop/bad cop, the "regimes" tasked Qatar with the mediation mission between Sudan's regime and the "rebels" in Darfur.

At first glance, the principality of Qatar's mediating between the Sudanese regime and the Darfur rebel movements was a positive move. After further examination, it was clear the plan was coordinated among the regional cartel with the aim of blocking international intervention in Sudan. Qatar's regime, which owns al Jazeera, is influenced by the Muslim Brotherhood, and its oil industry funds the most radical jihadi programs on the television network. The priority to the "brotherhood" of authoritarian regimes and jihadi organizations is to ensure that no UN, international, or Western intervention leads to self-determination for Darfur or sanctions on Khartoum. By inviting the Darfur groups to sit down in Doha with the regime's representatives, Qatar could sink the international campaign to save Darfur. Showing that both sides were making progress and negotiating would make a good impression on the international community and allow Khartoum to buy time and possibly survive the ICC indictment and go back on the offensive. Most Darfur leaders realized the motives behind this maneuver, and Abdul Wahid Mohamed el-Nur rejected it, signaling that from exile in Paris, he would seek international intervention, not Qatari or Arab League mediation.

The Oppression of the Beja

The Beja people live in the eastern part of Sudan along the Red Sea. They are another African ethnic group oppressed by the jihadist regime in Khartoum. According to their main organization, the Beja Congress, the eastern Sudan blacks have been denied cultural, social, and economic rights by the ruling elite in the capital.

In January 2005 thousands of impoverished Bejas carried out public protests in Port Sudan, in which they asked for essentially the same things the population of Darfur was calling for: greater political representation, wealth-sharing, jobs, services, and so on. They were met with violent suppression by local security forces and regular army troops, during which at least twenty were killed, more than 150 arrested, and thousands more displaced from their homes, mostly improvised shacks in crowded coastal slums.

According to some Beja leaders, this reinforced the notion that armed struggle was the only thing Khartoum understood, and they encouraged hundreds of young Beja men to join the armed wing of the Beja Congress. When the government arrested several key Beja Congress leaders in March 2006, it poured gasoline on the fire. It was at this point that Eritrea took the initiative to propose itself as a facilitator of peace talks.[68]

According to Ibrahim Ahmed, the U.S.-based representative of the Beja people who leads the Beja Organization for Human Rights and Development, it became clear that the eastern part of Sudan, with Port Sudan as the main urban center, had become a target for ethnic cleansing, with the goal of removing the native people and settling Arab communities funded by the regime and oil-producing governments in the region. "Funds from Libya and the Arab Gulf are being offered to the regime to displace the African indigenous populations and replace them with Arab settlers," Ibrahim Ahmed told me. "Khartoum is arguing that the Beja people and their presence along the coast of Sudan are obstructing the Red Sea from becoming a fully Arab lake."

In addition to ethnic cleansing, Sudan's regime has been using the Beja areas to establish jihadist military camps to train individuals and groups aiming at operations in Somalia and Ethiopia and internationally.

The Oppression of the Nubians

Aside from the historical reference to the ancient name of Sudan, the term "Nubia" today refers to a land and an ethnic group inside Sudan struggling for freedom. The modern-day Nuba mountains lie in south Kordofan, a province (now a state) in the geographical center of Sudan, chiefly inhabited by a cluster of peoples indigenous to the area. They are black African, followers of Islam, Christianity, and traditional religions, but their homeland is within the political boundaries of northern Sudan.

In the early 1990s, the Islamist regime waged an ethnic-cleansing campaign against the Nubians in order to "Arabize" their homeland. As researcher Alex de Waal wrote: "This was the first step in an unprecedented military assault, accompanied by a radical plan for population relocation. The idea of planned displacement and the concept of 'peace camps' for the relocated had existed for several years, but this was the first time that the government was envisaging its use throughout an entire region. In addition, mass rape appeared as an instrument of policy. The intent was to wholly clear the Nuba mountains of Nuba people. The campaign was justified by explicit reference to jihad."[69]

By way of comparison, the Nuba area is larger than the entire West Bank and Gaza, or the Lebanese republic. Just imagine the uproar if Israel was bulldozing the entire Palestinian population east of the Jordan River. The attempt to cleanse the Nuba is already of that magnitude—and the Arab League, the OIC, the African Union, and the UN are silent on the bloodshed. In a meeting with lawmakers from the Nuba area who were visiting Washington I was told that after Darfur, these mountain Africans will also demand freedom.

Conclusion

The people of southern Sudan will be heading to the polls in 2011 to decide their future. If they decide for self-determination, eight million Africans will be on their way to statehood. Separation may not be accepted by the jihadi regime in Khartoum. It would take away a portion of the country where important resources, including gas and other minerals, are located, as well as a segment of the Nile River. Additionally, if and when southern Sudan becomes independent, the other oppressed nationalities of Sudan with African identity, such as Darfur, the Beja, and the Nuba mountains, will also request the same right to self-determination.

Ideologically, the regime in Khartoum, controlled by a staunch Pan Arabist and Islamist elite, cannot accept allowing territories once under the "Caliphate" to revert to their original inhabitants. The jihadi regime in control of Sudan cannot make peace with its own populations, and it is only when a democratic alternative takes over in the Arab center of the country that the nationalities at the periphery will be able to coexist within a new confederated Sudan or between separate and associated countries. Khartoum's Islamist regime will fight self-determination for the south and will suppress Darfur, the Beja, and the Nuba population.

The Arab liberal and democratic opposition to the "National Congress Party" of Bashir and to the Islamist movement founded by Hassan Turabi has an obligation to unite in a bid to form a future government in the center. Only a democracy win in Khartoum would stop future wars and ethnic cleansing against the African people of Sudan. An alliance between the Arab Muslim democratic opposition in the north and the African ethnic movements in the south, east, and west of the country is the only coalition that can eventually bring back freedom and democracy to Sudan and put a stop to the totalitarian fantasy of a new "Caliphate" invading black Africa.[70]

12

The Greater Maghreb: The Most Violent Jihadists and Their Nemesis

The native populations—the nations and tribes that lived in North African and the Greater Middle East before the invasion of their lands by the armies of the Caliphate in the seventh century C.E.—from Egypt to the Atlantic Ocean, across the deserts of Libya, Tunisia, Algeria, and Morocco, all the way down to Mauritania, have three things in common. First, they are all native North African; second, they have all submitted to the rule of one Islamic empire for centuries; and third, they have been and continue to be subjected to oppression by Arab nationalist regimes and to extreme violence by modern-day jihadists. These populations include, in order from largest population to smallest; the Berbers of the Maghreb (mostly Morocco, Algeria, and parts of the Sahel), the Copts of Egypt, and the blacks of southern Mauritania. The Arab Muslim majorities in these countries are also deprived of full liberties and face human rights abuses. Both demographic majorities and minorities are suppressed politically, but ethnic minorities are put under several layers of pressure. In many parts of the Greater Middle East and the Arab world, cultural, linguistic, and religious minorities are pressured to alter their "identity." The North African native ethnicities have been bullied for centuries, but more aggressively so in modern times, and have been prevented from achieving cultural and political emancipation.

While Arab Muslim majorities were oppressed on political grounds, non-Arab Muslim communities were suppressed based on their very existence and identity. Throughout the Greater Middle East, there is a struggle between the forces of authoritarianism and jihadism (even though jihadists are often pitted against each other), on the one hand, and civil society, in particular its minorities, on the other.

In North Africa as a whole, the scenario repeats itself in many nations, although with local differences and cultural and historical diversity. Most governments are authoritarian, with different levels of assertiveness. Libya is the only full-fledged dictatorship, holding thousands of political prisoners. Muammar Qaddafi's regime, inspired by extreme Arab nationalism, socialism, and political Islamism, has been in power since 1970. In Egypt, Tunisia, Algeria, and somewhat in Morocco, multiparty systems exist, but according to opposition movements, the governments are under the control of authoritarian elites and have been holding political prisoners for years.

The debate about the march of democracy in these four countries continues, and experts look at several factors to determine legitimacy. First, they consider the fact that the ruling elites maintain a state of pressure and control over their opposition and civil society in general. The North African Arab countries aren't yet at the democratic level of Turkey, Israel, or Cyprus, their trans-Mediterranean neighbors. However, a second look at the evolution of political systems in these countries shows a stark difference between the four multiparty constitutions in Morocco, Algeria, Tunisia, and Egypt and the raw dictatorship in Libya, which resembles the regimes in Syria, Iran, and Sudan rather than its own immediate neighbors. In the four nondictatorial but authoritarian countries of North Africa, opposition movements have access to newspapers and can criticize the government (to a certain extent), and their members can be elected to the legislatures. In Morocco, the constitutional monarchy is constantly criticized by its opposition, but there is a margin of freedom in its criticism. In Algeria, Tunisia, and Egypt, the opposition parties can organize and run for elections in various ways. The Muslim Brotherhood in Egypt, even though it seeks a regime change and the establishment of an emirate instead of a republic, still controls a large bloc of members in the Egyptian assembly.

Many studies over the last decade have shown that democracy movements in North Africa, as in the Arab region as a whole, are getting better organized and more vigorous and are making inroads in acquiring more civil rights. The democratic forces in North Africa are still far from achieving the full liberalization that would enable their countries' civil societies to enjoy the freedoms achieved on the northern shores of the Mediterranean. Two main challenges face the liberating process: the threat of jihadism and the severe oppression of ethnic and religious minorities.

The question of democracy in the various regions of North Africa is complex. It has a diamond shape. On the top sit the regimes; below on equivalent points are the secular opposition and the jihadist forces; in the center area of the upper triangle is a mostly suppressed civil society; and in the bottom area of the diamond sit the oppressed non-Arab and non-Muslim minorities. Regimes try to maintain a balance between containing the Islamists and fighting the jihadists on the one hand, while on the other hand delaying the expansion of significant democratic reforms. But, in at least two countries, state ideologies continue to reject the full emancipation of their ethnic minorities. This struggle can be illustrated by the state of the minorities in Algeria and Egypt, and by the slavery issue in Mauritania.

The Berbers

Along with the Copts of Egypt, the Berbers are among the oldest inhabitants of the North African continent. Their experience is similar to that of the Native Americans in the United States. As in all similar cases of ethnic identification, the origin and identity of the Berbers are disputed by historians, and they are questioned by politicians and ideologues of modern times.

Arab nationalists, Islamist historians, ideologues, and politicians alike reject the idea that these populations have a legitimate right, as native North Africans, to self-determination and independence or even to autonomy and self-rule. The Islamists, and naturally the jihadists, argue that since the entire area was justly conquered by the Caliphate thirteen centuries ago, not only must it revert to an Islamic empire, it must also oppose the rise of small independent states, even Muslim states. The Islamists who support a return to the Caliphate believe the large countries of Morocco and Algeria must disappear so that the Caliphate can be established, so it is impossible to even consider the rise of a country for the Berber nation across the Maghreb, in the western part of the North African plateau. However, Islamists invite the Berbers, since they are already Muslims, to join the drive of Salafism and jihadism and be equal to the Arab ethnics in their jihad to reclaim the just Caliphate.

The Arab nationalists in the region, mostly socialists and authoritarians, use nuanced arguments to reject the right of Berbers to self-determination. Qaddafi of Libya often boasts that Berbers are also Arabs, because, as he puts it, "They came from the Arabian peninsula some four thousand years ago," well before the Arab invasion of the continent. Qaddafi and his Arab nationalist acolytes attempt to claim that the Berbers are Arabs, too, even if they refuse to acknowledge it. It would be as if the Anglo-Saxons of North America had told the Native Americans, "You're Europeans and came from Eurasia some ten thousand years ago, so you're not more native than us and your lands are ours."

Short History of the Berber Struggle

The ancient Berber nations—also called Mazigh or Amazigh—came from Afro-Hamitic origins and inhabited the areas between Morocco and western Egypt, settling several areas as far south as the Sahel. Their multiple kingdoms met with the Phoenician settlers who founded Carthage, and Berbers formed the bulk of the population of the Carthaginian empire. After the end of the Punic Wars, the Berbers were conquered by the Romans, the Byzantines, and the Vandals, but were able to maintain their cultures across the centuries. Their regions were identified as Numidia, Mauritania, and several others. Christianity spread into North Africa in its first centuries and the new city of Carthage became the seat of North African Christianity, in parallel to Alexandria, which was the patriarchate of the Copts. Significant Jewish communities settled in the Berber areas as of the first century C.E. After invading Egypt under the command of Amr Ibn al A'as, the Caliphate's armies progressed through the Sahara toward the Berber nations and were met with strong resistance in 642 and 669 C.E., particularly in areas of today's eastern Algeria and Tunisia.

The Arab conquest of the Berber areas was a benchmark in their history similar to the Anglo-Iberian conquest of the Americas. It marked a total change in dominant culture, a significant mutation in ethnic majorities, and a shift in religious affiliation.

After a series of battles that began in Cyrenaica (present-day Libya) and spreading to several parts of what is today the west of North Africa covering Tunisia, Algeria, and Morocco, Caliphate forces led by generals and emirs appointed from the Arabian Peninsula defeated the Berber resistance and added these vast areas of the continent to the expanding empire from the east. The Arab forces gathered in Kairouan south of the city of Tunis and advanced toward the Atlas range and the plains surrounding it. The original Berber homelands fell under the *Fatah* of North Africa, which would use the northern coasts to invade Spain.

Unlike previous conquerors, the Arab rulers insisted on full assimilation. Since the early seventh century, a process of Arabization and Islamization has brought large segments of the Berber populations into the fold of the new identity. It is important to note that while a Berber resistance slowed the process of assimilation, a number of the indigenous tribes joined the conquerors, as had been the case in Syria and Mesopotamia.

One notable Berber who took the banner of the Caliphate was none other than Tariq Bin Ziad, the illustrious commander of the invading forces that landed in Spain and defeated the Visigoth Christian armies around 715 C.E. In his honor, the rock dominating the passage to Iberia was called Jebel Tarik, mutating in European languages to Gibraltar. Tariq led the Caliphate armies across Iberia, giving first the Umayyads, then the Abbasids what no leader of the Islamic empire ever imagined: a piece of Christian Europe. The area was rich with water and fertile land and would be named by the conquerors Andalus—or the land of the Vandals. However, the general who was to the Caliphate what Cortés was to the Spanish empire centuries later wasn't honored as he should have been. As soon as he secured the victories in Andalusia, the Arab elite of Damascus dispatched rulers to seize power on behalf of the pure Arab dynasty of the Umayyads, known for their disdain of other ethnicities, particularly those from Africa, even if they were Muslim.

The most famous Berber in Arab history was treated like a second-class citizen, despite his achievements, which brought immense riches to the Arab-led Caliphate in the Levant.[1] "He simply wasn't an ethnically first-class citizen" says Ferhat Mehenni, the leader of a modern-day Berber autonomist movement in Algeria, "because he wasn't from the ruling class, the Arabs who moved from the east since the conquest."

The Tariq narrative is highly symbolic of the centuries that followed up to the present day. The Berbers developed into two groups.

First, there were those who Arabized and became part of the Arab
settler population coming from Arabia and the Levant. They would
be the equivalent of the mestizos of Hispanic America, a mix of
white Europeans and Native Americans. The Arabo-Berbers who
converted to Islam, some argue, might very well be today the demographic majority across the region, from Morocco to Algeria. The
second group was those Berbers who didn't Arabize and maintained
their pre-Arab cultural heritage, particularly in enclaves throughout
the Maghreb.

With the loss of the Andalus, the Caliphate's western frontiers
regressed to northern Morocco. Arab rulers of the Maghreb, fearing
further incursions by the Europeans, relaxed the process of Arabization of the Berbers. In the sixteenth century, the Ottoman Sultanate
claimed all of North Africa, appointing its bureaucrats as *Walis* in the
Maghreb. Both historical developments gave a mild break to the Berber areas, allowing their culture to survive for a few more centuries
while still under the yoke of a Sultanate. Gradually, Turkish rule receded and European powers began colonizing the Maghreb in 1830,
with France occupying Algeria, Morocco, and Tunisia, while Spain
secured northern Morocco and Italy took control in Libya. Both
Arabs and Berbers found themselves under Western occupation.

With the settling of European populations in Algeria in the
mid-nineteenth century, French authorities attempted to secure
the support of the Berbers against the mounting influence of Arab
nationalism and Wahabism throughout the Arab population. For
decades two tendencies competed within the Berber Amazigh communities. One trend promoted the idea of solidarity with the Islamic
identity in the Maghreb against French colonial rule, and the other
argued that the real ethnic threat was Arab nationalism.

Historians of the Berber peoples share the ambivalence that characterized the evolution of their political movements. While many
Berbers joined the struggle against the French all the way to the
independence of all Maghreb countries, others focused on obtaining autonomy and independence for Berber nations. The choice for
these native "nations" in the Maghreb was to either join the Arab
nationalist movement, particularly in Algeria, against the French and
form postcolonial secular countries, or struggle directly for one or
more Berber states. The dilemma was harsh. Being mostly Muslim or
Islamized, the Berbers were not immune to the call of jihad against

the infidel colonialists. Arab nationalists, though secular, often used the call for the *Grand Jihad contre la France* to mobilize the Amazigh tribes for the resistance. French-Algerians and local authorities played the song of Berber autonomy versus future Arab domination.

In the end, the majority of Berber political leaders chose to side with the ethnic Arabs against the French rule, and three Arab states emerged in the Maghreb: Morocco, Tunisia, and Algeria, all former provinces of the Arab and Ottoman Caliphate.

In Morocco, independent since 1956, the ethnic Berber population is estimated at 40 percent, while in modern-day Algeria, independent since 1962, the group forms a strong minority of about 30 percent. However, if counted with the "Arabo-Berbers," the Amazigh-ancestry population may be about 70 percent or more of the entire Maghrebi population. As in Sudan, the original Arab settler population is smaller than the native North African population. However, the mixed population in the Maghreb is mostly influenced in its political choices by the dominant establishment of the Arab nationalists and the Islamists, even though in its daily cultural life it connects with both roots, Arab and Berber. Morocco's Berbers, with much greater numbers, especially in the Atlas Mountains, and living under a constitutional monarchy that has established blood ties to many of their tribes, feel more comfortable than their Algerian kin. Even in moderate Morocco some Berbers fear the rise of jihadism as a threat to their way of life and to the few shy steps toward electoral democracy, which weren't accomplished without difficulty.

In contrast, in the Arab Republic of Algeria, which reached independence from France in 1962, the Berber question is more dramatic. In the center of the Berber struggle in Algeria is a Berber region seeking autonomy, Kabylia. This region is stirring the questions of self-determination and democratization as never before in the entire Maghreb.

The Kabyle Question

The Berber populations are spread throughout the region, from smaller communities in Libya, Tunisia, and Egypt, to larger groups in the Sahel such as the Tuareg in Mauritania, Mali, and Niger, all the way to Burkina Faso. The largest Berber "nations" are found in the Maghreb. Among them the Chleuh (francophone plural of Arabic

"Shalh"), the Tashelhiyt of south Morocco, numbering about 8 million, the Riffians of north Morocco, and the Chaouia of Algeria. However, the most autonomous trends of Berber ethnonationalism are found in the people of the Kabyles of northern Algeria, who to a large degree have kept their original language and culture.

Geographically, Kabylia is situated immediately to the east of Algiers. Mostly mountainous, the region is home to some 5 million Kabyle Berbers. Most of them are concentrated in the three Berber provinces of Tizi Ouzou, Bejaia, and Bouira. Some 50 percent of the populations of the provinces of Setif, Bordj Bou Arreridj, and Boumerdes are also Kabyle speakers. In addition, half of the 3 million people of Algiers are Kabyles. Due to its poverty and population density, Kabylia has been the source of more than half the Algerian immigrants in France. Having been among the oldest areas of resistance on behalf of Berber culture, Kabylia erupted several times in the past few decades to demand cultural autonomy, including its rights to Berber education in the Amazigh language.

Ferhat Mehenni, the president of the Kabyle Autonomy Movement (MAK), spoke with me during meetings at the U.S. Congress in fall 2009, at which he briefed members about the situation in his home country, saying:

> The Kabyles are conscious of their heritage and their long history stretching from before the Arab conquest. Our ancestors refused to Arabize and we maintained our language, the Amazigh. For centuries, completely isolated from the outside world, our people struggled to maintain its identity in its mountainous homeland while Umayyads, Abbasids, and Ottomans ruled the entire region along with their vassals. Under the French, our population sought its autonomy, but Kabyles joined in the resistance to build an independent, free, secular, and pluralist Algeria, where Arab and Berbers, including Kabyles, Muslims and non-Muslims alike, would live in justice and peace. Instead, after liberation, Arab nationalists ruled Algiers and rejected the Kabyles' demands for autonomy. Since then, we are struggling for the most basic rights, the right to be ourselves and the right to be different even as we live together.

Mehenni, like many other Kabyle leaders, lives in exile in France and serves as traveling ambassador to the world on behalf of his ethnic community. In Washington, interest in his cause began with stunningly simple questions. "Who are the Kabyles? Who are the Berbers? Are you Arabs? What religion are you?" asked the lawmakers, think tank officials, and even journalists. Such questions are never asked about the Palestinians, let alone about the Israelis or the Kurds. Why is there ignorance about this population of 5 million, while Westerners are so well informed about the people of Kosovo?

The Kabyles have stood up for their cultural and political rights since the 1970s but have been suppressed by the ruling National Liberation Front (FLN), a North African version of the Baath in Syria and Iraq. Demands for teaching and using Amazigh as a national language were systematically rejected by the regime, busy with the "Arabization process."[2]

The forcing of Arabic language and culture on the Berbers in general and the Kabyles in particular by the FLN was perceived by these minorities as a form of "ethnic cleansing," according to Alex Medouni, representative of the Kabyles in Washington, D.C. "The Kabyles were subjected to nonstop suppression since day one of the independence, first by the Pan Arabist and socialist elite in Algiers for three decades. And when the military regime was sidelined after the Cold War, the replacement of the regime, still Arab nationalist and backed by the army as well as the rising Salafi Islamists, resumed the pressure. The Kabyles haven't had a respite since the departure of the French, even though they were at the forefront of the liberation war."[3] A first generation of exiled Kabyles left the country early on to continue the struggle from overseas. A number of exiled intellectuals maintained the idea of a Berber homeland or at least an autonomous Kabylia."[4]

In the 1980s it was unthinkable in the Arab nationalist circles of the Levant, as well as in the Maghreb, that non-Arab minorities would be recognized as dissatisfied. From the Kurds in Iraq to the Berbers of Algeria, it was an untouchable subject. During these years of struggle while the Cold War raged, I wrote about their cause in the monthly newspaper I was publishing in Beirut. In an environment extremely hostile to anyone who raised the issue of minorities in the Arab world, my writings were attacked as "inciting for fragmentation of the region by advancing the notion that there are unhappy minorities in the Arab world."[5]

The Kabyles and Jihadists in the Algerian Civil War

In 1991, the Islamic Salvation Front (FIS) won the first multiparty election in Algeria with a slim margin. Although the Islamists were in the minority, a large segment of the population, including many Berbers, voted against the old authoritarian FLN-backed candidates. But the FIS made its intentions clear that once in power they would establish an Islamist regime, with no room for a secular multiparty system. In reaction, the secular Government backed by the army shut down the FIS and canceled the results of that election. Since then, many Islamist Salafists have resorted to violent jihadist methods and waged a terror war in the country.

Algeria's civil war throughout the decade was essentially waged by the jihadists of the Salafi Group for Call and Combat (GIA), who not only fought against the government, but also attacked the secular segments of civil society.[6] Algerian civilians, both Arabs and Berbers, suffered immensely at the hands of the jihadists and also fell victim to government counterstrikes. More than 140,000 civilians were killed, many in savage slaughter at the hands of the Salafi terrorists.[7] Ethnically both Arabs and Kabyles were targeted by the blind terror of the Salafists. Women, children, elderly, artists, civil servants, and musicians were killed or maimed.

The jihadists assassinated civilians in an effort to spread terror among seculars and moderates.[8] In particular, the killing of the famous Kabyle singer Lounes Matoub signaled an escalation between the mostly Arab jihadists and the Amazigh Kabyles. Matoub, who was assassinated in the district of Tizi Ouzou, Kabilia's capital, represented the pride of the Berbers.[9] In addition to the general civil war between the Salafists and the government, and the jihadists' targeting of secular symbols in the country as a whole, a confrontation began between the jihadists and the Kabyles.

The clash between the terrorists and this particularly moderate and secular community of Berbers had clear, deep ideological roots. On the surface, the Salafi Islamists of the GIA were an extreme form of jihadists, akin to the Taliban in their fundamentalism. Their call for a radical Islamist state would naturally clash with the mostly secular and liberal Kabyles. Beyond this ideological division the jihadists represented, in the eyes of the Amazigh-speaking Kabyles, a resurgence of the old Caliphate, whose invasion centuries before had led to the collapse of the Berber nations.

The struggle between the jihadists and the Kabyles was a fight between the resurgent totalitarian Caliphate and liberal democracy, between the past and the future. The confrontation in the Kabyle and other Berber areas resulted in trauma and devastation for millions of civilians who stayed in Algeria and many more who left.[10]

Kabyles and the Future

After 9/11 and the Iraq War of 2003, two developments shed a different light on the Kabyle struggle. First and foremost, in the framework of the war with the jihadists worldwide, the Kabyles as a nation were positioned, thanks to the Salafists of Algeria, as a resistance movement against the totalitarian terrorists.[11] While it is true that al Qaeda in the Maghreb (AQIM), the new outfit of the Algerian and Moroccan jihadists since 2006, had recruited among Kabyles before, it is also true that the Berber society in northern Algeria and across the region was more resentful of and resistant to the Salafists' agenda than others. Secular Kabyles are the toughest intellectual challengers of the ideologues of al Qaeda.

Beyond the ideological clash, other developments in the region have inspired the Kabyles. "We saw the Kurds being granted their basic rights by a member of the Arab League, Iraq, a few years after the fall of the Baath," Ferhat Mehenni told me. The musician-turned-political-leader was making a logical parallel. Why can't the Kabyles, and the Berbers in general, be treated like the Kurds of Iraq and granted autonomy, local government, and cultural and educational institutions? Both Kurds and Kabyle are non-Arab ethnicities stuck in an "Arab" state. In the end, they should be given their rights or let go.

Mehenni also mentioned Darfur and the blacks of Sudan, another Arab country that resisted granting rights to its own minorities. Unlike Kurdistan or Darfur, Kabylia didn't experience massacres of the size seen in Iraq and Sudan. "But it all depends on who is in power in Algiers," said Medouni, the American Kabyle leader. "If the jihadists take over in Algeria, both Arabs and Kabyles will pay the price," he rightly concluded.

The difficulty in Algeria is the triangular struggle between the government, the jihadists, and the Kabyles. The Kabyles accuse the regime's elite of obstructing the recognition of Berber Amazigh identity. Algiers' recognition of the Kabyles is crucial for this pre-Arab people. "Our government rushes to the international forums to support the rights of Palestinians thousands of miles away but does not recognize the rights of its own people in Kabylia," says Mehenni. One day on al Jazeera I widened the parameters by asking why the Arab League sought justice for Gaza and demanded withdrawal of armed forces from the West Bank but didn't do the same for Tizi Ouzou. The ethnic claim by the Kabyles is legitimate and must be addressed by the international community and by the Algerian government.

The other reality is that the government in Algeria is fighting a hard battle against al Qaeda and the local terror groups. Many Algerian Arabs are seculars and humanists, and they are fiercely resisting the onslaught of the Salafists. The international community must help the Algerian government to confront the jihadists at the same time it facilitates a dialogue between Algiers and Tizi Ouzou. This was my suggestion to members of the U.S. Congress, the European Parliament, and NGOs focusing on human rights in the region.

The best solution would be to encourage the formation of a coalition of liberal Algerians and Kabyles and other Berbers. Undoubtedly, this would form a democratic majority in Algeria. Between a coalition and the secular government of the country, a front would be established, and al Qaeda would be isolated. Once that is achieved, the democratic culture can advance across the country, and in the end, the center will recognize the periphery. But by the summer of 2010, Mehenni and the Kabyles formed a government in exile. He told me: "Freedom cannot wait—we are moving forward."

Arabs and Kabyles—if they both commit to democracy—can achieve a real revolution against the totalitarian doctrines of the jihadists. The problem is finding the courageous minority that will begin the reform in the majority, so that democracy prevails in Algeria and eventually in the entire Maghreb.

On the shores of North Africa, there are two winds blowing: the nightmare of Jihadism and the hope of democracy.

13.

The Copts and Liberals:
Egypt's Rising Democrats

Why is the world community one-eyed when it comes to ethnic and religious minorities in the Middle East?" This question has been repeated for decades by speakers and participants in conferences on human rights and democracy organized by the region's dissidents. I have often had to answer this question, particularly when the subject was one of the most marginalized ethnicities of the Greater Middle East: the Copts of Egypt. There is one fact that is unchallengeable, inescapable, and constant: The Copts face injustice not only at home but also at the hands of the entire region's regimes, dominant political culture, and the United Nations. They are subjected to this treatment for one simple reason—they aren't recognized as a people with their own identity, history, religion, and aspirations. Unlike the Berbers, the Kurds, the Palestinians, or even the Jews, the Copts are not even counted as a "nation" deserving of rights. This continues to be their struggle in Middle Earth, even though they descend from ancient civilizations that built the pyramids, advanced science, and created objects that fill the world's museums with overwhelming evidence of high culture.

"Why aren't we treated like the Muslims of Kosovo, Bosnia, Gaza, or Chechnya even though our numbers are higher than all of these nations combined?" asked Dr. Shawki Karas, who passed away in 2003 and was the founder of the American Coptic Association based in New Haven, Connecticut. Karas never missed an opportunity, in North America or anywhere else in the world, to speak on behalf of his community, which he believed was "the most marginalized of all peoples in the Middle East."

In the last forum organized by the Coalition for the Defense of

Human Rights in the Islamic World in Washington in 2002, at which Karas and I both spoke, he took the issue of the Copts to its deepest moral ground. "We are a people of fourteen millions inside the most populous Arab country, Egypt. The Copts are among the oldest Christians in the world, among the poorest, and have been denied their basic rights since the seventh century continuously. Even those nations who were occupied, brutalized, or massacred were at least recognized at some point as existing peoples, and at times in their tumultuous history, they tasted freedom and enjoyed their identity. But never the Copts: They are the underdogs of the underdogs."

Karas, who left his native Egypt in the early 1960s, fleeing the oppression of the Arab nationalist and socialist regime of Gamal Abdel Nasser, settled in America and became a successful social-behavior professor at the University of Connecticut. Since the early 1970s he has organized other exiled American Copts and formed an association advocating freedom for his people in Egypt. I met Karas in Washington in 1991 at what was then the first minisummit between Egyptian Copts, Assyrians from Iraq, and Lebanese Christians to discuss the common fate and destiny of Middle Eastern Christian minorities in light of the continued persecution led by the jihadists in the region. His was a voice for justice I listened to for decades, and one that remains in my memory even though he has passed away.

My first contact with the Coptic issue occurred a few months after I wrote a series of articles in the daily *al Ahrar* (*The Free Ones*) in Beirut in 1980, when dramatic events took place in Egypt. Coptic neighborhoods in Cairo and villages in Upper Egypt were raided by armed militia of the Jemaa Islamiya (Islamist Groupings), an offshoot of the Muslim Brotherhood and precursors of militant Salafists. During these bloody events Copts were killed, raped, kidnapped, and tortured, and many in Lebanon and the West learned for the first time not only that there was a Christian minority in Egypt, but that it numbered in the millions.

In researching the history of the Copts, I learned of the existence of an entire district of Christian Copts with Cairo called Shubra. The sheer size of that Christian nation, anchored around the Nile River since ancient times, was mind-boggling. There were more Copts in a Cairo neighborhood than Palestinians living in Gaza or than the entire population of Greek Cyprus or East Timor. There were more Copts than the citizens of Kuwait, Bahrain, or Lebanon. They are not a population existing on a few streets here and there or in some dispersed villages in the desert. The Copts were and are still the largest Christian population in the Middle East, and they are almost as numerous as the Kurds or the Berbers in three or four states. An anti-Coptic campaign swept across Egypt only a few years after President Sadat signed a peace treaty with Israel in 1979. How can this be happening in a country that is receiving large amounts of foreign aid from the United States? I asked myself at the time.

As these events were unfolding, President Sadat, whom I respected and admired for his courage in traveling to Israel and surprising his enemies with his intention to make peace, acted strangely. He ordered the incarceration of both the attackers and the victims. Thousands of jihadists and Copts were arrested and jailed for "incitement and involvement in confessional incidents." It was illogical, particularly for a president who was assailed by all the region's radicals, to equate the armed Islamist militias and the Copts, who were clearly the victims.

Sadat was assassinated by a cell of jihadists during state-sponsored celebrations a year later.

The Copts in History

The Copts are the direct descendants of the ancient Egyptians who lived under the pharaohs. They are to that ancient civilization what today's Mayans and Incas are to the pre-Columbian civilizations in Central America. Hamitic ethnically, the Copts are distant cousins of the Berbers in North Africa. The term Copt or *Gypt* is associated with Egypt (*Eh Gypt*, meaning "the land of the Copts"). The Copts were Christianized by St. Mark, who was based in Alexandria. Egypt's Coptic culture existed under the Byzantine Empire before the Arab conquest of the Nile Valley. As with other ancient nations in the region, the expansion of the Caliphate into Egypt had historic consequences for Coptic identity and sovereignty. In a stunning parallel with other struggles in the region, the events of the mid-seventh century C.E. remain—in the eyes of Copts—at the root of their identity even though their real crisis today is about democracy and suppression.

The armies of the Caliphate, led by Amr Ibn al A'as, erupted in Egypt in 648 C.E. and defeated the Byzantine forces in several battles, taking one Egyptian city after another. In the north, Alexandria was seized and its library burned. The Copts, being Christian, fell into *Dhimmi* status and were able to survive—if they chose to—as second-class citizens with rights codified by Caliph Umar for Jews and Christians, the People of the Book. Gradually, many Copts converted to Islam and became Arabized while a strong minority maintained their original culture. There were sporadic uprisings against the Caliphate's governors of Egypt by the native population in the late seventh century.

The shrunken Coptic Christian community kept the use of the ancient Egyptian language and its religious rituals for as long as it survived. Unlike the Christians of Lebanon, who enjoyed a mountainous enclave from which they built a homeland while awaiting the fall of the Ottoman Empire, the Copts had no other choice, in the flatlands of Egypt, than to submit to whoever ruled the Nile River. With time, cultural erosion took place, and use of the original Coptic language shrank until it was used only in church. Copts, Arabized Copts, and Arab émigrés formed the population under the various Caliphates, which produced the Egyptian language, a mix of the tongues of ancient Egypt and Arabia.

In the nineteenth century two European interventions energized the shrinking Coptic community and placed it back on the national chessboard. First was Napoleon's campaign against the Mameluks, who dominated Egypt on behalf of the Ottomans, a campaign which lasted from 1798 to 1801. The French "rediscovered" the Copts of Egypt and used their services in translation and cultural interpretation. After the withdrawal of the French, the Copts were once again persecuted until the British occupied Egypt in 1882. Arab nationalists and Islamists viewed the British colonial era as a Western occupation, while it was perceived as a period of relief for the pre-Arab native ethnic groups.

From the late nineteenth century into the mid-twentieth, the Copts of Egypt regained ground socially, economically, and politically. For the first time since the seventh century, a Christian Copt, Boutros Ghali, the grandfather of Boutros Boutros-Ghali, the former secretary general of the United Nations, occupied the office of chief executive of the land, holding that office from 1908 until his assassination in 1910.

The Copts saw the emergence of two trends in their midst as World War I ended. A core group of nationalist Copts saw the collapse of the Caliphate and the crumbling of the Ottoman Sultanate as a historic opportunity to claim a Coptic homeland, based on President Woodrow Wilson's fourteen principles, including the right of self-determination, which granted many small nations in Europe their own states. This movement sought the creation of a Coptic state in Upper Egypt. Another movement among the Copts, led mostly by the growing business community and the upper class, preferred an association with moderate and patriotic elements from the Arab Muslim majority to build a modern-day republic in Egypt, even a constitutional monarchy. The Wafd Party, a mainstream centrist and patriotic movement led by Saad Zaghlul, opposed both the monarchy and British rule. Perceived as liberal by many Coptic intellectuals, the Wafd was the strongest alternative to the rise of the Muslim Brotherhood, the real nemesis of the Christians of Egypt. The Copt elite, still enjoying British protection in the 1920s and 1930s, projected that a Coptic state wasn't achievable and opted for a potential democratic Egypt over a resurgence of the Caliphate if the Brotherhood gained power.

Empowered by public and religious education in the early twentieth century, the Copts of Egypt gained in numbers and were invited to serve in the bureaucracies under the British and the constitutional monarchy. Meanwhile, Egypt as a whole was witnessing profound political and social changes. With the departure of the British after World War II, Arab nationalists and the Muslim Brotherhood reignited pressures against Copts and against Egyptian liberals in general, particularly within the state institutions. The corruption prevailing inside the monarchy's bureaucracy helped incite action against the regime. Arab nationalists and Islamists used the defeat of the Egyptian army in the first Arab-Israeli war in 1948 to wage a relentless campaign against King Faruk's government. In 1952 a coup, led by the "Free Officers" representing the nationalists and Islamists inside the armed forces and led by Mohammed Neguib, ousted the king.

The Copts' Fate under the Republic

During the two years that followed the "revolution-coup," an odd situation prevailed in Egypt. On one hand a number of political parties operated on the assumption that the fall of the monarchy would bring about full freedom and that a liberal system was on its way. On the other hand, hard-core Arab nationalists under the leadership of Colonel Gamal Abdel Nasser plotted for a second coup to dislodge Neguib and do away with potential postmonarchy liberalism.

During that two-year window, the Coptic movement, led by attorney Ibrahim Hilal, started to openly recruit membership after having declared the formation of the first Coptic political party in history, the Hizb al Umma al Kubtiyya (Party of the Coptic Nation). In only three days, more than ninety thousand became members, and hundreds of thousands applied. Hilal emerged as the leader of the largest ethnic minority in the region, bypassing the Kataeb Party of the Lebanese Christians.[1]

In 1954 Nasser staged a coup, dislodged Neguib, and declared an Arab socialist republic in Egypt. All parties and movements that didn't pledge allegiance to Pan Arabism and his leadership, including the Muslim Brotherhood, were banned. Across the country, monarchists, liberals, democrats, anti-Nasser conservatives, and even the communists, despite the fact that Nasser was an ally of Moscow, were rounded up or exiled. The Coptic party was disbanded and its leadership arrested. Hilal was later released but didn't have an active role in politics again. However, a wave of young Copts left the country for exile in the United States and the West. Among them were Selim Naguib, who would lead the movement out of Canada, Shawki Karas in the United States, and later on, Louis Rufail in Lebanon.

After the death of Nasser in 1970, Anwar Sadat replaced him and started preparations for the October war of 1973. According to Khalil Kallada, who led one of the exiled Coptic groups in Lebanon during the 1970s, between 1967 and 1973 a number of Coptic nationalists of the Diaspora called for the establishment of an autonomous Coptic province in the Sinai after the Israeli withdrawal, in an area that, according to Kellada, "would be representative of the native population of Egypt from pre-Arab times. All the Copts would have to do is resettle on their national soil in the Sinai where they could enjoy a secular form of life and freedoms, away from the threat of the extremists. The Coptic province would be associated to Cairo within a federation." But these plans, considered dangerous by the Arab nationalists of Egypt and the region, weren't even considered by the Israelis, who had control over the Sinai, according to the exiled Copts.

Soon enough the October/Yom Kippur War of 1973 washed away the dreams of the small faction of Coptic nationalists as Egypt and

Israel settled their conflict first with a cease-fire, and later through Sadat's historic visit to Jerusalem and the signing of the Camp David Agreement. The Sinai was returned to Egypt with the end of the war. The "peace" achieved between the two governments didn't bring democracy to Egypt or basic rights to the Copts. Under Nasser, the security services suppressed all other political parties, including the Muslim Brotherhood. The Pan Arabist socialist regime, like its Baathist sisters in Iraq and Syria, was a one-party regime; all other forces were crushed—monarchists, liberals, conservatives, Islamists, Copts, and even the communists. Under Sadat, the business communities were given more freedom, but the radical Arab nationalists and the Islamists turned against the regime for having signed an agreement "with the Zionists." The Copts supported the peace treaty, first, because they weren't part of the global Arab-Israeli feud over Palestine, and second, because they thought that with the end of the state of war, democratization would be introduced. That didn't happen.

The Muslim Brotherhood, particularly its offshoot the Jemaa Islamiya and other jihadists, waged a campaign against the Sadat regime to punish him for signing a peace treaty with the *kuffar* (infidels) and at the same time unleashed attacks against the Christian Copts across the country as "objective allies of the Jews and Israel." In 1979, jihadists began a violent campaign against Coptic villages, neighborhoods, and individuals. Egyptian liberals were targeted as well. The anti-Islamist Muslims of Egypt, freer under Sadat, raised their voices, demanding further liberalization of the country. Core liberal intellectuals such as Faraj Foda and Nawal Saadawi felt they could pressure the government to relax laws and regulations regarding basic freedoms now that Egypt had shifted allegiance from the Soviet Union to the United States.

Ironically, the Egyptian government, still run by the same security agencies and bureaucracies, hit back against the violent Islamists, but to strike a balance suppressed the Copts as well. Samuel Shehata, an exiled Coptic leader, told me in Beirut in early 1981, "Sadat was establishing a balance of terror between the terrorist Jemaa Islamiya and the unarmed second-class citizens in Egypt so that he can withstand the huge pressures he was under from the entire Arab world, including Syria, Iran, and the Wahabis, for having signed the Camp David Agreement." The Copts, in other words, were paying the price of signing an agreement with Israel because the other Arab regimes were opposed to peace.

On June 17, 1981, a series of incidents took place in one of the poorest and most populous neighborhoods of Cairo, El Zawya el Hamra. Coptic homes and churches were targeted and burned.[2] News reports and witnesses spoke of wide attacks by the Jemaa Islamiya against these Coptic neighborhoods, home to a million people. Attacks occurred in Upper Egypt as well. According to Coptic sources, twenty-two civilians were burned in their homes and businesses in El Zawya el Hamra during the riots. The Egyptian internal minister, General Hassan Abu Basha, declared that eighty-one Coptic Christian citizens were killed, over one hundred were seriously wounded, and eighty homes were looted and destroyed. The Coptic associations in the Diaspora, however, said not a single jihadist was ever arrested or prosecuted for these crimes.

Sadat ordered arrests on both sides—the attackers and the attacked. Thousands of jihadists and Copts were incarcerated; it would be as if both Nazis and Jews had been arrested for making trouble in Germany in the 1930s. Moreover, the Egyptian government put the head of the Coptic Orthodox Church, Pope Shenouda III, under house arrest in the abbey of Wadi Natroun in Egypt's Western Desert. These incredible measures, targeted at the unarmed ancient community of the country, were followed by a series of speeches delivered by Sadat at the National Assembly. To my amazement, particularly after I had praised the Egyptian president for his courage for engaging in peace discussions, and also for granting merciful asylum to the cancer-stricken shah of Iran, I heard Sadat harshly attacking the old and peace-loving Pope Shenouda for being responsible for the violence against the Copts. I was shocked when Sadat attacked the Coptic Diaspora leaders, including Shawki Karas in the United States. "I'll make you into a hamburger," shouted Sadat, speaking of Karas. Then he turned his fury on Beirut and attacked those voices encouraging the Copts to sedition. At first I didn't know who he was talking about, since Lebanon's politicians never discussed the issue of the Copts. Then I realized that he probably meant my articles in *al Ahrar* from the previous year.

Years later when I met with Egyptian diplomats and academics and asked them about the strange behavior of Sadat at the time, I was told that the pressure coming from the regimes on the outside and the

Islamists on the inside was unbearable. "He had to show that he was not with the infidels against Islam," explained a seasoned former diplomat. "The Copts were Christians and no one in the West was claiming to protect them. Besides, unlike in Lebanon or in southern Sudan, they weren't armed and couldn't organize a resistance. They were the ideal scapegoat. By hitting them, he would buy time and satisfy the powerful Islamist circles in Egypt, particularly the Muslim Brotherhoods, so that he could claim he was a righteous Islamic leader."

I am not sure this was the only explanation, but one thing is certain: President Sadat was under threat from the jihadists. On October 6, 1981, as he was reviewing a military parade commemorating the October war with Israel, he was assassinated by jihadists who had penetrated the army and were members of the Islamic Jihad of Egypt, which years later would merge with al Qaeda. Sadat wanted to show the Islamists he wasn't betraying the cause of the *Umma*, but the jihadists killed him regardless.

That dramatic episode convinced me further, even nine years before the end of the Cold War, that totalitarian ideologues cannot be negotiated with when it comes to the core of their doctrines. Despite the assassination of the Egyptian president by jihadists—the same who waged attacks against the Copts—Shenouda and many of his followers still spent time under house arrest or in jail before they were released. The rest of the decade was still dangerous for Copts and Egyptian liberals, but the bulk of the jihadi wrath turned toward Afghanistan, the land of holy struggle against the Soviets.

The Copts in the Post–Cold War Era

When the Soviet Union collapsed, many ethnic groups in the Greater Middle East felt the time had come for self-determination and democracy. The sight of the Soviet republics parting ways, of Czechoslovakia breaking up peacefully, and especially of menaced ethnic groups' receiving international protection in the former Yugoslavia and in northern Iraq left the region's minorities with hope that in a post-Soviet era, the oppressed would eventually be recognized.

That assumption didn't take into account the power of the brotherhood against democracy. In the former Yugoslavia, the OIC had no choice but to stand in support of its coreligionists, the Muslim minorities. In Iraq the OIC wasn't able to intervene with or against

Kurdish autonomy in the north, because both parties were coreligionists. In Egypt, the Copts didn't have any chance to see the Arab League or the OIC pressing an Arab and Islamic government to grant a non-Muslim minority any additional rights. The Copts aren't Arab or Muslim, and thus they are on the bottom of the ladder. Since they have no geopolitical assets, as do the Lebanese Christians, or a military force, as do the southern Sudanese, they were doomed to isolation despite their large numbers. Last but not least, the Copts were too dispersed inside their own homeland. Unlike most other minorities such as the Kabyles, Kurds, and Maronites, they had no home or enclave.

While the Mubarak government was seen in the West as friendly, cooperative, and essential in protecting the Camp David Agreements, it was criticized by many Copts for not doing enough to stop the continual attacks against their community in Egypt. So, as the new post-Soviet era unfolded and the international community rushed to help Kuwait against Saddam, and pressured Israel and the Palestinians to reach a peace agreement, the jihadists resumed their attacks against the Copts.

On May 12, 1990, in the city of Alexandria, a group from Jemaa Islamiya ambushed and murdered a Coptic priest and six other Coptic Christian citizens. No jihadist was prosecuted for these crimes. On May 4, 1992, in the village of Manshyet El-Nasr, a group of jihadists killed twelve Copts in their field; in 1994, jihadist attacks took place against St. Mary's Monastery in the villages of El-Mouharak and El-Qousya; in 1996, hundreds of armed members of Jemaa Islamiya attacked the Coptic village of El-Badary; in 1997, jihadists killed twelve Coptic Sunday school students in the village of Abu Quorcas. Again, there was no forceful intervention from the state against the Jemaa Islamiya. More killings took place in the Nagi-Hammady district of Bahgoura, and in 1998, only a few months after Osama Bin Laden declared war on "infidels" worldwide, Copts were murdered in the village of El-Kosheh. Fearing jihadist reprisals, Egyptian authorities arrested a thousand Copts along with a number of Islamists. Throughout the 1990s, these incidents evoked no international response, even though in other countries, such as Bosnia and East Timor, the international community was actively assisting targeted communities.

In December 1999, El-Kosheh was attacked, resulting in the deaths of twenty-one Copts and the destruction of 260 Christian homes and businesses. During the violence, local police forces either stood passively watching the mayhem, or worse, according to Coptic sources, became actively involved in the attacks. Ninety-six suspects were arrested and prosecuted by Egyptian tribunals; however, an Egyptian state security court acquitted all of them.

In February 2001, according to the Coptic associations, security forces stormed and destroyed with bulldozers the Coptic Church of St. Bola in Shobra Elkhaima after the local bishop asked for permission to hold prayers.

Post-9/11: The Violence Continues

While in most other areas of the region, international attention focused on the fate of persecuted minorities and in general on the democracy struggle, the Copts reported continuing attacks by jihadists and shortcomings by their own government. In February 2002, a Coptic church and thirty-five homes were burned by armed jihadists. In April 2003, a security unit inexplicably bulldozed the Charity Isle of Patmos, a Coptic Christian Center that provides treatment for mentally and physically handicapped children and orphans. In August, security forces were ordered by the local governor to destroy a fence surrounding the historic fourth-century monastery of St. Anthony in El Zaaferane. The monks in residence at this monastery used their bodies as shields to prevent the Egyptian government security forces from attacking the monastery. In October, dozens of Copts were arrested, many of them converts from Islam to Christianity. On Friday, November 7, the village of Gerza-Ayiat-Giza was attacked by a force of five hundred jihadists.

The jihadists in Egypt and throughout the region were part of a trend toward fighting against the *kuffar* as directed by al Qaeda on websites and in its messages aired on al Jazeera. This trend was visible in Iraq, in Nigeria, and Indonesia, where non-Muslims and secular Muslims were assaulted by jihadists. In 2005 several Coptic churches, houses, and shops were targeted in Kfar Salama as was the "Church of the Two Swords." Christian attorney Sabri Zaki was assassinated in his office.[3]

The following year witnessed a sharp escalation in jihadi attacks against the Copts, first against churches in Alexandria, and then against the villages of al Hammam in Assiut province, Hijaza Kabali in Qana province, and Kafar Salma in Sharqiya, culminating with the beheading of a Copt in Assuan. In 2006, after more jihadi attacks, Coptic families began to flee. In 2007, the attacks widened further as the Jemaa Islamiya and their supporters attacked the villages of Bemha el Iyyat, Safat Midum, Kum Umbo, northern Luxor, the Church of Mary in Dakhila, and dozens of other locations. The jihadist campaign didn't slow in 2008, with attacks in several villages. In 2009, the jihadists hit Luxor. In early 2010, anti-Copt incidents were still taking place, particularly in Nag Hamadi in the province of Kana.

The jihadi violence was aimed not only at neighborhoods, towns, and villages but also at individuals in urban areas, including professionals, women, and students. NBC linguist and Islamist expert Dr. Jacob Kyriakes, himself of Coptic ancestry, told me in 2005 that "quantitatively and qualitatively the anti-Coptic campaigns have reached a critical mass leading to ethnic cleansing as many families are seeking relocation inside Egypt or political asylum abroad."

A sign of the times emerged at an international Coptic conference in Washington during the summer of 2010, where I spoke. The youngest participants in the conference, attending from the four corners of the planet, were the most determined to fulfill the aspirations of "their people." One of them declared: "It has been too long. We've been living in captivity on our own land, Egypt. It is time to rise for freedom."

Egyptian Liberals Targeted

Although the Copts are the most harshly treated community in Egypt and among the worst treated in the region, it is important to note that the jihadists and the authoritarians also singled out the liberal segments of society. During the 1990s, as I continued to monitor the violence against the Copts, I began listening carefully to the messages from the various liberal groups and intellectuals in Egypt, realizing that their success meant the expansion of democratic culture in the most populous and influential Arab country and one of the leading Sunni countries in the world.

For the beleaguered Coptic minority to achieve equality in its own homeland, the democracy and liberal camp had to rise and win the hearts and minds of most Egyptians. The situation in the Nile country was complex. On one hand were the authoritarian regimes since the revolution-coup of 1954, and the ruling elite, unwilling to open up the system to real pluralist culture. On the other hand were the dangerous and influential jihadists, including the Muslim Brotherhood and the more extreme Jemaa Islamiya and Islamic Jihad, which had no agenda in Egypt other than the establishment of an emirate, à la the Taliban. Arab nationalists and communists, if they had their way, would establish a totalitarian state.

The only two groups that would advance the cause of democracy and freedom were the minorities—the Copts and the liberals. A coalition between Egyptian liberals and the Copts could actually form a numerical majority, but only if the democrats in Egypt were empowered to reach out to the real societal majorities, women, youth, and labor forces. Unfortunately, the modern political history of Egypt didn't give the liberals a true chance to mobilize. As in other Arab countries, the passage from the fall of the Ottomans and their Sultanate, to European colonialism, to the rise of republics was extremely rocky for the democracy seeker.

The opening for the development of a pluralist culture in Egypt began, ironically, with British control at the end of the nineteenth century. Previously, the country had been ruled by dynasties and governors either answering to the Caliphate or seeking to become one—the Umayyads, Abbasids, Fatimids, Mameluks, and Ottomans, with the brief interlude of reformer Mohammed Ali in the early nineteenth century. With the spread of education and the adoption of secular constitutions under British rule, a modernist elite, followed by a growing middle class, developed in the urban areas. Even the revolts against the British, inspired by patriotism and to some degree by Arabism, were to an extent seeking a liberal republic.

The rise of the Wafd Party in the early twentieth century signaled the possibility of Egyptian liberalism. By the late 1950s, as the British withdrew, the secular Wafd obtained from King Faruk a reduced monarchic power and an expansion of the constitutional norms. Egypt was on its way to a Mediterranean-type democracy, until the revolution of 1954. Under the first short-lived revolution led by Neguib, the debate between factions over the withdrawal of the military and the rise of a real republic was close to achieving the goals of a Kerinskylike democracy, as in Russia before the Leninists took over in

October 1917. But Nasser's coup transformed the state into a Soviet-like regime with one party, one chief, and a Pan Arabist ideology. The Egyptian socialist and Pan Arabist dictator suppressed all other forces, starting with the liberal democrats, but also the socialists, the communists, and later the Muslim Brotherhood. Between 1954 and the death of Nasser in September 1970, the liberal political and intellectual elite were obliterated. Most activists were jailed, eliminated, or forced into exile. Some attempted to organize opposition abroad, with little success. The broadcast *Misr al hurra* (Free Egypt) by Egyptian exiles out of southern France in the 1960s was one of these attempts.

Under President Sadat, a relaxation of repression against the opposition was felt across the country, but state police and agencies still ruled the republic. In preparing for the Yom Kippur War, the regime wanted to rally public support and minimize domestic stresses. Ironically, as soon as the war was over and Sadat engaged in negotiations leading to his historic peace treaty with Israel, state repression refocused on the Islamists and Arab nationalists who opposed peace, while Western-inclined liberals saw less suppression.

With the signing of the Camp David Agreements in 1978, and the subsequent Egypt-Israel peace treaty in 1979, the jihadists waged a full-scale war against the regime, backed politically by the ultra–Arab nationalists and the left wing. The business community and segments of liberals took advantage of the shift to resurface.

The election of Hosni Mubarak in 1981 was a continuation of Sadat's agenda but without the heavy legacy of the peace agreements. The equation in Egypt remained the same for decades—jihadists rising against the regime, the Muslim Brotherhoods mobilizing from within the system for their Caliphate, the communists in the opposition, the business community and bureaucracies thriving, liberals becoming more vocal, although not as free as in liberal democracies, and Copts harassed by the jihadists and critical of the government.

Post-1990 Liberals

With the collapse of the Soviet Union, human rights abuses in Egypt and around the world came into focus in the West, with liberals becoming more aware of the impact of their actions. Cairo was receiving large foreign-aid packages from Washington and significant aid from the European Union, which gave Western governments some leverage in terms of intervening—however slightly—on behalf of dissent. In the early 1990s, dissidents became more vocal in their demands for liberalization despite a firm but cautious response from the government. One has to note that what liberal opposition was able to say and do under Mubarak since 1990 was dramatically wider than what they achieved under Sadat, and certainly drastically different than under Nasser. The march was on, but at a very slow pace.

One of the impediments to a faster evolution toward liberalization was not the government, which was agreeing to small concessions, but the Islamist movements, which were becoming more radical and intolerant on ideological grounds. Indeed, how could the liberals struggle for democracy and obtain large concessions from the authoritarians when the "other opposition," the Muslim Brotherhood, was waging a massive countercampaign to impose the hijab, separation of the sexes, and discrimination against the Copts? Every concession obtained by the liberal opposition from the Mubarak regime was seized by the Muslim Brotherhood as an opportunity to impose their reactionary ideology. If students obtained more power for their unions, the Islamists would impose gender apartheid on campuses. The triangular zero-sum game between the regime, the liberals, and the Islamists is reminiscent of the struggle in the Weimar Republic between the government, the liberals, and the National Socialists.

My first encounter with a genuine Egyptian liberal of international dimension was on my campus in Florida in 1995 when we were visited by celebrity author Nawal Saadawi at the invitation of the Women's Studies Department. Knowing about the mounting jihadi threat in Egypt and the powerful influence of the Muslim Brotherhood, I was eager to listen to Saadawi's message firsthand. And indeed I was served well as she lectured my graduate students with a clear message: She was feminist, progressive, and liberal. While she criticized U.S. foreign policy and Israel, which was expected, she also tore apart the Islamist agenda and pounded the Mubarak regime. Saadawi represents the daring story of women's struggles in the heart of the Arab world. She later told me, "The seeds I am planting will flourish with future generations of women, and you'll see they'll be the ones to defeat the fascists." Years later I saw the first fruit of her work in several spots in the region. Another noted Egyptian liberal,

Saad al Din Ibrahim, a distinguished social scientist and director of the Ibn Khaloun Center in Cairo, became internationally known as he raised the issue of human rights, democracy, and religious minorities in Egypt in a difficult decade separating the end of the Cold War from the war with the jihadi terrorists. Ibrahim paid the price of his temerity by being jailed and abused.

Egyptian Liberals after 9/11

The strikes of 9/11 produced a new context internationally, favoring the rise of democratic agendas. In Egypt two peculiar movements expanded in the years following the U.S.-led efforts against al Qaeda and for democratization. One movement was secular and populist, Kefaya, and the other Islamic reformist, al Qur'aniyun. The "It's Enough" movement, or Kefaya, was initially established to oppose the reelection of President Mubarak, after twenty-four years of his presidential mandate.[4] Starting as a grassroots coalition of movements in 2005, Kefaya demonstrations peaked in that same year. A new face of Egypt's liberal community is Ayman Nour, a politician who challenged President Mubarak as a contender but also as an organizer before he was jailed by authorities. Although Nour, who launched the Ghad Party (Tomorrow's Party), was a harsh critic of the United States and United Kingdom for their invasion of Iraq in 2003, both Western nations pressured Mubarak to free him from jail, with President Bush, in 2006, calling for his release at a conference on dissent.

In conjunction with the secular liberals, Islamic "reformists" have also risen in the post-9/11 era. The "Koranists" or al Qur'aniyun claim they began in 1979 but flourished in the early twenty-first century as they spread their anti-jihadist views. Their leaders, particularly Dr. Ahmad Subhi Mansour, now based in North America, and the followers of the movement are "intellectual Muslims who believe in Islam as 'the religion of freedom, democracy, tolerance, justice, peace, and human rights.'" According to Mansour, "They fight the terrorist culture from within Islam, using the Koran as the only source of legislation." The International Koranis Center, the doctrinal hub of the movement, provides literature opposed to the Salafist view of the jihadists. The Koranists of Egypt, according to their leaders, are "victimized by both the Muslim Brotherhoods and the regime." Another voice critical of the Islamists is that of the Sufi Muslim movement, which strongly believes in the spirituality of Islam, as opposed to the jihadi agenda of the Jemaa Islamiya and its Salafist web.

An emerging former Islamist from Egypt is Tawfik (or Tariq) Hamid, who once was a member of the Jemaa Islamiya but reversed course and became a staunch secular thinker and advocate.[5] During several meetings I held with Hamid in Washington in 2009 and 2010, he argued that "the only way to defeat the jihadists was to use the Koran intelligently and interpret the verses differently." Interestingly, he believes that the government in Egypt "can help in the ideological battle against the Salafists and stop the expansion of the jihadists before they take over." Tawfik believes the government, even under Mubarak, can mobilize al Azhar in the right direction to counter the Muslim Brotherhoods. "All energies must come together to contain and reverse the Islamists," argues this medical doctor who lectures to audiences worldwide. "It is only then that democracy can battle its way into life."

The Future of Democracy and Freedom in Egypt

There are still significant barriers and difficulties to overcome before full democracy and pluralism can take root in Egypt. This is evident in the frustrations of Coptic leaders abroad and liberal activists on the inside. In three consecutive Diaspora congresses, held in Zurich in 2004, in Washington in 2005, and in New Jersey in 2006, Coptic leaders declared their rejection of the current state of affairs in Egypt and demanded international intervention to stop the ethnic cleansing of their people. In Egypt, for the first time in modern history, Copts are taking their protests to the streets after their homes and villages are attacked. In 2009, thousands of Copts demonstrated in the streets after a series of incidents targeting their churches.

In a sense, the Coptic nonviolent uprising has begun. I expect the protest among Copts to grow, particularly as other nations and communities in the region expand their political coverage in the media, and advocacy for this group spreads around the world.

The secular and liberal forces in Egyptian society are also expected to continue to rise. Khairi Abaza, a senior fellow at the Foundation for Defense of Democracies in Washington and an expert on Egypt, said in several forums, "There is a feeling inside Egyptian society that change must come, but there is also another feeling that change must not go backward." When I asked him how change could go backward in Egypt, he simply replied, "Look at Iran. Change came in 1979 but it drove the country backward even as the public thought it had achieved an important change. In Egypt, society in general seeks change but it all depends on who is achieving that change, forces that would add to the progress being made in terms of social and political development or forces that would take away the achievements of past generations."

Socialist MEP Paulo Casaca is more explicit: "If the Muslim Brotherhood advances even at the expense of the current authoritarian regime, the post-Mubarak era will be totalitarian. But if change is achieved gradually at the hands of democracy and secular forces, Egypt could influence the entire Arab world and the Sunni countries in general."

As an observer of the battle for change in Egypt, I see four armies set to engage each other over the future of the country. One is the army of the Muslim Brotherhood with its ultranationalist Pan Arabist allies. This force wants to bring down the regime and establish an anti-Western, nondemocratic state. This army would end up establishing one building block for the Caliphate. Another army is the current regime, which is swinging between the status quo and small changes, too tiny to satisfy the majority of Egyptians. Within this institutional force, the armed forces are the real defenders against the jihadist beast, but only as long as the public supports them. A third army is the populist and dissident forces that oppose the regime. They are not Islamist ideologically, but are deeply influenced by anti-Western propaganda and culture. The populist force could be used by the Muslim Brotherhood to topple the regime. The last army is the dissidents who wish to move the country toward liberal democracy, but are too weak to win and too abandoned to move forward. Next to them are the Copts, who are isolated and attacked on all flanks.

The only conclusion one can draw from this equation is that in the end the final battle will be between the jihadists and their allies and the democrats and their Coptic allies. Egypt either will be transformed into a Talibanlike country or will move forward to a humanist destiny of pluralism, tolerance, and democracy.

14.

Arabia's Liberals: How the Peninsula Produces Jihadism *and* Its Antidote

Fourteen of the nineteen terrorists who massacred thousands in America on 9/11 were Saudi Arabians; we have a problem with Arabia." This sentiment was repeated on the airwaves in the weeks, months, and years following the September 11 attacks in New York and Washington.

This simple accusation against an entire country, while extreme to some, was legitimate to many others. That a dozen or so jihadists who committed suicide attacks in the United States happened to be of Saudi extraction shouldn't indict an entire population or incriminate the government of the Kingdom. It is inaccurate, unjust, and inefficient. Besides, the Saudi authorities are in a state of war with al Qaeda and its followers. Bin Laden and Zawahiri have often blasted the government of Saudi Arabia and most other countries in the Peninsula, including Yemen's government.

At the same time, there is not a shred of doubt that there is a "problem" in Arabia, and it is at the root of the terror that hit the heart of America. Even before 9/11, I considered that a movement originating in Arabia was responsible for the massacres, wars, and miseries striking the region and the international community. That movement comes from the totalitarian ideology of the Salafist jihadists in their different forms and shapes, and their doctrine of doom originated in the Peninsula, though it has been reshaped and repackaged in other countries, including the Emirate of Qatar, via its powerful funded media, al Jazeera, and projihadi diplomacy. The fourteen terrorists of 9/11 are only one product of the factory that has produced hundreds of thousands of identical clones around the world and has millions of supporters.

Every illness has its antidote embedded in its original habitat, and this is the case for jihadism, which erupted from its Arabian birthplace. Indeed, across the region, in the very desert countries that witnessed the rise of old Salafism, extreme puritanism, and Wahabism, small signs announcing the rise of democracy activists and reformists can be detected. Shy, feeble, and perhaps inconsequential in the world of real politics, nevertheless the liberals of Arabia do exist. Time and recognition will provide them the platforms, the relevance, and ultimately the tools to help spread the culture of tolerance and pluralism in a highly important area of Middle Earth.[1]

The historic challenge to these dissidents isn't only about promoting a set of values. Progress in humanism and internationalization of the democratic culture is gradual and is a result of a development in the general political culture of the region or country in question. The real and imminent challenge for the Peninsula's liberals, or at least its humanists, is to counter, contain, and begin the ideological confrontation of the hard-core jihadists, who enjoy deep support in the dominant intellectual elite. To Salafists, Arabia in general and the Saudi Kingdom in particular are the center of the earth, where legitimacy and material support are generated.

There are three points of strength that the jihadists draw from Arabia—two they seek to dominate and one they already control. First and foremost, Arabia's Hejaz province along the Red Sea harbors the two most important religious shrines of Islam, Mecca and Medina. Whoever manages those cities holds tremendous influence and leadership in the Muslim world. That is a goal yet to be fulfilled by the hard-core Islamists. Saudi Arabia is in fact a religious country, but the extreme Salafists, the al Qaeda crowd, want it to become a Talibanlike state. The second source of power is the immense resource of oil within the borders of the Arabian monarchy. This richness of historic proportions, never before available in this size in one subregion of the world, has had a dramatic influence on the expansion of Salafism in general and the Wahabi stream in particular. The third point of strength is funding of the indoctrination processes by Arabian sources throughout the Middle East and around the world. For decades it has been the single leading factor in the rapid rise of jihadism internationally.

When we realize the power of jihadism in the Peninsula and the formidable force by which it is backed, we can understand the titanic difficulties of the mission of democracy advocates in those sandy lands. That mission involves not only moving democratic principles forward, as in other postcolonial regions in the world, such as Latin America, Africa, and parts of Asia, but also establishing the mere existence of political and cultural pluralism, a notion at odds with Salafi jihadism. The battle for freedoms in the Arabian Peninsula may well be, my own observations and research suggest, the most difficult on the planet, and much more challenging than liberalizing China, Myanmar, or Cuba. But the stakes are even higher than in any other part of the world. If democratization were to move forward in the Peninsula, even against unfathomable odds, the results would affect the entire Muslim world and beyond. This is why the small efforts by reformists, as minute as they are, need to be viewed in the context of the power the jihadists have in their support from the political, economic, and theological elite of the Arabian Peninsula.

Arabia in History: From Happy to Tense

The Romans used to call the Peninsula *Arabia Felix,* meaning "Happy Arabia." For thousands of years before the common or Christian era and before the rise of the Islamic empire, the large, barren lands of the Peninsula were called by its own inhabitants the *Jazeera,* or the "Island," in reference to being surrounded by water on three sides: the Persian Gulf, the Indian Ocean, and the Red Sea. The insulation of the mostly nomadic tribes living on that island (geographically a peninsula) caused isolation from the Levant.

No great conqueror of the Middle East ever invaded the Jazeera before the Caliphate. Egyptians, Hittites, Assyro-Babylonians, Persians, Greeks, and Romans marched east, west, and north of the Peninsula, but never seized its territories. One could argue that there is nothing to conquer in a desert. There were, however, important urban cultures in the southern parts of Arabia, including in the kingdoms of Yemen, as well as southern Hejaz, particularly the city of Mecca. The heavy price of crossing these enormous deserts to capture cities already trading with the upper Middle East wasn't worth it. This geological boundary provided insulation and isolation to the Semitic Arab-speaking tribes for centuries, but at the same time kept them in a nomadic state, allowing Mecca to become the federal capital for trade and political influence in the entire region. Roman and other historians saw this stability of the web of roaming Bedouins in the desert and the Meccan bourgeoisie as a source of happiness, in the sense that no foreign invasion affected the authentic way of life in that area. That state of affairs changed abruptly in the seventh century C.E. with the eruption of the Islamic state.[2]

When we examine the history of Arabia, or any other area in the world that is relevant to modern-day politics, we do not refer to the faith narrative, because it has an unchallengeable dimension of its own. The social history of Arabia can be divided into periods before and after Islam, or more precisely periods before and after the rise of an organized Pan Arab power, embodied by the Caliphate and by local royal and tribal elites.

The era before the unified state that brought all tribes under one flag is commonly called *A'ssr al Jahilyya* or Age of Ignorance by Islamic historians. This title asserts that before the advent of Islam, the people of the Peninsula weren't aware of salvation. In sociological history, this was pre-Islamic or pre-Caliphate Arabia. Its population was mostly tribal, pagan, Christian, and Jewish. The rise of the Islamic state didn't affect the Peninsula's ethnic identity but had an impact on its former religions, mainly Christianity, Judaism, and the polytheist deities. The early Muslim armies established a theological government in the Peninsula, which became a *Khilafa*, or Caliphate, after the death of the Muslims' commander and Prophet, Mohammad bin Abdullah.

Since that radical transformation in the Arabs' motherland in the seventh century, and as the armies of *Fatah* (conquest) left the Peninsula to conquer the lands of the infidels, the original home of the Arabian tribes became a region in the Caliphate for centuries. Ironically, though Jazeera was the birthplace of the Caliphate, within a few short years, the first dynasty of Arab caliphs, the Umayyads, moved the capital to Damascus, in 667, and the Abbassid dynasty moved it to Baghdad in 750. The Arab age of conquests and empire peaked outside the Peninsula, but the Hejaz remained the holy land of the empire. Mecca and Medina became the destination of pilgrimage forever. Even though the centers of gravity of the Arab empire moved far beyond the original homeland, the area remained a sort of sacred or venerated territory for Arab settlers from Spain to Persia.[3]

The Ottoman Empire moved the capital of the Caliphate to Istanbul, unseating the Arab leadership and installing the Turks. But

Mecca remained naturally the first shrine, giving the Arabs of the Hejaz and the rulers of the holy city a prominence lost by the Arab settler and emigrant communities in the upper Middle East, who fell to the second level of importance under the Ottomans.

For four centuries before the collapse of the Turkish Sultanate, the Peninsula had three types of Arab establishments. The leading group was the governors of Mecca, particularly the Hashemites, closest in line to the family of the Prophet. The second group was the emirs and rulers of the other Arabian provinces under the Ottomans, such as Yemen, Kuwait, Qatar, and Oman. The last group was the federations of tribes that escaped the yoke of the Turks, among them the al Saud, in the Riyadh oases and throughout the Rub' al Khali, the desolate part of southern Arabia's desert.

The only Arabs who have never been under Ottoman domination were the central Arabian tribes led by the Saudis. Since the end of the nineteenth century, the followers of Mohammed Abdel Wahab, an Arabian who called for an extreme Salafist doctrine, united with the central Najd tribes in an attempt to challenge Ottoman rule in the Peninsula. The movement was identified as "Wahabi," the first contemporary Islamist movement. Since then, the Wahabi and Saudi movements have been perceived as one, although the tribal confederation's interest was in seizing power in the Peninsula and taking back Arab lands from the Ottomans into Arab hands, while the interest of the Wahabis were fundamentally ideological, and their goal was seizing the Caliphate.

World War I deeply affected the shape and the destiny of Arabia and its future democracy challenge. Britain became the ally of the Hejaz's Sherif Hussein against the Ottoman Empire, as the Hashemites were hoping for a Greater Arabian Kingdom encompassing the Peninsula, Iraq, Syria, and Palestine. The Meccan establishment led by Sherif Hussein aimed to restore an independent Arab monarchy, which most likely would have been moderate, as is the modern Jordanian monarchy, the only surviving part of the Hashemites. In 1924, the Najd tribes under Abdel Aziz al Saud invaded the Hejaz, brought down the Meccan establishment, and erected a Wahabi kingdom with a capital in Riyadh. The future of Arabia and the region was affected for decades to come.[4]

Modern Arabian Peninsula and Wahabism

The postcolonial Arabian Peninsula witnessed the emergence of a core state and periphery countries differing in size, population, and political systems. In the center, the Saudi Kingdom rose as the most powerful and influential entity in post-Ottoman Arabia. It controlled Mecca and Medina, the holiest shrines of Islam, and soon enough its elite were blessed with enormous oil dividends as Western companies developed the seemingly endless oil fields. To its south were two poor republics, mostly tribal northern Yemen and heavily Marxist-penetrated southern Yemen. Eastern Arabia was composed of formerly British-dominated principalities stretching from Kuwait to Qatar, Bahrain, Oman, and the United Arab Emirates' federation. With the exception of southern Yemen, which was under Soviet influence, the rest of the Peninsula benefited from Western protection, either by Great Britain or by the United States.

During the Cold War, Saudi Arabia and the rest of the Arabian principalities situated themselves in the U.S.-led camp against the communists but didn't shift toward liberal democracies in their own political systems. As in the rest of the Arab world, the Peninsula's governments and regimes were opposed to pluralism and in most cases did not observe basic human rights as prescribed by the Universal Declaration of Human Rights.

The political system most unlike liberal democracy was undoubtedly the Wahabi regime in Saudi Arabia. Openly claiming its adherence to orthodox Salafism, Riyadh's political establishment enforced the tenets of Wahabism inside the Kingdom in all aspects of life: tight implementation of Sharia law, creation of a religious police—the Mutawwa—and full segregation of women within the country. The system recognizes only one religion, Islam, and one form of it, Sunni Salafism in the Wahabi form. All other religions are illegal. In addition, the regime doesn't allow the formation of political parties or electoral representation. There is no voting process under Wahabism. The country is ruled by an absolute monarchy and an elite class consisting of thousands of emirs. Last but not least, the female population of the Kingdom is denied—by international standards—all basic rights of political, social, and economic participation in public affairs. One stunning example is that women not only may not interact with males, but may not even drive cars. In short, the Kingdom is founded on Islamist Wahabi principles, which are strictly enforced.

The guardians of Salafism are the circles of radical clerics who are in charge of the regime's compliance with religious tenets. These organizations include the Council of the Assembly of Senior Qadis and the Higher Council of Qadis. Control of political and religious power has been tight, solid, and unshakable for decades. Leading theologians and scholars have long been the backbone of the doctrine upon which the regime draws for its legitimacy. Without elections, political parties, or any other form of sociopolitical representation, the country is held morally and ideologically by the blessing the clerics provide to the rulers.[5]

This Wahabi power within the regime could be compared to the communist core within the Soviet Union. Not all Saudis are Wahabi, nor are all members of bureaucracy and government, but Wahabi Islamism is the state ideology, and escaping it would be the equivalent of rebelling against Orthodox communism in the Soviet era. Many Saudi males, at various levels of government, are critical of Wahabism just as members of the Communist Party of the USSR were of their own system. Yet the regime is too grounded in theological material for significant reform to develop naturally from within the institution at the pace needed to meet modern-day democratization.[6]

Not only has the core clerical subregime maintained a strong grip on domestic matters, but it also controls the country's international policies. Under Wahabi guidance, Riyadh has adopted policies and steady campaigns at regional and international levels to satisfy the Salafi agenda since World War II. During the Cold War, the Kingdom invested heavily in funding institutions, associations, and government entities throughout the Greater Middle East and beyond to spread the Islamist Salafi doctrine in public affairs. Millions of petrodollars were spent to support education, social, medical, and economic projects in the Arab world, with the goal of developing a vast constituency supportive of the Islamists and segments of society influenced by the calls of jihadists. The "Wahabi agenda" favoring tight Sharia, gender segregation, and a jihadist view of international relations and conflicts constitutes, along with Khomeinism and Baathism, the majority of opposition to the rise of liberal democracy, pluralism, and peace in the region.

Ironically, even though the political leaders of the Kingdom have shown signs of pragmatism and have initiated peace projects to solve the Arab-Israeli conflict, the other arm of the regime, the Wahabi clerics, has maintained an irreconcilable attitude toward world politics. The ideology they promoted created currents of thoughts and movements that fiercely opposed democracy, women's equality, equal rights for non-Muslim communities, and a two-state solution in Palestine. The marriage between the Saudi establishment and the Wahabi clerical bloc bound the monarchy to rigid rules, preventing reform and in some cases mere social modernization in the country. The most closed system in the region, excluding the Taliban's, is also challenged by social and intellectual movements seeking liberalization and freedoms. Even the Wahabis can be opposed inside their own den.

Opposition to the Wahabis

Inside the Kingdom, two important regions are at odds with the central power in Riyadh and continue to claim distinctiveness from what they perceive as Najd domination of the country. Ironically, the largest province that is somewhat critical of the Saudis is the Hejaz, home to the holiest shrines of Islam, Mecca and Medina. The Hejazis, who in general are more moderate and open than the Wahabi-influenced elite ruling in Riyadh, have maintained some resentment since the Saudi invasion of their "country" in the 1920s. The Hejaz existed as an independent state during the brief peace-conference era following World War I. Its officials and delegations participated in the negotiations for a new Middle East before the Hejaz was overrun by the Wahabi forces and united with Najd by military force. The remnant feeling of "Hejazism" still prevails in many parts of the province, stretching from today's Jordan to Yemen's northern borders. The Hejaz-Najd tension, though inconsequential geopolitically, indicates a trend toward future claims of decentralization that could be developed by the political elite.

The future of the Hejaz, within a unified Arabia, could be good news for the Peninsula and the region. However, the development of liberalizing tendencies in the most sensitive area in the Arab and Muslim world, and most daringly in the cities of Mecca and Medina, would be the equivalent of an intellectual revolution. "Just think of the most important shrines of the Muslim world becoming gradually the producers of tolerance, pluralism, and eventually liberal ideas," a number of Hejazi human rights activists (who obviously preferred to remain anonymous) told me during a conference in Washington in the late 1990s.

The suppression of women not wearing the full garb in Jeddah, Arabia's main civilian port city, was much less frequent than in the rest of the country, particularly in Riyadh. On some of my media panels, callers from the Hejaz, including some from Mecca, displayed discontent with the severity of the Mutawwa (religious police) and the radical clerics. Evidently, these were only subtle signs and not hard indications that the majority in the Hejaz would be more comfortable with a relaxation of the tough measures. It was often remarked to me that the "Hashemite legacy in the Hejaz was all but eliminated." The original Meccan establishment had historical ties to the Hashemite dynasty, which was ejected from the Hejaz at the beginning of the last century and is now in power in Jordan. "Imagine the birthplace of Islam ruled by the same spirit as the Jordanian monarchy," say Hejazi activists.

One can conclude that the ideological grip of the Wahabis on the spiritual center of Islam is not that tight. It is a long shot, but hope exists that a new and younger generation of reformists in Hejaz pressing for openings in the system may well see freedom and democracy in the not-too-distant future.

The most challenging relationships are between the Shia population of eastern Saudi Arabia and the regime's hard-core clerics. The Ihs'a province, where most Saudi oil fields are located, has a non-Sunni majority. The Shia opposition claims the Wahabi regime practices systematic suppression of the religious minority in those areas.

Ali al Yammi, the director of the Washington-based Saudi Human Rights Council, stated in a congressional briefing I was part of in July 2010 that "the regime keeps the Shia population in a state of economic underdevelopment for the purpose of weakening their political participation in the system." Yammi, who was forced into exile, is among those identified as hard-core liberals opposing the system as a whole.

Ali al Ahmad, the director of the Gulf Institute in Washington, argued in testimony and briefings to the U.S. government that "the Wahabi regime is the root cause of the expansion of Islamist and jihadist ideologies not only in the country but throughout the region."

Ahmad, who is from Shia-dominated eastern Arabia, told me, "The extremist Salafists who influence the regime resent the Shia community in the Kingdom and fear a revolution is brewing in those areas."

In contrast, Saudi officials told me that the tensions in the Shia areas "are Iranian-made and the result of their incitements." The government believes, according to a high-ranking advisor I spoke with, that Tehran's regime is funding a Hezbollahlike organization in the Dhahran areas in Saudi Arabia to direct attacks against Riyadh's authorities. Al Yammi told me, "Arab Shia in Saudi Arabia have a cause of their own, they don't need Iran's mullahs."

Perhaps both sides have a point. On one hand, the Shia community in eastern Arabia is in fact targeted by the Wahabi regime, which not only suppresses the Sunni moderates and liberals, but also targets the Shia. On the other hand, the Iranian regime is attempting to penetrate this community to establish a pro-Iranian movement on the Peninsula. In short, the populations of that area are sandwiched between the Wahabis and the Khomeinists.

Often, Saudi Arabia is described as monolithic and insensitive to modernity and liberalization. This description would be correct if the country consisted only of Wahabis. In fact, not only are the Hejaz and the eastern part resentful of the Salafi powers, but segments of Saudi society, and surprisingly many of the high-ranking emirs and royals, are also skeptical. The Wahabi network with its clerics, sympathizers, bureaucracies, and emirs is similar to the old guard of the Soviet Communist Party, and the country is under their spell. Yet the segments frustrated with the extreme Salafis are present in all sectors indicated above. Indeed, there are emirs not enamored of the hardcore Wahabis.

Some interpret the recent slow moves by the king to ease doctrinal control over the destinies of Saudi women as a step in the right direction and a counterpoint to the hard-core clerics. Across bureaucracies, opposition exists to the extreme brand of Wahabism. We cannot yet call these forces reformist, as they do not advance a full-fledged organized program like the Green Movement in Iran. It is important to note that the Wahabi machinery is not alone; it faces discreet countermoves by the more moderate Islamist web inside the Kingdom.

Those most relevant to the possibility of democratization in Saudi Arabia are the real liberal dissidents, mostly ordinary citizens who have captured the importance of pluralism and human rights in their lives. Today in the Wahabi Kingdom there are the beginnings of what could become an unparalleled counterjihadi force, not very different from the prodemocracy groups emerging in Afghanistan, Iran, and the rest of the region. At this stage of the region's modern history, individual dissidents and intellectuals within a totalitarian environment are as valuable as mass movements vying for democratization. We can clearly see signs of this burgeoning reform phenomenon in Saudi Arabia. More and more Saudi writers, both young and seasoned, are rejecting extreme Salafism and the jihadi concepts and calling for equal rights for women. Their writings are not limited to Western press but also appear in Arab media, including notably on Elaph .com and Aafaq.com. More young Saudis have been seen participating in highly artistic youth shows on regional television, including the Lebanese equivalent of *American Idol, Star Academy.* These appearances attracted attacks by radical clerics in Saudi Arabia and threats against the LBCI, Lebanese Broadcast Corporation International, but to no avail.

In addition, young Saudi females have been relentless in following trendy fashion around the world in secret and in the security of their homes. I recall seeing the phenomenon of Saudi female rebellion against suppression in the 1980s when I boarded flights in the Mediterranean. As soon as the female passengers flying from Saudi Arabia to a European destination were up in the air, many niqabs and hijabs were exchanged for more revealing Western clothing. In the last few years, a battle for the celebration of Valentine's Day was waged across Saudi Arabia. Despite calls by Wahabi leaders to ban the "*Kafir* feast," younger and younger Saudi women are finding ways to purchase goods and celebrate the event across the land. As in Iran, an underground of intellectual and social resistance to Wahabism is gradually expanding.

I consider the following components significant to the continuing struggle in Saudi Arabia: First, there is the ever-increasing globalization and the increasing access of younger elements of society to the outside world; second, the increasing number of young Saudis in chat rooms and social networking sites will form a counterculture leaning gradually to pluralism and eventually to the democratic process; and finally, the younger Saudi women teaching their children a variant of the austere Wahabi curriculum will slowly lay the groundwork for an alternative education.[7]

In my conversations with educated Saudi citizens from various realms of society, I came to the conclusion that a march toward a more open society and pluralist political system will inevitably emerge. The question is when and after what kind of social upheaval. The Wahabi core of the regime is among the most resilient in the world. All aspects of public life are either in the hands or under the control of Wahabi elites. The rigorous application of Sharia laws based on Salafi interpretation leaves little room for liberal interpretation. In short, the development of a classical form of opposition to the Wahabis is unlikely, but not impossible. There is no significant coordination between those citizens in civil society who seek liberalization, those within government—including these at the highest levels who push slowly for reform—and the open opposition of the dissidents. The dissidents vie strongly with the entire government, including its pragmatists. Individual citizens conduct their little pushes in their daily lives in isolation from dissident narrative and from government sympathizers. Unlike the situation in Iran, where the opposition has come together to isolate the radicals, the Wahabis of Saudi Arabia are the strongest element in the center of the regime and are suffocating their opponents one at a time.[8]

Another problem for the rise of change in the Kingdom is the apologist position of the United States and the West. The centers of power on both sides of the Atlantic are overwhelmingly under the influence of the oil lobbies, with the Wahabi pressure groups at their core. The Western "partners" of the oil powers of Arabia, including mainly the American and European associates in the petronetworks, have formed a formidable obstruction for any prodemocracy policy toward the Peninsula initiated by the United States or the other liberal democracies. "While Washington and Brussels rushed to support dissidents in Eastern Europe, Latin America, Myanmar, and other areas, there were no open pressures on the Kingdom on behalf of its dissidence," according to Ali al Yammi.

However, the pro-Wahabi pressure groups operating in the West and in the United States are more important in the battle for democracy in Arabia. Consider this: For reformists in Arabia to receive support from the international community in general and from the United States in particular, they need to convince America's decision-makers, both in the government and in the NGO community, of their cause. The powerful Wahabi lobby in the United States has been able to delegitimize the idea of U.S. support to democracy in the Peninsula, let alone the region as a whole, making the task of reformists in Arabia nearly impossible. They are facing systematic suppression by the Wahabis, are dispersed in their efforts, and are totally abandoned by Western governments.

The Reformers on the Periphery

Outside Saudi Arabia, Arabian activists for freedom and democracy fare differently from one country to the next. In Yemen, geopolitics has determined the potential for liberalization and democracy. The country has undergone dramatic changes and faced several crises affecting the movement toward greater democracy since independence in the 1960s, when it became one greater Yemen, and then again when it was unified after conflict in 1994. Before the union of the early 1990s, southern Yemen was ruled by a communist regime that suppressed alternatives, while northern Yemen was ruled by conservative tribal elites also unfriendly to political pluralism. Liberals had no wiggle room on either side of the border. Political parties and elections were allowed in unified Yemen, but under the solid grip of President Ali Abdallah Saleh, who has ruled the country in an authoritarian manner since the 1990s.

"Yemen's active liberals still have a hard time organizing politically within civil society," argues Munir al Mawari, a Yemeni political activist and journalist. He told me in 2005 during meetings at the Foundation for Defense of Democracies in Washington that "the south, being more secular and progressive, wants to bail out. The southerners regret the union because they haven't found pluralism and democracy; instead they found themselves locked in a classical authoritarian country." Mawri also projected the potential explosion of a rebellion in the northernmost part of the country, led by the Shia movement known as the Hawthis. Both were proven accurate just a few years ago.

In 2008, a protest movement arose in the south calling for local autonomy. A year later, at the instigation of Iran's regime, the Hawthis in the northern tip of the country waged an armed rebellion against Saleh's government. Meanwhile, the entrenched Salafi jihadi movement of Yemen, which has a strong and historical participation in al Qaeda's activities, began launching operations against the government's institutions and security forces.

The multidimensional conflict of Yemen isn't helping the liberal elements in the country. Under an authoritarian government unwilling to yield more freedoms, threatened by two jihadist movements, one to the north backed by the Khomeinists and one in the center backed by the Salafists, the democracy advocates are struggling against three layers of pressure—two from the terrorists and one from government. Even as the country is sinking into a multidimensional, quasi–civil war, Yemeni workers for human rights, intellectuals, and secular democrats are expanding in numbers and influence among younger generations, even though the jihadists are recruiting as well.

In this beautiful country, as in other Arab areas, the race is also on between the Islamists who stubbornly indoctrinate and incite for jihad and the resolved democracy activists who are pushing gradually toward civil society. Yemen is the poorest of all Arab Peninsula countries, but its secular intelligentsia is the most promising, if given a chance to grow and express itself.

The other Gulf monarchies present common features regarding their democratic tendencies. In all these countries—Kuwait, Qatar, the United Arab Emirates, Bahrain, and Oman—a margin for multiplicity of political parties was opened, and in most of these principalities governments are open to criticism. The dynastic order in these monarchies is somewhere between constitutionalism and strong family rule. A survey of the global evolution of the Gulf political systems leaves observers with little doubt on the big picture: Authoritarianism is omnipresent on essential matters of political power, but openness prevails regarding economics and business.

Social matters continue to be under pressure by the Islamists. Across the board, prodemocracy activists are pushing for free debate and have been able to publish criticism online and in print, and in many instances were even able to demonstrate. "It is a contained and sometimes controlled freedom," charges Omran Salman, chairman of Arab Reformers, a U.S.-based NGO, which published the second influential liberal site online, Aafaq. "The ruling elite, mostly backed by oil dividends and protected from outside threats by the United States and the West, knows it should give some space for political activities and even opposition so that their image is not tarnished in the international community, but there are limits to political tolerance. It is basically about not challenging the legitimacy of these regimes, or in fact the families ruling these principalities," said Salman in briefings to the U.S. Congress in 2009. Salman, a native of Bahrain, promotes liberal democracy throughout the Gulf. "We're calling for full equality for women, fundamental rights for minorities, the end of wars, and advancement inside the Arab world, and of course in the Gulf area."

According to officials from Kuwait and Bahrain, political pluralism is moving forward in their countries, but they need to keep in mind the systemic threats represented by the jihadists. Government officials, including those in the United Arab Emirates and to some extent in Oman, seem to imply to outside observers that they will gradually absorb steps toward political tolerance, but only as much as national security against radicalism and jihadi threats would allow.

In Kuwait, the Salafists exert significant pressure on the ruling family of al Sabbah to delay secular reforms and rights to women. Kuwait's political establishment also fears outside threats, including Iran's meddling. The small, oil-rich principality has already experienced occupation at the hands of another totalitarian regime, during Saddam's invasion of 1990. Some of Kuwait's press, such as the daily *as Siyassa* and its daring editor, Ahmad Jarallah, has been very vocal in criticizing both the Khomeinists and the Salafists. Some of Kuwait's academics, including the former president of its university, have also been outspoken in responding to the jihadi agenda, including on al Jazeera. Kuwait's reformists, prodemocracy movement, women's movements, and open-minded emirs are a potential force for change in the future.

The same scenario replicates itself in Bahrain, the United Arab Emirates, and Oman, with local differences all related to ethnic and religious makeup. In Bahrain and the United Arab Emirates, the presence of large Shia contingents is used by the Iranian regime to subvert the existing governments and extort from them. In Oman, attempts were made by the Iranians to incite tension between Sunnis and the *Abadhiyya* Muslim community. Across the Gulf, democracy advocates are pressed between Salafi militants and Khomeinist menace, while governments are very wary of reforms that would allow the jihadists to seize more power.

Qatar's Jihad against Democracy?

Unlike most moderate principalities of the Gulf, Qatar's regime has developed a rather unusual attitude over the past couple of decades.

While on the surface it is classified as a moderate country economically and politically, its regime has engaged in two policies to the detriment of democratic culture and in support of oppressive regimes in the region. While hosting a large U.S. military base and promoting a pro-Western image, Doha's ruling family launched the jihadist TV Channel al Jazeera in 1996, opening a new era in the region where Salafi ideologies got an enormous boost at a time when secular and liberal democrats were persecuted across the board. The channel is fully funded by Qatar's oil and other state-run companies and supports jihadism over democracy and liberalism. It has had significant effects on the region's political culture.[9]

The Islamists were endorsed by al Jazeera's powerful broadcasts at the expense of liberation for women, minorities, and youth in the Arab world. Many commentators in the region assert that Qatar's ruling elite, from the emir's entourage to its foreign ministry, are influenced by the Muslim Brotherhood.

"The *Ikhwan*'s influence in Qatar's decision-making is manifest, clear, and progressing," said Egyptian political expert Magdi Khalil in Washington during meetings in 2006. "The foreign minister, the prime minister, and the country's emir are solidly behind al Jazeera's jihadi line and provide endorsement to leading ideologue Sheikh Yussuf al Qardawi," he added. "The narrative of the al Jazeera broadcast, funded and protected by the Qatar regime, openly supports the Islamists, the jihadists, and the Salafists, which translates into anti-democracy, -pluralism, and -minorities."

Hameed Ghuriafi, senior analyst and writer for Kuwait's *as Siyassa*, told me, "The Qatari regime represents the sophisticated version of traditional Islamism. While its rulers claim modernity, they align themselves with the Iranian regime, Hezbollah, and the Assad regime against the peoples of Iran, Syria, and Lebanon." Ghuriafi, who expresses the views of many Arab liberal writers, said: "The rulers of Qatar perform the work of the authoritarians and the jihadists in the region, but as diplomats and propagandists. Look how they've created the greatest propaganda tool in the hands of the Muslim Brotherhood and see how they provided forums and legitimacy to the antidemocracy forces in the region. They helped Hezbollah seize power in Lebanon, broke the isolation of the Assad regime, signed strategic agreements with Iran's regime, and helped Omar Bashir of Sudan escape the International Criminal Court."

These views are largely echoed by liberal journalists, including those on the reformist website Elaph and leading analysts such as Nadim Koteish from Mustaqbal TV in Beirut: "We haven't seen Qatar funding media and projects to help the oppressed in the region but the oppressors, unfortunately," Koteish told me.

Depressed Arabia?

A journey into the world of dissidents, democracy activists, and women's struggles in the Peninsula would leave you with two findings. On the one hand, certainly the majority of the population is not living the Roman-described happiness of Arabia. Salafism is too oppressive, either directly, inside the Wahabi Kingdom, or by influence, throughout the other countries of this subregion. The road to democratic reforms will be long and difficult, full of setbacks and of interim accommodations. The land of the ancient Arabs may have to wait for the lands of the former Caliphate outside the Peninsula to produce democratic achievements before it can move forward. Arabians may well have to wait for neighboring regimes to see their democracies emerge before experiencing democracy at home.

But on the other hand, I can see hope growing across these desert states. As I argued in this chapter and in my lectures on political change in the Middle East, small changes in difficult places are equivalent to big changes in easier societies. The symbolic gestures toward easing restrictions on women and youth in Saudi Arabia; the works by prominent Saudi female writers on freedom; the rising voices of dissidents and democracy activists in Yemen, Kuwait, the United Arab Emirates, and Bahrain; and some manifestations of courage within the bureaucracies in these countries may not yet match the megapower of the authoritarians and the jihadists, but I can see progress in this core part of Middle Earth. Once the ideas are out the rest will unfold irreversibly.

15

Islamists versus Muslim Democrats:
The War for the Soul of the Muslim World

On October 4, 2004, at a hotel in Washington, D.C., more than 750 delegates from various Middle Eastern American communities gathered to celebrate "Freedom and Democracy in the Greater Middle East." For the first time Lebanese, Syrians, Iraqis, Iranians, Egyptians, Sudanese, Libyan, Saudis, Yemenis, Bahrainis, Palestinians, Mauritanians, and others, all believers in pluralism and the rejection of totalitarian ideologies, came together to promote democracy. In addition to all the national identities, there were also Copts, Assyro-Chaldeans, Kurds, Darfuris, Berbers, Jews, Aramaeans, Arabs, and a plethora of ethnicities from the region in attendance. As a general coordinator of the event, I had the privilege of meeting and exchanging ideas with dozens of delegations and intellectuals, political cadres, and human rights activists. What brought them together was the increasing awareness of the common struggle for freedom in the Greater Middle East.

I called the event a "Middle Eastern American Revolution," as it was the very first time almost all ethnic and religious communities in exile were represented by organizations and leaders who were determined to push for change in the region, despite the oil-producing regimes, the authoritarians, and the jihadists. While the bulk of the participants in that benchmark event were non-Muslim and non-Arab representatives, such as Maronites, Assyro-Chaldeans, and Copts, the novelty was that "new" Muslim and Arab activists were surfacing in Washington, as they were in other Western capitals. They represented not only a democracy-seeking trend within their communities, but also a new breed of men and women who had witnessed the horrors of totalitarianism in the region and terrorism in the West and decided to act for political and ideological change in their communities and in their mother nations.

Zuhdi Jasser, a Muslim activist who spoke at the conference, said, "This is a beginning for a new era in Mideast American history." Zainab al Suwajj, the courageous Arab woman leading the Islamic American Congress, and a speaker at the event, said, "The mass graves in Iraq shook off the basis of our consciousness." Mohammed Yahia, from Darfur's exiled community, stated: "We saw Christians coming to our aid when we black Muslims were massacred by the Janjaweed." In short, we were witnessing the slow emergence of "Muslim democrats," who out of their exile in the West were signaling to civil societies in the region that time for democratic change, or even peaceful revolutions, had come. The Washington gathering was a symbolic event, and was preceded by a number of meetings I attended that were dedicated to engaging activists and intellectuals from the region or in exile who were eager to start a wider democracy movement.

While the antidemocracy agenda was easy to identify and understand in the West, the identity and ideology of Muslims who opposed authoritarianism were less understood and often marginalized by Western elites. Therefore, this last chapter is dedicated to the Muslim intellectuals and activists who have been, and will continue to be, at the core of resistance against the jihadists. Questions remain about their ideas, doctrines, and attitudes toward core values. "How do they reconcile with religion and the political culture produced by the Islamists?" ask observers in the West. Muslim democrats have answers and they have tried to convey their view to the world, but to no avail.

Dissidents' Rallies

I've met and interacted with producers of ideas representing the opposing camps, the Islamists, the "Muslim Democrats," and all those in between. From my younger years at school to the time I began publishing in Beirut, to the decades lived in America, I came to understand the deep difference between the two trends within what some have been calling "political Islam," but which I describe more accurately as "Muslims in politics." Thirty years of reading, debating, and researching allowed me to distinguish between those in the region who want ultimately to crumble the ideas produced since the Enlightenment and the Universal Declaration of Human Rights and those who want to move away from theocracies and empires.

The Islamists and their radical version, the jihadists, are on the most extreme end of the movement seeking to revert to the empires. They want to reestablish a Caliphate with rigid implementation of Sharia laws. The Islamists have shown a capacity for adapting to geopolitical situations and have produced parties and platforms that are electoral on the surface but quickly convertible back to the Islamist-run state as soon as victories are scored. The other authoritarians, Baathists, waver between absolutism and concessions to international standards. However, in the end, this entire web aims at maintaining a balance between opposition to pluralism and the return to the Caliphate. Yet you have Muslims who were born and raised in Islamic societies but have come to believe that the Caliphate and all its tools are a matter of the past and that humanity must move beyond religious empires, much as humanist Christians have bypassed "Christian empires" and moved into the secular stage of history.

Christians, by way of comparison, managed to unlink their faith from the affairs of state and history, even though the values contained in their religion still guide many among them, even when it comes to politics. In the secular modern world, governments and international organizations do not represent and are not guided formally by religion. Humanist Muslims, whose works have appeared in many stages of Islamic history, argued similarly, although with greater difficulty, that societies can be inspired by but should not be tied to the will of organized religions. Some have called them reformists because they have to undergo a reform of the official version of Islamic history, which was mostly influenced by the Caliphate. Others may call them humanists, secular, or even republicans. There are valid arguments for using all these labels, although it is in fact democracy that constitutes the ultimate dividing line.

Muslim democrats are as diverse and varied in their views as believers in democracy in all other cultures. They may be liberal, conservative, socialist, nationalist, feminist, or environmentalist, but they all believe in the higher values of international law, universal human rights, gender equality, and pluralism. These beliefs are what distinguish this body of activists, politicians, legislators, leaders, youth, women, intellectuals, and other segments of civil societies within the

Muslim majority countries (particularly in the Greater Middle East) from other political forces.

Following the Washington democracy conference, I had the opportunity to participate in a number of Muslim democrat forums and conventions, mostly in the United States but also in Europe, during which I became more and more convinced that dissidents rising against the totalitarian ideologies emanating from the Middle East are the only real moral and political force that can produce change. On March 3, 2007, the "Secular Islam Summit" conference of Muslim dissidents was held in St. Petersburg, Florida, and issued a declaration calling for reform within the Islamic world. During the sessions, at which I spoke about international law as an umbrella for democracy platforms in the Middle East, speakers represented different points of view about how to oppose the authoritarian systems. While speakers such as Tawfik Hamid and Zuhdi Jasser advocated reforms within the religious and political institutions, others, such as Ibn Warraq and Wafa Sultan, called for abandoning the theological framework altogether. The community of dissidents was united in rejecting the modern-day "Caliphate" but seemed to have different views regarding how to perform the reformation, a very natural phenomenon in the world of oppositions.[1]

In the St. Petersburg summit I was able to engage many of these dissident leaders and project the impact of their ideas and ideals. Wafa Sultan, whom I met for the first time at the event, but whom I have seen in action on al Jazeera, takes the fight "all the way to the core," as she told me. "The issue is really in the essence of the Islamic theology and how Islamic powers have used this theology to perpetuate their grip on powers," she argued to me. Ibn Warraq builds a doctrine on how this power had produced "an Islamic imperialism."[2] He told me dissidents in the Islamic world are organizing as if in an age of pre-Enlightenment. Tawfik Hamid, whom I met for the first time at the conference, advocates an approach that goes through the same text but with a different interpretation. "I can use the same paragraphs from theology and refute jihadism," he told me. Zuhdi Jasser focuses on the democratic way of life in America as a response to the message of Islamism. "I can be a Muslim but I don't need to be an Islamist" is his motto.

The St. Petersburg Declaration moved toward abandoning the theological injunctions and adopting global humanism, rather than clinging to religious texts and trying to reinterpreting them. The dissident debate had begun.

During the summer of 2007, a much wider conference on "democracy and security" was held in Prague, with many Middle Eastern dissidents in attendance. On June 5 and 6, dozens of writers and democracy activists from the Middle East were invited by a number of European think tanks to testify before an international forum of politicians, intellectual, and media. Many world leaders participated, including U.S. president George Bush, Estonian president Toomas Hendrik Ilves, former Czech president Vaclav Havel, former Spanish prime minister José Maria Aznar, and a roster of lawmakers and diplomats, as well as former and current dissidents from the Soviet Bloc and other regions of the world, including Senator Joseph Lieberman, former Soviet dissident Natan Sharansky, and chess player and politician Garry Kasparov. Among the Middle Eastern figures present were Palestinian activist Bassem Eid, Iraqi MP Mithal Allusi, Iranian student leader Amir Abbas Fakhravar, Libyan dissident Mohammed al Jahmi, Syrian reformer Farid Ghadri, Egyptian human rights activist Saad al Din Ibrahim, Syrian exiled MP Ma'moun al Homsi, Iranian crown prince Reza Pahlevi, and Iranian exile Mohsen Sazegara.[3]

The Prague meeting was certainly the most impressive show of dissidents' solidarity to date. I observed the passion with which the region's democracy activists expressed their views, particularly Mohammed al Jahmi from Libya, whose brother was lingering in Qaddafi's jails; Mithal Allusi of Iraq, whose two sons were assassinated by terrorists in Baghdad; Ma'moun al Homsi, who recounted his fleeing from Syria's Assad regime, and Amir Abbas Fakhravar, who testified about the students' struggle in Iran.

Most poignant for me was the sight of the former Soviet dissidents embracing the current Caliphate's dissidents. I had the privilege of meeting almost all of these struggling figures and listening to their stories, and I had the honor of meeting Vaclav Havel and many of those who knew what it was to seek freedom during the totalitarianism of the Cold War.

In my presentation I criticized the unwillingness and inability of international organizations to stand by democracy dissidence in the Greater Middle East even though these entities were tasked by their constituents and funded to raise the profile of victims of human rights abuse. I compared the actions of the United Nations and the industry of democracy advocacy in dealing with injustices in Latin America, Asia, South Africa, and the former Soviet Bloc to their inaction in the Muslim world, and particularly in the Greater Middle East. It is only when the international community raises the profile of dissidents and democracy movements in the Muslim-majority countries of the region that the power of the totalitarian ideologies will recede.

One other benchmark gathering I had the privilege of participating in was the forum organized by the International Humanist and Ethical Union to address the questions of the so-called Islamophobia and Defamation of Religions initiatives pushed by the Organization of the Islamic Conference (OIC) through their representatives at the Human Rights Council of the UN in Geneva. Participating in the panel were two leading figures in the Muslim democrats' network in the West, Danish MP Naser Khader, originally from Lebanon, and Tarek Fatah, a Canadian broadcaster and human rights activist, originally from Pakistan. This first salvo at a UN location drew the attention of media and many NGOs. The conference, billed as "An Analysis and Discussion of Religion and Freedom of Expression at the Human Rights Council," was held on September 17, 2008, and chaired by Roy Brown, IHEU main representative, UN Geneva. Naser Khader, one of the most focused Muslim liberals, led the charge: "What the Islamists do is to lobby their view not just throughout the Islamic world, but now we also see them pushing in the doors in forums that should only allow admission for those with a democratic passport, so to speak."

Kadher then went to the heart of the matter: "Islamists on the march are being met with invitations into forums and agendas where they have nothing—and I mean nothing—to contribute with. They will say that their agenda is only pointed at the Islamic world. But that is a lie. Islamists' sole goal is to conquer the whole world, not just a bit of it: everything. They are prepared to the teeth to let this fight go on and on, to take bit by bit. And we are making it very easy for them. We act like we got caught in the headlights—just because an organization like the OIC says that they—and they alone—speak for all the Muslims. Only in this case we are naïve democrats (Naïvocrats, as I like to call them). We do think that OIC speaks for every Muslim. But they don't. They don't for a bunch of my other friends—democratic modern Muslims to whom religion is a private matter, not a public boxing ring with Islam in one corner and democracy in the other. OIC in my opinion only speaks for their sugar daddies in Saudi Arabia."[4]

Tarek Fatah moved forward in his arguments, pointing out that "almost all Muslims live under dictatorship and oppression." He argued that Islamists are using the OIC to validate policies traumatizing Muslim societies.[5] In his speech at the ONG forum at the UN in Geneva, he said:

> Barely a day goes by without news of gross violations of human rights of Muslims living in so-called Islamic countries. Whether it is honor killings of sisters and mothers or the harassment of gays and calls for their death; whether it is imprisonment of political opponents or attacks on minorities, we Muslims who live in the West are constantly reminded of the rights we enjoy under secular parliamentary democracies as individual human beings. Life in the OIC countries is the reason why millions of Muslims have escaped and taken refuge in Europe and North America. We are testament of their failures. They rule their populations with a sense of entitlement that they believe are their God-given right, and millions suffer under their tutelage. I urge you to not fall for the charm offensive of those who falsely claim to speak on behalf of Muslims and Islam. They do not, and their record speaks for itself.
>
> Why should Muslims only enjoy human rights and freedom of expression to discuss their own religion where they live as minorities, yet never be able to do so where they form a majority? Why should I fear for my life simply because I ask why so many Muslim societies have failed despite their enormous natural wealth? Islam is a religion, but Islamism is a political ideology. They are not the same despite what the OIC claims. Everyone has a right to practice Islam without fear of persecution. However, Islamism is nothing more than the use of Islam to secure power over an already marginalized community of Muslims. Proponents of Islamism had better be prepared for criticism, not just from non-Muslims, but from Muslims, who have been the primary victims of this totalitarian ideology.[6]

The *Daily Times* of Pakistan interpreted Fatah's arguments as if the "Islamists are using the OIC to validate actions and policies that have resulted in the creation of traumatized and dysfunctional societies across the Muslim world."[7]

In my own speech I argued that those speaking officially and internationally on behalf of all Muslims failed to represent the segment that struggled for pluralism and human rights, as defined by international consensus. I warned that creating legislation that would sanction those who allegedly "defame" religion can and will be used to stifle dissent and opposition in Muslim-majority societies. I projected that dissident and democracy NGOs will eventually act internationally to assert their view and represent the segments in the region's societies that are committed to internationally accepted values of democracy.[8]

The panel and the NGOs present at the forum seemed to solidify the idea that a super regime in the region was playing the oppressive role of a modern-day Caliphate and obstructing Muslim democrats from expressing themselves and moving their civil societies toward the rest of international society in the quest for equality and freedom.

Gradually, the voices for change are making progress, as politicians and legislators lend their ears to the new generation of reformers. In July 2009 Representative Sue Myrick of the U.S. House of Representatives hosted a Moderate Islam Summit in Congress, which was attended by six organizations, all proponents of secularism in politics while still diverse in their views of the world and of the ways to make progress happen in the Greater Middle East. Among them were Dr. Hedieh Mirahmadi, president of an international educational NGO; Zeyno Baran, the director for the Center for Eurasian Policy at the Hudson Institute; Syrian reformer Farid Ghadry; Manda Zand Ervin, Iranian women's reformist; Dr. Ali Alyami, director of the Center for Democracy and Human Rights in Saudi Arabia; Omran Salman, Arab Reformists Project; and Dr. Zuhdi Jasser. Discussions were followed by meetings with U.S. officials from various branches, focused on helping the moderates counter radicalization in their homeland is and reach out to fellow moderates in the region.

The summit didn't have an immediate impact on the U.S. government's policy as a whole, but a dynamic was created, within which democracy advocates in the community became bolder in signaling their views to the public. Alyami pushed for an all-out reform on theological and political grounds, while Mirahmadi and Jasser wished for an adaptation of Muslims to present-day secular politics, aside from the debate on theological transformation.

In Europe similar interests are slowly emerging. On March 20, 2010, a number of think tanks from Germany, the Netherlands, Spain, Austria, and the European Studies Center, in coordination with the European branch of the International Republican Institute, held a transatlantic summit on political Islam. The aim of the meeting, attended by the president of the European Center Right (then the majority at the European Parliament), Wilfried Martens, was to find ways to engage and moderate the phenomenon of "political Islam."

My presentation focused on the difference between Islamists and Muslim democrats. I argued that the latter were not yet found in formal political parties in the Middle East but were active as NGOs, networks, student and labor unions, women's groups, politicians, and bureaucrats. From Morocco to Iran, those who believe in the same international value system are omnipresent and acting, but they need to be identified and helped. In fact, liberal democracies must not only find them, but also partner with them.

The Media's Muslim Democrats

Confronted by the Islamist propagandists and the authoritarian powers, these alternative voices of Muslim democrats, seculars, conservatives, reformists, or intellectual revolutionaries have started to be heard, first in the region but also in some quarters in the West. Liberal websites such as Elaph and Aafaq regularly post pieces by reformists living in the region. Even more centrist and conservative publications such as Pan Arab *al Hayat, al Sharq al Awsat*, and *al Nahar*, although not necessarily endorsing the push for democracy, are allowing liberal commentators to publish strong criticism of the regional oppressive order, particularly on the cultural level. A growing number of journalists and analysts are pounding readers with strong arguments about change, challenging the jihadists, and the idea that the Islamists and the authoritarians are the sole representatives of the majority of Muslims in the Middle East. One of them, Shia Lebanese commentator Nadim Koteish of *al Mustaqbal*, told me, "If you look at the numbers coming from below, the liberal voices have most likely bypassed the fundamentalists, but the guardians of the political culture are still from the other school." Hazem Saghieh, a seasoned left-wing writer who used to publish in the ultra–Arab nationalist daily *As Safir* when I was living in Beirut, is now posting significantly liberal pieces out of his new residence in London.

The Political Map of "Muslim Democrats"

The forces for change inside the Muslim-majority countries in the Greater Middle East are not monolithic. Rather, they are as diverse, divided, and dispersed as regular political movements and parties in stable democracies. The examples of post-Saddam Iraq, post-Taliban Afghanistan, and post-Syrian-withdrawal Lebanon all show that once the weight of dictatorship or occupation is removed, the layers beneath rise up. What replaces a totalitarian elite is not necessarily a liberal democratic culture, but a transitional stage in which forces of change vie to seize the moment. The first battle is between those who wish to establish another totalitarian regime, or bring back the old one, and those who wish to move toward democracy. In Iraq, the Baathists, al Qaeda, and the pro-Iran Islamists moved in to obstruct the weak democracy, and the battle is still on. In Afghanistan, the Taliban came back to dislodge the new government, which wasn't yet a full liberal democracy, to say the least. In Lebanon, the Cedars Revolution was immediately challenged and pushed back by Hezbollah and the pro-Syria forces.

In these examples, one sees that the forces of change are in the majority (with the exception of Lebanon, where prodemocracy Christians are a large bloc). A snapshot of the region shows a string of democracy forces (with non-Muslim democrats in countries such as Lebanon, Iraq, Sudan, and Egypt) battling the oppressive sitting elites or returning suppressive forces. The Allawi coalition and some Kurdish forces in Iraq, the Cedars Revolution in Lebanon, the Green Movement in Iran, the secular opposition and the African movements of the south, Darfur, and the Beja areas in Sudan, the liberal and Kabyle groups in Algeria, reformers in Syria, dissidents in Libya, and democracy activists throughout the region form the vertebra of the regional movement toward democracy. And there are politicians and bureaucrats within state apparatuses from top to bottom who also support the democracy movement, as is the case in Jordan, Morocco, the Gulf, and, within limits, in Saudi Arabia.

Before moving forward, Turkey has stepped backward in terms of liberal democracy. Turkey has been a peculiar case, with secular and democracy forces struggling to improve liberties under a string of military and civilian governments for decades. The forces of democracy were found in all areas of politics but often contained under the strict boundaries imposed by the Kemalian republic. Pluralism was achieved by the 1980s and opposing parties were formed, but always under the watchful eyes of the military. Ironically, the military was the guardian of secularism against the return of old Islamism of the Ottoman days or the takeover by communists during the Cold War. Turkey was anticlerical, as a balance with its Caliphate past. Its democratic secular forces, mostly in its west, didn't penetrate the deeper countryside, which remained ultraconservative. In later years the Islamist political forces were successful in taking over the conservative Muslims, and with them obtaining majorities in the Parliament, leading them, in their latest form, the AKP, Adalet ve Kalkimnha Partisi (Justice and Development Party), to firmly control government. The Islamists of the AKP—although moving gradually in the domestic realm—seized the centers of power, pushing back the army and the secular politicians before the liberals moved into the countryside to educate about non-Islamist democracy.

The Voices of Democratic Change

In the world of Muslim democrats there is a rich mosaic of thinking, doctrines, ideas, and backgrounds. The melting pot of ideas we see through the growing body of literature is a genome for the future of the region, and will determine if democracy can prevail one day. There are several types of intellectuals and activists who spearhead ideas of change. The following are not the only kinds of dissident, but are those I had the privilege to meet, know, read about, hear, or view. They are a sampling of a wider range of courageous men and women, both in the region and in exile.

Ex-Muslims

Ex-Muslims promote fundamental reforms in religion as a path to change in politics. These intellectuals have broken away from the theology of faith and decry the use of religion altogether by Islamists.

Ibn Warraq is among the oldest figures in this school of thought. He is the author of the book *Why I Am Not a Muslim,* in which he describes the problem in both theological and historical dimensions, terming it "Islamic imperialism." I heard and met Ibn Warraq at a conference in Washington in 1994, at which he made his case to a coalition of dissidents. Ayaan Hirsi Ali is the outspoken Dutch MP who was threatened by jihadists in her country before she quit and sought political asylum in the United States. Born in Somalia, her life story and thoughts are featured in a popular book titled *Infidel.*[9] She wrote the screenplay and did the voiceover for *Suppression,* a film by Theo Van Gogh, a documentary on the treatment of women in Islamic societies. Hirsi Ali is well received by intellectual audiences and is known for her courage in speaking directly, as she did in an open letter to President Obama about the subject.[10] I served with her on a panel in New York in 2008 on the UN's unbalanced approach to fighting for underdogs in the Middle East. Last but not least is Dr. Wafa Sultan, a Syrian-born psychiatrist, now based in Los Angeles, California. Sultan, whom I met in Florida, is a secular Muslim who believes that "Islam is stuck in the Middle Ages" and needs to be reformed fully.[11] Sultan's most controversial appearances were on al Jazeera in a cross fire with radical clerics.

Progressives

There is a "progressive" category of reformers who do not engage in opposing theology but heavily criticize the politics and socio-economics of the ruling elites in the region as well as the radical Islamists. Among the many seen as progressives (although they may wish to identify their work otherwise) are: Ammar Abdelhamid, a Syrian secular Muslim whose writings on Syrian youth's sexuality have certainly confronted the traditional thinking on the issue in conservative and Baathist-dominated Syria.[12] Abdelhamid, a charismatic young leader who began his life as an Islamist before he turned into a hard-core liberal, promotes nonviolent methods to transform the culture from authoritarian to democratic, starting with Syria. I met him at several conferences and learned further about the trends in Syria's civil society, all encouraging. Dr. Shaker al-Naboulsi is a Jordanian author based in the United States, a strong proponent of secularism whom I met often in debates on Arab TV. Al-Naboulsi is a seasoned scholar whose writings on Aafaq and Elaph—in particular his articles "The Arab Progressive: The Arabs are Still Slave to a Medieval Mentality" and "Islamist Democracy?"—illustrate the emerging liberalizing trend.[13] "I know what our society feel and think deep down. Way below the surface of dogma, our people are just like other people, seeking the same human goals. When it comes to this, the jihadists can't beat us," he told me after we participated in a joint round table on Arab TV. Munir al Mawari is a Yemeni journalist based in Washington. His articles underlined the fact that there is no one Arab global view, and that the dominant elites are in control of the radical message.[14] Bahrain-born Omran Salman, cited in an earlier chapter, leads the Arab Reformists Project. Salman is an outspoken advocate for opposing the narrative of the Islamists.[15] Based in Canada, Tarek Fatah and Irshad Manji are heavyweights in the liberal progressive wing of Muslim democrats. I have had enlightened discussions with both of them. Fatah, originally from Pakistan, is a secular Muslim who advocates for gay rights and opposes Sharia law. He was a founder of the Muslim Canadian Congress in 2001.[16] Irshad Manji, well received in liberal milieus, was born in Uganda to parents of Egyptian and Gujarati descent and is based in Canada. Manji self-identifies as a secular Muslim, lesbian, and feminist. She is the director of the Moral Courage Project at New York University. Her best-known book is *The Trouble with Islam Today*.[17] Mona Eltahawy is an Egyptian-American journalist based in New York City and an influential progressive. She is an outspoken commentator on Muslim women's issues, and her articles appear often in Western liberal publications.[18] Last but not least, there is El-Farouk Khaki, a Tanzanian based in Canada, a founder of Salaam, a gay Muslim support group. He cofounded the Muslim Canadian Congress.

Western-Based Religious Reformers

Western-based religious reformers seem to be in the majority of dissidents at this stage, particularly those focusing on reforming religion or, more precisely, reinterpreting the texts in a manner that would marginalize the jihadists and open the path for democracy and pluralism. Dr. Tawfik Hamid, also known as Tarek Abdelhamid, is an Egyptian doctor who once was (as he details it in his writings) a radical Islamist, but renounced radicalism and "sought to reform Islam based on peaceful interpretations of core Islamic texts." Dr. Hamid and I had long conversations about long-term strategies to encourage reforms. "It will take time, but we must begin by developing another narrative of religion to encourage freethinking, liberal views, and democracy," he told me.[19] Ahmad Subhi Mansour is another Egyptian scholar whom I met and who seeks theological reform. A graduate of Al-Azhar University in Cairo, Mansour was later expelled as a professor there for being an enemy of Islam for his interpretations and was imprisoned for two months. He founded the Egyptian Society for Enlightenment in 1993, and after a fatwa was issued calling for his assassination, he fled to the United States. He now operates the International Koranic Center.[20] Dr. Muhammad Tapir-ul-Qadri, a former Pakistani lawmaker now based in the United Kingdom, issued a six-hundred-page fatwa against the use of terrorism. He is the founder of Minhaj-ul-Quran, a worldwide movement that promotes a nonpolitical, tolerant Islam.[21] Abdul Hadi Palazzi, one of the first Western-based scholars I met in the 1990s, is an Italian sheikh who is the secretary general of the Italian Muslim Association. He preaches traditional Islamic views over extremism and advocates dialogue between Jews and Arabs.[22]

Western-Based Secular Scholars

In the West, we've seen a growing number of Western-based secular Muslim scholars developing new approaches to reforms and responding to the world vision of the Islamists and the jihadists. I've met and interacted with some of this new generation of scholars, among them Turkish-born Dr. Zeyno Baran, who published a recent book, *The Other Muslims: Moderate and Secular.*[23] In it she presents a group of Western-based Muslim scholars, including Bassam Tibi, addressing different aspects of the battle for Islam's renaissance and coexistence with secular democracy and international human rights standards.

Other notable secular Muslim scholars are Asra Noumani, an American of Indian descent, who founded Muslims for Peace,[24] and Iraqi-born Kanan Makiya, the author of *The Republic of Fear* and *Cruelty and Silence.*[25] In Canada, political scientist Salim Mansur is a leading member of Canadians Against Suicide Bombing.[26] In the Netherlands, scholar Nasr Abu Zayd was exiled from Egypt after he was declared an apostate. He now teaches humanism and Islam at a university in Utrecht.[27]

Civic and Community Leaders

Over the past few years a number of Muslim civic and community leaders have emerged on both sides of the Atlantic as beacons of anti-jihadism. Enjoying the freedom of liberal democracies, this new generation of activists seems to have become the nucleus of a future Western-based leadership of the prodemocracy movement in Islamic politics.

Dr. M. Zuhdi Jasser is of Syrian descent and the chairman of the American Islamic Forum for Democracy. Jasser, whom I met after 2001 and identified as one of the most articulate and focused Muslim-American leaders, has developed a strong voice in the Muslim-Islamist debate. He hosted a documentary on the struggle between Muslim moderates and Islamists, initially produced to air on PBS, but after the network refused to broadcast, it was aired on other media and online.[28] Dr. Hedieh Mirahmadi is the president of a think tank dedicated to antiextremism in Islam. Mirahmadi, a follower of Sufism, has been very active in the United States, Britain, and South Asia in promoting moderation. I met with Mirahmadi often in the U.S. Congress and on panels and witnessed her successes in the debate.[29] Naser Khader, whom I met in Europe, is another star of the democracy reform movement in Islamic politics. A member of the Danish Parliament and of Lebanese descent, MP Khader fought back against the vast network of Islamists in Denmark and in Europe and has become, to many Muslim democrats, a leading figure for future Islamic politics in the West and perhaps internationally. Maajid Nawaz and Ed Husain are British Muslims of Pakistani descent, based in the United Kingdom and founders of Quilliam, a counterextremist think tank. They have been helping British authorities devise policies to counter the influence of Wahabism and encourage pluralism in Muslim communities.[30] Hassen Chalghoumi, a Tunisian cleric who founded the Conference of Imams to promote interfaith understanding in France, is an outspoken supporter of the burka ban proposed by the French government. In France, Bassam Tahhan, a Syrian intellectual who has taught in Paris since 2006, believes Islam needs a reformation similar to Protestantism. Also in France, Tunis-born Al-Afif al-Akhdar advocates a secular Islam and is outspoken against the Wahabi version of Islamic law.

Liberal Voices from the Region

The Greater Middle East has many men and women struggling for democracy and freedom. Some countries, such as Lebanon, Iran, Iraq, and Sudan, have witnessed vast popular movements. Some activists have been noticed in the international arena. In Lebanon, the debate on democracy has been thriving, particularly since 2005. Beirut had its days of freedom for Muslim (and also Christian) liberal intellectuals before the war of 1975. Since the Syrian invasion in 1976 and the domination of most Muslim areas by Islamist and jihadist militias, including, since the 1980s, domination by Hezbollah in the south, in Bekaa, and south of the capital, the human rights activists and democracy advocates in Muslim civil society were put under increasing pressures. The assassination of writer Mustafa Jeha in the early 1990s was the signal for the freedom retreat. Outside Lebanon, dissidents and freedom fighters have been emerging in most countries.

Joshua Muravchik, in his book *The Next Founders*, listed seven whom he described as "Models for a Rising Generation."[31] He listed two dissidents I have met and discussed issues with—Mithal Allusi and Ammar Abdelhamid. Allusi, described as "the Politician" of dissent, is a member of the Iraqi Parliament and leads campaigns to democratize and liberalize the system. Abdelhamid, who started as an Islamist in his younger years, leads a human rights NGO, Tharwa, and works on democratizing Syria's civil society. Mohsen Sazegara, who was part of the Iranian regime's apparatus in its early Khomeinist years, was persecuted by the rulers and ended up in the West as an advocate for pluralism. Palestinian human rights activist Bassem Eid is among the most daring in his community in challenging not only Israeli authorities but also Palestinian Authority and Hamas apparatuses. In Egypt, Hisham Kassem is seen as a bold publisher advocating a free press, and in Kuwait, feminist and member of Parliament Rula Dashti emerges as a role model for future women in democratic politics. Saudi women's rights activist Wajiha al-Huwayder is a journalist based in Saudi Arabia who frequently publishes in *Al-Watan*, but the Saudi paper has recently stopped publishing her writings, particularly as they criticize the core Wahabi system. Also in Saudi Arabia, another ascending voice is that of journalist Mansour al-Nogaidan, who believes that Islam needs a reformation.[32] Ayad

Jamal Eddin, an Iraqi Islamic scholar, has become a loud voice calling for reforms not only in the political realm but also in the concept of jihad and its derivatives. A very effective debater I have heard often on Arab airwaves, Jamal Eddin has become an inspiring image to younger generations of Arabs, including bloggers and activists who are leveling criticism against the very foundation of the ideology of jihadism. From Egypt, a liberal political thinker, Tarek Heggy, whom I met and who lectures at major universities and think tanks on reforms in Egypt and the Middle East, has become another model for younger generations seeking democratization.[33] In Jordan, journalist Rana Hussein helped launch the National Jordanian Committee to eliminate so-called crimes of honor.[34] In Bahrain, Ghada Jamshir, a women's rights activist, advocated for reform of the country's Sharia courts and has founded the Women's Petition Committee. Also in Egypt, Ali Salem, a playwright, voices criticism of extremism. One of the most powerful voices of humanism and democracy in the Muslim Middle East is a Shia cleric from Bahrain, Diya' al Mussawi, who has been fending off the arguments of the jihadi propagandists and opening the intellectual path for a Muslim-based revolution against jihadism.[35]

Undoubtedly the messengers for democracy in the Middle East have been active, sacrificing, and are the prelude to the revolutions to come. The few names I cited, and others unnamed in this book, are the vanguard, the tip of the iceberg. At this stage of history one can see them as the Davids facing off against endlessly powerful Goliaths. But the future will reveal, as history has revealed in other regions of the world, that the underdogs who are willing to fight for freedom are much more numerous than one thinks.

Looking Into The Future

I T IS NOW WELL ESTABLISHED THAT THE WORLD COMMUNITY IS facing an increasing threat by jihadist and radical forces, regimes, and organizations. The menace of Salafist and Khomeinist terrorism and mass destruction targets countries and cities on five continents in addition to the ongoing wars in the Greater Middle East, from Afghanistan to Somalia, passing by Iraq, Yemen, Lebanon, and beyond. It is also a fact that these forces are attempting to deepen their control of the region's peoples, resources, and destinies. Thus, as we look into the future of these conflicts and the opportunities for world peace, we can clearly see the link between the control of the region by radical forces and the war waged against democracies worldwide. As long as jihadi regimes, forces, and their allies oppress civil societies in their own midst, they will continue to assault the free world. For by controlling large areas of the Greater Middle East, antidemocracy forces have been using and continue to use the immense riches of the region, including its vast oil reserves, to build enough power to maintain their regimes and dominant political culture and use the latter's benefits to achieve their goals of wider, if not world, domination.

As was the case with the previous totalitarians—Nazism, fascism, and Bolshevism—it will take a gigantic effort to defeat these global threats in order to save the free world from disasters and salvage the populations under oppressive regimes. In the cases of the Nazi, fascist, and militaristic powers that rose in the 1930s and provoked World War II's genocides, it took force to defeat force and achieve liberation. In the case of the Soviet Union, it took steadfastness in the free world and symbolic solidarity with the dissidents inside the iron curtain. However, in this century's battle with jihadi totalitarianism, it will take a more complex, longer-term, and even a greater all-out world campaign to defeat the antidemocracy forces and free the captive nations they sequester.

The forces crushing the underdogs in the region have long arms inside the West, something their predecessors, the twentieth-century totalitarians, didn't. With petrodollars at work and apologist influence metastasized across bureaucracies, academia, and media, Middle Eastern authoritarians have established a Western-based support system. Democracies are now threatened both from the region and inside their countries. The rules of the game have changed. The global equation is like a triangle: The Greater Middle East's civil societies are suppressed by jihadi totalitarians while Western democracies are threatened by these same forces. Hence, the equation between the Free World and the Greater Middle East is locked into a vicious circle. Western democracies will continue to be the targets of antidemocracy forces in the region as long as democracy is not prevalent in the bases of these jihadist or totalitarian countries.

At present, the reality is that Western liberal democracies and other members of the international community can spare themselves and future generations from more lethal strikes, urban chaos at home, and overseas wars only by enabling democracy forces in the Arab and Muslim world to win their war of ideas. Ironic but true, at this stage of the conflict, well-established and older democracies can be saved only by as-yet-unborn democracies and the underdogs fighting for freedom in the region. New York, Washington, Paris, London, Moscow, and New Delhi can know peace of mind and have their economies recover only inasmuch as the political culture changes toward freedom in Tehran, Damascus, Riad, Khartoum, and Tripoli. The feared homegrown jihadists mushrooming in the West and casting the shadow of greater unrest over the megalopolises of the world can be shrunk to annoyances only if the factories of indoctrination of the Middle East become museums of past radicalization. Great powers and advanced democracies have seen their fate being ultimately linked as never before to the weakest segments of societies in the third world. Military intervention alone won't solve this conflict. It is now clear that the battle will be won when democratic forces defeat the ideologies producing terrorism at home, in the midst of the region's civil societies.

But at the same time there is no illusion that the weak segments of these societies, which reject jihadi and other totalitarian violence, can win this war alone or at least in the time frame hoped for in the international community. Students, women, and minorities in Iran, not recognized by the outside world as the legitimate voices of the Iranian people, are threatened by the Pasdaran and the Basij forces. Civil society NGOs in Lebanon cannot face off with the megapower of Hezbollah's armies. Darfur's population, the Nuba and Beja communities, are defenseless against the Khartoum regime. The Kabyles aren't able to make their claim accepted by the Pan Arabist powers in Algeria. And across the region, reformers in Syria, Saudi Arabia, Yemen, the Gulf, and beyond are isolated in their struggle. If under the presence of NATO and other forces in Iraq and Afghanistan it is still very difficult for women and progressive sectors to rise, what would then be the case in their absence? In short, the forces of change (toward pluralism, not jihadism) can eventually, decades from now, reach their goals by their own means, during which time the totalitarians can threaten the entire planet. A nuclear Khomeinist Iran, an al Qaeda–controlled Saudi Arabia, a Hezbollah-dominated Lebanon, a Hamas-led Palestinian state, an Iraq divided between Salafists and the Mahdi army, an Egypt under the Muslim Brotherhood, and a North African Horn and Sahel increasingly penetrated by the jihadists will menace international relations like no other force before. Democracies' national security and stability cannot withstand hyper-levels of homegrown terror. The region won't free itself by itself in a historic time that would avoid a worldwide drama. The planet must help Middle Earth defeat the threat and reach freedom. The question is, how? And the most pressing part of it is, how do we know the change is happening? How do we measure the progress?

Here is where answers are difficult to digest, the future is hard to fathom, and the developments needed to occur may seem shocking to the political establishments on both sides of the Atlantic and the Mediterranean. The future of the region can go either backward toward the establishment of Salafist emirates and Khomeinist republics as a first step to a forthcoming apocalyptic Caliphate à la the Taliban or à la Khomeini, or the future of the Greater Middle East will look like nothing we've seen before in history: a land of peace, democracy, freedom, and pluralism. The authoritarian regimes and hybrid forms of power such as dictatorships, authoritarianism, Baathism, or ultranationalism will succumb to one or the other direction, abruptly or gradually.

A brighter Middle Earth in its final shape would see the end of jihadism and oppression: In Iran the ayatollahs' regime would be gone, replaced by a democracy where ethnic minorities would be recognized and their right for self-determination consecrated. Liberal men and women would be elected to office and a multiparty system would thrive.

In Afghanistan, the Taliban would be disarmed and transformed into a marginal Islamist movement, as would be their counterparts in Pakistan. Politics on both sides of the borders would be normalized and parliamentarian. In Iraq, a federal system would finally be installed with rights to all minorities, while Salafists and Khomeinists would be reduced to harmless Islamist clubs debating the past with no impact on people's lives or security.

In Syria, the Assad regime would be removed and political prisoners freed. Coalition governments and local cultural autonomies would ensure a healthier political process in the country as the Baath Party would be reformed and its control of state and army banned. In adjacent Lebanon, Hezbollah would be disarmed and its dictatorship of the Shia community ended. Lebanon would finally be reorganized as a federation with a democratic nonsectarian process instead of the confessional regime. Cultural and ethnic pluralism would be recognized.

In Gaza, Hamas militias would be decommissioned and a duly elected Palestinian Authority would enter negotiations with Israel, leading to a settlement of the half-century quarrel over security and lands. A viable Palestinian state would emerge naturally. Jordan and Morocco would continue reforms under their constitutional monarchies, as would Kuwait and the rest of the Gulf principalities. Yemen, like Egypt, Tunisia, and Algeria, would witness a mutation from authoritarian populism to healthier democracy.

Sudan's oppressed ethnicities would be freed and slavery abolished. The south, Darfur, Nuba, and the Beja peoples would be granted self-determination. Northern Sudan would witness the end of the genocidal regime and the rise of an Arab democracy. In Somalia, Eritrea, and across the Sahel, gradual pushes for empowerment of civil societies would take place as jihadists and authoritarians would be marginalized.

Saudi Arabia would surprise the world if democracy were to win eventually. By gradations or due to crises, change would transform the Wahabi system into a constitutional monarchy as elections would eventually be practiced. Women would be allowed to drive cars and one of them would one day become the prime minister of the country. Incredibly, Mecca could become the capital of reform in the Muslim world as Karbala and Qom could play similar roles for the Shia.

Turkey would come back to a secular, albeit liberal, culture, after the AKP adventures are over. Courageous future leaders would recognize the Armenian genocide, accept Kurdish culture, and pull out from Cyprus. Such a Turkey could lead the Turkic-speaking areas of the world into development and advancement.

One can imagine a Grand Middle East where ethnic and religious minorities—such as the Copts, Kurds, Assyro-Chaldeans, and others—would be free to be on their own or continue the joint partnership with the larger communities. A fully free and democratic region could finally afford an integrated economy in which the dividends of oil would be invested in growth and technologies.

There wouldn't be poverty in Gaza or in Darfur nor in Yemen and Somalia, because the region has enough resources to move societies into middle-class status. Pan Arabism would be transformed into an Arab common market to compete with the other large transnational economies of the world.

If Middle Earth is freed, the planet would have a better chance to face the challenges of the future. And for that to happen, democracy must be assisted in order for it to survive and to thrive. The region is not an exception because of differences in religion; rather it has been made into a black hole rejecting pluralism because of the tight grip by elites under the banner of a totalitarian set of ideologies.

Revolution is coming to Middle Earth. It is up to the international community to make that happen in this generation or in future ones, with the price it could cost humanity. Either democracies will help democratic revolutions in the Middle East, resulting in peace finally emerging from the rubble of history, or civil societies will be abandoned by greedy Western elites, and the most dangerous and barbaric forces in the history of the world will seize Middle Earth, bringing horror and destruction to the entire planet.

Walid Phares
Washington, D.C.
July 4, 2010

NOTES

INTRODUCTION

1 See, for example, "A New Approach to Safeguarding Americans," Remarks by John O. Brennan, Assistant to the President for Homeland Security and Counterterrorism, offered at the Center for Strategic and International Studies, Washington, D.C., and published in *Foreign Policy* on August 6, 2009.

1. THE MISSED CENTURY

1 The hijab (pronounced hejaab) is a head cover traditionally worn by religious Muslim women but claimed to be theologically mandatory by Islamic fundamentalists. The Arabic word means to curtain or veil.

2 See Bat Yeor, *The Dhimmis: Jews and Christians under Islam*, Dickinson University Press/Associated University Presses, 1994.

3 On Michel Aflaq's thought, see Qasim Sallam, *Al-Baath wal Watan Al-Arabi*, in Arabic, with French translation ("The Baath and the Arab Homeland"), Paris, EMA, 1980.

4 One recent account of the conquest can be found in Hugh Kennedy, *The Great Arab Conquests: How the Spread of Islam Changed the World We Live In*, Da Capo Press, September 11, 2007.

5 Sharia, body of Islamic Law. See Noel James Coulson, *A History of Islamic Law* (Islamic surveys), Oxford University Press, 1964; also Majid Liebesny and J. Herbert, eds., *Khadduri. Law in the Middle East: Volume I: Origin and Development of Islamic Law*, Washington, D.C.: The Middle East Institute, 1955.

6 On the status of non-Muslims in Islamic law, see Antoine Fattal, "Le statut légal des non-musulmans en pays d'Islam," *Revue Internationale de Droit Comparé*, 1960, vol. 12, issue 2, pp. 439–42; also see Bat Yeor, Miriam Kochan, and David Littman, *Islam and Dhimmitude: Where Civilizations Collide*, Fairleigh Dickinson University Press, December 2001.

7   See Murray Gordon, *Slavery in the Arab World,* New Amsterdam Books, January 25, 1990.

8   On mandates in the Middle East, see Nadine Meouchy and Peter Sluglett, eds., *The British and French Mandates in Comparative Perspectives/Les Mandats Francais Et Anglais Dans Une Perspective (Social, Economic and Political Studies of the Middle East and Asia),* Brill Academic Publishers, bilingual ed., January 2004.

9   On Arab nationalism see Adeed Dawisha, *Arab Nationalism in the Twentieth Century: From Triumph to Despair,* Princeton University Press, December 2, 2002.

10 On Ibn Taymiyya, see Muhammad Abd al-Halim Hamid, *Maan ala tariq al-dawah: Shaykh al-Islam Ibn Taymiyah wa-al-Imam al-shahid Hasan al-Banna* (*Together on the Path of Dawa, Sheikh of Islam Ibn Taymiya and the Martyr Imam Hasan al Banna*) (*Silsilat "Nahwa al-nur"*) (Arabic ed.) (unknown binding).

11 See Mordechai Nisan, *Minorities in the Middle East: A History of Struggle and Self-Expression,* McFarland & Company; 2nd ed., September 2002.

2. THE 1990S

1   See Kanaan Makiya, *The Republic of Fear: The Politics of Modern Iraq,* University of California Press; 1st ed., June 15, 1998.

2   See Roger Azzam, *Liban L'instruction d'un Crime—30 ans de Guerre,* Cheminements, Paris, 2005.

3   After the Yom Kippur War of October 1973, oil-producing regimes in the region organized an oil boycott aimed at the West in reprisal for its support of Israel. See Jay Hakes, "35 Years After the Arab Oil Embargo," *Journal of Energy Security,* October 6, 2008; see also Karen R. Merril, *The Oil Crisis of 1973–1974: A Brief History with Documents* (The Bedford Series in History and Culture), Bedford/ St. Martin's, February 22, 2007.

4   On this topic, see Martin Kramer, *Ivory Towers on Sand: The Failure of Middle Eastern Studies in America,* Policy Papers, No. 58, Washington Institute for Near East Policy, October 1, 2001.

5   Ibid.

6   See Publications of the Prince al Waleed Center for Muslim-Christian Understanding, Georgetown University. Also see *Islam and Democracy,* John L. Esposito and John O. Voll, Oxford University Press, paperback, May 9, 1996.

7   See John Entelis, *Islam, Democracy, and the State in North Africa,* Indiana Series in Arab and Islamic Studies, paperback, October 1, 1997.

8 See the articles published by Dr. David Hoile, a public affairs consultant and the director of the European-Sudanese Public Affairs Council ESPAC since 1998.

9 Ismael Royer in *IViews,* September 15, 1999.

10 CNN, July 3, 2003; see also "Lashkar-e-Taiba in America: A Convicted Terror Recruiter Plays Victim of the NSA," Stephen Schwartz, *Weekly Standard,* December 16, 2008.

11 On the unknown persecution worldwide, see Paul Marshall and Lela Gilbert, *Their Blood Cries Out,* Thomas Nelson, March 12, 1997.

12 Robert Kaplan *The Arabists: The Romance of an American Elite,* Free Press, 1995.

13 Thomas F. Farr, *World of Faith and Freedom: Why International Religious Liberty Is Vital to American National Security,* Oxford University Press, 2008.

14 See, for example, *As Safir,* Beirut, July 2, 2000.

3. Lights from the Window

1 *Ghazwa,* from Arabic "raid," is used by contemporary jihadists to claim a jihad attack on an infidel enemy, emulating the historical raids conducted by the Caliphate or early Islamic conquests in the Middle East.

2 Francis Fukuyama, *The End of History and the Last Man,* Free Press, 1992.

3 See Patrick Goodenough, "US Policy Shift on Durban Racism Conference Draws Concern, Criticism," CNC News, Monday, February 16, 2009.

4 Paul Marshall, "Four Million: The Number to Keep in Mind This November," *National Review,* August 27, 2004; also Stewart Stogel, "Bin Laden's Goal: Kill 4 Million Americans," *NewsMax Magazine,* Wednesday, July 14, 2004.

5 Jean-Marie Colombani, "Nous sommes tous Américains," *Le Monde,* September 13, 2001.

6 The Ninth Extraordinary Session of the Islamic Conference of Foreign Ministers in Doha, Qatar, "expressed its concern over the possible consequences of the fight against terrorism . . . in Afghanistan, and underlined the necessity of ensuring the territorial integrity of Afghanistan and its Islamic identity. It rejected the targeting of any Islamic State under the pretext of fighting terrorism." AP, AFP, al Jazeera, October 10, 2001.

7 I raised this point in the second book of my trilogy on pluralism,

published in 1979, *Al Taadudiya fil Aalam* (*Pluralism in the World*), Kasleek University, June 1979.

8 Bernard Lewis, *What Went Wrong: Western Impact and Middle Eastern Response,* Oxford University Press, 2002.

9 Walid Phares, "Middle East: The Unfinished Symphony," *Lebanese American Journal,* May 1991.

10 See "Arab Summit Embraces Iraq, Snaps at US," NewsMax.com, March 29, 2002. See also "Arab Summit Adopts Saudi Peace Initiative," CNN, March 28, 2002.

11 See Fouad Ajami, *The Foreigner's Gift: The Americans, the Arabs, and the Iraqis in Iraq,* Free Press, 2006.

4. DEMOCRACY SABOTAGED

1 Sheikh Dr. Yussuf al Qardawi is the chairman of the World Union of Clerics and the ideological mentor of al Jazeera TV. He is based in Qatar and is recognized as the main inspirer of the Muslim Brotherhoods worldwide.

2 Bernard Lewis, "Bring Them Freedom, or They Destroy Us," Real Clear Politics, September 20, 2006. Article is adapted from a lecture delivered by Bernard Lewis on July 16, 2006, onboard the *Crystal Serenity,* during a Hillsdale College cruise in the British Isles.

3 BBC, CNN, November 6, 2003.

4 White House, Reuters, BBC, Fox News, November 19, 2003. Speech at Whitehall Palace.

5 See Stanley Kurtz, "Saudi in the Classroom, A Fundamental Front in the War," *National Review,* July 25, 2007.

6 See History News Network, "Nicholas De Genova Explains What He Meant When He Called for a Million Mogadishus," April 21, 2003. See also Tom McGhee, "No Job, No Money for Churchill," *Denver Post,* July 7, 2009.

7 Walid Phares, *The War of Ideas: Winning the War against Future Jihad,* Palgrave, 2007.

8 See Tony Blair, "A Battle for Global Values," *Foreign Affairs,* January/February 2007.

9 From State Department official website at www.state.gov.

10 See James Traub, "Persuading Them," *New York Times,* November 25, 2007.

11 Barbara Ferguson, "Karen Hughes Resigns After Failing to Improve the US' Image Abroad," *Arab News,* November 2, 2007.

12 See Michael Rubin, "Is American Support for Middle East Dissidents the Kiss of Death?", *AEI Middle Eastern Outlook,* December 5, 2006.

5. Freedom and Its Obstructors

1 See "Religious Freedom Is a Growing Priority," *Middle East Quarterly*, September 1997.

2 See John Bolton, *Surrender Is Not an Option: Defending America at the United Nations*, Threshold Editions, 1st ed. (November 6, 2007).

3 "Bolton Resigns as UN Ambassador," *USA Today*, December 4, 2006.

4 See Kenneth R. Timmerman, "Live from Qatar: It's Jihad Television: The al-Jazeera TV Network," *Insight on the News*, March 2004.

5 Walid Phares, "Jihad TV: Al Jazeera, the Global Madrassa," *National Review*, March 26, 2003.

6 See Mohammed El-nawawy and Adel Iskandar, *Al-Jazeera: The Story of the Network That Is Rattling Governments and Redefining Modern Journalism*, Basic Books, August 2003; Walid Phares, "The War on Iraq" (*"Al harb ala al Iraq"*), *Philadelphia Inquirer*, Thursday, April 22, 2004; Judea Pearl, "Another Perspective, or Jihad TV?," *New York Times* and *International Herald Tribune*, January 17, 2007.

7 Javid Hassan, "Top Judge Blasts Al-Hurra TV's Ideological War," *Arab News*, March 9, 2004.

8 Joel Mombray, "Television Takeover: US Financed al Hurra Is Becoming a Platform for Terrorists," *Wall Street Journal*, March 18, 2007.

9 See Dafna Linzer, "Lost in Translation: Alhurra—America's Troubled Effort to Win Middle East Hearts and Minds," *ProPublica*, June 22, 2008. See also Daniel Nassir, "We Do Not Spread Propaganda for the United States," *Middle East Quarterly*, Spring 2008, p. 63.

10 See Kenneth R. Timmerman, "Sen. Tom Coburn: Voice of America Harming U.S. Interests in Iran," *NewsMax Magazine*, Wednesday, February 14, 2007.

11 Editorial, "Voice of the Mullahs: Public Diplomacy Takes a Pro-Islamist Tilt," *Washington Times*, April 14, 2010.

6. The Taliban's Nightmare

1 For a summary of rise of al Qaeda and the Taliban in Afghanistan, see Laurence Wright, *The Looming Tower: Al Qaeda and the Road to 9/11*, Vintage (August 21, 2007).

2 Ihsan Hijazi, "Madrid Envoy Dies in Beirut Shelling," *New York Times*, April 17, 1989.

3 The Khartoum conferences under the auspices of Dr. Hassan Turabi, leader of the National Islamic Front of Sudan, gathered representatives from various Islamist and jihadist groups around the world to discuss future strategies in the region and against the West.

4   Press release, "Revolutionary Association of the Women of Afghanistan (RAWA)," March 23, 1997, http://www.rawa.org/oic.htm.

5   W. L. Rathje for *Discover Archaeology*, "Why the Taliban are Destroying Buddhas," in *USA Today*, March 22, 2001.

6   "Taliban Leader, Omar, Boasts of Eventual Victory," CNN, September 20, 2009.

7   RAWA press release, op. cit.

8   On radical clerics in Arabia, see Erick Stakelbeck, "Sleeping With the Enemy," *FrontPage*, July 13, 2004; see also Mamoun Fandy, *Saudi Arabia and the Politics of Dissent*, St. Martin's Press, 1999.

9   I wrote a chapter on sexual apartheid in my book *The War of Ideas: Jihadism against Democracy*, Palgrave, 2007.

10 "Sufi Mohammed 'Hates Democracy' and Calls for Global Islamic Rule," Deutsche Presse-Agentur, February 18, 2009.

11 As Sahab (al Qaeda publishing house), English transcript of the interview with Mulla Nazeer Ahmad, the emir of the mujahideen in South Waziristan, September 4, 2009.

12 NEFA Foundation, May 2009, http://www.nefafoundation.org/miscellaneous/FeaturedDocs/nefatalibanqa0509.pdf.

13 The center was led by Nina Shea, with Paul Marshal as senior researcher. Later the center was hosted by the Hudson Institute after Freedom House's board was pressured by Saudi lobbying to let go of criticism of Islamist regimes in the region.

14 "Fears Over Afghan Convert Trial," BBC, March 22, 2006.

15 See unama.unmissions.org/Portals/UNAMA/SG%20Reports/09sept25-SGreport.pdf. See also snapshot of security situation leading up to recent elections, http://unama.unmissions.org/Portals/UNAMA/SG%20Reports/09july23.pdf. See also Annual Report on Afghanistan to the Human Rights Council, March 2009, and the Annual Report on the Protection of Civilians in Armed Conflict in Afghanistan, January 2009 (highlights multiple cases wherein the Taliban targeted and killed aid workers, raped women and children, kidnapped and killed journalists, sought to disrupt the electoral process, and so on).

16 Established following the Bonn Agreement of December 2001: http://www.aihrc.org.af/English/. See also obstacles facing AIHRC in their annual report from 2008, on pp. 63–64, available at http://www.aihrc.org.af/Rep_Annual_2008.pdf.

17 Adam Entous, "Taliban Growth Weighs on Obama Strategy Review," Reuters, October 9, 2009.

18 President Obama's speech at West Point, Reuters, ABC, December 1, 2009.

7. MESOPOTAMIA RISES

1 Articles published in the monthly *Beit Nahrain,* Modesto California, 1982–90.
2 Kanan Makiya, *Republic of Fear: The Politics of Modern Iraq,* University of California Press, 1998.
3 I made those points in "Iraq and the New World Order, the Unachieved Symphony," *Lebanese American Journal,* March 1991.
4 Paulo Casaca, *The Hidden Invasion of Iraq,* Acacia Books, 2008.
5 French Poet Jean de la Fontaine wrote a poem about this story titled "*Le Lièvre et al Tortue*" (*Lièvre* is Hare).
6 See Reuel Marc Gerecht, "On Democracy in Iraq: It Is Starting to Take Roots," *Weekly Standard,* vol. 12, no. 31, April 30, 2007.
7 Interview with Paulo Casaca, European Parliament, Brussels, April 2009.
8 Chelsea Carter, "Iraq Orders Security Shakeup after Baghdad Blasts," Associated Press, December 9, 2009.

8. THE CEDARS REVOLUTION

1 See Boutros Daou, *Tarikh al Mawarna: History of the Maronites,* vol. III, Kasleek University Publications, 1980.
2 *Sawt al Mashreq,* Beirut, October 1982.
3 The meeting with President Helou took place in his residence in Kasleek, as he was visited by a delegation from the Union Libanaise Francophone headed by Sami Phares, the author's brother.
4 For an overview of the first years of the Lebanese war, see Marius Deeb, *The Lebanese Civil War,* New York: Praeger, 1980. In Arabic, see Pierre Khoueiry, *Hawadeth Lubnan* (*Lebanon's Events*), three volumes, Junieh, 1977.
5 In AFP, Radio Damascus, al Baath newspaper, July 20, 1976.
6 See reports by Human Rights Watch, Amnesty International, and the U.S. State Department between 1992 and 2004; see also briefings at the U.S. Congress's committees of Middle Eastern affairs.
7 Scott Wilson, "Syrian Ex Official Says Assad Threatened Hariri," *Washington Post,* December 31, 2005.
8 "Lebanese Minister Marwan Hamade Wounded in Beirut Blast," *Daily Star,* Beirut, October 1, 2004.
9 See a special report published by *Al Nahar* daily on January 15, 2005, featuring interviews with Lebanese émigré leaders who worked on issuing UNSCR 1559.
10 Erich Follath, "New Evidence Points to Hezbollah in Hariri Murder," *Der Speigel,* May 23, 2009.

11 Mustafa Jeha, *Mihnat al Aql fil Islaam* (*The Crisis of Mind in Islam*), Beirut, 1987.

9. Syria's Reformers

1 Known as the Sykes-Picot Agreement, signed in 1916. For this topic and a background on Syria's history, see Philip Hitti, *History of Syria Including Lebanon and Palestine*, Gorgias Press LLC, 2002.

2 On Syria's modern history see Jack Morrison, Adam Woog, and Arthur Goldschmidt, Jr., *Syria (Creation of the Modern Middle East)*, Chelsea House Publications, 2008.

3 Michel Aflaq, *Al Baath al Arabi al Ishtiraki* (*The Arab Socialist Baath*), Beirut, 1964 (multiple publishers).

4 See Barry Rubin, *The Truth About Syria*, 1st edition, Palgrave Macmillan, 2007.

5 *Al Muharer al Arabi* (*The Arab Liberator*) is a Pan Arab weekly published in Beirut and owned by Syria national Nouhad Ghadri.

6 The monitoring entities include Human Rights Watch, Amnesty International, the European Parliament, and U.S. congressional committees on human rights, as well as Syrian and Lebanese human rights organizations, 1970–2000.

7 See, for example, the well-known apologist biography of the Syrian dictator by British journalist Patrick Seale, *Asad: The Struggle for the Middle East*, University of California Press, January 11, 1990.

8 Northeastern part of Syria, also known as *Hassaka*.

9 Journalists at the *Guardian*, *New York Times*, and *Le Monde* welcomed the appointment of Bashar as good news for democracy. On academic apology, see, for example, David Lesh, *The New Lion of Damascus: Bashar al-Asad and Modern Syria*, Yale University Press, 2005.

10 Nouhad Ghadri gave several briefings in Washington D.C., to members of Congress and administration officials in 2007.

11 From an interview with Ma'moun al Homsi in Prague in June 2007.

12 See Lee Smith, "A Liberal in Damascus," interview with Ammar Adhelhamid, *New York Times*, February 13, 2005.

13 See Hazem Saghieh, "Let Us Welcome Michel Kilo," *Lebanon Now*, May 27, 2009. See also Rhonda Roumani, "Syria Frees Five Political Activists: Released Opposition Leader to Create New Liberal Party," *Washington Post*, January 19, 2006.

14 CLIME, Center for Liberty in the Middle East, Washington D.C.

15 See "Syria arrests dissident writer," BBC, May 15, 2006. See also Amnesty International Report, "Syria: Prisoner of Conscience, Riad Seif," September 2001.

16 Briefings to various offices and committees in Congress, 2003–2006, by Farid Ghadri.

17 Statements by Walid al Muallem, Syria's deputy foreign minister, *Al Arabiya,* October 30, 2009.

18 Michael Ledeen, "Syria and Iran Must Get Their Turn," *National Post,* April 7, 2003.

19 Michel Abu Najm, interview with former Syrian vice president Abdel Halim Khaddam, *Al Sharq al Awsat,* January 1, 2006. See also Khaddam interview with *Al Arabiya,* December 30, 2005.

20 Among the pro-Syria academics who maintained a regular and intelligently crafted commentary on the necessity of engaging Assad was Professor Joshua Landis, director of the Center for Middle East Studies and associate professor, University of Oklahoma. Married to the daughter of a Syrian General, Professor Landis maintains a very active weblog, *Syria Comments,* in favor of the regime.

21 See "Iraq and Syria Recall Envoys in Bomb Suspects Row," Reuters, August 25, 2009. See also Martin Chulov, "Baghdad Car Bombs Blamed on Syria and Islamists by Iraqi Government," *Guardian,* December 9, 2009.

22 From briefing in Congress, the Anti Terrorism Caucus of the U.S. House of Representatives, July 15, 2009.

23 See, for example, Joshua Landis, "Is Syria Ready for Democracy?" *Syria Comments,* March 12, 2005.

24 The annual conference of the Florida Society for Middle East Studies, held at Florida Atlantic University.

25 From Haytham Manna website.

10. The Green Revolution

1 For a background on Persian history, see Percy Molesworth Sykes, *A History of Persia,* Hesperides Press (November 4, 2008). See also Lindsay Allen, *The Persian Empire,* University of Chicago Press, December 20, 2005. On the Caliphate's conquest of Persia, see Efraim Karsh, *Islamic Imperialism: A History,* Yale University Press.

2 For a sociological and economic analysis of Iran's modern history, see Ervand Abrahamian, *A History of Modern Iran,* Cambridge University Press, July 28, 2008; recommended reading for the geopolitical history of modern Iran under the Khomeinist revolution is Amir Taheri, *The Persian Night: Iran under the Khomeinist Revolution,* Encounter Books, March 25, 2009.

3 Hamid Dabashi, *Theology of Discontent: The Ideological Foundations of the Islamic Revolution in Iran,* New York University Press, 1993.

4 I had analyzed this doctrine in a series of articles published by the daily *Al Ahrar* in Beirut during 1980, particularly in an article titled *"Thawra Takhattat hudud biladaha"* ("A Revolution Heading beyond Its Borders"), *Al Ahrar,* May 1980.

5 On the Iran-Iraq War see, for example, Ervand Abrahamian, *A History of Modern Iran,* Cambridge, 2008. See also Efraim Karsh, *The Iran-Iraq War, 1980–1988,* Osprey Publishing, 2002.

6 See, for example, Kerim Yildizand Tanyel B. Taysi, *The Kurds in Iran: The Past, Present and Future,* Pluto Press, 2007.

7 On Ahwaz Arab struggle, see, for example, Peter Tatchell, "Iran's Anti-Arab Racism: Iran Treats Its Arab Minority as Second-Class Citizens. Now It Is Planning to Hang Six of Them after Rigged Trials Held in Secret," *Guardian,* Friday, October 26, 2007; "Iran: Defending Minority Rights: The Ahwazi Arabs," report by Amnesty International, May 16, 2006; and Daniel Brett, "Iran's Forgotten Ethnocide," in *Arab Media Watch,* originally published in *The Arab,* March 2008.

8 See R. Farzanfar, *Ethnic Groups and the State: Azaris, Kurds and Baluch of Iran,* Massachusetts Institute of Technology, 1992. See also Selig S. Harrison, "Pakistan's Baluch Insurgency," *Baloch Voice,* July 3, 2009; Malek Towghi, "Ethnic Cleansing in Iranian Baluchistan," *Baloch Human Rights International;* BalochOnline, August 30, 2009.

9 See Salman J. Borhani, "The Azeris of Modern Iran," *The Iranian,* August 4, 2003; Brenda Shaffer, *Borders and Brethren: Iran and the Challenge of Azerbaijani Identity,* MIT Press, 2002.

10 Read, for example, Farideh Tehrani, "The Truth Inside," *National Review,* October 15, 2002.

11 "Jihad against Love: Valentine's Day Invades the Middle East," *Front Page Magazine,* February 14, 2005.

12 See Elaine Sciolino, "Student Unrest in Iran," *New York Times,* July 13, 1999, see also "Iran Student Protests: Five Years On," BBC, July 9, 2004; Neil MacFarquhar, "Iran Latest Protests Are Seen as the Toughest to Stop," *New York Times,* June 16, 2009.

13 See "Student Demonstrations in Iran," *Voice of America,* December 19, 2002. See also Nazila Fathi, "4th Day of Protests in Tehran, and Demonstrations Spread," *New York Times,* November 12, 2002; Margaret Warner, "Student unrest in Iran," on *Jim Lehrer News Hour,* PBS, June 18, 2003.

14 Borzou Daragahi, "Iranian Exile Speaks Out against Militia He Once Supported," *Los Angeles Times,* July 9, 2009.

15 Amir Fakhravar, "Call It What It Is: Iran's Revolution," *Daily News* (New York), January 3, 2010.

16 See, for example, "Workers Rights," *International Campaign for Human Rights in Iran,* January 2006.

17 Marvin Kalb, "Report on Hezbollah and Western Media," Harvard Kennedy School of Government, Shorenstein Center on the Press, Politics and Public Policy, 2007.

18 I wrote an article about the subject that year; see Walid Phares, "A Mid East American Revolution Is Coming," *Front Page Magazine,* October 1, 2004.

19 See "Ledeen Calls for a Speedy Democratic Revolution in Iran," hoder.com weblog, July 11, 2002.

20 See, for example, Michael Ledeen, *Freedom Betrayed: How America Led a Global Democratic Revolution, Won the Cold War, and Walked Away,* AEI Press, October 1996.

21 See Meir Javedanfar and Yossi Melman, *The Nuclear Sphinx of Tehran: Mahmoud Ahmadinejad and the State of Iran,* Basic Books, 2007.

22 Martin Walker, "A Democratic Revolution in the Middle East?" *The Globalist,* March 29, 2005.

23 "Iran Arrests Student Editor over Insulting Islam," AFP, May 5, 2007.

24 Saul Gonzales, "Beaming Back," *PBS NewsHour,* June 19, 2003. See also Juliette Niehuss, "Why Washington Needs Iranian Students," *Asia Times,* July 23, 2003.

25 Ledeen, *Freedom Betrayed.*

26 Eli Lake, "Iran Advocacy Group Said to Skirt Lobby Rules" *The Washington Times,* November 13, 2009.

27 See Jacki Lyden, "Iranian Women Activists Gain Momentum," interview with Fariba Davoodi Mohajer on *All Things Considered,* NPR, March 17, 2007.

28 *Results of Survey in 28 Centers of Iranian Provinces: Iranians' Values and Attitudes,* Tehran: Ministry of Islamic Guidance, 2004, pp. 78, 84.

29 Mohammad Maljoo, "Worker Protest in the Age of Ahmadinejad," *MERIP* 241, Winter 2006.

30 "For Workers Revolution against the Islamic Dictatorship: No to All Wings of the Mullah Regime," *Internationalist,* June 2009.

31 Amir Taheri, "Repression and Resistance: Urban Workers, Women, Students, Teachers, and Ethnic Minorities against the Regime," *National Review,* June 16, 2009.

32 Walid Phares, "Iran—The Uprising Is On and There's No Turning Back," FoxNews.com, June 20, 2009.

33 "Iranian Killed in Protest Was Willing to Be 'Shot in Heart,'" *Telegraph,* November 15, 2009.

34 Bahman Bakhtiari, "Is Iran Going to Change? There Is a Chance," *Salt Lake City Tribune,* January 5, 2010.

35   Robert Tait, "Iran Opposition Leader Mousavi 'Ready to Die' for Reform," *Guardian*, January 1, 2010.

36   Heshmat Tabarzadi, "What I See on the Frontline in Iran: Regime Change Is Now Our Movement's Rallying Cry," *Wall Street Journal*, December 17, 2009.

37   Arash Sobhi, "Cannons, Guns, Basiji, Prison, Torture or Execution; Has No Effect on Us Anymore," Planet Iran (translated from Farsi), December 6, 2009.

38   "Obama Refuses to 'Meddle' in Iran," BBC, June 19, 2009; "Obama's Iran Abdication," *Wall Street Journal*, June 18, 2009.

39   Fuad Ajami, "Obama's Persian Tutorial: The President Has to Choose between the Regime and the People in the Streets," *Wall Street Journal*, June 22, 2009.

40   Mark Landler, "Obama Resists Calls for a Tougher Stance on Iran," *New York Times*, June 19, 2009.

41   Peter Speigel and Jay Solomon, "U.S. Retracts July 4 Invites It Gave Iran," *Wall Street Journal*, June 25, 2009.

42   Walid Phares, "Obama Must Stand Up for Iranian Reformers," *NewsMax Magazine*, Wednesday, June 24, 2009.

43   Tariq Alhomayed, "Acting as if Iran is Not Present," *al Shaq al Awsat*, June 2009.

44   "Hezbollah Accuses West of Fomenting Turmoil in Iran," *Africa Asia*, June 2009.

45   "Venezuela's Chavez Backs Ahmadinejad amid Iranian Protests," *Miami Herald*, June 20, 2009.

46   See, for example, Robert Baer, *The Devil We Know: Dealing with the New Iranian Superpower*, Three Rivers Press, August 18, 2009.

47   Hassan Daioleslam, "The Strange New Friend of the Iranian Demonstrators," *The American Thinker*, January 8, 2010.

48   Clare Lopez, "Rise of the Iran Lobby: Tehran's Front Groups Move on—and into—the Obama Administration," Center for Security Policy, February 2009.

49   Amir Fakhravar, "Call It What It Is: Iran's Revolution," *Daily News* (New York), January 3, 2010.

11. Hell in Sudan

1   I wrote about this in my article "The Sudanese Battle for American Opinion," *Middle East Quarterly*, March 1998.

2   Samuel Cotton, *Silent Terror: A Journey into Contemporary African Slavery*, Writers & Readers Publishing, February 15, 1999.

3 Mashrek Institute, citing Dominic Mohammed's estimate of 2.5 million killed either during battles or as a result of disease and starvation, *Middle East News Wire,* December 1997. Christian Solidarity International reports 1.5 million casualties in various reports aired by CBN, February 4, 1997.

4 In 1992, Chevron sold its concessions back to the Sudanese government, which later subdivided these concessions into smaller exploration blocks. Arakis Energy of Canada signed a production-sharing agreement with the government for three concessions.

5 Robert Collins, *The Southern Sudan in Historical Perspective,* University of Tel Aviv, The Israel Press, 1975, p. 36.

6 Gabriel Warburg, *Islam, Nationalism and Communism in a Traditional Society,* Frank Cass, 1978, p. 98.

7 Quoted in Dustan Wai, *The African-Arab Conflict in the Sudan,* Africana Publishing Company, 1983, p. 67.

8 Quoted in Warburg, *Islam, Nationalism and Communism,* p. 153.

9 Wai, *African-Arab Conflict,* pp. 105–9.

10 Ibid., pp. 125–41.

11 Pierre Arbanieh, "Mas'alat Janub as-Sudan: Ila Ayna?" *Sawt al-Mashreq,* Beirut, December 1983.

12 Nicholas Khoury, "Aslamat Janub as-Sudan," *Sawt al-Mashreq,* Beirut, January 1984. See also Mordechai Nisan, "Sudanese Christians: Tribulations in Black Africa," *Minorities in the Middle East: A History of Self Expression,* McFarland, 1991, pp. 193–205.

13 Dominic Mohammed, "Jihad in Africa: The Islamization of Southern Sudan," lecture at Florida International University, November 9, 1995.

14 Francis Mading Deng, "The Identity Factor in the Sudanese Factor," in *Conflict and Peacemaking in Multiethnic Societies,* Joseph V. Montville, ed., Lexington Books, 1990, pp. 354–56.

15 Steven Wondu, U.S. representative of the SPLM, at a conference of the Coalition for the Defense of Human Rights Under Islam, Washington, D.C., May 2, 1997.

16 *Middle East News Wire,* January 15, 1994.

17 *Middle East News Wire,* March 15, 1997.

18 Ryek Machar, "The Sudan Conflict: The SPLM/SPLA-United Calls on America to Support the People of South Sudan in their Struggle for Self-Determination, National Liberation and Independence in the Sudan," United States Institute for Peace, April 12, 1994.

19 *New York Times,* July 19, 1992.

20 Remarks during the symposium "The Impact of Islamization on International Relations and Human Rights," Unitarian Methodist Church Saint Andrew, Washington, D.C., March 30, 1997.

21 *Al-Musawwar,* Cairo, January 24, 1997, pp. 26–27.

22 *Al-Nafir,* July 14, 1996; author's interview with Sheikh Makin, leader of the Nuba Mountains Liberation Movement, Washington, D.C., May 5, 1997.

23 Christian Solidarity International reports that "some, like Jacob Aligo lo-Dado, have been arrested, beaten, and tortured. His crime? He objected to a government mandate that required all students to speak Arabic and study the Koran. Today scars mar his back and serve as a testimony." CSI report, quoted on CBN, November 23, 1997.

24 John Eibner and Caroline Cox, *Evidence on Violations of Human Rights in Sudan,* Christian Solidarity International, April 1996.

25 Associated Press, July 15, 1996.

26 Its acts are fully documented by human rights organizations (such as Human Rights Watch and Amnesty International), journalists, the United Nations, and many others.

27 *Middle East News Wire,* February 1994.

28 David Littman, "The U.N. Finds Slavery in the Sudan," *Middle East Quarterly,* September 1996, pp. 91–94; Caroline Cox, member of House of Lords, United Kingdom, "Slavery in Sudan," submitted to the U.S. House Committee on International Relations, Joint Subcommittee Hearing with the Subcommittee on International Operations and Human Rights and the Subcommittee on Africa, March 13, 1996. Two American reporters traveled to southern Sudan and actually bought back black slaves from northern traders; they reported on this in the *Baltimore Sun,* June 16, 1996.

29 "Fact Sheets" issued by the Sudanese embassy in Washington: "Sudan Condemns Slavery," February 2, 1997; February 5, 1997; "Sudan Opposes Terrorism," February 6, 1997.

30 Sean Gabb, "Truth and the Sudan Foundation: A Debate Between Sabit Aley and Sean Gabb," October 22, 1997, at http://www.sufo .demon.co.uk.

31 Agence France-Press, March 19, 1997.

32 The Sudan Foundation, http://www.sufo.demon.co.uk.

33 Hizbullah of Lebanon; the Palestinian Hamas and Islamic Jihad; the Islamic Salvation Front (FIS) of Algeria; Jeman Islamiya of Egypt; Muslim Brethren-inspired political parties from Jordan, Yemen, and Lebanon, as well as the Baath, Nasserite, and other Arab nationalist organizations.

34 *An-Nahar, as-Safir,* March 12, 1997.

35 Agence France-Press, March 11, 1997.

36 "Sudan Ambassador to Ethiopia, Usman al-Sayyid, Reports Visit of Israeli Intelligence Official to the South," Sudan News Agency, September 2, 1997.

37   *Al-Hayat,* May 9, 1997; *Middle East News Wire,* April 15, 1997.

38   See Gabriel Warburg, "Hot Spot: Egypt and Sudan Wrangle over Halayib," *Middle East Quarterly,* March 1994, pp. 57–60; *As-Safir,* April 10, 1997.

39   *Middle East News Wire,* March 14, 1997. See also Charles Jacobs, "No Relations with Slavers: AASG Asks Clinton to Freeze Oil Deal with Sudan," *Middle East News Wire,* January 30, 1997.

40   Agence France-Press, March 10, 1997.

41   Agence France-Press, Reuters, March 24, 1997.

42   Former Sudanese minister of information Bona Malwal, interview with the author in Miami, October 11, 1995.

43   The four organizations were the Assyrian National Congress, the American Coptic Association, the World Lebanese Organization, and the South Sudan Movement of America. See *Beit Nahrain Magazine,* Modesto, Calif., Fall 1992.

44   A. M. Rosenthal, "The Well Poisonous," *New York Times,* April 29, 1997.

45   Reverend James Kennedy, leader of the Coral Ridge Ministry, aired by Trinity Broadcast Network, September 24, 1997.

46   Chris Mitchell said, "the fourteen-year-old civil war pits an Islamic government in Khartoum that has been waging a jihad, a holy war, against the largely Christian and animist south," Christian Broadcast Network, February 4, 1997.

47   See, for example, the report by Jeff Barthel of the UN's World Food Program, CBN, November 23, 1997.

48   See *AASG Newsletter,* November 1995.

49   Charles Jacobs, "A New Abolitionist Movement," *The Forward,* May 24, 1997; Samuel Cotton, "The Slavery Issue: A Crisis in Black Leadership," in *Slavery in Africa Today,* Sabit Aley, ed., paper presented at Columbia University at the first abolitionist conference, 1995, pp. 37–41.

50   Interview with the author in Washington, D.C., April 10, 1997.

51   Samuel Cotton, "Abolitionist Convention for Sudan," presented at Columbia University, March 12, 1995; "Sorrow and Shame: Brutal North African Slave Trade Ignored and Denied," *New York Weekly,* March 22, 1995.

52   Samuel Cotton, "Abolitionist Convention for Sudan," presented at Columbia University, March 12, 1995; "Sorrow and Shame Brutal North African Slave Trade Ignored and Denied," *New York Weekly,* March 22, 1995.

53   Clarence Page, "Africa's Dirty Secret: Slavery in Our Time," *Washington Times,* May 3, 1995; Clarence Page, "Tolerating Slavery in Africa," *Washington Times,* July 7, 1996; Sabit Aley, "Genocide and

Slavery in the Sudan: The Farrakhan Connection," *Slavery in Africa Today,* Sabit Aley, ed., collection of articles, First Abolitionist Conference, 1995. See also Nina Shea, *In the Lion Den,* Broadman and Holman Publishers, 1997, pp. 31–35.

54 Nat Hentoff, "Averting Our Eyes from Slavery, *Washington Post,* December 27, 1997.

55 Interview with the author, Washington, D.C., May 14, 1997.

56 Address to the general assembly of the Coalition for the Defense of Human Rights under Islamization, December 15, 1995.

57 Interview with the author, Washington, D.C., October 29, 1997.

58 Congressional Record, Senate, November 2, 1997, p. S11698.

59 Senate Foreign Relations Committee, Subcommittee on the Middle East, hearing on Persecution of Religious Minorities in the Middle East, April 30, 1997.

60 Interview with Steven Wondu and Nina Shea, conference on Human Rights Under Islam, Washington, D.C., May 2, 1997.

61 Press release, United States Information Agency, November 4, 1997.

62 News release under Daily State Department Briefings, United States Information Agency, November 5, 1997.

63 IRIN-Reuters, "Sudan: A Who's Who of the Darfur Groups in Sirte," November 1, 2007.

64 http://www.savedarfur.org.

65 Sudan: Anything Is Possible if ICC Indicts President," *Humanitarian News and Analysis,* project of the UN Office for the Coordination of Humanitarian Affairs, January 22, 2009.

66 Michael Slackman, "Often Split, Arab Leaders Unite for Sudan's Chief," *New York Times,* March 30, 2009.

67 "Turkey Defends Bashir Invitation," *Tehran Times,* November 9, 2009. See also Turkish daily *Zaman,* November 7, 2009.

68 Dan Connell, "War & Peace in Sudan: The Case of the Bejas," *Social Sciences Research Council,* February 27, 2007.

69 Alex de Waal, "Averting Genocide in the Nuba Mountains, Sudan," *Social Sciences Research Council,* December 22, 2006.

70 Scott Baldauf, "Sudan Opposition Parties Forge Alliance," *Christian Science Monitor,* September 9, 2009.

12. THE GREATER MAGHREB

1 See Michael Brett and Elizabeth Fentress, *The Berbers,* Blackwell N.Y. and London, 1996; "The Unification of North Africa by Islam," p. 81; "The Arab Conquest," p. 83; "The Revolt of the Berbers," p. 87; and "Arabization of North Africa," p. 120.

2   See Mohand Khellil, *La Kabilie our l'Ancetre Sacrifie*, l'Harmattan Press, 1979.

3   See Said Sadi, *Culture et Democratie*, Editions Parentheses, 1987.

4   See Mohand Khellil, *l'Exil Kabyle*, l'Harmattan Press, 1989.

5   Some of this criticism was leveled in the daily *al Liwaa* by Sheikh Mustafa al Juzu, academic Fuad Shahine, and the Nasserite Movement of Kamal Shatila. More criticism was produced by a leading Salafi Islamist ideologue, Fathi Yakan, in his jihadi newsletter.

6   See Amnesty International Algeria, "Civilian Population Caught in a Spiral of Violence," November 18, 1997.

7   See "The Embattled Arians of Algeria: Radical Islamism and the Dilemma of Algerian Nationalism," p. 3; "Historical and Unhistorical Approaches to the Problem of Identity in Algeria," p. 138; and "Algeria Contested Elections," p. 191. In Hugh Roberts, *The Battlefield Algeria: 1988–2002*, Verso, February 2007.

8   Sebastian Rotella, "Algerian Security Forces Kill Islamic Radical in Gun Battle," *New York Times*, February 10, 2002.

9   "Algerian Singer Killed in Terrorist Ambush," *Independent*, Friday, June 26, 1998.

10 "Riots without End?", p. 287, and "The Kabyle Cockpit," p. 292, in *The Battlefield Algeria: 1988–2002*, op. cit.. See also R. Baduel, *L'Algerie Uncertaine*, Edisud, 1994.

11 See Ben Evensky, "New Ally in the War Against Al Qaeda?" FoxNews.com, January 28, 2010.

13. The Copts and Liberals

1   See *Nashrat al Umma al Qobtiva*, newsletter published in Beirut, Fall 1981. See also *La Revue du Liban* weekly magazine, November 1980.

2   Reuters, Agence France-Press, June 17 and 18, 1981.

3   Michael Slackman, "Egyptian Police Guard Coptic Church Attacked by Muslims," *New York Times*, October 23, 2005.

4   "'Kifaya' in Egypt," *Washington Post*, March 15, 2005, p. A22.

5   Tawfik Hamid, *Inside Jihad: Understanding and Confronting Radical Islam*, Abdelhamid, May 6, 2008.

14. Arabia's Liberals

1   See Habib Trabelsi, "Princess Amira's Statement about Driving Deals Heavy Blow to Conservative Current in Saudi Arabia," *Saudi Wave*, February 13, 2009.

2   See G. Lankester Harding, "Inside Arabia Felix," *Saudi Aramco World*, January/February 1965. See also Robert Hoyland, *Arabia*

and the Arabs: From the Bronze, Age to the Coming of Islam (Peoples of the Ancient World), Routledge, 2001.

3 Hugh Kennedy, *The Great Arab Conquests: How the Spread of Islam Changed the World We Live In*, Da Capo Press, 2008.

4 See Louis Alexander and Olivier De Corancez, *History of the Wahabis (Founders of Saudi Arabia)*, Ithaca Press, 1st English ed., December 1995.

5 See Alexander Bligh, "The Saudi Religious Elite (Ulamas) as Participant in the Political System of the Kingdom," *International Journal of Middle East Studies* 17, 1985, pp. 37–50.

6 See Guido Steinberg, "The Role of Wahabi Scholars in Saudi Arabia: Political Islam Hindering Reform," Qantara de, October 30, 2006. See also David Van Biema, "Wahhabism: Toxic Faith?" *Time*, September 7, 2003.

7 See Habib Trabelsi, "Princess Amira's Statement about Driving Deals Heavy Blow to Conservative Current in Saudi Arabia," *Saudi Wave*, February 13, 2009. See also "The Saudis Argue about Sexual Equality: Are Women on Their Way at Last? With the King's Permission, the Debate Is Hotting Up," *Economist*, April 29, 2010.

8 See Roger Hardy, "Saudi Arabia's Bold Young Bloggers," BBC, October 17, 2006. See also "Saudi Liberals Advance Agenda with New TV Show," Reuters, Friday May 18, 2007.

9 Kenneth Timmerman, "Live from Qatar: It's Jihad Television: The al-Jazeera TV Network Is Osama bin Laden's Favorite Satellite Channel, a Station Financed by the Emir of Qatar, a U.S. Ally," *Insight*, February 11, 2002.

15. ISLAMISTS VERSUS MUSLIM DEMOCRATS

1 See Susan Jacoby, "Diverse Muslims, Violent Islamist Fundamentalism," *Washington Post*, April 19, 2007.

2 Ibn Warraq, *Why I Am not a Muslim*, Prometheus Books, May 1995.

3 Summary of the conference in *Journal of Democracy*, vol. 18, no. 3, July 2007, pp. 186–88.

4 Naser Khader, "World War Three Is Here," *Europe News*, September 17, 2008.

5 Khalid Hasan, "OIC Effort to Modify UN Human Rights Declaration Opposed," *Daily Times of Pakistan*, September 20, 2008.

6 The text of the speeches can be found at http://www.iheu.org/node/3275.

7 Khalid Hasan, *Daily Times of Pakistan*, op. cit.

8   "A Modern Day Inquisition," *The American Thinker,* December 9, 2008.

9   Ayaan Hirsi Ali, *Infidel,* Free Press, 2007.

10 Ayaan Hirsi Ali, "Obama Should Speak Truth to Islam Because Others Can't," *The Australian,* June 15, 2009.

11 Wafa Sultan, *A God Who Hates,* St. Martin's Press, 2009.

12 Lee Smith, "A Liberal in Damascus," *New York Times Magazine,* February 13, 2005.

13 Elaph, July 8, 2004. English translation at *MEMRI,* September 20, 2004.

14 See Munir al Mawari, "The Neo-Reactionaries Invade the Arab World," *al Sharq al Awsat,* October 5, 2003.

15 See Omran Salman, "Misguided Muslim Groups: Focus Should Be on Extremists' War against the West," *Philadelphia Inquirer,* August 31, 2006.

16 See Tarek Fatah, "Burn Your Burka," *National Post,* October 9, 2009.

17 Irshad Manji, *The Trouble with Islam Today,* St. Martin's Press, 2004.

18 Mona Eltahawy, "Lives Torn Apart in Battle for the Soul of the Arab World," *Guardian,* October 20, 1999.

19 Tawfik Hamid, *Inside Jihad: Confronting Radical Islam,* Abdelhamid, 2008.

20 Ahmad Subhi Mansour, "The False Penalty of Apostasy (Killing the Apostate)," *Ahl Al Quran International Islamic Center.* Originally published in Arabic in August 2006.

21 Muhammad Tapir-ul-Qadri, *Creation of Man: Fatwa on Suicide Bombings and Terrorism,* Minhaj-ul-Quran International, 2010.

22 Abdul Hadi Palazzi, "The Islamists Have It Wrong," *Middle East Quarterly,* Summer 2001.

23 Zeyno Baran, *The Other Muslims: Moderate and Secular,* Palgrave/Macmillan, 2010.

24 Asra Noumani, *Standing Alone in Mecca: An American Woman's Struggle for the Soul of Islam,* Harper One, 2005.

25 Kanan Makiya, *Cruelty and Silence: War, Tyranny, Uprising, and the Arab World,* W.W. Norton, 1994.

26 Salim Mansur, "Long, Bloody Road to Islam Reform," *Toronto Sun,* February 27, 2010.

27 Nasr Abu Zayd, *Reformation of Islamic Thought: A Critical Historical Analysis,* Amsterdam University Press, 2006.

28 See "It's Time to Root Out Political Islam," *Arizona Republic,* January 9, 2010.

29 See "Traditional Islam: Our Road Map to Peace," *World Organiza-tion for Resource Development and Education*, www.worde.org, May 2010.

30 See Ed Husain, *The Islamist*, Penguin Books, 2007. See also Maajid Nawaz, "Why I Joined the British Jihad—and Why I Rejected It," *Times Online*, September 16, 2007.

31 Joshua Muravchik, *The Next Founders: Voices of Democracy in the Middle East*, Encounter Books, 2009.

32 Mansour al-Nogaidan, "Losing My Jihadism," *Union Leader*, July 28, 2007.

33 Tarek Heggy, *The Arab Cocoon: Progress and Modernity in the Arab Societies*, Vallentine Mitchell, 2010.

34 Rana Hussein, "Lets Talk about Virginity," *Al Raida Magazine*, vol. XX, no. 99, Fall 2002/2003.

35 "A Breath of Islamic Fresh Air: Secular Muslims Are Creating Signs of Hope: Don't Knock Them, Says Peter Riddell," *Church Times*, March 30, 2007.

INDEX